The Church and Western Culture
An Introduction to Church History

Tom Streeter

Bloomington, IN Milton Keynes, UK
authorHOUSE®

AuthorHouse™
1663 Liberty Drive, Suite 200
Bloomington, IN 47403
www.authorhouse.com
Phone: 1-800-839-8640

AuthorHouse™ UK Ltd.
500 Avebury Boulevard
Central Milton Keynes, MK9 2BE
www.authorhouse.co.uk
Phone: 08001974150

© *2006 Tom Streeter. All rights reserved.*

No part of this book may be reproduced, stored in a retrieval system, or transmitted by any means without the written permission of the author.

First published by AuthorHouse 10/10/2006

ISBN: 1-4259-5349-2 (sc)
ISBN: 1-4259-5350-6 (dj)

Printed in the United States of America
Bloomington, Indiana

This book is printed on acid-free paper.

Contents

Preface/Ackowledgments	VII
Introduction: Why study history?	XI

PART ONE — THE APOSTOLIC AGE 30 - 100 AD — 1

1.	The Church is Introduced into History: 30 AD	3
2.	The Gospel Is Established: 30 - 100 AD	14
3.	The New Testament is Written: 45 - 100 AD	23
4.	The Persecutions Are Initiated: 64 AD	32
5.	The Destruction of Jerusalem: 70 AD	40

PART TWO — THE PATRISTIC AGE: 100 - 500 AD — 45

6.	Ante-Nicene Period: 100 – 325 AD	47
7.	The Council of Nicea: 325 AD	76
8.	Post-Nicene Period: 325 - 500 AD	94

PART THREE — THE MIDDLE AGES: 500 - 1500 — 133

9.	The Rise of the Papacy: 500 - 600	135
10.	Mohammedanism: 622 AD	140
11.	Charlemagne: 800 AD	149
12.	The Great Schism of 1054	158
13.	The Zenith of the Papacy: 1100 - 1300	164
14.	The Crusades: 1095 - 1270	169
15.	Eucharistic Controversies: 1215	177
16.	The Renaissance: 1200 - 1600	182

PART FOUR	THE MODERN PERIOD: 1500 - PRESENT	197
17.	THE PERIOD OF REFORMATION: 1500 - 1700 AD	201
18.	THE PROTESTANT REFORMATION	216
19.	THE AGE OF REASON AND REVIVAL: 1700 - 1870 AD	267
20.	THE AGE OF THEOLOGICAL DIVERSITY: 1870 - PRESENT	377
BIBLIOGRAPHY		409
ENDNOTES		415

PREFACE

This book was given birth through the men's discipleship ministry within our local church. It contains what men, engaged together in learning about their faith, wanted to know about the history of the church. They asked questions, and gradually, in answer to their inquisitive minds, this volume developed and was brought to life over a ten year period. In a very real sense, it is "our book." No doubt there are better books dealing with church history, but this one has a special kind of significance because of its origin within our church community. Our men's training, which requires a two year period, covers three main areas: *church history*, *theology*, and *worldview*. Thus, this volume represents one part of that triad. After concentrated study in these three areas, many of our men state that it was the time spent in the church history section that was most enlightening and influential.

Our focus in this volume is upon church history, but as all discover, the history of the church cannot be easily separated from the ebb and flow of history in general. This volume is a primer, a beginning, for those who want to be better informed about some of the church's history and formation, both theologically and institutionally. Like all written works, there was the challenge of what to include and what to leave out. The questions helped. Some of the questions I knew from having worked for over 40 years in pastoral ministry, but contemporary issues always bring about new questions and insights, and this is probably reflected in this work. Together we have come to realize the life-giving influence, perspective, and direction gained from stepping outside our own moment of time and learning from the people and events that preceded us.

*Dedicated to the men of
Zionsville Fellowship.*

Special thanks to the following people

Deb Bissell and Jean Godsman for assistance in preparation of the manuscript.

My co-workers, Eric Bobbitt and Keith Ogorek, for their important roles. Ten years ago Eric and I began discussing and creating the original ideas for training men in our church and, together, committed ourselves to "disciplemaking." Keith participated in one of our first groups, has since joined our church staff, been involved in training others, and has encouraged and overseen the publication process.

Susan Albers, Laura Dunshee, David Herbon, Jay Parks, and Judy Streeter read the manuscript and offered most helpful suggestions.

Don and Marie Miller and Rob and Debbie Wingerter provided comfortable and quiet places for thought, research, and writing.

INTRODUCTION:

Why study history?

> *History is a massive shadow that hovers over our every step. The successes and follies of the past generations loom large on the path behind us, surround us in our present circumstances, and beam an occasional light on the divergent crossroads that lie ahead. We may not like the accumulated tendencies of the human race, but we ignore them at our own peril. As Churchill and Truman wisely advised, to dismiss history and the experiences of others as irrelevant, only augments our risks of repeating humankind's failures.*[1]

Henry Ford said, "History is more or less bunk."[2] Whatever Ford intended by the statement, modern mass culture seems to have embraced it as a common attitude. Even if people say they disagree with the idea of Ford's statement, most reflect a general passivity when it comes to history. Typically, people make no effort to acquaint themselves with the past except in some sentimental or utilitarian fashion, and a wide range of people believe that because of technology and the future's promises, not much may be gained by looking into the past.

Ford's statement stands in contrast to George Santayana's adage, "Those who ignore the past are condemned to repeat it."[3] He believed history to be a great teacher, and if we turn our backs, we do it to our own peril. The popular historical writer, Will Durant, wrote: "For the present is the past rolled up for action, and the past is the present unrolled for our understanding."[4] Thinking in this same vein, T. S. Eliot remarked that we have been condemning the rising generation to a new form of provincialism: to the provinciality of time, which imprisons men and women in their own little present moment.⁵

> *Eliot perceived that most of what we know is learnt through history—public or personal history. For only the past is knowable—civilization's past and our family's past. Upon the rippling surface of the deep well of the past lies an evanescent film we call the present, dissolving and sinking even as one reads these phrases; while the future... remains quite unknowable. If ignorant of the past, we drift bewildered on the well's surface....⁶*

G. K. Chesterton reminded us that history gives our ancestors a vote. Specifically he wrote, "Tradition means giving votes to the most obscure of all classes, our ancestors. It is the democracy of the dead."⁷

In modern culture, there is neglect, almost disdain, for history. This is sad because history is a story about "us." There is a common human nature shared by people in every age who face over and over the same issues, opportunities, problems, and the same mortality. In our ancestors, we see ourselves. They are there for us to learn from, to teach us lessons that help keep us from the same mistakes, and inspire us to believe and strive for the good and great. The past is more than just events and dates. It is filled with actual people with real lives who possessed important thoughts and ideas. The accumulation of wisdom through the ages serves us well when we receive it in the present.

> *Lacking a knowledge of how we arrived where we stand today, lacking that deeper love of country which is nurtured by a knowledge of the past, lacking the apprehension that we all take part in a great historical continuity—why, a people so deprived will not dare much, sacrifice much, or take long views. With them, creature comforts will be everything; yet, historical consciousness wanting, in the long run they must lose their creature comforts too.⁸*

In the book, *Here We Stand*, edited by James Boice and Benjamin Sasse, the fifth chapter contains the following thought-provoking paragraph:

> "All attempts to interpret the past," wrote H. Richard Niebuhr, "are indirect attempts to understand the present and its future." While there has always been a fairly deep antipathy in American culture toward the past and an obsession with the present and future, Christianity is a religion dedicated to remembering. Again and again in Scripture, especially in the Psalms, believers are called upon to remember what they believe, why they believe it, and to pass the stories of redemptive history down to their children. The prophets do not simply encourage blind optimism toward the future, an attitude that permeates modern society, but rather recall the people of God to their theological roots: This is what the Lord says: "Stand at the crossroads and look; ask for the ancient paths, ask where the good is, and walk in it, and you will find rest for your souls" (Jer. 6:16). All too often, even believers search for that spiritual rest in a frenzied delight in the new and improved rather than in the tried and tested. As goes the culture, so goes the church these days and in this time and place, in the words of Walter Lippmann earlier this century, "Whirl is king."⁹

Blaise Pascal, the mathematical genius, physicist, and creative Christian thinker, lived from 1623-1662. Os Guinness cites Pascal as an example of one who knew the value of history.

> For those who do desire to rise above their times or stand outside their cultures, there are three sure ways. In ascending order, they are travel, history, and direct knowledge of God—and there are few lives and testimonies which are more help with the two deepest of these than that of Blaise Pascal.¹⁰

To the Christian, history must not be viewed simply as a series of happenstance events. A sovereign God governs and directs history. History is also replete with examples of God's hand at work. The term, "direct knowledge of God," refers to knowledge which one has discovered for himself, something one learns from firsthand experience, not something handed to him from someone or somewhere else. Guinness further illustrates the problem modern man has created for himself because of his preoccupation with the present and disdain for the past:

> *As typical people, most of us are prone to the curse of "homo-up-to-datum," Daniel Boorstin's apt term for the illusion that the closer we are to instant total information, the nearer we are to wisdom. Of its many consequences, one of the more fatuous is that we seem to know everything about the last twenty-four hours but next to nothing about the last twenty-four years, let alone the last twenty-four centuries.*[11]

So, why study church history?

The Effects of Modernity

The effects of the modern world are powerful. Because of this, it is both important and necessary that we find other reference points. If all we know is the present, then our only option is to compare ourselves to ourselves, become locked in the "provinciality of time," and become victims of the dominant spirit of the age. What is "modernity?" The word speaks of all the technology, globalization, marketing schemes, consumerism, commercialism, amusements, lifestyles, and attitudes that go together to define our modern world. It is a double-edged sword that cuts two ways, bringing both benefits and difficulties. We all appreciate our cars, computers, refrigerators, and other modern conveniences, that help simplify our lives. However, uncritical acceptance of modernity is a serious matter. It has been observed that modernity does not lead first to heresy, but to idolatry. In our modern world, we find ourselves being deeply affected because we have few other reference points apart from our modern times.

> *Evangelicals, once known as "the serious people," are now in serious disarray. Nowhere is this more damaging than in our captivity to modern idols in our churches and our hearts. We evangelicals can justly call ourselves heirs of America's first faith. But we who should be guardians of the faith are falling victim to the world's first and worst sin against faith. We are idolizing the products of what the Bible calls the "imagination of our hearts." We have uncritically bought into the insights, tools, and general blessings of modernity. (Modernity is the character and system of the world that the forces of modernization and development have produced.) This has led us to idolize modern approaches to life, such as politics, management, marketing, and psychology; we have also fallen prey to powerful modern myths, such as change, technique, relevance, and need.*[12]

Social scientists have identified two primary models that govern the way Americans handle their lives: the *therapeutic* and the *managerial*. These two approaches are based upon the need we sense, in a ever-changing culture, to gain control of our lives. The therapeutic approach has to do with finding ways that make us feel good about ourselves. The managerial model lends itself to learning "techniques" that enable us to govern our lives, from our jobs and finances to the "handling" of our families. The latter is illustrated in the number of "how to" books one finds in today's bookstores. These are examples of the products of modernity.

History provides a different perspective. Four days after his arrival in Wittenberg, Germany in 1518 to teach at the newly-founded university, Philip Melanchthon delivered his inaugural address to the incoming student body. He encouraged them in their pursuit of a life of the mind, and spoke of the essential elements. They should "burn with a love of what is right...[and have] a zeal for elegant literature."[13] They should study philosophy and logic, and other subjects that would help them in the natural world. Along with these, he promoted history as central to their studies.

> *In this matter history is absolutely necessary, for even if I tried, I could certainly not find anything in the whole world of learning that would be more worthy of praise. This is what tells what is beautiful, bad, useful, useless, more fully or better than Chrysippus and Crantor ever could. No aspect of life, either public or private, can do without it. It is to this that the administration of urban and domestic affairs is indebted...no one can see the work of civil business being tended to by its own spirit rather than by history...unless I am mistaken...every type of art flows from history.*[14]

History Is Revelation

God has revealed himself in the world. If He had not done this, He could not be known. This revelation has occurred in a general sense and in a special sense. *Special Revelation* is God showing himself in the Bible and in Jesus Christ. *General Revelation* is God showing himself in the natural world, in the nature of man, and in the providential flow of history.

Special Revelation:	**General Revelation:**
The Bible	Nature
Jesus Christ	Image of God in Man
	Providence (God's rule over history)

The Christian view of history is teleological; that is, it has meaning and is moving toward a goal. If God designed history and it is moving toward a goal, then we should understand that it is not merely a series of unrelated or disconnected events. Rather, God oversees and directs history both generally and particularly.

Generally, God directs history by his *providence*.

- His providence is seen in his benevolence to all people by ordering the natural world, sending sun and rain (Matthew 5:45).
- He provides food for all people (Acts 14:15-17).
- Providence is God's attention concentrated everywhere at once.

Particularly, God orders history by *direct intervention*.
- He disciplined his nation Israel (Deuteronomy 28:15-68) but will also restore them (Deuteronomy 30:1-10); He judged Egypt for injustices against Israel (Exodus 7-11), and, God raises up and removes rulers (Daniel 2:21).
- There are evidences from history, other than from the Bible, which seem to indicate God's intervention. (The preservation of the people of Israel, the Church's long history, Constantine and "the sign of the cross," the death of Arius, the fall of Rome, Irish Christianity, the founding of America, the evacuation of Dunkirk and the battle of Midway in World War II...and several other examples raise the question of Divine providence.) Anyone who investigates the records of history should not be surprised to find some remarkable "coincidences."
- The Bible indicates that history as we know it will be culminated by God's direct involvement.

Historical evidence is not often consulted because it is not easily accessible. One must investigate the historical records, and this takes work. Further, studying history involves the matter of interpretation, which means that it takes time to both gather the data and learn methods of interpretation, in order for accurate understanding to unfold.

The Bible Is History

The 66 books of the Bible were not written in a vacuum, separated from the events of human life. They are very much rooted in history. As the periods and events described in the Bible are studied more closely, it becomes apparent that there is a connection with secular history. As a matter of note, secular histories give substantial support to people, places, and events recorded in the Bible. Various biblical writers provide data in their texts indicating the importance they placed on their texts being recognized in a specific historical setting.

When we read the Bible, we are reading history. As a record of history, the Bible gives an account of the origin of the universe, the earth, and mankind. The stories are presented not as myths, but as real events in a world made and governed by God. Even parts of the Bible not normally thought of as historical, are nevertheless, historical documents, produced by real people living in the real world at a point in time. The letters of the New Testament provide valuable historical information alongside the doctrinal instruction that is given.

History Helps Interpret the Bible

Sometimes church councils, creeds, and other traditions of the church are viewed as dusty and antiquated products—events and records from a time that have no relevance to our day. The truth is, they provide us with information and insights that actually help us interpret our times. The commentaries, sermons, histories, and letters of teachers, theologians, and writers of history contain a richness not often found today. Sometimes, their insights amaze us. In most cases, theologies written by such people as Ignatius, Irenaeus, Tertullian, Augustine, Aquinas, Luther, Calvin, Melanchthon, and many others, provide the theological foundations upon which most of our modern theologians and Bible teachers build their thoughts, whether they know it or not. When we refer to their works, we are studying the ones who originally built the theological frameworks followed today.

History Provides Heroes

For those devoted to God and his kingdom, the pages of the Bible provide accounts of lives that have inspired people of faith for centuries. They are stories we hold to and never want to forget. But God's work did not stop at the end of the New Testament, and the stories do not stop either. Along with the heroes found in the first century and before, there are 19 more centuries that present God's work continued in the lives of devoted men and women that should not go unnoticed. We find that there have been gallant men and women who fought with both mind and sword, heroes possessed of virtue, and of great and noble accomplishments. Sometimes when truth and justice needed to be defended, our heroes picked up the sword or led armies to defeat an enemy. At other times, it was the power of a reasonable faith that prevailed. Their influences were both temporal and eternal.

"Are there any heroes today?" is a question we sometimes hear. Maybe it is because we have given up our heroes of the past that we are unable to identify any in the present. Perhaps we no longer know what a hero looks like. When we live at a time when "celebrity-ism" prevails, and image rules over reality, it is important to locate reference points that help us find our way. In his book, *The Image*, Daniel Boorstin reminds us of who to emulate.

> *The hero is distinguished by his achievement, the celebrity by his image or trade mark. The hero created himself; the celebrity was created by the media. The hero was a big man; the celebrity is a big name... The hero is made by folklore, sacred texts and history books, but the celebrity is the creature of gossip, of public opinion, of magazines, newspapers and the ephemeral images of movie and television screen. The passage of time, which*

establishes the hero, destroys the celebrity... The dead hero becomes immortal. He becomes more vital with the passage of time.[15]

Enter the past and perhaps you will discover some new heroes of your own, and see, as well, that God not only orchestrates history, but reveals himself in the passage of time.

PART ONE
The Apostolic Age 30 - 100 AD

OVERVIEW

Christianity has Jewish roots. Born in the midst of a Jewish community, the church was first known as a Jewish sect. After a time, it became apparent that there were major differences between the followers of Jesus and Judaism. The life and teachings of Jesus Christ brought a moral and theological revolution to the world. As the distinctives of Christianity became apparent to the Christian believers themselves, the church had a major impact upon the first century world.

The clarity and reality of its message stood in stark contrast to the mythological and superstitious paganism of its day, and its doctrine of salvation carried it beyond the limits of Judaism to "all the world." Starting as a small group in Jerusalem, it began to expand into important parts of the Roman Empire and became entrenched in the city of Rome by the end of the first century. The apostles were careful to present the message first to the Jews, but under the guidance of the Holy Spirit, soon realized they possessed a message for the whole world. The apostles themselves made efforts to go to the most distant places with the gospel.

The first century was characterized by establishing the church in every place the gospel was proclaimed. The church also had to come to grips with the central issues of the doctrine and meaning of the message that had been given to them. The growth of the early church was not without opposition as there was the threat of false teachings within and the continuing threat of persecution from without.

CHAPTER ONE

The Church is Introduced into History: 30 AD

The church began in or around the year 30 AD, in Jerusalem on the Day of Pentecost (the fiftieth day after Passover). What was perceived in its beginning as a small, local movement within Judaism, was transformed into a far-reaching community of many different peoples, crossing boundaries of race, languages, economic status and cultures. Less than 300 years after its beginning, Christianity became the favored religion of the great Roman Empire.

Why do we date the church's beginning at 30 AD? The following two paragraphs are from Austin's *Topical History of Christianity*.

> *The City of Rome was approximately 780 years old, and in the Greco-Roman world, the calendars of men counted from the founding of that colossal capital of the empire (AUC—"ad urbe condita"). But along the northwest coast of the Sea of Galilee, in the small province of Palestine, lay an average-sized city called Capernaum, from which was about to be launched such startling ideas and world-shaking events, that in centuries to come people would date their calendars not by AUC but by AD—Anno Domini, "in the year of the Lord." Thus, the year AUC 780 would be more easily recognized as the year AD 27. "The Lord" to which the new dating referred was a 33 old carpenter from the village of Nazareth who was named Jesus!*
>
> *The reason for Jesus being thirty years old rather than 27 in the year AD 27 (as would be supposed if the Christian era dates from his birth) rests in an error of*

> calculation by Dionysius, a Scythian monk who started the Christian calendar in the first half of the 6th century. The biblical record informs us that Jesus was born during the last few months of the reign of Herod the Great. Roman records indicate that Herod died in AUC 750, not in 754, as Dionysius miscalculated. The birth of Jesus was, therefore, sometime prior to 4 BC. There is no 0, so from 1 BC to AD 1 is one civil year, and from 4 BC to AD 4 is seven years. Thus, Jesus began his ministry at the age of 30 in the year AD 27.[16]

We can deduce from what Austin has written that the founding of the church probably occurred in 30 AD. We arrive at this number by adding three years from the beginning of Jesus' public ministry (27 AD). Since we know that he had a three-year public ministry beginning when he was thirty, and that he died when he was 33 years old, 30 AD marks the beginning of the church.

Stages in the Church's Development

Definite stages can be traced in the church's development and expansion. Many church historians and Bible students cite the following steps in the church's growth.

The first stage, of course, began with the birth of the church (Acts 2). With the coming of the Holy Spirit upon the 120 gathered in the upper room, as Jesus had predicted, the church was born. On that same day, following the preaching of Peter to Jewish pilgrims gathered in Jerusalem for the festival of Pentecost, 3,000 were baptized. All of the first church members were Jews and soon were seen as a new sect or movement within Judaism. There were many other Jewish sects: Pharisees, Sadducees, Zealots, Hellenists and Essenes, etc. Those converted at Pentecost and immediately following came to be known as "Nazarenes," meaning they were followers of Jesus, the man from Nazareth. These new converts went on living their lives very much as before—they spoke Aramaic (the common Semitic language spoken in the New East at that time), they continued going to the temple to pray, they observed the Jewish dietary laws, and they practiced circumcision. Their distinguishing marks were baptism in the name of Jesus, diligent regard for what was known as "the apostles' doctrine," meeting together for fellowship, worship, the breaking of bread, and their commitment to "having all things in common."

A second stage concerned the addition of Hellenistic Jews to the existing Aramaic community (Acts 6). Hellenists were Jews who followed the Greek customs, spoke Greek, but retained their Jewish faith. As the gospel spread among the Jews, it spilled over into these Jewish communities, with their Greek backgrounds. Thus, the test of bringing two cultural groups together was faced. Quarrels developed between the two groups because those from the Greek background believed that their widows were being overlooked in the daily distribution of food taking place in the Christian community (Acts 6). Seven leaders from among the Hellenists were appointed to solve the problem of overseeing the distribution of food to the widows. Among them was a young man named Stephen, who emerged as a preacher. In his preaching, he brought an indictment against Jerusalem's Judaism and condemned the temple and its worship. For this, he was stoned as a blasphemer and was the first known Christian martyr. His preaching also brought suspicion upon the Hellenists, and they had to flee from Jerusalem to Samaria, the Mediterranean coast, and Antioch. There they became missionaries to the Jews who lived in those areas.

A third stage involved the gospel being preached to the Samaritans. This is recorded in Acts 8, and the key person is Philip the evangelist. When a persecution broke out against the church, followers of Christ were scattered throughout Judea and Samaria. We are told that Philip, because of this dispersion, went to Samaria and proclaimed Christ. Many were converted and the church was established there. The Samaritans were a mixed race of Jew and

Gentile, but their religious roots were Jewish. They held to the Pentateuch, to circumcision, to Messianic hopes, and celebrated the Passover and Pentecost, but they had a temple of their own on Mt. Gerizim. The Jews and Samaritans hated each other. When Philip went and proclaimed the Christian message to them, and they believed, the gospel had been preached across all Jewish lines and was ready for the next step.

A fourth stage carried the message to the Gentiles (Acts 10, 11). This involved Peter taking the gospel to the Gentile, Cornelius, and his household. Peter was motivated by a vision to go to Cornelius. While Peter was preaching to the household of Cornelius, the Holy Spirit came to them in ways similar to the day of Pentecost, and Peter welcomed them into the church through baptism. This caused Peter to realize that it was not necessary to become a Jew before embracing the Christian faith, and he returned to Jerusalem to explain what had occurred. Though this was a major hurdle, his explanation persuaded the church in Jerusalem to accept the fact that the gospel was for Gentiles as well as Jews. From this time on, the Christian faith was no longer strictly tied to Judaism.

A fifth stage involved the missionary journeys of Paul and his colleagues. The first of these missionary journeys began at the city of Antioch (Acts 13). Antioch became the starting point for the evangelization of the Roman Empire. Paul and Barnabas joined together for this first missionary journey. They journeyed through Asia Minor entering the synagogues to preach to the Jews and then to the Gentiles, without imposing upon them Jewish practices. Following this initial missionary journey, Paul and his teams made several tours, all of which involved the proclamation of the gospel and the establishment of churches. Finally, he ended up in Rome where he had a powerful ministry and, it seems, helped establish the church that became the world center for Christianity. No doubt Paul was the greatest theologian and greatest missionary leader of the apostolic period. His theology and his missionary strategies have served to set the standard for others in all ages who have sought to continue the work of the church. It is important to note that everywhere Christ was proclaimed, churches resulted.

To summarize, the church spread in the following fashion: (1) from Aramaic Jews to (2) Hellenistic Jews to (3) Samaritans (half Jew, half Gentile) to (4) Gentiles and then (5) became a world religion as Paul carried the message into the wider segment of the Gentile world.

The Apostolic Period extends from the birth of the church in 30 AD to the death of John the apostle around 90-100 AD, covering a period of about 70 years. The church began in Jerusalem, moved through Palestine, and gradually extended through Syria, Asia Minor, Greece, and Italy. The most prominent centers of Christianity were Jerusalem, Antioch, and Rome. These represent respectively the mother churches of Jewish, Gentile, and catholic or universal Christianity. The nationalities reached in the first century were Jews, Greeks, and Romans, and the main languages used were Hebrew, Aramaic, and especially the Greek language. This period covered the reign of 10 Roman emperors, beginning with Tiberius (14-37 AD) and ending with Domitian (81-96 AD). The entire list of emperors includes Tiberius, Caligula, Claudius, Nero, Galba, Otho, Vitellius, Vespasian, Titus and Domitian.

What Happened to the Early Church Leaders?

The apostolic period of church history was characterized by great missionary zeal that resulted in the ever-expanding growth of the church. There can be no doubt that the apostles of Jesus Christ saw it as their responsibility to proclaim the gospel and establish the church to the ends of the earth. Jesus had commanded them to "go into all the world," and this is precisely what they did.

The 12 Apostles

Peter

Peter's leadership and initiative established him as one of Christianity's greatest heroes. His name heads all the lists of the apostles given in the Gospels of Matthew, Mark, and Luke, and in the Book of Acts. Peter preached the gospel throughout Pontus, Galatia, Bithynia, Cappadocia, and Asia.

According to tradition, Peter eventually went to Rome where he preached and supervised the missionary efforts of the early church from the center of the empire. Exactly when he went to Rome and how long he stayed is uncertain. He was martyred sometime during the reign of Nero (54-68 AD), probably in the year AD 65 during the first great persecution against the church. He and Paul might have been killed at or about the same time. Tertullian, an ancient Christian writer, who died about AD 225, says that Peter was crucified. Eusebius (AD 265-339), known as "the father of church history," adds that Peter suffered head downwards, at his own request.

Andrew

When we become acquainted with Andrew in the New Testament, we find him to be a disciple of John the Baptist. Andrew witnessed Jesus' baptism, was impressed by John's declaration that Jesus was "the Lamb of God," and decided to meet him. This meeting convinced him that Jesus was the Messiah, and he resolved to follow him. Thus Andrew became Jesus' first disciple.

Andrew is a Greek name that means "manly." He seems to have been one who had a quiet strength of character and helpfulness upon which others could rely. What we know of his later ministry comes through Eusebius, who reports that Andrew preached in Scythia, an area which is now Russian territory between the Black and Caspian Seas. The apocryphal *Acts of Andrew* tells us that he preached the gospel and suffered martyrdom by crucifixion in Greece. Tradition also says he was crucified on an X-shaped cross and its replica has since been called "St. Andrew's Cross." Later tradition maintains that his body was taken to Constantinople and during the Crusades was transferred to the town of Amalfi in Italy.

James, the Son of Zebedee

James is the only one of the 12 apostles whose martyrdom is recorded in the New Testament (Acts 12:1, 2). During a persecution of the church, Herod Agrippa I, king of Palestine (AD 42-44), had him beheaded. As far as we can tell, he is the first of the 12 to be martyred. There is a legend that James' accuser was so impressed by James' courage during his trial that he repented of what he had done, professed his belief in Christ, and was himself condemned to death. Seventeenth century Spanish tradition says that he preached in Spain and that his headless remains are buried in Santiago de Compostela. For this reason, within Catholicism, he remains the "patron saint of Spain."

John

After Pentecost, John worked closely with Peter in preaching the message of Christ. Paul, in his letter to the Galatians, states that the three outstanding leaders in the church at Jerusalem were Peter, James, and John.

There is strong, early tradition which indicates that after many years John went to Ephesus and followed Timothy who had been the leader in the church there. Apparently Timothy, who had been assigned to Ephesus by Paul, was beaten with sticks (probably around 79 AD) until he died, and a strong leader was needed. Available information states further that John was later taken to Rome to be martyred, miraculously escaped, but later, under the persecution initated by Domitian (81-96), was banished to the island of Patmos. The following is reported in *The Fragments of Papias* (70-155 AD):

> *After Domitian, Nerva reigned one year. He recalled John from the island and allowed him to live in Ephesus. At that time he was the sole survivor of the twelve disciples, and after writing the Gospel that bears his name was honored with martyrdom.*[17]

John died sometime after 90 AD. This is why we say the Apostolic Period ended around 100 AD

Philip

Though Philip is listed as one of the 12 apostles, the New Testament tells us very little about him. There are a number of traditions surrounding Philip: he preached the gospel in central Asia Minor and later died a natural death in Hierapolis (in Egypt) after the destruction of Jerusalem; he had three daughters; he was crucified under the emperor Domitian. Part of the difficulty in these traditions comes from the tendency in the second century to confuse Philip the apostle with Philip the evangelist who appears in the Book of Acts.

Bartholomew

Church historian, Eusebius, reports that in the third century Pantaenus met some people in India who had knowledge of Jesus Christ. Eusebius says that they showed Pantaenus a copy of the Gospel of Matthew in Hebrew which they maintained had been brought by Bartholomew when he came there to preach and establish churches. The name "India" was used indiscriminately by the early writers. It is probable that "India" was Ethiopia or Arabia. Other traditions claim that Bartholomew traveled with Philip and Thomas.

Thomas

The later work of Thomas is associated with Parthia and India. It is probable that he evangelized the "Christians of St. Thomas" in the

Malabar Coast of India, as they claim he did. A group of "Thomas Christians" in southwest India still worship in an ancient church said to have been founded by Thomas. Tradition holds that Thomas was martyred by spearing near Madras in AD 72, and was buried at Mylapore, a suburb of that city.

Matthew

It is said that after making many converts in Judea, Matthew went to evangelize nations of the East. It is probable that he labored in Ethiopia and was martyred there.

James, the Son of Alphaeus

Traditionally, James, the son of Alphaeus, and James "the brother of the Lord," have been regarded as the same person. Despite the fact that we know nothing of James' activity during the ministry of Jesus, he emerges to be a man of considerable importance in the early church. Two early historians tell us that James was put to death shortly before the destruction of Jerusalem in 70 AD. The Jewish historian Josephus reports that James and some others were stoned to death on the orders of the high priest, Annus, in 62 AD. Hegesippus, a second century historian, supplies vivid details of James' death. He tells us that James' enemies placed James on a pinnacle of the Temple and urged him to deny publicly that Jesus was the Messiah. Instead, James gave a rousing vindication of Christ. Furious, his enemies cast him from the Temple. Finding that the fall had not killed him, they began to stone him. As they did so, it is reported that James prayed for his persecutors. Eventually, he was beaten with a club and was buried at the place where he died.

Jude or Thaddeus

Luke's Gospel and the Acts of the Apostles name him Jude, or Judas, but Matthew and Mark call him "Thaddeus." There is no doubt that this is the same person. "Thaddeus" is most likely a descriptive name introduced to distinguish him from the traitor

Judas Iscariot. Traditionally, Jude, the apostle, had been thought to be the brother of James, "the brother of the Lord," but nowadays most scholars challenge this identification. There is a Western tradition that Jude preached the gospel in Mesopotamia, then went to Persia with Simon where they evangelized, made many converts, and finally were martyred there.

Simon, the Cananaean

The New Testament lists Simon as one of the twelve, but gives him no further mention. Luke and Acts call him "the Zealot." He was probably given this title because he belonged to the radical Jewish faction that opposed Roman rule in Palestine. The Zealots thought of themselves as the agents of God's righteous wrath against idolatry and any other transgression of the Law. They were convinced that acceptance of foreign domination and payment of taxes to a foreign ruler were blasphemy against God. Their tactics were similar to those used by political terrorists today: they killed frequently, attacking both foreigners and Jews who they suspected of collaboration. The Zealots were the chief instigators of the Jewish rebellion against Rome in 66 AD. During the next few years they gained control of Jerusalem by the suppression or murder of those who opposed them. Even after the fall of Jerusalem in 70 AD, they still maintained small pockets of resistance.

Some early Christian writers identify Simon with Simeon, son of Clopas, who according to the historian Hegesippus, succeeded James as head of the Church in Jerusalem. An Eastern tradition maintains that he died peacefully in Edessa, but this conflicts with a Western tradition that holds that he was martyred with Jude in Persia.

Paul

Though he was not one of the twelve, no account of the activities of early church would be complete without mention of the apostle Paul. Sometime after his conversion, Paul embarked on his apostolic ministry to the Gentiles. He undertook three missionary journeys, made countless converts to Christianity, and established several churches to which he wrote his well-known epistles. After his third journey, he returned to Jerusalem where some Jews accused him of bringing Gentiles into the inner court of the Temple. A riot ensued and Paul was arrested. Eventually, when he appealed to Caesar in virtue of his Roman citizenship, he was taken to Rome where he was put under house arrest for two years. There is no certain information about Paul after the aforementioned. Some think he made two more missionary journeys to Spain and Macedonia. Traditionally, he is said to have been martyred, by beheading, on the Ostian Way at a place called Aquae Silviae. His martyrdom probably occurred in 64 or 65 AD

The historian Eusebius wrote the following comments about the dispersion of the apostles:

> *It is said that this Mark traveled to Egypt and was the first to preach there the Gospel which he had written, and that he was the first to found churches in Alexandria itself.*[18]
>
> *The holy apostles and disciples of our saviour were dispersed throughout the inhabited world. Thomas, according to tradition, was assigned the country of the Parthians (Matthew obtained Ethiopia, Bartholomew upper India), Andrew Scythia, John Asia where he lived: he died at Ephesus. Peter seems to have preached to the Jews of the Dispersion in Pontus, Galatia, Bithynia, Cappadocia and Asia; finally having come to Rome also, he was crucified head downwards, having himself asked that he might suffer in this way. What need we say of Paul who, from Jerusalem to Illyricum, fully proclaimed the gospel of Christ and finally bore witness at Rome under Nero? These are the express words which Origen uses in the third volume of his Commentaries on Genesis.*[19]

Chapter 2

The Gospel Is Established: 30 - 100 AD

Today, as we read the New Testament, the message of the gospel seems quite clear. As apparent as it might seem to us, it was not quite as evident to the early Christians, especially as they tried to establish the essential elements of the gospel. From its inception, the meaning of the message given by Jesus Christ to his disciples was sorely challenged. Bound together by the resurrection, the teaching of the apostles, and the sacraments, the embryonic church spread throughout Judea. In this growth, there was also the process of "figuring out" or interpreting the meaning of "the apostles' doctrine."

Judaizers

The first major test came through the Judaizers. The Judaizers believed that the gospel was true but it was ineffective without the addition of Jewish law, namely, circumcision. This was, perhaps, the first entrance of legalism into the church. Paul's concern for the Judaizers is expressed throughout his writings. When he says, "Beware of the dogs...beware of the false circumcision," he is speaking of those who brought this legalistic element into the Christian teaching. Not only did they seek to affect the content of the gospel, they literally "dogged" Paul, trying to undo what he taught. They said his gospel was "too easy." They believed that to say a person was "saved by grace alone" would lead to a license to sin. Paul entered into heated debates with the Judaizers and believed that what they preached was "distorted" and, in fact, was "another gospel"...that it did not even come close to representing the true gospel of Jesus Christ. Throughout the church, he saw the temptation to adopt the ideas of the Judaizers and this represented a grave danger. This issue became so great that within 20 years of its founding, the church stood at the brink of a split.

A climax came in dealing with this issue in 50 AD, when the Jerusalem Council met to address questions related to the teaching of the Judaizers. This is described in Acts 15. The chapter begins with this explanation, "And some men came down from Judea and began teaching the brethren, 'Unless you are circumcised according to the custom of Moses, you can't be saved.' When Paul and Barnabas had great dissension and debate with them, the brethren determined that Paul and Barnabas and certain others of them, should go up to Jerusalem to the apostles and elders concerning this issue." The conclusion of the council was that nothing could be added to the work of Christ: a person is saved by grace alone.

This issue gave birth to the first church council, set a precedent and a pattern, and gave justification for future councils to be held when needed. The goal was to establish apostolic doctrine in relationship to this issue. Paul's concerns in relationship to the teaching of the Judaizers can be found particularly in the book of Galatians. Although the official position of the Jerusalem council was made clear, the Judaizers continued for some time to cause agitation throughout the church.

Gnostics (Docetists)

A second challenge to the doctrine of the church came in the form of Gnosticism, a theological-philosophical system born out of Greek thinking. The word *gnostic*, comes from the Greek word *gnosis*, which means "knowledge." The word *docetism* comes from the Greek, *dokeo*, which means "to seem" or "to appear." The basic belief of the Gnostics is what is known as dualism, meaning that the world is divided into two cosmic forces: good and evil. Good is identified with the spiritual world and evil is identified with the material world. It is more accurate to say that Gnosticism was not a singular religion but a series of movements within a wider range of thought. Each movement offered a way of enlightenment by a religious leader or philosopher who possessed "the gnosis," the special knowledge about life. The human problem, as they saw it, was that the pure light of heaven in the soul of man had become contaminated through matter and had to be redeemed. In the process of redemption, the Gnostics believed that there were basically three groups of people: (1) a higher or enlightened spiritual class that lived by gnosis, higher knowledge, or secret wisdom; (2) a lower spiritual class that lived by faith; and (3) a spiritually disadvantaged class that could not come to gnosis regardless of how good a teacher they studied under. This was actually a strange type of predestination.

Various Gnostic ideas filtered into Christian teaching because of the emphasis that the spirit was good and material was evil. The "flesh" was part of the material creation and needed to be overcome. To many, this seemed compatible with Christian doctrine.

The Gnostics believed in an ultimate Supreme Being who was far removed from the physical creation but had allowed a lesser god to create the universe. Since the Supreme Being could have no contact with the material world, the Gnostics explained the origin of the material world through a series of emanations. They taught that there was a long chain of divine creatures, each weaker than the one before it (its parent). One might think of God as a kind of sun, the emanations would be the sunbeams, extensions of His own nature, but distinct from Him. Each emanation was capable of creating other "supernatural" beings but of lesser power and wisdom. It was one of these powers that created the material world. He was powerful enough to create, but not wise enough to see that creation was an error. He is the God of this world and the one known as the God of the Jews.

This system came into direct conflict with Christian teaching about the person of Christ. The problem, of course, was that if Christ were truly God, how could He possess a material body? According to their teaching, the eternal Son of God did not become human or suffer on the cross; He only appeared to do so. Because Christ was "spiritualized," His true humanity was denied. Thus, there was no true sacrifice for sins and salvation was achieved through knowledge. As Gnostic teaching began to influence Christianity, various ideas began to emerge to explain his appearance as a human. Fundamental to their thinking was the idea that the Ultimate Deity sent one of his subordinate powers called "Christ" into the world to free men from the bonds of matter. Of course, it would not do to have this Son of God possess a material body. To overcome the problem of Jesus having an actual body, they taught that what people saw was merely a human appearance—a ghost, hallucination, or phantom. Others devised a more complicated explanation, saying that at the baptism of Jesus the true Christ descended into the human named "Jesus," and at, or just before his crucifixion, the true Christ left him. The true Christ could not be crucified. They taught that Jesus' resurrected body was a phantom. It is interesting that the first challenge to the church was not a denial of Christ's deity, but a denial of his humanity. The one apostle who gave special attention to the failures of Gnosticism was John. It is apparent that the teaching of Gnosticism had made its way into Christian circles due to the attention John gave in making it clear that Christian teaching stands in contradistinction to Gnostic philosophy. Though he does not mention the terms *gnosis*, *Gnostic*, or *Gnosticism*, in his gospel and in I and II John, he addresses issues pertaining to Gnosticism (cf., John 1:14; I John 4:1-3; II John 7).

Apostolic Doctrine

The existence of these false religions, or aberrations from the doctrine taught by the apostles, forced the early Christians to come to grips with the essential elements of their faith. Was it possible to draw clear lines between the true worship of Jesus Christ and the wide series of religious ideas and practices of the Greek, Roman, and other middle-eastern religions? Because a large number of people came to faith out of these backgrounds, many of their old ideas were carried with them into Christianity. Thus, besides the persecutions they experienced, the church was faced with many internal uncertainties.

It is important for us to remember that though the Old Testament Scriptures were known and treated as inspired by these early Christians, the New Testament canon had not yet been developed. It was not until well into the third and fourth centuries that final recognition would be given to the books that now comprise the New Testament. Therefore, it is rather amazing to see that the apostolic church was able to discern clearly the content and meaning of Christian doctrine.

How was this done? First, it seems apparent that truth was preserved in the writings of the apostles. Even though the canon would "officially" be recognized much later, all of the New Testament books were written in the first century. Those known as apostles, and those associated with the apostles, were naturally trusted as ones able to communicate accurately what Jesus had taught. The book of James was written in or around 45 AD. Soon after the mid-century, Paul's writings were circulating among the churches, shortly followed by the four Gospels. So, as the writings of the apostles and those close to the apostles began to appear, they were collected, copied, and read in the churches. However, it is important to remember that though these writings were highly trusted, they had not yet been recognized as "Scripture."

Second, along with the New Testament books, creeds began to emerge as a means for communicating the basic and essential elements of the Christian faith. The earliest developed were called baptismal creeds. They were first used to prepare converts for baptism but soon were used for other purposes, such as distinguishing between genuine belief and false teaching. In the first century church, these creeds were held in high regard and were included as part of "the tradition" ("the teaching") of the apostles (II Thess. 3:6; I Cor. 11:2). The word *creed* comes from the Latin *credo*, "I believe," or *credimus*, "we believe," and were simply distilled versions of the broader content of Christian doctrine that was being assembled and taught at that time. It is probable that some of these creeds existed as summaries of the teachings of the apostles prior to the composition of the New Testament. They then made their appearance in the New Testament books when they were written. Examples of biblical passages thought to be creeds are:

I Timothy 3:16

Great is the mystery of godliness:
He appeared in a body,
    Was vindicated by the Spirit,
Was seen by angels,
    Was preached among the nations,
Was believed on in the world,
    Was taken up into glory.

It is likely that this text from I Timothy was also sung by the church because common practice was to put doctrine into musical settings.

Acts 4:12

Neither is there salvation in any other,
for there is no other name under heaven
given among men, whereby we must be saved.

Romans 10:9, 10

That if you confess with your mouth,

> "Jesus is Lord," and believe in your
> heart that God has raised Him from
> the dead, you shall be saved. For with
> the heart man believes unto righteousness
> and with the mouth confession is made
> unto salvation.

I Corinthians 15:3, 4

> For I delivered unto you as of first
> importance what I also received, that
> Christ died for our sins according to
> the Scriptures, and that He was buried,
> and that He was raised on the third day
> according to the Scriptures.

Ephesians 4:4-6

> There is one body and one Spirit,
> just as also you were called in one hope of your calling
> one Lord, one faith, one baptism, one God and Father
> who is over all and through all and in all.

It is also most likely that the earliest copies of the *Apostles' Creed* began to be circulated in the late first or early second century. In its first version, it was called the *Old Roman Creed* and reads as follows:

> I believe in God almighty
> And in Christ Jesus, His only son, our Lord
> Who was born of the Holy Spirit and the Virgin Mary
> Who was crucified under Pontius Pilate and was buried
> And the third day rose from the dead
> Who ascended into heaven
> And sits on the right hand of the Father
> Whence he comes to judge the living and the dead
> And in the Holy Ghost

The holy church
The remission of sins
The resurrection of the flesh
The life everlasting.

This creed went through several revisions until it became the *Apostles' Creed* that we know today. It was put into its "final" form around 700 AD. In its later version, the creed adds the line, "Maker of heaven and earth." In this, it repudiated the Gnostic idea that the created world is evil and the work of an evil or inferior god. Statements in the creed that point to the full humanity of Jesus, such as, "born of the Virgin Mary," and "crucified under Pontius Pilate," stated to the Gnostic that Jesus was flesh. The phrase in the creed that states concerning man's future, "The resurrection of the flesh," is aimed directly at the Gnostics, stating that the body is not an evil thing to be discarded, but a gift of God to be enjoyed and something so essential to the nature of humanity that it is included in the resurrection.

Another document, which dates from the end of the first century or beginning of the second century, is the *Didache*, also called *The Teaching of the Twelve*. It was a church manual designed to teach new converts and give guidance in the practice of the Christian life. It contains references to the Lord's Prayer and prayers of thanksgiving used at the celebration of the Eucharist. It also contains instructions on the practice of baptism and the Lord's Supper.

All of these short creeds and collections of the apostles' teachings served to help summarize the content of Christian doctrine. They played a more important role than we might imagine. Even though the New Testament canon had not been developed, Christian truth was being preserved. Interestingly, when the time came to apply tests to those books thought to be canonical, they were judged by the "teaching" or doctrine handed down and collected by the church throughout the first century. This is just the opposite of today. When we want to test a doctrine or a teaching, we test it against the Scriptures. In their day, they tested what was thought to be Scripture against what was known as Christian doctrine.

A third and very important way Christian truth was preserved was through the development of the apostolic ministry. The early church was built upon apostolic foundations. This included two important elements: doctrinal foundations and governmental foundations. Men trained by the apostles became stalwarts in protecting the doctrine and guiding the church. Through the efforts of the apostles, bishoprics were developed that provided unity of doctrine and practice of church life. These bishops worked together in various ways. They protected what they perceived to be the doctrine handed down from the apostles, gathered sacred writings, guided the church in its worship, and developed life in the Christian communities. This organic process gave a dynamic to the life of the church and also provided order and consensus in maintaining oneness and doctrinal purity.

Chapter 3

The New Testament is Written: 45 - 100 AD

The "Holy Bible" of the church of the first century was the Old Testament. It was their authority as they sought to defend and establish the church in its early days. When we are told that certain Christians "searched the Scriptures daily to see if these things were so," it was the Old Testament that was the object of their investigation. It is clear from the quotes in the book of Acts that the early Christians saw the Old Testament as Scripture and sufficient. There is no indication that the church desired any other religious literature, and it would have seemed to them sacrilegious and dangerous to add anything to this "ancient treasure."

However, the apostolic church, beginning sometime around 30 AD, began coming into possession of a body of religious literature; and, it was growing. This caused the leaders of the church to consider the meaning of this and what should be done about it. Some of it bore marks of special significance and other had questionable traits. The New Testament literature came into existence in general, and the gospels in particular, because they espoused special ideas about the *life* and *teaching* of Jesus Christ. Both of these aspects were deemed important. What could be said (written) that would give an accurate account of the uniqueness of the person of Christ? But Jesus also espoused a certain teaching or philosophy. How could this be accurately preserved?

During the first 20 years after the ascension of Christ (30-50 AD), the facts concerning the person and teaching of Jesus were circulated and preserved orally—by word of mouth, oral testimony, and tradition. In Palestine at that time, training seems to have been generally, if not exclusively, oral. The rule among some rabbis was, "Commit nothing to writing," because it was believed that such an act would lead to slothfulness in learning. If one were to write it down, he would be dependent upon what was written and the mind would remain inactive. Rather, truth could be brought into a person's life through an attentive and active mind. So, the people were trained in oral learning. Through custom and training they were used to hearing, paying close attention, and remembering. Some became so proficient they could memorize most, if not all, of what a teacher or speaker presented as he spoke. It is worth noting how many times in the Old Testament references are made to the Word of God being read to the people. The people of the east, not dependent upon textbooks and notebooks, listened and developed retentive memories and accurate repetition to such a degree that this method was trusted for communicating—even the gospel. This, to them, was the normal way to communicate so that succeeding generations would have the same truth and carry on the same traditions.

An illustration of the belief in oral and catechetical (question and answer) instruction can be seen in the way the apostles addressed the matter of training Christians and taking the gospel to others. The first books of the New Testament were not written until 15 or 20 years after the founding of the church. The apostles were in Jerusalem long enough to shape a common narrative and tell it to the church. By the time the first persecution and scattering of Christians occurred around 34-35 AD (Acts 8:1-4;11:19), the apostles and their co-workers went everywhere "preaching the word," which meant they were telling the story of Jesus and salvation—his birth, life, death, resurrection, and ascension. This oral gospel was being circulated throughout Palestine and throughout the mission fields. Luke speaks of Theophilus as having received catechetical instruction, "by word of mouth" (Luke 1:4). Luke also made reference to others before him who had taken it in hand to "draw up a narrative" concerning matters well established "among us." Was this a reference to the other writers of the gospels only, or was it a reference to the writings of other eyewitnesses who were concerned that the message be preserved? Those who could give an accurate account of the life and meaning of Christ through oral instruction were thought of as "ministers of the Word". Recent papyrus discoveries in Egypt have produced scraps of papyri containing sayings of Jesus, as well as other matter. Could Luke's reference be to the writings of those now categorized as apocryphal literature?

So, from the founding of the church, the story of Christ and salvation was transmitted largely through oral means (30-45 AD). In the next period (45-100 AD), we have the origin of the New Testament. The need arose for placing oral teaching and preaching into written form. There are several reasons why:

- The number of persons who could give personal testimony to what Jesus did and said was rapidly becoming smaller as eyewitnesses, friends, and those taught by Jesus died.
- Christianity was spreading far beyond the limits of Palestine and needed a written record.
- Unlike the quiet life of the isolated Jewish people, regions beyond Palestine were characterized more by the hurry of life and crowding of events, so it was not safe to trust memory and oral transmission.
- It was easy for pagan influences or interpretations to be attached to the gospel.

Because of these events and the accumulation of literature about Jesus Christ, it became necessary to separate what was reliable from what was suspect. It became clear that a body of New Testament literature was being produced that would stand alongside the Old Testament Scriptures. The apostles themselves, because they were the closest to Jesus, saw it important to put their knowledge into written form. Along with them, certain companions of the apostles wrote. It was finally recognized that all of the New Testament was written by an apostle or a companion of an apostle. Though all of the New Testament was written between 45 and 95 AD (most written between 50-70 AD), it took many more years for full and complete recognition. (See section on "Canon" under the "Patristic Period.") Even though the church's final stamp of approval did not come until the fourth century, many of the books were recognized in the first century as having authority.

Another influence that necessitated the development of a recognized New Testament canon, and at the same time caused its delay, was the emergence of two other types of literature: *apocryphal* and *pseudepigraphal*. The word *apocrypha* comes from the Greek word, *apokrupha*, meaning "secret or hidden." The Middle English word meant "not authentic." *Apocryphal* books were those argued by some to be canonical or semi-canonical. Those books long held to be New Testament apocrypha or extra-canonical literature are:

The Teaching of the Twelve (The Didache)
The Epistle of Barnabas
The First Epistle of Clement
The Second Epistle of Clement
The Shepherd of Hermes
The Apocalypse of Peter
The Acts of Paul, including Paul and Thecla
The Seven Epistles of Ignatius
The Gospel of Pseudo-Matthew
The Protevangelium of James
The Gospel of the Nativity of Mary
The Gospel of Nicodemus
The Gospel of the Savior's Infancy
The History of Joseph the Carpenter
The Epistle of Polycarp to the Philippians

The word *pseudepigrapha* means "false writings" or "falsely ascribed." *Pseudepigrapha* are those writings that claim to be produced by biblical writers or in biblical times. Listed in this literature are gospels, acts, epistles, and apocalypses.

The Gospel of Matthew
The Gospel of Bartholomew
The Acts of Thomas
The Acts of Matthias

The Gospel of Barnabas	*The Acts of Philip*
The Gospel of Matthias	*The Acts of Thaddaeus*
The Gospel of Thomas	*The Epistle of Paul to the Laodiceans*
The Gospel of Peter	*The Apocalypse of Peter*
The Gospel of Philip	*The Apocalypse of Paul*
The Acts of Paul	*The Apocalypse of Thomas*
The Acts of Peter	*The Apocalypse of John,*
The Acts of Andrew	"*The Theologian*"

There are some values to be found in both the apocryphal and pseudepigraphal writings. They reveal some of the traditions of the early church; they contain some of the earliest documentation of the canonical books of the New Testament; they form a bridge between the apostolic writings of the New Testament period and the patristic literature of the third and fourth centuries; and they contain much of historical value about the practices and policies of the early church.[20] In general, they are found to be unacceptable due to lack of substantiation and verification of authors, along with certain inaccuracies. They reflect the ascetic, Docetic and Gnostic tendencies and heresies of early Christianity…they show a popular desire for information not given in the canonical Gospels, such as the childhood of Jesus, and the lives of the apostles…they display an unhealthy desire to find support for doctrinal interests and heretical teaching under the guise of apostolic authority…and [display] fanciful embellishments of Christian truth (e.g., Mary worship).[21]

Thus, because of the variety of literature being compiled, it became necessary to discern which works deserved recognition as "Scripture." The standards of authenticity had already been set by the Old Testament Scriptures. *Which writings could equal them in Divine authorship?* became the question in producing a New Testament canon. The books that began to be recognized and used immediately were many or most of the ones we have in our present-day New Testament. Their authorship, composition, and time of writing can be characterized as follows.

The Gospels

The Gospel of Mark, according to most authorities, was the first gospel written and the date given is around 50 AD. Interestingly, Mark was not an apostle but he was a disciple of one of the very important apostles. The bishop and church historian, Eusebius (270-340 AD), quotes from bishop Papias (70-155 AD), who said that John the Elder, who we believe to be John the Apostle, said the following: "Mark indeed became Peter's interpreter, and wrote accurately as many things as he remembered of the things said or done by Christ… For neither did he hear the Lord, nor did he follow Him; but afterwards he attended to Peter… So Mark committed no error in thus writing some things as he recalled them; for he took thought of one thing, not to omit anything that he heard, nor to make any false statement therein."[22]

The Gospel of Matthew was the second account written about the life and teaching of Jesus and may be dated about 58 AD. Matthew was a disciple of Christ and was appointed an apostle by Jesus. Prior to becoming a follower of Christ he had been a customs officer, a Roman tax collector, and as such he would have been skilled in taking notes and making records. He was an eyewitness of the person, works, and teachings of Christ. His personal observations, his contact with other apostles and probable conversations with Jesus' father, Joseph, presumably account for his "sources." According to Papias, Matthew made notes in Hebrew of the sayings of Jesus, called the *Logia of Matthew*. He wrote what we know as *The Gospel of Matthew* in Greek, and it is quite possible that many, if not all, of these sayings were incorporated into his Greek gospel.

The Gospel of Luke was most likely written about 59 or 60 AD at the city of Caesarea. Luke was not an apostle, but was the close companion of the Apostle Paul. He accompanied Paul on his missionary journeys and was with him in meetings with other apostles. He seemed to be well educated, was a physician, and proved himself an able historian. He explains in the beginning of his gospel that the sources of his writings were written documents and eyewitnesses.

The Gospel of John, it is believed by a majority of scholars, was written at a date later than any of the other gospels. Some have argued that it was written sometime prior to the fall of Jerusalem in 70 AD. However, most agree that his gospel was written at Ephesus as late as 90-95 AD. This would mean that the gospel might have been written as many as 30 years after the Synoptic Gospels (the first three). In one sense, it might be said that John had no "sources." He was close to Christ, being "the disciple that Jesus loved." He was with Jesus from the beginning of his ministry, and his ripe age, his mature thought, and his spiritual insights made his work original. His view is different. The other gospels view Christ more from the earthly point of view while John views him from the heavenly, focusing on the deity of Christ. As time passed, John probably saw it necessary to provide this view of Christ for the church, especially in light of the heretical views that were being promoted at the end of the first century.

The Epistles

James, who is thought to be the Lord's brother, wrote his epistle at Jerusalem around 45 AD to encourage Hebrew Christians who had been suffering persecution under Herod Agrippa I (Acts 12). The date of its composition makes it the first New Testament book.

I Thessalonians and II Thessalonians were written from Corinth during 52 to 53 AD while Paul was on his second missionary journey.

Galatians and 1 Corinthians were written on Paul's third mission trip, probably from Ephesus in 57 AD. On that same journey, he wrote *II Corinthians*, probably in the same year, and probably from

Philippi. As he continued on this trip it is conjectured that he wrote *Romans* while he was in Corinth in 58 AD.

Ephesians, Colossians, Philemon, and Philippians were written during Paul's first Roman imprisonment in 63 AD and are generally referred to as the "prison epistles."

I Timothy and Titus were probably written around 63 or 64 AD after Paul was released from his first imprisonment and *II Timothy* during his second imprisonment in 64 or 65 AD. These three letters are known as the "pastoral epistles" because they deal with qualifications of pastoral leaders as well as care of church members.

I Peter, II Peter, I John, II John, III John, and Jude are referred to as the "general epistles." There is little agreement regarding the dates of their composition, but it is probable that *I Peter* was written around 63 or 64 AD, *II Peter* about 64 or 65 AD, *Jude* about 66–68 AD, and *I, II,* and *III John* about 90-92 AD.

Hebrews is perhaps the most unusual of New Testament books. This is due to the fact that its authorship still stands in question. Some argued that Paul wrote it; others were sure he did not write it; and yet others remained uncertain. It was one of the last books to be admitted into the canon and that was largely through the influence of Augustine and Jerome. Ironically, it is one of the most doctrinal of books and is loaded with either quotations or allusions to the Old Testament, and this is the main reason it was accepted. Most agree that if an apostle did not write the book, an acquaintance did. It is believed it was written about 64 or 65 AD.

History

Acts has been satisfactorily proven to be the work of Luke, also the author of the Gospel of Luke. It is also agreed that it was written about 63 AD. Besides being an eyewitness of much of the early history of the church, he had access to Peter, Philip, Paul, and others who were their companions.

Prophecy

Revelation was written by John, who is taken to be the Apostle John. His source for the book was direct revelation from the risen Christ in signs, symbols, and visions. Two dates are suggested for its composition, 68 and 96 AD. The latter date is preferred by most scholars.

Chapter 4

The Persecutions Are Initiated: 64 AD

Paulus Orosius, a church historian and church leader who lived around the turn of the fifth century, catalogues ten major persecutions that occurred against the Church during the first 300 years of its existence. The rulers and the dates of their reigns are listed below. The names in italics represent the most severe persecutions.

Nero (54-68 AD)
Domitian (81-96 AD)
Trajan (98-117 AD)
Marcus Aurelius (161-180 AD)
Septimus Severus (202-211 AD)
Maximus Thrax (235-238 AD)
Decius (249-251 AD)
Valerian (253-260 AD)
Aurelian (270-275 AD)
Diocletian (284-305 AD)

These persecutions came during the time Roman emperors were trying to maintain control over a disintegrating empire. The great years of Rome had passed. Rome was founded in 753 BC and had experienced progressive growth to greatness, which culminated under Julius Caesar who ruled from 60 BC to 44 BC.

Period of Persecutions

During the next 250 years—actually until 312 AD—there were many more emperors with several calling themselves "Augustus," which meant that each one was to be received as "a god among the gods," making emperor worship a familiar part of the religions in the Roman world. Each time one of these men declared himself to be a god, there was usually the accompanying motive to gain control over an empire continuing to disintegrate, and so persecutions also accompanied his rule.

It is a curious fact that some of the best of the Roman emperors—Trajan, Marcus Aurelius, Decius, and Diocletian—were harsh to Christians, while some of the worst in terms of personal morality and ethics left them in peace.

Why Christians Were Persecuted

Roman authority was very tolerant of the variety of religions found in the vast Roman empire. Wherever Roman armies raised the standard of Rome, they almost always found some kind of new religion. As long as these new religions had no problem adding homage or worship of the emperor to their ceremonies, Rome seldom interfered. This was almost always the case.

When Christianity first appeared, it was considered to be a sect of the Jews. The Jews, with their fanatical loyalty to one true God, and their willingness to turn their land into a blood-soaked wilderness before they would acknowledge any other deity, were made an exception. They received immunity from worshipping in the Roman way with its worship of many gods, including emperor worship. For a time, Christianity operated under this "covering" until it became apparent that there was a difference. Four distinctives might be noted that set the Christians apart and caused them to be persecuted.

The first distinctive concerned their relationship to the Jews. For a while, Christians found protection under the Jewish system because they were viewed as a Jewish sect. Since initially all the believers in the Church were Jewish, they therefore lived under the Roman law designed to allow the Jews to continue with their own religion and culture. They actually met in Jewish synagogues, which served to secure their position. However, after it became apparent to the Jews that there was a major distinction between them and the Christians, the Jews rejected the Christians and removed them from synagogue worship. Thus, the Christians lost the protection they had under the immunity granted to the Jews since the time of Julius Caesar.

Second, the Christians were more aggressive than the Jews in trying to make converts throughout the empire. Like the Jews, they refused to worship the emperor. Unlike them, they were doing their utmost to reach people with the gospel, even from among the emperor's subjects. So, their attempts at spreading the gospel was seen as causing unrest. The problem of Rome was maintaining unity. Anything that did not contribute to this was brought under suspicion. Christianity was the first religion in history to perceive its beliefs as being for the world. Christ was needed by all mankind. Other religions were content to allow people of other faiths to function on their own without interfering. They did not see evangelism as necessary; whereas, the followers of Christ did.

Third, the Christians maintained a distinctive lifestyle. Tertullian explained that Christians had the reputation of living aloof from the crowds. The word used to describe the New Testament Christians was the Greek *hagios*, often translated "saints," and meaning, "holy ones." Moral and ethical behavior accompanied their faith in Christ. In trying to be distinctive in this way, the Christians were sometimes thought to be anti-social or disinterested in social or governmental issues. Along with this came suspicion. At one point they were accused of cannibalism because they were said to be eating flesh and drinking blood in their meetings. This, of course, stirred up public sentiment against them.

Fourth, and the primary reason, in arousing suspicion and bringing persecution upon the Christians was their rejection of the pagan gods and emperor-worship. Christians were not persecuted because they worshipped Jesus. They were persecuted because they worshipped "Jesus only." The Roman world was a world of mixture—syncretism—when it came to religious life. There were many gods and nobody cared who worshipped whom so long as their worship did not disrupt the unity of the state, and included the worship of Caesar. Because the Christians would not bow to Caesar, or any other god, they were seen as troublesome rebels. They would not have had such problems if they had worshipped Jesus and just added emperor-worship, but they would not worship any man. It was because of this that they were called "atheists." This charge was coupled to the fact that many within the empire could not understand "imageless" worship. As a result, they blamed the Christians for insulting the gods of the state.

Two Great Persecutors in the First Century

Nero

Lucius Domitius Ahenobarbus was his given name, but he became Nero Claudius Caesar Germanicus V, and the last Roman emperor in the line of Julius Caesar. He was born at Antium on the sea coast, December 15, 37 AD. He was 31 years of age and in the 14th year of his reign when he died on June 9, 68 AD.

His father was Enaeus Domitius Ahenobarbus, a man from a well-known family of Rome, but not in the line of the emperors. His mother was Agrippina, the Younger, daughter of Agrippina the Elder, sister of the emperor Caius (also called "Caligula"), and niece of the next-to-be emperor, Claudius. When Nero was born, his father predicted that any offspring born of himself and Agrippina could only prove disastrous for the public. Both of them were very volatile people. At the age of three, Nero lost his father, and most of the estate was taken through the covetousness of the emperor

Caius (Caligula). In the year 39 AD, Agrippina, Nero's mother, was banished from Rome because Caius suspected she was involved in a plot against him. Thus, Nero was deprived of his mother and, at the same time, left with nothing. With Agrippina absent from Rome, Nero's aunt, Domitia Lepida, took responsibility for the boy and placed him with two tutors, a dancer and a barber. These two would have a life-long effect on him.

On the occasion of Claudius' ascension to the throne in 41 AD, Agrippina, being his niece, was recalled from her banishment, and Nero was restored to his mother. From this point in time, Agrippina worked in every possible way to see that her son become emperor, which, in fact, occurred on October 13, 54 AD.

Perhaps one of the better summaries of Nero's life is offered by Philip Schaff:

> *The glorious first five years of Nero's reign (54-59) under the wise guidance of Seneca and Burrhus, make the other nine (59-68) only more hideous by contrast. We read his life with mingled feelings of contempt for his folly, and horror of his wickedness. The world was to him a comedy and a tragedy, in which he was to be the chief actor. He had an insane passion for popular applause; he played on the lyre; he sung his odes at supper; he drove his chariots in the circus; he appeared as a mimic on the stage, and compelled men of the highest rank to represent in dramas or in tableaux the obscene of the Greek myths. But the comedian was surpassed by the tragedian. He heaped crime upon crime until he became a proverbial monster of iniquity. The murder of his brother (Britannicus), his mother (Agrippina), his wives (Octavia and Poppaea), his teacher (Seneca), and many eminent Romans, was fitly followed by his suicide in the thirty-second year of age. With him the family of Julius Caesar ignominiously perished....*[23]

The event which launched Nero's persecution and made him the first major persecutor of the Christians, was the burning of the city of Rome in 64 AD. Bruce Shelley gives the following account:

> *In the year 64 AD, during the reign of Emperor Nero, fire broke out in Rome. For six days and nights the fire burned. The greater part of the city was laid in ashes. The rumor circulated that Nero himself had caused the city to be set on fire. This aroused great hatred among the people of Rome against the emperor. To turn this hatred away from himself Nero accused the Christians of having set the fire. The accusation certainly was not true, but large numbers of Christians were arrested and a terrible persecution followed. Many Christians were even crucified. Some were sewn up in the skins of wild beasts; then big dogs were let loose upon them, and they were torn to pieces. Women were tied to mad bulls and dragged to death. After nightfall Christians were burned at the stake in Nero's garden. The Roman people who hated the Christians were allowed to come into the garden, and Nero drove around in his chariot enjoying the horrible spectacle to the full. It was probably during this persecution that the apostles Peter and Paul suffered martyrdom in Rome.*[24]

Peter and Paul probably died in 64 or 65 AD. Many believe that Nero burned Rome with the intention of rebuilding a grander and more glorious city and calling it "Neropolis." The church historian, Eusebius, reports the following:

> *They say that in the reign of Nero, Paul was beheaded at Rome itself, and that Peter likewise was crucified, and this story is confirmed by the association of the names of Peter and Paul with the cemeteries there, which has lasted to this day. That is also affirmed by a churchman, called Gaius, who lived in the time of Zephyrinus (199-217*

AD), Bishop of the Romans. When discoursing in writing with Proclus, the head of the sect of the Phrygians, Gaius in fact said this of the places where the sacred tabernacles of the said apostles were laid: "But I myself can point out the trophies of the apostles. For if it is your will to go to the Vatican or to the Ostian way, you will find the trophies of those who founded this church".[25]

Domitian

Domitian ruled from 81-96 AD. He became the second emperor to be known for his persecution of Christians, which began in 85 AD. After a promising beginning, he became as cruel and bloodthirsty as Nero, and practiced self-deification. He began his letters with words like, "Our Lord and God commands...," referring to himself. He required his subjects to address him as "Lord and God." He ordered gold and silver statues of himself to be placed in the holiest place of the temples. It was reported that when he seemed most friendly, he was the most dangerous.

Domitian was a cruel and savage ruler who not only persecuted Christians but put to death some of the chief citizens of Rome. To get money to pay for the games and the entertainments he provided to amuse and keep the people happy, he prevailed upon the rich and plundered large portions of their wealth. Another twisted ambition was that he searched for the direct descendants of King David and for the relatives of Jesus...fearing they might have aspirations to rule.

He also searched for Christians. When he found them, they were charged with holding disorderly meetings at night, being of a rebellious, turbulent spirit (because they could not support emperor worship or the public festivities related to this worship), being cannibals, and and causing famine, pestilence, and earthquakes that afflicted any of the Roman provinces.

When Christians were brought before magistrates, they were administered a test oath of their loyalty to the emperor or to the empire. If they refused the oath, death was pronounced against them. If they confessed themselves to be Christians, the sentence was the same. The various punishments inflicted included: imprisonment, racking, burning, scourging, stoning, hanging, boiling in oil, and banishment, which seemed to be one of Domitians favorite ways of dealing with trouble-makers. Some notable Christians persecuted or martyred under Domitian's rule include:

- John the apostle, who was banished to the Isle of Patmos during this persecution (Revelation 1:9). One tradition says he was also boiled in oil but survived. John died sometime around 95-100 AD.
- Timothy, bishop of Ephesus, had been discipled by Paul. Timothy probably served the church in Ephesus until sometime during Domitian's reign and it is reported that he stood against the idolatry of the city, and, consequently, was beaten with sticks and died two days later.
- Dionysius, the Aeropagite, was an Athenian by birth (Acts 17:34). He was educated in all the significant literature of Greece and went to Egypt to study astronomy, making several observations about the eclipse of the sun. On his return to Athens, he was highly honored for his achievements and, in time, became the senator of that city. He had become a Christian through the ministry of the apostle Paul (Acts 17). Because of his "purity of manners," he was appointed bishop of the church in Athens. He had held this position for two years when he was seized and beheaded with the sword.

CHAPTER 5

The Destruction of Jerusalem: 70 AD

In 66 AD, Palestine was a boiling pot. Pompeii had conquered Jerusalem in 63 BC; consequently, after years of Roman rule and oppression, the Jews had become exasperated with the insensitivity of Roman governance. The Romans had pushed the Jews increasingly into subjugation, setting up rulers from outside Palestine, raiding the temple occasionally to make up for what they said were unpaid taxes, and pushing the Jewish merchants and farmers deeper into debt. The Jews were showing signs of revolting.

Finally, in May 66 AD, an organized rebellion broke out against the Romans. Although the Jews were divided into numerous factions, several charismatic and radical leaders, especially from among the Zealots, stepped forward to inspire the people and organize them into fighting units. In July 66 AD, the Jews stormed Jerusalem, burned the palace, killed the Jewish high priest, and attacked the local Roman garrison, slaughtering many of them. This was followed by an appeal to end the Roman subjugation of the Jews. By September 66 AD, the anti-Roman Jewish extremists had full control of Jerusalem. Jewish revolts broke out elsewhere in Caesarea, Damascus, and Alexandria. The Jews had defied Rome without a single ally. To do this in that age was akin to putting a knife to one's own throat. But the Jews were appearing to get the upper hand. However, years of bloody strife would follow, ending in catastrophe for the Jews.

Vespasian

When Nero, who was emperor at the time, was informed of the rebellion, he sent his most famous general, Vespasian, to Palestine with a large army numbering around 60,000 to discipline the unruly Jews. Vespasian's campaign against the Jews began in the year 67 AD, from the Syrian port town, Ptolemais (Acco). Because the Jewish resistance was strong, he first secured the Mediterranean port towns, then he marched on slowly and cautiously toward Jerusalem. The general's plan was to lay siege against Jerusalem and then slowly tighten the noose. But the campaign came to a halt in the summer of 68 AD when an event occurred that kept him from completing the victory. Nero killed himself! Following his death, chaos and an ensuing civil war broke out in Rome. Because Vespasian was a candidate to become emperor, he returned to Rome. Three emperors, Galba, Otho, and Vitellius, ruled in rapid succession, and, like Nero, came to violent deaths. Then, on July 1, 69 AD, Vespasian was proclaimed universal emperor. He restored order and security to the city of Rome.

Titus

To carry on the job in Palestine, Vespasian had left his son, Titus, as general of the forces. Ten years later, Titus would be the Roman emperor. Following Vespasian's appointment as emperor, the Roman legions, led by Titus, once again moved against Jerusalem. By the end of the year 69, all Judea, except for Jerusalem and three strongholds along the Dead Sea, were under Roman control. In April 70 AD, the siege of Jerusalem began, and this time there would be no relief. This happened shortly after Passover when Jerusalem was filled with Jewish people who had come from the countryside and from towns and cities throughout Judea and were forced to remain in the city. The horrors that followed in Jerusalem are almost indescribable. The siege would last for five months. The Jewish Zealots rejected every offer from Titus for surrender or some sort of compromise. They ended the lives of their own people who spoke of surrender. They made attacks down the Kidron Valley and inflicted great losses on the Romans. For a period the Romans crucified hundreds of Jewish prisoners (as many as 500 a day), but this only created more anger and tenacity on the part of the Jews. Finally, a famine began and thousands died daily.

By May, half the city was in control of the Romans. Titus offered terms of surrender to the Jews but they contemptuously refused. In July, Jewish strongholds within Jerusalem began to crumble. On July 5, the fortress (castle) of Antonia, which was near the temple, was taken by surprise attack at night. This, of course, prepared the way for the destruction of the temple. On July 17, 70 AD, the daily sacrifices at the temple stopped. This was because all hands were needed to defend the area. The last and bloodiest "sacrifice" was at the altar of burnt offerings where thousands of Jews, who had crowded around it, were slaughtered. Soon after, the temple began to be destroyed as fires raged around and in the temple area. It was burned on the August 8, 70 AD. As the temple burned, the battles in the area continued to rage. Josephus reports that the hill on which the temple stood was seething hot, the entire hill seemingly engulfed in flames, but that the blood around the temple was more significant than the flames. The ground was hardly visible because it was covered with corpses. Josephus says that over these heaps of bodies, the Roman soldiers pursued fleeing Jewish fugitives.

The number of Jews killed during the siege and the concluding battles numbered around 1,000,000. Josephus reports 1,195,000. About 97,000 were taken captive and sold into slavery, or sent to the mines, or selected for the gladiatorial games in various Roman arenas.

The temple, and large portions of Jerusalem, was razed to the ground. In September, the last stone was removed from the temple area and it became a plowed field. Small bands of the Jewish resistance remained throughout the land, but Titus would move with his troops over the next three years to wipe out these groups. This included laying siege to the determined band that occupied the mountain fortress called Masada. It was on April 15, AD 73, when the people of Masada committed mass suicide rather than surrender.

There have been conflicting reports as to what Titus' thoughts were as he marched into Jerusalem to bring about its destruction. Josephus reported that Titus wanted to save the temple as a sign of Roman toleration and moderation. However, another report from the Roman historian Tacitus, preserved by Sulpicius Severus, indicates that Titus wanted to destroy the temple.

> *Titus first took counsel and considered whether he should destroy so magnificent a work as the temple. Many thought that a building, which excelled all mortal works in sacredness ought not to be destroyed, for if it were saved, it would serve as a token of Roman moderation, whereas its destruction would display an eternal mark of savagery. But others, on the contrary, including Titus himself, expressed the opinion that the temple ought most certainly be razed, in order that the Jewish and Christian religions might be more completely abolished; for although these religions were mutually hostile, they had nevertheless sprung from the same founders; the Christians were an offshoot of the Jews, and if the root were taken away the stock would easily perish.*[26]

There is no question that the Romans had an appreciation for art and beauty, but the difficulty presented by these two monotheistic religions—Judaism and Christianity—had long been a thorn in Rome's side. If the destruction of the temple would diminish, or put an end to, the ideas and activities of one or both of these groups, all the better.

For the most part, because the Jews were so stubborn and hard to deal with, they had been exempted from laws of worship and sacrifice under the Roman system. Because Christianity was seen as a variety of Judaism, it enjoyed protection under the Jewish umbrella. By 70 AD, it had become apparent that there were large differences between Christianity and the Jewish faith. Following the destruction of Jerusalem, they were no longer identified with one another. From this point on, Christianity would have to make a way on its own, independent of Judaism. Both, however, continued to be persecuted.

PART TWO
The Patristic Age: 100 - 500 AD

OVERVIEW

The word "patristic" comes from the Greek word pater, which means "father." This period, distinctively known as that of the "Church Fathers," is a time rich in stories and in the development of important Christian doctrines. The age marks a transition from the leadership of the apostles to those who followed them. It is the time characterized by the development of the office of bishop. Bishoprics were understood to be the localization of the apostolic office, and bishops were men who occupied positions of leadership in the larger cities and exercised their office over a territory or region. As the church continued to expand, and the leaders of the church sought to maintain unity, the term "catholic" became popular. The word meant that the church was universal and the same everywhere. It began to be called "the One, Holy, Catholic, and Apostolic Church." It was marked by episcopal leadership and a universal vision. In this period, Christianity became a world religion as it reached to the boundaries of the Roman Empire. By the middle of this period a strong relationship developed between state and church. Christianity became the favored and established religion of the empire, and there was increasing institutionalizing of the church. Coupled with first century Christianity, three stages of church growth can be observed: the apostolic church was predominantly Jewish; the ante-Nicene church, Greek; and the post-Nicene church, Roman.

Chapter 6

Ante-Nicene Period: 100 – 325 AD

The period, dated from 100-500 AD, is marked by many important people and events. Two characteristics give it special distinction and these provide the basis for outlining the period: (1) it is the age of the church fathers, and (2) the occurrence of the important and consequential Council of Nicea. It is called the Patristic Period because it recognizes those who led the church after the apostles. Early on, the leaders of this time were called bishops, and later, *papa* or *pater*, out of respect for their sacrificial leadership and position. The title suggests something like the term "senior pastor" that is used today. The entire age is divided nearly in half by the Nicene Council in 325 AD; hence, we have the "ante-Nicene" and "post-Nicene" periods. These terms provide the outline for studying this stage of church history. The period can be divided into three sections: the Ante-Nicene Period (the period from the end of the apostolic age to the council), the Nicene Council, and the Post Nicene Period (from the time of the council to around 500 AD).

What happened to the church after its foundation-layers died? Who were these new leaders and how were they prepared to continue the work of the apostles? Where would the disciples of the apostles take the church? It was Paul who laid out the injunction and philosophy of training others: "And the things you have heard from me in the presence of many witnesses, the same commit to faithful men who shall be able to teach others also" (II Timothy 2:2). These men called "church fathers" were those who led the church out of the first century and into the second. Many were first-hand witnesses to the ministry of the apostles. Their achievements are many:

- ✧ They lived through the time known as the "classic age" of persecution. The persecutions initiated by Nero and Domitian in the first century continued until the ascension of Constantine to the throne in 312 AD. More Christians were martyred in this period than during the time of the apostles.
- ✧ They were the human instruments who gave us the New Testament. Church leaders wrestled with the issues of canonicity, provided the primary evidences for the books we now have in the New Testament, and decided upon the final list that we find in our Bibles today.
- ✧ Many heresies appeared in the second, third, and fourth centuries, and the leaders of the church proved themselves well-equipped and able to offer arguments that still amaze and educate us today.
- ✧ The church which emerged from the apostolic age was poor in earthly possessions. Though it was suspect, tolerated, outlawed at times, poor, and often persecuted, by the end of the period it had conquered an empire with the gospel.

The high repute given to the church fathers in the early church can be seen in the words of Athanasius, who lived in the fourth century. The catholic faith, says he, "is that which the Lord *gave*, the apostles *preached*, and the fathers have *preserved*; upon this the church is founded, and he who departs from this faith can no longer be called a Christian."[27]

Ante-Nicene Fathers

This period is distinguished by several leaders whose lives were characterized by deep dedication and care for the church. Among these are those usually referred to as the Apostolic Fathers (distinguished from the church fathers, in general). The Apostolic Fathers are the earliest Christian writers outside of the New Testament…their writings form a bridge between the New Testament and the Apologists who wrote in the second century.[28]

The Apostolic Fathers noted here are Clement of Rome, Ignatius, and Polycarp.

Clement of Rome

Clement of Rome was esteemed almost as much as the Twelve Apostles in the early Church, and his letter to the Corinthians was regarded by many almost on par with the New Testament canon.[29] It is believed that he was born around 30 AD and died in 101 or 102 AD. Some scholars think he is the Clement referred to in Philippians 4:3. Clearly he was trained by the apostles and became a prominent leader in the church at Rome. Schaff states that he "was a disciple of Paul and Peter, to whom he refers as the chief examples for imitation."[30] There is strong evidence that he was the third bishop of the church in that great city, serving sometime between 92 and 102.

In, or about the year 96 AD, a letter was written from the church in Rome to the church at Corinth and the authorship is ascribed to Clement. It is called *I Clement* and was written to urge members in the congregation at Corinth to end their revolt against their elders and submit to their authority. Some of the elders in the church had been deposed and it is apparent from the letter that Clement was deeply concerned.

> *After an introduction in which he calls to their remembrance the fine spirit of their Church in former times, Clement launches into a series of exhortations concerning such Christian virtues as love, penitence, and humility in order to inspire obedience to his later Admonitions... The heart of his argument appears in chapters 42-44 and centers around the fact that the elders and deacons were provided for by the apostles, who in turn were sent out by Christ, and Christ was sent out by the Father... This section is followed by a long prayer in which his intense desire for the unity of the church is clear. A final exhortation to unity concludes the work.*[31]

This letter from Clement has been assigned the most prominent place among the writings of the Apostolic Fathers in recent times because it is the earliest Christian writing apart from the books of the New Testament.[32] His letter is also valuable because of its many quotations from the Old Testament. It is interesting to note in chapter 25 that Clement uses the pagan story of the Phoenix rising from the ashes as an illustration of the resurrection.[33] This may be the main reason this letter was not included in the New Testament canon. Clement gives valuable information as to the state of ministry in his time, the history of the Roman church, and the martyrdoms of Peter and Paul.[34]

There is another letter called *The Second Epistle of Clement* which is given some importance because it is regarded the earliest surviving sermon outside of biblical literature. Because its style is somewhat different than *I Clement*, its authorship is uncertain.

Ignatius

It is not known for certain when Ignatius was born, but he apparently died in the year 107 AD. Coxe reports the dates of his life as 30-107 AD.[35] Some historians place his death as late as 117. Little or nothing is known of his early life. Tradition says that he and Polycarp were fellow pupils of John the Apostle. He served as bishop of the church in Antioch and was known as a devoted pastor. The Emperor Trajan arrived in Antioch in the year 107 and threatened persecution to all who refused to sacrifice to the Roman gods. Of course, Ignatius refused, and as leader of the church, was made an example. Ten Roman soldiers arrested him, he was tried for the said crime, found guilty, and Trajan condemned him to be thrown to the wild beasts at Rome. Taken from city to city, staying in different jails, the Roman soldiers led him to the capital of the empire for his execution. He received visitors along the way and his guards permitted him to visit Christian congregations whose members and bishops had not been arrested…As Ignatius passed through Smyrna he was received with honor by Polycarp, bishop of the congregation there.[36]

> *On the way to martyrdom he wrote at least seven epistles. From Smyrna he wrote to the churches in Ephesus, Magnesia, Tralles, and Rome; from Troas he wrote to Smyrna and Philadelphia and to Polycarp, bishop of Smyrna. These epistles are the most important documents of the period.*[37]

In his letters to the churches, Ignatius expresses his thanks to the members of the Christian community who had traveled to bid him farewell and shown him kindnesses, warns them to be faithful amidst future persecutions, and urges them to maintain the unity of the church.[38] In his letter to Polycarp, Ignatius urges this bishop of Smyrna to "stand firm like an anvil under the hammer," and instructs Polycarp on carrying out his duties.[39] Ignatius was 40 to 50 years older than Polycarp.

Ignatius was deeply concerned and showed special insight regarding the unity of the church. The word "catholic" is derived from the Greek word meaning "universal" or "the same everywhere." One of its earliest appearances is in the writings of Ignatius of Antioch.[40] He said, "Wherever Jesus Christ is, there is the Catholic Church."[41] By the end of the second century the term was in wide use.

> *With unusual insight into the controversies yet to come in the church, he insisted on the reality of both the divinity and humanity of Christ, and upheld the office of bishop as the best hope for unity in Christianity. Ignatius may have been the first to use the threefold order of bishop, elder, and deacon.*[42]

He was one of the first to oppose Gnostic or Docetic tendencies in the church, teachings which emphasized purity of the spiritual and evil contamination of the material. Ignatius insisted upon the revelation of Christ in the flesh as an antidote to this false teaching.

Ignatius was a great teacher and had the ability to state a truth concisely. From his letter to Polycarp we have the following examples, noted by Dr. Coxe.[43]

- Find time to pray without ceasing.
- Every wound is not healed with the same remedy.
- The times demand thee, as pilots the haven.
- The crown is immortality.
- Stand like a beaten anvil.
- It is the part of a good athlete to be bruised and to prevail.
- Consider the times: look for Him who is above time.
- Slight not the menservants or the handmaids.
- Let your stewardship define your work.
- A Christian is not his own master, but waits upon God.

It is reported that on December 20, 107 AD, Igatius was thrown to the lions in the amphitheater at Rome and that in only a few minutes nothing was left of his body but a few bones. These were carried back to Antioch as a memorial to those who were pastored and taught by him.

Polycarp

The leading Christian figure in Roman Asia in the middle of the second century was Polycarp, bishop of Smyrna.[44] Though the dates of his birth and death cannot be stated with certainty, scholars believe Polycarp's life dated from 69-156 AD. Traditionally he is described as a disciple of John the Apostle and was known, instructed, and probably ordained by the apostles. His well-known disciple, Irenaeus of Lyon, has given a clear description of Polycarp.

> *But Polycarp was not only instructed by the apostles, and conversed with many who had seen Christ, but was also, by apostles in Asia, appointed bishop of the Church in*

> *Smyrna, who I also saw in my early youth, for he tarried [on earth] a very long time, and, when a very old man, gloriously and most nobly suffering martyrdom, departed this life, having always taught the things which he learned from the apostles, and which the Church handed down, and which alone are true… He it was who, coming to Rome in the time of Anicetus [bishop of Rome] caused many to turn away from aforesaid heretics to the Church of God, proclaiming that he had received this one and sole truth from the apostles—that namely, which is handed down by the Church.*[45]

If Polycarp was born in 69 AD, it means that he was born one year before the destruction of Jerusalem and, more than likely, knew the Apostle John for several years. He served as bishop for many years in his hometown of Smyrna, located in what is now western Turkey. He was known and revered for his purity of life, simplicity, and steady manner, rather than the profundity of his teaching. *The Epistle of Polycarp to the Philippians*, written by him, is still available, and reveals him to be a sweet and honest man who won the respect of everyone for his kind and gentle ways. He was seized during the severe persecution of Christians under Emperor Marcus Aurelius and was asked to renounce his faith. Before a large crowd in the city square, he was brought before the governor who commanded him to curse the name of Christ.

> *The governor called to the people, "Polycarp says he is a Christian." Then the mob let loose, "This is the teacher of Asia," they shouted, "the father of the Christians, the destroyer of our gods."*[46]

When asked to "curse Christ," Polycarp refused, with this reply, "I have served him eighty-six years, and he has done me no wrong; how can I blaspheme the king who saved me."[47] He was then burned at the stake.

There is a letter which was circulated following Polycarp's martyrdom, written by the church he pastored at Smyrna, and addressed to "the Church in every place." It is called *The Encyclical Epistle of the Church at Smyrna*, and it was written to explain the circumstances surrounding his martyrdom and his conduct during the ordeal. Following is part of the letter which contains Polycarp's final prayer, offered after he was bound to the stake.

> *They did not nail him then but simply bound him, and being bound like a distinguished ram [taken] out of a great flock for sacrifice, and prepared to be an acceptable burnt offering unto God, looked up to heaven and said, "O Lord God Almighty, the Father of thy beloved and blessed Son, Jesus Christ by whom we have received the knowledge of Thee, the God of angels and powers, and of every creature, and of the whole race of the righteous who live before thee, I give Thee thanks that Thou hast counted me worthy of this day and this hour, that I should have a part in the number of Thy martyrs, in the cup of thy Christ, to the resurrection of eternal life, both of soul and body through the incorruption [imparted] by the Holy Ghost…may I be accepted this day before Thee as a fat and acceptable sacrifice, according as Thou, the ever truthful God, has foreordained, had revealed beforehand to me, and now hast fulfilled. Wherefore also I praise Thee for all things, I bless Thee, I glorify Thee, along with the everlasting and heavenly Jesus Christ, Thy beloved Son, with whom, to Thee, and the Holy Ghost, be glory now and to all coming ages. Amen.*[48]

Justin Martyr

His given name was Falvius Justinus, and he was born just near the end of the first century or the beginning of the second, so his life is usually dated 100-166 AD. He was a Gentile, a Greek, and was born in a town in Samaria near Jacob's well. The town, called Flavia Neapolis, was named after the Roman emperor Flavis Vespasian, who planted a colony there after the destruction of Jerusalem. He must have come from a family of some wealth because he was well-educated and traveled extensively. He was well-read in the philosophies of his day, and is acknowledged as the first Christian author of the second century and the founder of Christian literature. Justin is the first among the fathers who may be called a learned theologian and Christian thinker.[49] Since the word "theologian" did not come into use until sometime later, he has been called the first Christian philosopher. Combining philosophy and Christian doctrine with his personal skills made him the foremost apologist of the second century. He is one of the first to see the importance of combining faith and reason.

As a young man he saw truth as the greatest possession and thus began a search into various systems of thought. He first studied Stoicism, then Pythagoreanism, then became fully engaged with Platonic thought. He was overpowered by the perception of immaterial things and the contemplation of eternal ideas of truth, beauty, and goodness.[50] When he first heard the gospel, he was fascinated by the idea that the *Logos*, the divine Word, was operating always and everywhere. He was especially interested in this emphasis in the *Gospel of John* but did not see the importance of the resurrection and divine grace. To him, salvation would come by contemplating and embracing the *Logos*. Fortunately, while he was still young, he came to understand the true meaning of the gospel.

> *He thought he was already near the promised goal of his philosophy—the vision of God—when, in a solitary walk not far from the seashore, a venerable old Christian of pleasant countenance and gentle dignity, entered into a conversation with him, which changed the course of his life. The unknown friend shook his confidence in all human wisdom, and pointed him to the writings of the Hebrew prophets who were older than the philosophers and had seen and spoken the truth, not as reasoners, but*

> *as witnesses. More than this: they foretold the coming of Christ, and their prophecies were fulfilled in his life and work. The old man departed, and Justin saw him no more, but he took his advice and soon found in the prophets of the Old Testament as illuminated and confirmed by the Gospels, the true and infallible philosophy which rests upon the firm ground of revelation. Thus the enthusiastic Platonist became a Christian.[51]*

He went on to become a Christian teacher and apologist and devoted himself to the defense of Christianity at a time when it was greatly attacked. In particular, he taught and wrote against Gnosticism and, at one point, spent quite some time in Rome where he argued against, and it is reported, defeated Marcionism, a brand of Gnosticism. On another occasion he traveled to Ephesus where he exerted effort to win a well-known Jew named Trypho and his followers to the Christian faith. He returned to Rome where he settled as a Christian teacher, living there from around 150 AD until his death. Three of his works survive.

- *Dialogue With Trypho*, which is the record of a long and friendly debate with Trypho.
- *Apology I*, which is a defense of the Christian faith, written to the Emperor Antonius Pius.
- *Apology II*, which is a letter written to the Emperor Marcus Aurelius and the Senate, in which Justin argued the philosophical truth of Christianity and explained Christian practices.

It is reported that in 166 AD he was arrested and put on trial for being a Christian. He was called upon to renounce his faith by making an offering to the gods. He refused to deny Christ, and through the instigation of a Cynic philosopher, Crescens, Justin and six other Christians were scourged and beheaded. Thus, he is known to us as "Justin the Martyr," or simply, "Justin Martyr."

Irenaeus

Irenaeus (120[?]-202 AD) was a Greek, born in Asia Minor into a Christian family.[52] All evidence points to the fact that he was born in Smyrna and raised in the teaching and practices of the Eastern Church. Thus, he enjoyed the instruction of the illustrious and venerable Polycarp of Smyrna,[53] and of "other elders" who, many believe, were immediate or second generation disciples of the original apostles trained by Jesus. While still a young man he moved to Lyon, located in what is now France. Between Smyrna (in Turkey) and Marseilles in Gaul (France), a brisk trade route had developed. It was probably due to this that Christianity was easily introduced into that region. Polycarp had sent one of his former students, Pothinus, into Celtic Gaul as a missionary and he established a church center in Lyon. Later, Irenaeus was sent to assist Pothinus, becoming one of his presbyters (elder). In 177 AD, the emperor, Marcus Aurelius, initiated a severe persecution in that area, aimed primarily at Lyon and Vienna. In that year Pothinus was martyred and after his death Irenaeus was appointed bishop in Lyon. And, as far as we know, he labored there with great success amidst many dangers until the end of his life. Thus, his life and work introduce us to the church in the Western outposts.

As bishop, Irenaeus promoted large missionary and literary efforts. Accounts indicate that under his leadership almost the entire population of Lyon was converted and the church became a center from which missionaries were sent to other parts of France and Europe. He also became known for his efforts in apologetics and polemics which formed the basis for the publication of his writings. An apologist defends the church against heresies from without and a polemicist contends with errors or heresies within the church. Irenaeus was especially concerned with the pseudo-Christian problem of Gnosticism. He opposed the teaching of this sect which he saw infecting the church (salvation through mystical, supernatural knowledge passed on to special initiates, blending aspects of old pagan mystery religions with the gospel). His most well-known and powerful writing was *Against Heresies* in which he insisted that the apostles had not passed on special private secrets to insiders. His work was very influential in protecting the church of his time against Gnosticism and today he is still read by theologians and historians.

Another concern Irenaeus had was church unity, and thus, promoted the idea of a "catholic" church. He was an opponent of all error and schism in the church and was, on the whole, the most orthodox of the ante-Nicene fathers.[54]

> *Irenaeus is the leading representative of catholic Christianity in the last quarter of the second century, the champion of orthodoxy against Gnostic heresy, and the mediator between the Eastern and Western churches. He united a learned Greek education and philosophical penetration with practical wisdom and moderation. He is neither very original nor brilliant, but eminently sound and judicious…He is familiar with Greek poets (Homer, Hesiod, Pindar, Sophocles) and philosophers (Thales, Pythagoras, Plato) who he occasionally cites. He is perfectly at home in the Greek Bible and in early Christian writers, as Clement of Rome, Polycarp, Papias, Ignatius, Hermas, Justin Martyr, and Tatian…We plainly trace him in the influence of the spirit of Polycarp and John [the apostle]. "The true way to God," he says, in opposition to the false Gnosis, "is love. It is better to be willing to know nothing but Jesus Christ the crucified, than to fall into ungodliness through overcurious questions and paltry subtleties."*[55]

Another important feature in the ministry of Irenaeus was his emphasis upon the Scriptures. He was the first among the patristic writers to make full use of the New Testament.[56] Even though the New Testament canon had not been completely agreed upon,

Irenaeus talked of the New Testament Scripture alongside the Old Testament.[57] To the first century church the "Scriptures" meant the Old Testament. By appealing to the Gospels, and the writings of the apostles and their associates, Irenaeus led the church in beginning to recognize the writings we now call the New Testament.

Not much is known about the life of Irenaeus after the year 190 AD, but it is reported that he died a martyr in the persecution under the emperor Septimus Severus in 202. It is also said that he was buried under the altar of the Church of St. John in Lyon.

Tertullian

Fiery, courageous, bold, brilliant, articulate, original, fresh, dogmatic, exteme, and eccentric are some of the words that have been used to describe Tertullian. He was a man of strong convictions, and never hesitated to express them without fear or favor.[58] Tertullian was the passionate apologist, polemicist, and ascetic of the North African church. He was also the first important theologian to write in Latin and is known as the father of Latin, Western theology.

> *Indeed, he was one of the greatest Latin writers ever and it is said that pagans used to read his works simply to enjoy the style. As a fifth-century writer put it, 'almost every word he uttered was an epigram and every other sentence a victory.' Or as a modern author said, Tertullian 'possessed an ability rare among theologians: he is incapable of being dull.'*[59]

Quintus Septimus Florens Tertullianus was born around 150-60 AD in the North African city of Carthage where his father was serving as captain of a Roman legion. Carthage was considered second in importance only to Rome. He received a liberal Greco-Roman education, having studied rhetoric, law, and the classics. His writings disclose an extensive knowledge in history, philosophy, poetry, and ancient literature, along with his knowledge of theology.

He was skilled in both the Latin and Greek languages. All who have studied him realize that he was a man of exceptional and varied intellectual skills. He is reported to have lived to a very advanced age and his death is placed as late as 240 AD.

He became a proficient lawyer and taught public speaking and practiced law in Rome, where he was converted to Christianity.[60] "To his thirtieth or fortieth year he lived in heathen blindness and licentiousness,"[61] says Schaff, and became a Christian around 197 AD, meaning he probably became a follower of Christ after age 40. Observing the courage of Christian martyrs was one of the major influences in his conversion. Immediately he became an advocate for the Christian faith through his writings and continued to write for the rest of his life, producing a large volume of Christian literature. Nothing is known of his private life or occupation, apart from the fact that he was married.[62] He held to a high view of marriage and family, but saw celibacy as the highest expression of self-denial and morality. He instructed his wife to remain a widow if he should die, or, at least, never to marry an unbeliever. Some scholars believe that his wife died young, because in Tertullian's later works there is no mention of her, and it seems that his attitude toward women and marriage became more and more negative as time went on.[63] Soon after his conversion, he felt drawn toward ministry in the Catholic Church and was ordained a presbyter (elder) in the church at Carthage.

At first he supported the mainstream Catholic Church, but sometime before 207 AD he began to become upset with the moral laxness of his fellow-clergymen and what he perceived to be the growing worldliness of the church. His disillusionment led him to join the ultra-severe ascetic group called the Montanists. Montanism emphasized separation from the world, a new outpouring of the Holy Spirit, charismatic activity, and the immanence of the New Jerusalem. They saw themselves as a group of "spiritual" Christians. Montanists had a distrust for church hierarchy and, therefore, set themselves apart from the "organized" church. Later, Tertullian broke with them and founded a movement that became known as the "Tertullianists" which continued into the fifth century. This group maintained a more orthodox stance than did the Montanists.

Tertullian was a prolific writer and is known primarily through his literary works. His concerns centered in three main areas: his *apologetics*, which considers Christianity's relationship to the Roman state and society, and defends Christianity against the heathen and the Jews; his *polemics*, which defends Christian doctrine against heresy; and his *practical works* which promote the moral and ethical behavior of Christians. Many of these works are still available today. His most well-known are: *Apology, Against Marcion, and Against Praxeas*. His *On the Soul* is the first known Christian writing on psychology. *On Baptism* is the earliest extensive work about baptism. He wrote in a witty, pithy, original, fresh style, and was known for his short statements that were filled with meaning. In *Apology*, written to the Roman governor of his province, he defends the Christians as the best and most loyal citizens of the Empire, and points out that the persecutions against them were a failure because, first, they were unjust, but also, because every time they were killed, they multiplied. One of the more popular passages in *Apology* states:

> Nor does your cruelty, however exquisite, avail you: it is rather a temptation to us. The oftner we are mown down by you, the more in number we grow; the blood of the martyrs is the seed of the church.[64]

The core of this statement from Tertullian later became popularized in the maxim, "The blood of the martyrs is the seed of the church."

In *Apology* we find "the first plea for religious liberty, as an *inalienable right* which God has given to every man, and which the government in its own interest should not only tolerate but respect and protect."[65]

Tertullian's *polemic works* are chiefly occupied with refuting the Gnostics. He was deeply committed to the authority of the Scriptures and preferred biblical answers to life's issues. He saw Greek philosophy as the parent of heresy and wrote:

> *What has the academy to do with the church?*
> *What has Christ to do with Plato?*
> *What has Athens to do with Jerusalem?*[66]

In his little tract, *The Soul's Testimony*, we have a beautiful and simple argument that man's soul was made for God.

> *Here the human soul is called to bear witness to the one true God: it springs from God, it longs for God; its purer and nobler instincts and aspirations, if not diverted and perverted by selfish and sinful passions, tend upwards and heavenwards, and find rest and peace only in God. There is, we may say, a pre-established harmony between the soul and the Christian religion; they are made for each other; the human soul is constitutionally Christian.*[67]

Tertullian's works abound in new words and new expressions. As he defined the nature of God and the relationship between the members of the Trinity, he gave us the words *Trinity* and *consubstantial*. His theology focused upon man's corruption and God's salvation, the great Pauline themes of sin and grace. Considering his times and his behavior, it is amazing that Tertullian was not martyred or excommunicated from the Catholic Church, or both. But he lived to a great old age.

Clement of Alexandria

Known as Clement of Alexandria, he was born in Greece, most probably in Athens, to pagan parents. The dates of his life are fixed, approximately, from 150-215 AD. His given name was Titus Flavius Clemens, which may indicate that he was in some way descended from another Titus Flavius Clemens, nephew of the Roman emperor, Vespasian. The former Titus Flavius Clemens and his wife, Domitilla, were suddenly arrested and condemned on the charge of "atheism" (i.e., Christianity) by the emperor Domitian.

Raised in heathenism, it seems that Clement was well-studied in all branches of Hellenistic literature and educated in all the known systems of philosophy at that time. He was widely read in Greek pagan literature and quoted something like five hundred authors in his works.[68] In all his studies he found nothing that could give peace to his soul. It appears that at some point in his adult years he became a Christian, though we have no details as to when or how this happened. After becoming a follower of Christ, he took time to travel. One of his chief characteristics was a love and strong desire for truth, so, "by long journeys East and West he sought the most distinguished teachers, 'who preserved the tradition of pure saving doctrine, and implanted that genuine apostolic seed in the hearts of their pupils.'"[69] We do not know the names of any of the teachers he encountered except for Pantaenus, who was head of the catechetical school at Alexandria, Egypt.

Impressed by Pantaenus, Clement settled in Alexandria where he would remain for twenty years. There he studied under this illustrious teacher, became an elder in the church, and about 189 AD succeeded Pantaenus to become president of the catechetical school. Under the leadership of Clement and those who followed him, the school at Alexandria would become "the brains of Christianity," taking the lead for years to come in giving theological definitions to the Christian faith. The catechetical school became the leading Christian institution of the time and developed an extensive library. Many eminent men came from the school in Alexandria including Clement's star pupil, Origen, the church father and scholar.

Clement and the Alexandrians, unlike many of their Christian contemporaries, looked upon philosophy as the handmaid to Christianity. Combining the best of ancient philosophy with

Christian doctrine, Clement built a system upon the idea that although faith is sufficient for salvation, "the man who adds knowledge to faith finds even greater good."[70] He saw ignorance and error as more fundamental evils than sin.[71] The system of thought in Alexandria was purposely called "Christian Gnosticism" because it was an attempt to make Christianity appeal to the philosophical mind of that time (Gnosticism had been a major influence in the city). The teaching was "gnostic" because it asked the big questions of meaning; but it was "Christian gnosticism" because it retained orthodox answers.[72]

> *Clement's purpose was clear. He seized not only the external forms of expression of the contemporary pagan philosophers but also their problems. If, for example, he discussed the universe and its meaning (cosmology), so loved by the gnostics, he did not do it with the intention of proving these ideas wrong offhandedly and then discarding them quickly, but instead he pointed out how the fundamental religious questions about the creation of the world, the existence of evil in this life, and the salvation through the Word, Jesus Christ, found their last and deepest answer in Christian revelation. He wanted to be an apostle to the Hellenistic intellectual world. His purpose was not purely or even primarily theological, but pastoral. He aimed to win not arguments, but men to Christ, and lead them to salvation.*[73]

Clement continued to teach with great distinction in the city of Alexandria until 202 AD when the persecutions under Septimus Severus compelled him to flee. After that we find him in Antioch and then in Jerusalem. We do not know if he ever returned to Alexandria. The close of his career is wrapped in obscurity and he is thought to have died around 215 to 220 AD. Several of his works are still available, giving theological views and additional information on the church's life and customs in the Roman world of his time. Along with Justin Martyr and Irenaeus, it may be said that Clement helped establish the development of Christian literature. To him we owe also the oldest Christian hymn that has come down to us.

Origen

Pious, popular, and persuasive, Origen (185 [?]-254 [?]) stands out as one of the great figures of the ancient church.[74] He is known as the greatest scholar and most productive author of early Christianity, and distinguished himself as a sincerely spiritual man as well as a loyal churchman. He was born in Egypt and raised by devout Christian parents in Alexandria. Origen was baptized as a child and received training from his father who was probably a rhetorician, and possibly taught at Clement's catechetical school in Alexandria. While still a boy, he showed deep spiritual devotion and memorized large sections of Scripture. During the persecutions under Septimus Severus, his father, Leonidas, was captured, imprisoned, and finally martyred in 202 AD. Origen wished to die with his father but was prevented by his mother.

Due to the generosity of a wealthy widow, Origen was able to continue his studies. He then supported himself by giving instruction in Greek language and literature and by copying manuscripts.[75] Then, with the approval of Demetrius, the bishop of Alexandria, he assumed the leadership of a group of catechumens (those being trained for baptism and membership in the church). He did extremely well in training those under his charge and became known as an outstanding teacher. In the year 203 AD, while still only eighteen years of age, he was appointed president of the catechetical school of Alexandria, a position left vacant by Clement. He continued in that position for twenty years during which time his fame spread. Eusebius tells us that thousands, including many pagans, came to hear him and many were converted to Christianity.

> He was successful in bringing many eminent heathens and heretics to the Catholic church; among them a wealthy Gnostic, Ambrosius, who became his most liberal patron, furnishing him a costly library for his biblical studies, seven stenographers, and a number of copyists (some of whom were young Christian women), the former to note down his dictations, the latter to engross them. His fame spread far and wide over Egypt. Julia Mamaea, mother of the Emperor Alexander Severus, brought him to Antioch in 218, to learn from him the doctrines of Christianity. An Arabian prince honored him with a visit for the same purpose.[76]

All during his time of teaching and writing he continued to pursue the ascetic life. In misguided obedience to Matthew 19:12 (taking it literally), he castrated himself. Later he regretted and repented of this act.

While still a layman, Origen made a trip to Greece and Palestine about 227 to 230 AD. While there he was ordained a presbyter by a group of bishops in Caesarea in order to allow him to preach. His ordination infuriated Demetrius, bishop of Origen's home town of Alexandria, who excommunicated Origen and banned him from his teaching post in the school of Alexandria, and from preaching in the city. Consequently, he stayed at Caesarea, established a school which became famous, and continued his teaching and writing, as well as making occasional journeys. He wrote prolifically, with his works possibly numbering as high as 6,000. Later, Jerome would ask, "Who could ever read all that Origen wrote?"[77] His major writings can be divided into four groups:

- ✧ *Biblical.* These were his most numerous works. Origen produced a massive edition of the Old Testament in parallel columns, featuring Hebrew and Greek. He authored commentaries on almost all the books of the Old and New

Testaments, wrote homilies, and produced notes on specific passages of Scripture.
- *First Principles.* This is probably his greatest work and is important because it is recognized as the first systematic theology produced in the early church. It features the fundamental doctrines of the Christian faith divided into four books: on God, the world, freedom, and the Scriptures.
- *Against Celsus.* This was a reply to the anti-Christian work called *True Word*, written by the Platonist, Celsus, who made charges concerning the irrationality of Christians and the lack of historical foundations in the Christian faith.
- *Practical Works.* Among his practical works, the two most well-known are *Treatise on Prayer*, which features an exposition of the Lord's Prayer, and *Exhortation to Martyrdom*, written during one of the persecutions.

Origen also did some of the first systematic work in the area of biblical hermaneutics. Reflected throughout his sermons and commentaries is his belief that there are three levels of interpretation in any text of Scripture: (1) the literal sense, (2) the moral application to the soul, and (3) the allegorical or spiritual sense which relate to higher mysteries of the Christian faith. He preferred the allegorical method as a way to allow God to speak in deeper ways; but this became a controversial issue in the church. Philip Schaff writes: "Origen's greatest service was in exegesis...His great defect is the neglect of the grammatical and historical sense and his constant desire to find a hidden mystic meaning."[78]

No doubt Origen's methods of interpretation affected his views on some major doctrines. His view of the Trinity has left many questions and his view of the soul of man and salvation seems less than biblical. His thinking in these areas definitely connects him to the eastern mind. Some believe that he was the first to develop teaching on purgatory. According to Origen, the souls of men proceed through purification to reconciliation with God. Some souls reach purification and reconciliation with God in the present life, but others need more time; thus, a period of purgation is needed.

> *For him the essence of salvation is becoming like God, being 'deified' through contemplating him. The soul needs to rise from the world of becoming to the realm of being. The Word appeared to enable this. The knowledgeable Christian will penetrate beyond the earthly Jesus to the eternal Word and achieve salvation through contemplating him. This concept of salvation is thoroughly Greek and has more in common with Gnosticism than with biblical Christianity...Where Tertullian was the leading theologian of the western, Roman end of the Mediterranean, Origen's influence was paramount in the eastern, Greek-thinking world. From this time onwards there was an identifiable Eastern tendency in theology, deeply influenced by Origen's ideas.*[79]

Origen's mystical theology—that one advances from purgation to illumination to union—is the foundation of all later mysticism in the church.[80]

During the persecutions of Decius in 250 AD, Origen was seized along with hundreds of other Christians, put in chains, experienced the iron collar, and was severely tortured. He was then put in stocks and confined to a dungeon. Being advanced in years he died from the effects shortly thereafter. Three hundred years after his work, Origen was condemned as a heretic at the First Council of Constantinople in 543 and again at the Second Council of Constantinople in 553.[81]

Ante-Nicene Heresies

One of the challenges of the early church was the determination of true doctrine. The Ante-Nicene fathers worked hard to establish accuracy of belief. Consequently, the church leaders distinguished between orthodoxy and heterodoxy. The word *orthodox* comes from two Greek words, *orthos*, meaning "true" or "right," and *doxa*, meaning "opinion;" hence, orthodox translates to "truth" or "correct belief." *Heterodoxy* likewise comes from the Greek language and is made up of the two words, *heteros*, meaning "different" or "other," and *doxa*, which means "opinion." Therefore, the word *heterodoxy* translates to "different opinion" or "other opinion."

Second century church leaders believed heterodoxy was equal to sin because it refused to receive or adopt the accepted standard revealed by God and deposited in the church. Once the church, in council, had agreed upon its doctrine, the common word used to describe heterodoxy was "heresy" and those who promoted another, or different, doctrine were called "heretics." Several ante-Nicene heresies arose and were confronted by various theologians and teachers.

Marcionism

Date of origin: 140 AD. Marcion was a wealthy ship owner from northeast Asia Minor who came to Rome sometime before 140 AD and became an active member in the church. As a teacher, he began to advocate the heretical idea that there is a complete discontinuity between the Old and the New Testament, between Israel and the Church, and between the God of the Old Testament and the Father that Jesus came to reveal. He taught that the Gospel completely displaced the Old Testament and, therefore, excluded the 39 books of the Old Testament from his "Bible." Because he believed that it was unjust for God to favor the Jews, he excluded not only the Old Testament but all New Testament books that appeared to favor the Jews. This included Matthew, Mark, Acts, and Hebrews. He also eliminated sections of the New Testament, which did not coincide with his views, including I and II Timothy and Titus. By the time he was done, he had a New Testament version that contained a doctored version of Luke and ten of Paul's letters.

Marcion separated the God revealed in Jesus Christ (the God of love and grace) from the inferior god revealed in creation and the acts of Israel. He did not believe that Jesus was born of a woman; rather, he suddenly appeared one day in 29 AD as a grown man in the synagogue in Capernaum. He did not believe Christ came in the flesh, but only appeared to be. Marcion's view was that Christ was a new being on earth and was unlike any other person, except in appearance. His view was very much gnostic or docetic. Though he stated that Christ's life, crucifixion, and resurrection were necessary for salvation, he believed they were merely apparent, not real. There was a severe dualism in Marcion's teachings. He thought the body was evil, needing to be both denied and discarded. Thus, he was an extreme ascetic, seeking spiritual reality and rejecting the world. Since he believed that only the immaterial part of man could be redeemed, he rejected the idea of the resurrection of the body.

Marcion was excommunicated from the church in 144 AD but went ahead to form his own group of churches. These churches were established in many parts of the empire and were modeled after orthodox churches. They ordained their own clergy and had their own rituals. Many of these congregations continued into the fourth century.

Montanism

Date of origin: 156 AD. Montanism was a Christian apocalyptic (end time) movement. It took its name from Montanus, a Phrygian, who, shortly after his baptism as a Christian (156 AD), claimed to have received a revelation from the Holy Spirit. He believed he was a representative prophet of the Spirit, and would lead the church into its final stage. His followers were encouraged to regard themselves as an elite group of "spiritual" Christians. Montanus proclaimed the imminent advent of the New Jerusalem, the signal for which was to be a new outpouring of the Holy Spirit. Preparation for this advent was to be preceded by withdrawal from the world.

Aided by two women, Maximilla and Prisca (Priscilla), Montanus preached the soon-coming end of the world, austere morality, and severe penitential discipline. His movement forbade second marriages and refused forgiveness of sins that persons committed after baptism. Special fast days were called, and persecution was to be expected (even encouraged) so that the church would be a purified and fit bride for the coming of Christ. Martyrdom was emulated and seen as the ultimate sacrifice in terms of dedication and separation from the world. Montanus also called for less church hierarchy and more charismatic activity in the church (tongues and prophecy).

Montanism established several separate communities in which men and women alike were admitted to the eldership and episcopacy. Despite condemnations and continued opposition from orthodox Christian writers and the established church, Montanism did not disappear until about the middle of the sixth century. In the year 230 AD, the group was excommunicated at the Synod of Iconium. For a period of time, Tertullian joined the movement because he admired the Montanists' discipline and morality.

Monarchianism

Date of origin: AD 190. "Monarchianism" is a theological term coined by Tertullian who opposed the doctrine. It was a popular second and third century heresy that rejected the Trinity in order to affirm the unity of God and guard against the idea of polytheism. Sometimes Christians were accused of worshipping three gods. However, Monarchianism ended up rejecting the Trinity entirely. There were actually two forms of this teaching: (1) *Dynamic Monarchianism*, or, *Adoptionism* and (2) *Modalistic Monarchianism*.

Dynamic Monarchianism taught that Jesus was a unique person who was divinely energized by the Holy Spirit (occurring at his baptism) and called to be the Son of God. Or, he was "adopted" as the Son of God but did not possess divine nature. Jesus was a human like all others but, because he was able to maintain perfection in his humanity, was chosen to become the Son of God.

Modalistic Monarchianism, also called "Sabellianism" (named after a man called Sabellius, a teacher of this doctrine), maintained that there was not three persons in the Trinity, only one, who was God. He, however, expressed himself variously as three persons: Father, Son, and Holy Spirit. This doctrine emphasized the oneness (unity) of God but failed to recognize the three persons in the godhead. Sabellianism became the most popular form of Monarchianism and Sabellius its most energetic proponent. His followers became known as "Sabellians."

Monarchianism was vigorously opposed by leaders of the church, especially Tertullian and Hippolytus of Rome. Sabellius, who persisted in expounding his ideas, was finally excommunicated from the church. It has been stated throughout history that a heresy is a truth carried to an extreme. This certainly was the case with Monarchianism.

Manichaeism

Date of origin: 242 AD. Manichaeism is a form of gnosticism that originated in Babylonia. Its founder was a person of noble descent, called "Mani" (or, "Manes"), 216-276 AD. Manichaeism was long treated as a Christian heresy, but it is more clearly understood as an independent religion, drawing upon such diverse resources as Christianity, Zoroastrianism, and Buddhism. Zoroastrianism is a Persian religion founded in the sixth century BC by the prophet Zoroaster. It is characterized by the worship of a supreme god, Ahura Mazda, who requires men's good deeds for help in his cosmic struggle against the evil spirit, Ahriman. At about the age of 24, it is purported that Mani received a special revelation from God indicating that he was called to perfect the incomplete religions founded by earlier prophets—Zoroaster, Buddha, and Christ. About 242 AD, he undertook an extensive journey as an itinerant preacher, proclaiming himself as the "Messenger of Truth," the Paraclete promised by Christ. Traveling throughout the Persian empire and as far as India, he gathered a considerable following. He met with increasing hostility from Zoroastrian priests and was finally executed by them for preaching heresy.

The essence of Manichaeism was the principle of absolute dualism—the complete separation between the material and spiritual worlds. Human beings, created by God, were divine in spirit but they carried within them seeds of darkness, sown by Satan, because of their material bodies. Material bodies are a kind of "soil for evil." Because of its belief concerning the material world, Manichaeism regarded evil as a physical entity rather than a moral entity. Women were considered forces of darkness, binding men to the flesh. Manichaeian doctrine denied the reality of Christ's body and adopted the following from Christian teaching: baptism, the Eucharist, and the idea of the sacrament of the remission of sins at the time of death. Salvation, as taught by Mani, required liberating the soul from the material darkness in which it is trapped. This is achieved through strict celibacy and ascetic practices. Those who would become perfect are to set three "seals" on their lives: on the mouth, to speak only truth and to abstain from meat or impure food of any kind; on the hands, to refrain from war, killing or injuring life, and on the breast, to render impossible the world of the flesh.

One of the most popular of the Manichees was St. Aurelius Augustine who, in trying to escape a life of indulging the flesh, joined the group. There he remained for nine years and then left the group to write and speak against their beliefs and practices, as well as describe in his *Confessions* his own experience with the movement. Manichaeism died out in the West in the sixth century.

Arianism

Date of origin: early fourth century (317 AD). Arianism was a fourth century heresy named after Arius (250-336 AD), a presbyter in the Church of Alexandria in North Africa. Arius denied the full deity of the pre-existent Son of God. He held that the Son, while divine and like God ("of like substance"), was created by God as the agent through whom he created the universe. Arius said of the Son, "there was a time when he was not." Arianism became so widespread in the Christian church and resulted in such confusion and disunity that the emperor, Constantine, called for a church council at Nicea in 325 AD

Athanasius, a deacon in Alexandria, who later became bishop there, became distinguished at the Council of Nicea. He led the debate for orthodox Christianity and Arianism was condemned at the Nicene Council. The great statements that came out of this council stated that the Son was consubstantial (of the same substance or nature) and co-eternal with the Father—a belief formulated and stated in the Greek word *homoousios* ("of one substance"). The Arians had used the word *homoiousios* ("of like substance").

Through the questioning of Arius during the debates at the council, several of his doctrinal points became apparent. The overall effect was a denial of the deity of Jesus Christ. The Council of Nicea produced one of the great doctrinal statements of the Christian Church, the *Nicene Creed*. It is one of three that are universally accepted by all major communions of the visible church—Protestant, Catholic, and Orthodox. The most noteworthy "Arian-like" Christology in modern times is the teaching of the Jehovah's Witnesses.

Persecutions in the Ante-Nicene Period

Christians were not persecuted because they worshipped Jesus, but because they worshipped Jesus only. This was a disruption to the empire and, consequently, they were seen as rebels. The Roman world was a world of mixture or syncretism when it came to worship. There were many gods and nobody cared who worshipped whom so long as their worship did not disrupt the unity of the state and, usually, included worship of the emperor. Because Christians would not bow to Caesar, or any other god, they were seen as troublesome rebels. There were persecutions off and on from 30 AD to 312 AD of different severity and in various places. Never were there persecutions in all places in the empire at the same time.

Chapter 7

The Council of Nicea: 325 AD

The Council of Nicea is the "pivot point" of the first 500 years of church history. The council took place in the summer of 325 AD, with the years prior to this date known as "the ante-Nicene period," and the years following, "the post-Nicene period." Most historians would include the Council of Nicea in a list of the top 10 events in the history of the church. It is called the Council of Nicea because it was held in the small town of Nicea in the ancient country of Bythinia (which now is part of modern day Turkey). Today Nicea is called Iznek and is located just outside the city of Istanbul. In the year 325 AD, the city we know as modern Istanbul was renamed Constantinople, after the Emperor Constantine the Great. Before that it was called Byzantium.

Huge changes had taken place in the Roman world by the year 325 AD, which gave the church a freedom and rest she had not known. For 250 years, she had only known long periods of persecution under various emperors. As recently as the year 303 AD, the Emperor Diocletian had issued three edicts in rapid succession:

- ✧ Christian meeting houses were to be destroyed.
- ✧ All copies of the Scriptures were to be burned.
- ✧ All Christians were to be deprived of public office and civil rights.

Previous to, and along with these orders, Christian leaders were imprisoned and ill-treated.

In 312 AD, the Church was delivered from these persecutions when Constantine arrived at Rome after a long march from Spain.

From his childhood, he had been influenced by Christian ideas. His mother, Helena, was a Christian and several of Constantine's tutors had been followers of Christ. His father, Constantius, was emperor of the western Roman Empire and ruled from Cordova in Spain. When he died in 303 AD, Constantine replaced his father and became emperor of Gaul, Spain, and Britain. As stories came to Constantine from other parts of the Roman Empire relating the persecutions of the Christians, he did not like what he heard and resolved to deliver the Roman people from the leadership they were under. Though already favorable toward Christianity, he had a rather dramatic spiritual experience during the march from Spain that both confirmed his decision and motivated him. The fourth century church historian Socrates relates the thoughts that Constantine had as he marched to Rome, the heart of the empire, a city armed and seemingly invincible:

> *The Emperor Constantine, being informed of this, exerted himself to free the Romans from the slavery under [Maxentius who had assumed rule in 305 AD], and began immediately to consider by what means he might overthrow the tyrant. Now while his mind was occupied with this great subject, he debated as to what divinity's aid he should invoke in the conduct of the war [among the many gods in the Roman world, which one should he consult?] He began to realize that Diocletian's party had not profited at all by the pagan deities...but that his own father, Constantius, who had renounced the various religions of the Greeks, had passed through life far more prosperously. In this state of uncertainty, as he was marching at the head of his troops, a vision which transcends all description appeared to him. In fact, about that part of the day when the sun, after passing the meridian, begins to decline towards the west, he saw a pillar of light in the heavens in the form of a cross, on which were inscribed these words, "by this sign conquer." The appearance of this sign struck the emperor*

> with amazement, and scarcely believing his eyes, he asked those around if they beheld the same spectacle; and, as they unanimously declared they did, the emperor's mind was strengthened by this divine and marvelous apparition.[82]

Following this he prepared standards with the sign of the cross on the banners and his army and proceeded to Rome. He met the Roman Emperor Maxentius and his army in a battle just outside Rome at the Mulvian bridge and soundly defeated him. During the battle Maxentius fell into the Tiber River and drowned. Constantine became Emperor of the Roman Empire.

Since Constantine had become disposed toward Christianity, and possibly had become a Christian, he immediately lifted the persecution off all the churches and all the Christians. Though he did not make Christianity the state religion, he openly protected and favored the church. He saw to it that new men were prepared for pastoral ministry, church facilities were repaired, and new church buildings were built under his reign. However, it seems that having gained peace from enemies outside, the Church's enemy devised a plan to create a battle within.

In the summer of 325 AD, in the city of Nicea, the church was "forced" into holding a council on issues pertaining to Christology, the area of theology that deals with the person of Jesus Christ. The word *Christology* simply means "the study of Christ." Some of the most important doctrine concerning Christ was formulated during this time and has remained a foundation in the life of the Church. An outcome of the council was the famous *Nicene Creed*.

The Council of Nicea was precipitated by events that occurred in the year 318 AD. In the North African city of Alexandria, a theological battle broke out. The bishop in the city at that time was a man by the name of Alexander. At a presbytery meeting, he lectured on the subject, "The Unity of the Trinity." Present in the presbytery was an elder named Arius who, during the meeting, took issue with Alexander and said that he was teaching Sabellianism.

Sabellius was a man who had lived about 75 years before, and had taught that there was not a Trinity. Rather, his doctrine stated that God was one person who expressed himself in three different ways: sometimes as Father, sometimes as Son, and sometimes as the Holy Spirit. Sabellianism had been condemned at an earlier church council so it was a serious charge that he leveled at Alexander. Later, it became clear that Arius had something else in mind. He saw an opportunity to introduce his own novel doctrine. Arius introduced his famous dictum into the church and a great controversy arose. He stated, *"There was when the Son of God did not exist,"* or, to put it into a more contemporary expression, *"There was a 'time' when the Son of God did not exist."*[83]

This "time" that the Son of God did not exist happened before the universe was created, which helps explain why he did not use the word time in his original statement. Further, Arius said the Son was created out of nothing just as the original physical creation. No other man before had dared stand up and say that there was a time when the Son of God did not exist, because it was a serious claim. It took away his deity because it stripped him of one of the attributes of divinity—his eternality (that he always existed). To suggest that there was a time when he was created by God the Father—even out of nothing—meant that he was nothing more than a created being. One of the marks of deity is "un-created-ness."

Alexander and the other bishops of North Africa took great issue with Arius, but he refused to listen to them. He taught his doctrine wherever he went and gained somewhat of a following. Arius was not a young man, and he was an experienced logician. He had been trained in the schools of Greek philosophy and rhetoric and was able, in his speeches, to appeal to reason and logic, and could sway a crowd. He was actually admired by Alexander and others for his abilities.

After Alexander had tried to correct Arius of his error, and found it to be useless, he called together a large assembly of Egyptian bishops in 320 AD. At this counsel, Arius and his partisans were anathematized for their unwillingness to repent from their false teaching, and were excommunicated from the Church. Although he and his followers were removed from the church, he began to hold his own church services and teach his doctrine. He simply could not be quieted and sent letters throughout the empire defending himself and trying to gain a larger following. The "Arians," as they came to be known, continued to teach and worked hard to bring other bishops over to their side and, indeed, many people were brought into their churches.

Due to their aggressiveness, it became necessary to unveil the errors of the Arians. The specific tenets of their belief system that Alexander and his colleagues exposed were the following.

- *There was a time when the Son of God was not.*[84]

- *He who previously had no existence subsequently came into existence.*[85]

- *He was created out of nothing; like everything else, reasonable and unreasonable, and consequently was by nature liable to change, capable of goodness and sin.*[86]

- *God, knowing that He (the Son) would not deny Him, chose Him above all created beings, although by nature He had no higher claim than other sons of God, that is, than other virtuous men. If Peter or Paul had sought to reach the same perfection as Christ, their relationship to God would have been absolutely the same as that in which Christ stood.*[87]

- *There was a time when God was not the Father.*[88]

Even though the errors of Arius were exposed, matters only continued to deteriorate. The Arian controversy became so great that it reached the ears of the Emperor Constantine. Constantine was concerned about this issue and enlisted the services of a church leader by the name of Hosius, a famous and respected bishop who presided over the church at Cordova in Spain. Hosius had proved himself to be a man of faithfulness, was loved greatly by the emperor, and was known in the church throughout the empire. He was 70 years old, had been a bishop for 30 years, and was a "confessor" who had survived the persecutions under Maximian, the Roman emperor prior to Constantine. Those who had suffered for Christ in the persecutions, and whose bodies were maimed, scarred, or disfigured were called "confessors." They were highly respected and honored because they had remained true to Christ under severe sufferings. Constantine thought, due to his influence, Hosius might be able to bring the doctrinal conflict to an end.

The Emperor Constantine invited Hosius to his palace in Nicomedia (a town near Nicea), composed letters to Alexander and Arius, and sent them with Hosius to Alexandria to seek reconciliation between the two men. Hosius delivered the letters and sat down with the two adversaries but could not administer reconciliation. In fact, it became apparent that he was trying to accomplish the impossible because Arianism cannot be reconciled with apostolic doctrine. One position sees Christ as eternal and the other sees him as created, a creature. As sincere as the emperor's letter was, it did nothing to resolve the problem. After his visit with Alexander and Arius, Hosius returned and reported the proceedings to Constantine. This theological battle continued to rage throughout the Church until the emperor decided to take the initiative in calling a church council composed of Christian leaders from all over the Roman Empire. The church historian, Socrates, who lived in the fourth century, supplies us with the following information:

> But the evil had become too strong for the exhortations of the emperor, and the authority of him who was the bearer of this letter for neither was Alexander nor Arius softened by this appeal; and moreover there was incessant strife and tumult among the people.

When, therefore the emperor beheld the Church agitated on account of both of these causes, he convoked a General Council, summoning all the bishops by letter to meet him at Nicea in Bithynia.[89]

Socrates indicates that neither Alexander nor Arius could submit to the authority of the emperor or the authority of the highly esteemed churchman, Hosius. What was needed was a church council. It was understood in the early church that a council was the common and appropriate way to address church doctrinal and practice issues and deal with heresies. This dates back to the New Testament *Book of Acts*, chapter 15, where we find such a model. Throughout this entire ordeal it became apparent that the emperor himself was quite concerned and became agitated when his intervention proved futile. Another ancient historian, Theodoret, said:

> *The emperor, who possessed the most profound wisdom, having heard of these things, endeavored, as a first step, to stop up their fountain-head. He therefore dispatched a messenger renowned for his wit to Alexandria with letters, in an endeavor to extinguish the dispute, and expecting to reconcile the disputants. But his hopes having been frustrated, he proceeded to summon the celebrated council of Nicea; and pledged his word that the bishops and their officials should be furnished with asses, mules, and horses for their journey at public expense.*[90]

As indicated, Constantine initiated the matter by sending letters to all the bishops across the empire, inviting them, their elders and deacons to a council to be held in the town of Nicea. Constantine made good on his word and provided them everything at his disposal for their travel. He supplied ships as well as horses, mules, and donkeys, and paid for their food and lodging as they traveled.

Assembling under the call of the emperor gave a sense of urgency to their gathering. It was clearly understood that it was the responsibility of the bishops to protect the doctrine of the church.

So, they came to this council with a great deal of purpose. More than 300 bishops came with elders and deacons. Altogether, there were approximately 1,800 to 2,000 who attended.

The Council

The Council of Nicea began on May 25 and ended August 25, 325 AD. The initial business was to set forth opinions and to enter into debate. This involved summoning Arius and his followers to the proceedings. There were probably 22 men in the Arian party. The emperor had indicated that he wanted to be present for the "heart of the debates," when they were nearing a time of decision.

> *The bishops had several conferences among themselves previously to the day when they were to proceed to the formal decision of affairs, and on which, Constantine desired to be present.*[91]

When the conference began, various people began to be distinguished. Men were getting to know one another. They had come from all over the Roman world and many had not met before. As the conference continued, they grew in appreciation for the Church and for one another as they observed the variety of gifts present. The historian Eusebius of Caesarea gives a description of those who attended:

> *Among these holy ministers, some excelled by the wisdom and eloquence of their discourse, others by the gravity of their deportment and patience of labor; and others, again, by their humility, and the gentleness of their manners. Some of them were honored on account of their gray hairs, while others were recommended by their youthful vigor and activity, both of body and mind. Several of them had but recently begun to exercise the functions of their ministry. Some were confessedly eminent for knowledge and abilities…Others were esteemed on*

account of their past sufferings in the cause of our holy religion, still bearing in their bodies, like the great apostle of the Gentiles, "the marks of the Lord Jesus."[92]

As these preliminary discussions took place, it also began to become apparent who the gifted debaters were and who some of the new leaders in the church would be.

> Before the appointed time arrived, the bishops assembled together, and having summoned Arius to attend, began to examine the disputed topics, each one among them advancing his own opinion. Many of the bishops who were then assembled and, of the clergy who accompanied them, being remarkable for their dialectical skill, and practice in rhetoric methods, became conspicuous, and attracted the notice of the emperor and the court. Of that number, Athanasius, who was a deacon of Alexandria, and had accompanied the bishop Alexander, seemed to have the largest share in the council concerning these subjects.[93]

The term "appointed time" referred to the day appointed for the emperor's arrival and the beginning of the formal debates, which was June 19, 325 AD. As indicated, there was a young man from Alexandria whose name was Athanasius, and he became the primary spokesman for the historic orthodox position. Athanasius was 29 years old and this was not the last time his voice would be heard. He became a great theologian, teacher, and bishop of the Church of Alexandria and came to be known as one of the greatest leaders in the Christian faith. At the Council of Nicea, he defended the Christian faith against the false teachings of the Arians.

On June 19, after all the preliminary conferences had occurred, and the council was prepared to enter into its formal debates, the Emperor made his appearance. Everyone was impressed by the regality of his presence and by his humility. When he and his retinue reached the place in the assembly hall where a seat awaited him, he remained standing until invited to sit. Some accounts show how impressed and overcome he was in sitting among those present. Some who came were well-dressed and others showed the poverty in which they lived. The emperor was especially impressed with the "confessors" and walked among them touching, and even kissing, their wounds.

The leader of the conference welcomed the emperor to the council and then invited him to give a speech to those present. The following account is given:

> *When he was seated, the spectators all continued in silence, fixing their eyes upon the emperor, who, surveying them with a cheerful and serene expression of countenance, and employing a few moments to collect his thoughts, spake to the following purport, in a pleasant and subdued tone of voice. "It was, my dear friends, my most cherished wish, that I might one day enjoy the sight of this convention. Having been indulged in this desire, I return thanks to God, the ruler of all, who, in addition to innumerable other favors, has granted me this greatest of all blessings, to see you assembled together, and united in your minds. May no malignant foe disturb in future our public happiness. An internal sedition in the Church is, in my apprehension, more dangerous and formidable than any war in which I can be engaged; nor do foreign concerns, however unfortunate, affect my mind with so sensible a grief as this unhappy affair. After I had become victorious, by divine assistance, over all my enemies, I thought that it only remained for me to render thanks to God, and to participate in the universal joy with those, whose liberation he has accomplished through my agency and efforts. But when the unwelcome news of your dissension was brought to my ears, I conceived that the report should by no means be neglected; and hoping that by my interference, a remedy might be applied to the evil, I*

> sent for you all, without delay. Great is my satisfaction to see you assembled together. But I shall consider the object of my prayers and labors as fully obtained, when I shall behold you united in the purposes of promoting harmony and concord; which, as persons consecrated to God, it is your duty to preach and to inculcate on others. Endeavor then, my friends, ministers of God, and faithful servants of a common master and Savior, that the causes of your disagreement being, all the asperities of controversy may be smoothed by the dictates of peace. By pursuing this course, you will not only do that which is pleasing to God, who is exalted above all, but will confer an important benefit on myself, your fellow servant."[94]

The speech given by Constantine was pronounced in Latin, which was his vernacular tongue, but another person translated it into Greek, which was the language of the larger number of people present.

The formal part of the council then commenced and continued several days. The position of the Arians was once again presented and it was explained how the doctrine they had devised was in opposition to the apostolic faith. This was shown in the presentation of one word, which became the key for the whole conference. The word was the Greek word, *homoousios*, which means "of the same substance, or consubstantial." Consubstantial means "of the same nature or substance" and became the word used at the conference when referring to the true nature of Christ. The question was, "Is the Son of God of the same substance as the Father or of another substance?" Another way of asking the question is: "Is the Son of the same nature as the Father or of another nature?" The Arians kept using the word, *homoiousios*, which means, "of a like substance." The words look very much alike except for a slight difference in spelling; and, the slight difference in spelling indicates a big difference in meaning.

At this point it became clear that the Arians held the idea that humans could, in some way, become or bear a kind of "godness."

Their reasoning was that since Christ, who was created at a point in eternity, could be called "true God," humans too, at some point, might be called "gods." The diminishing of Christ's deity meant the elevation of man.

The greater number in the council saw the difference between *homoousios* (same substance or nature), and *homoiousios* (similar substance and nature), and agreed that Christ was of the same substance as the Father, not of a like substance.

The Conclusion

Arius and his followers were given one more chance to repent, and some did, but Arius and a few others held to their position. Their ideas were fully rejected by the council so the next step was to compose a document to which unanimous consent could be given, one which would reflect the agreement and common consent of the leaders as to what was the true doctrine of the Church. Hosius was given the responsibility of drawing up this document, which became the *Nicene Creed*. There were variations on the wording of the *Nicene Creed*, and there was some editing following the conference, but its important elements can be seen in the creed as we have it today.

> *We believe in one God, the Father Almighty,*
> *Maker of all things visible and invisible;*
> *And in one Lord Jesus Christ, the Son of God,*
> *The only begotten of the Father,*
> *That is, of one substance with the Father;*
> *God of God, light of light, true God of true God;*
> *Begotten, not made, consubstantial with the Father,*
> *By whom all things were made, both in heaven and in earth;*
> *Who for the sake of us men and on account of our salvation,*
> *Descended, became incarnate, was made man,*
> *And suffered, and rose again on the third day;*
> *He ascended into the heavens*
> *And will come to judge the living and the dead;*
> *[We believe] also in the Holy Spirit.*[95]

One can observe that the creed focuses upon Jesus Christ and precisely who He is. Other important beliefs of the Church are alluded to but not developed. Over the years the creed was added to until it became the creed we have today. There is an ending included in the original document that we do not have in our more contemporary version of the creed. It sets forth the consequences of anyone who would deny the essential doctrine contained in the creed. Of course, this was composed with Arianism in mind but would have application to anyone or any church body denying the deity of Christ.

> *But to those who say, "There was a time when He was not,"*
> *Or "He did not exist before He was begotten,"*
> *Or "He was made of nothing," or assert that*
> *"He is of other substance or essence than the Father,"*
> *Or that the Son of God is created, or mutable, or susceptible of change,*
> *The Catholic and Apostolic Church of God anathematizes.*[96]

It was on the basis of this creed that Arius and his companions were anathematized and excommunicated from the church. His writings were condemned as well. The action of the Council of Nicea was clear, concise, and severe. It is apparent that the Council of Nicea was both educational and had a great unifying influence upon the universal Church. Some church leaders during the conference vacillated upon what they did believe with regard to Christology. But by the end of the conference, there was unanimous agreement and a sense of "having come together." It seems that the emperor saw this clearly as a work of God—that the whole affair seemed guided by Divine Providence. The success of the council was felt deeply by many and, to Constantine, the logical conclusion to such a conference should be a celebration. Thus, the prince invited the participants to the royal palace for such an occasion. Magnificent entertainment was provided by Constantine and not one of the bishops missed the "imperial banquet." It is described in the following way:

> *The guards and soldiers, disposed in a circle, were stationed at the entrance of the palace with drawn swords. The men of God passed through the midst of them without fear, and went into the most private apartments of the royal edifice. Some of them were then admitted to the table of the emperor, and others took the places assigned them on either side. It was a lively image of the kingdom of Christ, and appeared more like a dream than a reality. At the conclusion of the splendid festival, the emperor courteously saluted every individual of the company, and presented his guests with rich and valuable gifts, according to their respective rank and merits. When they were about to separate, he took friendly leave of them, exhorting them to union, harmony and mutual condescension; and concluded by recommending himself to their prayers. Thus ended the great council of Nice...*[97]

God used this event to put a temporary stop on the arrogance and spread of Arianism, but such heresies die hard. In fact, forms of Arianism still exist within some cults today. From the time of the council, Arius and his followers refused to repent. Wishing to be a part of the Catholic Church, they let some time pass and then made an attempt to get back into the Church. The story unfolds in the following manner.

In the year 336 AD, 11 years after the council and just a year or so before Constantine died, Arius returned to say that he believed the *Nicene Creed*. The church historian, Socrates, reports what happened.

> *Meanwhile, the Emperor Constantine, being desirous of personally examining Arius, sent for him to come to the palace, and asked him if he would assent to the determination of the synod at Nicea. He, without hesitation, replied in the affirmative, and ascribed the declaration of faith in the Emperor's presence, acting with duplicity. The Emperor, surprised at his ready compliance,*

> obliged him to confirm his signature with an oath. Thus he did with equal conceit. The way he evaded, as I have heard, is this: he wrote his own opinion on paper and carried it under his arm. So, that he had sworn truly that he really "held" the sentiments he had written. That this is so, however, I have written from hearsay, but that he added an oath to his subscription I have myself ascertained from an examination of the Emperor's own letters.[98]

We should remember that it was in northern Egypt, at the city of Alexandria, that Arius began to assert his doctrine. His attempt to get back into the Church occurred near Constantinople, on the northern side of the Mediterranean Sea and was partly necessitated by the emperor's request that he come to his palace near Constantinople. Constantine was convinced of Arius's sincerity and desired religious unity. Therefore, Constantine ordered that Arius be received back into communion of the Church through the bishop.

The name of the bishop in Constantinople was Alexander. He had followed the movements and teaching of Arius over the years, was suspicious of him, and did everything he could to keep Arius out of the Church. However, he failed. He found no way to overrule the order of the emperor. It was announced on Saturday that Arius would be received and have communion in the church at Constantinople the next day, Sunday. Alexander, being quite distressed, went into the church sanctuary to pray. There was another person who went into the church with him whose name was Marcarius, an elder from the church.

At this particular time, Athanasius, who was now bishop of the church in Alexandria, had been exiled to Gaul (France). When Athanasius came out of exile, Marcarius told him what happened on the Saturday before Arius was to be admitted back into the church at Constantinople. On Saturday an announcement was made by the emperor that Arius and his colleagues would be received back into the Church. Theodoret relates what happened.

> *The bishop Alexander, deeply grieved at what he heard, went into the church and poured forth his lamentations, raising his hands in supplication to God, and throwing himself on the pavement in the sanctuary, prayed. Marcarius went in with him, and heard his prayers. He [Alexander] asked one of two things. "If Arius," he said, "is to be joined to the Church tomorrow, let me Thy servant depart, and do not destroy the pious with the impious. If Thou wilt spare Thy Church, and I know that Thou dost spare her, look upon the words of the followers of Eusebius, and give not over Thy heritage to destruction and to shame. Remove Arius, lest if he come into the Church, heresy seem to come in with him, and impiety be hereafter deemed piety." Having thus prayed, the bishop left the church deeply anxious, and then a horrible and extraordinary catastrophe ensued.*[99]

Arius and his followers were celebrating, believing that they had gained a great victory and vindication in their cause. Three historians—Theodoret, Sozomen, and Socrates—describe what happened. Theodoret records the bold response of Arius upon the prospect of being brought back into the Church: "Arius, emboldened by the protection of his party, delivered many trifling and foolish speeches…."[100] Socrates writes, "For going out of the imperial palace, attended by a crowd of Eusebian partisans like guards, he paraded proudly through the midst of the city, attracting the notice of all the people."[101] Then, something quite amazing occurred. Theodoret tells us that he "was suddenly compelled by a call of nature."[102] Socrates states it in the following way:

> *As he approached the place called Constantine's Forum…a terror seized Arius, and with the terror a violent relaxation of the bowels: he therefore enquired whether there was a convenient place near, and being directed to the back of Constantine's Forum, he hastened thither. Soon after a faintness came over him, and together*

with the evacuation his bowels protruded, followed by a copious hemorrhage, and the descent of the lower intestines; moreover portions of his spleen and liver were brought off in the effusion of blood, so that he almost immediately died. The scene of this catastrophe still is shown at Constantinople, as I have said, behind the shambles in the colonnade: and by persons going by pointing the finger at the place, there is a perpetual remembrance preserved by this extraordinary kind of death.[103]

Theodoret adds:

> [He] gave up the ghost, being deprived at once both of communion and life. Thus was the end of Arius. The followers of [Arius] were covered with shame, and buried him whose belief they shared. The blessed Alexander completed the celebration, rejoicing with the Church in piety and orthodoxy, praying with all the brethren and greatly glorifying God. This was not because he rejoiced at the death of Arius… but because the event plainly transcended any human condemnation. For the Lord himself passing judgment upon the menaces of the followers of [Arius], and the prayer of Alexander, condemned the Arian heresy, and shewed that it was unworthy of being received into the communion of the Church; thus manifesting to all that, even if it received the countenance and support of the emperor, and of all men, yet by truth itself it stood condemned.[104]

Socrates wrote:

> …and the report of it quickly spread itself over the city and throughout the world. As the king grew more earnest in Christianity and confessed that the confession of Nicea was attested by God, he rejoiced at the occurrences.[105]

When Constantine heard of this event, he regarded it as proof of perjury. This was the end of Arius, a contriver of false doctrine. The Council of Nicea provided a document that has been held by faithful communions of Christians, but it did not come without opposition and pursuit of the truth.

Chapter 8

Post-Nicene Period: 325 - 500 AD

This period marked a new relationship between the church and state. It would have been hard for those who suffered through the first three centuries to have imagined such a time. To them, suffering seemed to be a normal part of being a Christian and, most likely, they would have been suspect of peace between the state and the church. Nevertheless, it was true, and not only was the church given favored status, it could also speak into the affairs of the state. This time period was marked by significant development in the church while the state continued to deteriorate. Ironically, the age begins with the elevation of the church and ends with the fall of Rome.

Post-Nicene Fathers

This period is also known as the "Golden Age of Church Fathers." Many outstanding men rose to make valuable contributions through their ideas and writings, and have had a lasting effect on church polity and theology. At this point in the history of the church, we must note a distinction between "east" and "west," due to the use of two different languages (Greek in the east and Latin in the west), two different heads of the church (Rome in the west and Constantinople in the east), and two different minds (rational in the west and mystery in the east). Because of this differentiation, we place the church fathers of this time into two groups: the Eastern Fathers and the Western Fathers.

The Eastern Fathers

Eusebius of Caesarea

Eusebius (260[?]-339 AD), is known as "The Father of Church History." He wrote a history of the church from its beginning until the time of the Council of Nicea in 325 AD. His work is called *Ecclesiastical History* (History of the Church) and remains our best record of the early church from that time period. He also wrote *Chronicle*, which was a history of the world, and *The Martyrs of Palestine*, covering the Great Persecution of 303-313 AD. He was alive when Emperor Constantine come to power, greatly admired the Emperor, and wrote a work called *The Life of Constantine*. His *Ecclesiastical History*, although not particularly well-written by most standards, pioneered the way in the writing and cataloging of early church history and provided both a model and foundation upon which others built.

He studied and worked under the well-known Pamphilus of Caesarea and, in gratitude to him, took his name, becoming Eusebius Pamphilus. This gesture usually indicated the relationship of son or slave. Pamphilus was in charge of Origen's outstanding library at Caesarea and so Eusebius had access to very useful sources which helped in his writings. In addition to his histories, Eusebius also wrote many exegetical, doctrinal, and polemical works and was the founder of a theological school in Caesarea.

Eusebius was well-equipped to write about the horrible persecutions under Diocletian because they had a direct effect upon his own life. During these persecutions he fled first to Tyre and then to Egypt for a time. Finally, he returned to Caesarea and, in either 313 or 315 AD, was elected bishop of that city. Besides having experienced the persecutions first-hand, he would, within a few years, take part in the great Arian controversies that threatened the purity of Christian doctrine and unity of the Church. At first Eusebius was inclined to side with the Arians, but as the Council of Nicea progressed and the creed developed in written form, he joined with the majority in condemning the Arian doctrine and anathematizing those who continued to hold to its tenets. Eusebius actually presented the *Creed of Caesarea* as a model for the council, and after some corrections and modifications, it was adopted and named *The Nicene Creed*. This creed was the first major summary of the doctrine of Christology by the Church and, to this day, remains one of the most carefully worded and succinct statements of the Christian faith.

John Chrysostom

John Chrysostom (345 [?]-407 AD) has been called the greatest preacher and expositor of the Bible during the period in which he lived, and is considered the most prominent doctor of the Greek Church. Because of his oratorical skills, in the sixth century he was given, posthumously, the title "Chrysostom," which means "golden mouthed."

Born in Antioch in the middle of the fourth century, he was given the simple name, John. He was raised by his father, Secundus, who was an officer of high rank in the army, and his mother, whose name was Anthusa. Widowed when she was 20 years of age, Anthusa became solely responsible for, and the main influence in the lives of her two children, John and his older sister. Being a woman of intelligence, character, and devotion to God, she directed her son into a life of spiritual interest and enrolled him in the best schools of Antioch. He began a promising career in rhetoric (the study of the rules and principles of composition and communication) and elocution (the art of public speaking) in his home city and continued to be drawn toward a life of piety. It was probably in the year 370 AD that he was baptized and took up the monastic life. For ten years he lived in a cave outside Antioch and, because of such austerity and rigorous self-denial, damaged his health. His poor health forced him to return to Antioch where he became a deacon and later a presbyter.

> *For the next twelve years he preached at Antioch and turned out to be the greatest preacher in the Eastern Church. Chrysostom had no use for the pomp, luxury, and loose living which were so prevalent in the Church and in the Court, and made enemies in both circles by his moral earnestness and unsparing attacks. (On one occasion, after his elevation as Archbishop of Constantinople in 398 AD, he kicked out 13 bishops for simony and immorality).*[106]

The time at Antioch proved to be a period of great benefit and development for Chrysostom. There he studied under Diodore of Tarsus who introduced him to the world of biblical scholarship. In Antioch a particular type of biblical interpretation was taught. In contrast to the "allegorical school" found in Alexandria, Antioch was known for its "literal" interpretation of the Bible. There, great emphasis was placed upon the grammar and history of the Scriptures as primary means for biblical interpretation.

> *The Antiochenes insisted that the Bible should be interpreted according to its natural meaning, the "literal" sense as it was called. There was scope for typology (drawing parallels between God's dealings with man at different times), but not for fanciful interpretations which evaded the plain historical meaning of the text. Chrysostom adopted this approach.*[107]

No doubt it was because of such training, aligned with his natural skills that gave him the reputation of being the greatest preacher of his time. At a time when the texts of the Bible were often "spiritualized" or "allegorized," he and others, coming out of the school at Antioch, provided a more accurate and realistic interpretation of the Scriptures.

> *He preached regularly, normally working his way through an entire book of the Bible. These sermons were*

> then published as commentaries. He also preached sermons on specific subjects and wrote a number of treatises.[108]

Thus, he became known as an able and excellent Bible expositor, and his works became widely read and known. This expanded his reputation and influence. He was popular, lived in Antioch and remained there until 397 AD. In that year the bishopric at Constantinople, the capital, was vacated and a new bishop was needed. Chrysostom was chosen and "forced" to accept the post. There, in the Church of Sophia, he would preach to vast congregations. Though a position of greater influence, it was also a place of greater danger. Chrysostom lived a pure, simple life that was a rebuke to his highly placed parishioners in Constantinople.[109] Not one to back down, and always working for moral and religious reforms, he continued to preach against public, political, and private sins. He taught that there must be no divorce of morals and religion; the Cross and ethics must go together.[110] Tension existed continually between the Empress Eudoxia and Chrysostom and, in time, she began to plan how she might banish the great preacher. Her opportunity finally came when he "denounced her for her extravagant dress and for placing a silver statue of herself near St. Sophia where he preached."[111]

> The Empress Eudoxia, stinging from Chrysostom's public criticisms of her opulent living, teamed up with Chrysostom's jealous, unscrupulous rival, Theophilus, Patriarch of Alexandria, and found a pretext for putting Chrysostom on trial when Chrysostom welcomed four Egyptian monks known as "the tall brothers." Chrysostom's foes conspired to depose and banish him. Although recalled briefly by Eudoxia (after a public riot protesting Chrysostom's ousting threatened her palace), Chrysostom was formally and permanently exiled in 403 AD. [He was forced] to live in the desert town of Cucusus in the Taurus Mountains in the depths of Armenia, but continued to exert a profound influence by his letters. The empress

then ordered him transferred to the desert town of Pityus. He was forced to walk the whole way bareheaded under the blazing sun and collapsed and died in 407 AD.[112]

Those who attended him on his forced march heard his last words: "Glory be to God for all things." After his death he was vindicated and his body brought back to Constantinople and buried with honor.

Theodore of Mopseustia

Theodore (350[?]-428 AD) entered the monastery at Antioch, where he remained for about ten years, studied rhetoric, and learned the Antiochene method of biblical interpretation under Diodore. There, he became a good friend of John Chrysostom and, along with him, went on to become a great theologian and biblical exegete. Theodore has been rightly called "the prince of ancient exegetes."[113] Both he and Chrysostom had a healthy influence upon the methods of biblical interpretation in their day.[114] He would go on to oversee the work of the church at Antioch and serve as bishop of Mopseustia. When marriage and a secular career seemed powerfully tempting, his friend John Chrysostom persuaded him to remain committed to the ministry. He was ordained a presbyter in 383 AD, and after ten years in Antioch, became bishop of Mopseustia in 392 AD.

Theodore championed orthodox Christianity against the Arians during the controversies over the nature of Christ which wracked the Church during the 4th and 5th centuries... Theodore was a theologian and writer of considerable renown. He attended the great Council of Constantinople in 394 AD, preached before Byzantine Emperor Theodosius, and wrote a number of Biblical commentaries and treatises.[115]

Some of his writings had characteristics of Pelagianism, causing Theodore to be condemned posthumously in 553 AD as a heretic.

Many today believe this action was too severe and was actually imposed upon Theodore because his pupil, Nestorius, veered off into heresy. Pelagianism is a doctrine which teaches a kind of perfectionism, saying that there is no inherent sin in human nature; rather, sin is a matter of choice. Pelagianism is a denial of original sin.

Whatever might be said about actions following the death of Theodore, there is no question that he was a powerful influence during his lifetime and contributed to the security of Christian doctrine.

The Western Fathers

Athanasius

Athanasius (293[?]-373 AD) is known as "the father of orthodoxy"[116] because he faithfully held to the doctrine handed down from the apostles and appealed constantly to the authority of the Scriptures. We first hear of him when he was a deacon in the church at Alexandria. Probably educated from boyhood in the great north African city, he became secretary to Alexander, bishop of Alexandria, accompanied him to the Council of Nicea in 325, and rose to popularity during the debates concerning the nature of Christ. He became known as a great defender of the faith and, upon Alexander's death in 328 AD, succeeded him as bishop in the church at Alexandria. He remained bishop for forty-five years, dying in 373 AD. From the time he became bishop, life for Athanasius "meant living in constant tension and attack and experiencing banishment five times from Alexandria... and [he] so persistently clung to the Nicene faith as normative for the Church's Christology, that it is due entirely to him that Nicene Christianity triumphed."[117]

> *Athanasius' protagonists were Arius and Eusebius of Nicomedia. Arius, whose theory of Christology was known as Arianism, taught that Christ was not quite God and not quite man, but something in between.*

> *Athanasius insisted that salvation came only because the full and real Godhead came into union with the full and real manhood in Jesus Christ, and that Arianism was basically pagan.*[118]

Beginning around 317 or 318 AD, while Alexander was still bishop, a long and bitter dispute erupted between those who came to be known as "Arians" and the leaders of the church in Alexandria. This dispute would continue long after the conclusion of the Nicean Council. Because of his popularity, skill in logic, and effective public speaking, Arius was able to gain a rather large following. With politics, as well as theology playing a role, these tensions continued for years until, finally, Emperor Constantine called the Council of Nicea in 325 to resolve the matter. The council decided in favor of the Alexandrians and anathematized the Arians. One of the great and lasting outcomes of this council was the document that we call *The Nicene Creed*.

Another result that should be noted was the relationship that began to develop between the church and the state. As noted previously, the emperor presided over the council and paid the expenses.

> *For the first time the Church found itself dominated by the political leadership of the head of the state. The perennial problem of the relationship between the Church and state emerged clearly here, but the bishops were too busy dealing with theological heresy to think of that particular problem....Nicea cost the Church its independence, however, for the Church became imperial from this time and was increasingly dominated by the emperor.*[119]

Athanasius also compiled the first list of the 27 books that are today recognized as the New Testament. He is also the first of the eight great doctors (authoritative teachers) of the Church. These include Athanasius, Gregory of Nanzianzus, Basil, Ambrose, Jerome, Chrysostom, Augustine, and Gregory the Great.

Jerome

Jerome was born around 340 AD at Stridon, a town in northeast Italy at the head of the Adriatic Ocean. He died in the Holy Land at Bethlehem on September 30, 420 AD. He became one of the most learned, influential, and celebrated fathers in the Western Church. There are conflicting reports about his early years. Some suggest that he was raised a pagan, others that he was raised by Christian parents. Whatever his background, it is certain that he came from a wealthy family. He probably did not embrace the Christian faith until after leaving home. Around the age of 12, after having received a good education at home, he was sent to Rome where he studied Latin, Greek, and rhetoric under the famous rhetorician, Donatus. He read with great diligence and profits the classic poets, orators, and philosophers, and collected a considerable library.[120] He became prolific in languages, theology, philosophy, and writing. It was while in Rome that Christian faith was born in him. One influence was his visits to the catacombs. He tells us that "it was my custom on Sundays to visit, with friends of my own age and tastes, the tombs of the martyrs and Apostles, going down into those subterranean galleries whose walls on both sides preserve the relics of the dead."[121] An indelible impression was made upon him as he deciphered the inscriptions and viewed the remains of Christians.

His days in Rome were not without temptations and difficulties and Jerome was often disappointed in his own moral laxness and failure. In spite of this, he was baptized by Pope Liberius, probably in the year 360 AD, around the age of 19 or 20, and "resolved thenceforth to devote himself wholly, in rigid abstinence, to the service of the Lord."[122] After his baptism, Jerome divided his life between the east and the west, between ascetic discipline and literary labor.[123] Drawn to the monastic life, he left Rome with a few of his friends and his library. He traveled to Antioch, visited the well-known anchoret communities (those who had entered seclusion for religious purposes), and then lived for four years as a hermit in the Syrian dessert. During this time he had a "grievous struggle with sensuality."[124] Following this period, and just prior to the year 380 AD, he was ordained by Paulinus, bishop of the church at Antioch. Jerome consented to ordination on the condition that he not be obliged to serve any particular church, believing his calling to be that of a traveling monk and recluse.

Leaving the life of a hermit, he went to Constantinople where he studied the Scriptures for two years under Gregory, bishop of that city. He then returned to Rome as a teacher and as literary secretary to the leader of the church there, Pope Damasus. Jerome, in spite of his crusty disposition and strict asceticism, found a large audience among Rome's wealthy, upper class women, several of whom later insisted upon accompanying him to the Holy Land.[125] Through his influence upon these women, Jerome impacted the city of Rome. "Formerly," says Jerome, "according to the testimony of the apostles, there were few rich, few noble, few powerful among the Christians. Now it is no longer so."[126]

Though Jerome made many contributions during his lifetime that influenced the church and culture, two stand out. First, was his translation of the Bible out of the original languages into Latin. While at Rome, Jerome was commissioned by the pope to produce a new and improved Latin translation of the Scriptures. After the pope died, Jerome visited Egypt, Antioch, and Palestine. He founded a monastery in Bethlehem in 386 AD, where he settled down to a life of scholarship and translation. In this effort, he was accompanied by several of the previously mentioned influential Roman women.

> *In Bethlehem he presided over a monastery till his death, built a hospital for all strangers except heretics, prosecuted his literary studies without cessation, wrote*

several commentaries, and finished his improved Latin version of the Bible—the noblest achievement of his life.[127]

His Latin version became recognized as the authorized version of the Western Church for the next 1,000 years, its superiority being reaffirmed by the Council of Trent in 1546. *The Latin Vulgate* became the Church's reference for Ecclesiastical Latin, the language used by the Church and throughout universities for over a millennium. The term vulgate means "common speech or language, the vernacular, the vulgar." Jerome is distinguished because of his momentous work in Bible translation.

Second, he became the "most zealous promoter of the monastic life among the church fathers,"[128] and secured monasticism in the western Church. His love of the ascetic life caused him to champion it with his pen, and the later medieval popularity of the ascetic life in the West owed much to the writings of Jerome on this subject.[129] These writings on the values and profits of the monastic life laid foundations, provided guidelines, and influenced the development of monasteries and convents in the Western Church.

Beside his translation of the Bible, and his promotion of monastic life, his life's work also included commentaries on most of the books of the Bible. He was skilled in several languages, studied classical disciplines, had a profound knowledge of the early church writings, was a biblical scholar, and traveled a great deal, gaining a clear understanding of geography. Although a gifted preacher, expositor, and writer, Jerome was also remembered as a controversial and surly churchman.

Ambrose

Ambrose, (340[?]-397 AD), bishop of Milan, was one of the most distinguished fourth century church fathers. The first Latin church father from a Christian family, Ambrose was also born into power as part of the Roman family of Aurelius.[130] While he was still a child, his family had received the pope and other church and political leaders into their home. His parents demonstrate the influence Christianity had during this time among the wealthy and influential in the Roman world. His father had held the high position of prefect of Gaul, and his family, high in imperial circles in Rome, educated him in law for a political career.[131] By the time he was 30, he was governor in the northern provinces of Italy...but a career in law and politics was not to be his life's work.

When the bishop of Milan died in 374 AD, it was the laity of the city who demanded Ambrose succeed him. At first, Ambrose did not want to be an ecclesiastical leader because he was doing quite well in the political world. But the people wrote to the Emperor Valentian, asking for his approval and seal on their verdict. Finally, with pressure from both the people and the emperor, and believing this to be the call of God, Ambrose agreed. This demanded some immediate changes for him. He had not yet been baptized. So, he gave up his high position, was baptized, gave his money to the poor, took the position of bishop, and began a life of leadership in the church with special focus upon the Scriptures and theology.

His persuasive writings, eloquent preaching, and ascetic living made him deeply respected.[132] His education in rhetoric, law, and Greek, joined with his outstanding personal disposition, made him an effective scholar and communicator. His eloquence was celebrated.[133] He was given the title "doctor," or "authoritative teacher," in the Western Church. Because he was so well-equipped, and fearless, he exercised powerful influence upon his world in general and upon individuals in particular.

His most famous moment in the public arena came when he stood up to the Emperor Theodosius, refusing him communion and calling the emperor to repent for public crimes. The emperor was a professing Christian and favorable toward Christianity, wishing to make it the state religion. Along with this, he and Ambrose were friends, but circumstances occurred which caused the bishop to take severe action.

> In 390, local authorities imprisoned a charioteer of Thessalonica for homosexuality. Unfortunately, the charioteer was one of the city's favorites, and riots broke out when the governor refused to release him. The governor and a few others were killed in the melee, and the charioteer was freed. Fuming, Theodosius exacted revenge. He announced another chariot race, but after the crowds arrived, the gates were locked and the townspeople were massacred by the emperor's soldiers. Within three hours 7,000 were dead. Ambrose was horrified. He wrote an angry letter to Theodosius demanding his repentance. "I exhort, I beg, I entreat, I admonish you, because it is a grief to me that the perishing of so many is no grief to you," he wrote. "And now I call upon you to repent." He forbade the emperor to attend worship until he prostrated himself at the altar. Theodosius obeyed, marking the first time the church triumphed over the state.[134]

On two other occasions Ambrose contended with emperors and came out the victor. The significance of this becomes apparent because it set a new trend for relations between church and state. For the next thousand years, secular and religious rulers struggled to determine who was sovereign in various spheres of life.[135] Sometimes the church exercised the power; sometimes the state possessed the power. Ambrose and Theodosius were restored in their relationship, and the emperor had only the highest regard for the bishop. Theodosius is reported to have said, "I know no bishop worthy of the name, except Ambrose."[136] The emperor died in the bishop's arms and Ambrose was chosen to preach the funeral sermon at Theodosius' funeral. Ambrose related that he loved the emperor and felt the loss in the depths of his heart.

The influence of Ambrose was also profound in the life of another outstanding person. His preaching so deeply influenced the worldly Augustine that the young man was converted, sought baptism, and began a career which led him to be one of the greatest church leaders in history. Some think that the greatest achievement of Ambrose was winning and bringing Augustine into the church.

A lingering theological error in the church was Arianism. Ambrose supported the decisions and documents of the Council of Nicea. He fought hard and successfully for the establishment of Nicene Orthodoxy...[and] led the struggle for a church based firmly on the deity of Christ.[137] In this it is shown why he became renowned as an upholder and defender of Christian doctrine.

Overall, he demonstrated his ability in the areas of theology, preaching, and church administration. Some of his most important efforts lay in his dealings with the imperial court, the outcome of which was establishing theological and philosophical foundations of independence for the church. Ambrose wanted to make the state and its rulers respect the Church so that it might not transgress upon the rightful claims of the Church in the spiritual realm.[138] He asserted that the church should be entirely independent of the state. It was his maxim that the emperor is *in* the church, but not *over* the church.[139] Other contributions of Ambrose included hymn-writing and encouragement of congregational singing.

Two years after Theodosius died in the arms of Ambrose, the bishop himself fell ill and died on Easter eve in 397 AD, after serving as bishop of Milan for 23 years. The worries of the country were expressed by one writer: "When Ambrose dies, we shall see the ruin of Italy."[140]

Augustine

The most influential figure in Western history, Aurelius Augustine, was born in Thagaste, a small town in the Roman province of Nimidia in Northern Africa, on November 13, 354 AD.[141] His thought in theology, philosophy, and culture in general, would influence the world over the next 700 years. He has left us more books from that period than anyone else. The magnitude of his person and thought can be seen in the words of Frederick Copleston:

> *In Latin Christendom the name of Augustine stands out as that of the greatest of the Fathers both from a literary and from a theological standpoint, a name that dominated Western thought until the thirteenth century and which can never lose its lustre... Indeed, in order to understand the currents of thought in the Middle Ages, a knowledge of Augustinianism is essential.*[142]

His early life was influenced by his mother, Monica, a devout Christian, and his pagan father, Patricius, who provided a different example for Augustine. His mother tried her best to raise him in the Christian faith, had an early influence upon him, and due to many concerns, would spend the rest of her life praying for her son. In his home town of Thagaste, he began his education and learned the rudiments of Latin and Greek (which he hated). Both parents had great aspirations for their son, and worked hard to provide the money necessary to further his education. It was probably in the year 365 AD that Augustine left for the neighboring town of Madaura, where it was intended that he would take up studies in Latin literature and grammar. It was in this pagan town that he began to detach himself from the faith his mother had taught him. Because of the general atmosphere of the town, and his preoccupation with Latin literature, he began his life as "a sensuous, pleasure loving intellectual."[143] After five years in Madaura, Augustine moved on to Carthage, where his worldly living would continue, and several major influences would enter his life.

In 370 AD, the year in which his father died after having become a Catholic, Augustine began the study of rhetoric at Carthage, the largest city he had yet seen. The licentious ways of the great port and center of government, the sight of the obscene rites connected with cults imported from the East, and Augustine's own passions alive and on fire, combined to lead to his practical break with the moral ideals of Christianity. Before long he took a mistress, with whom he lived for over ten years, and by whom he had a son in his second year at Carthage. In spite of his irregular life Augustine was a very successful student of rhetoric and by no means neglected his studies.[144]

While in Carthage, he made what appeared to be a final break with Christianity. Tormented by the problem of evil within the Christian worldview (If God is truly good how could there be evil and suffering in the world?), he embraced the teachings of the Manicheans who taught a dualism, stating that there were two eternal and competing principles in the universe—two worlds: the one of light, love, mind, and spirit; and the world of darkness, evil, hate and the flesh.[145] To Augustine, this conformed to truth, to the way things really are, to what he saw in the world and what he experienced within himself.

> *Augustine, now detached from Christianity both morally and intellectually, returned to Thagaste in 374 and there taught grammar and Latin literature for a year, after which he opened a school of rhetoric at Carthage in the autumn of 374. He lived with his mistress and their child, Adeodatus...*[146]

As life in Carthage continued, Augustine began to lose some of his trust in Manichaeism. In 383 AD, he left for Rome because he had heard that the students there were of a higher quality than those in Carthage. He remained a year until he was awarded a teaching position in Milan as a professor of rhetoric. This would lead to some major changes in his thought and in his life. In Milan, he encountered the teaching of Ambrose. For several reasons, some political and some spiritual, Augustine lost most of his belief in Manichaeism, and having become somewhat of an academic skeptic, his mind and heart seemed ready to receive the gospel. However, there were many tensions still residing within Augustine. He had not given up his immoral ways as he continued to struggle with his strong passions. His mother wished him to marry a certain girl, hoping that marriage would help to reform his life; but, being unable to wait the necessary time for the girl in question, he took another mistress in place of the mother of Adeodatus, from whom he had parted in sorrow in view of the proposed marriage.[147]

By this time Augustine had become a spiritual mongrel.[148] He was raised a Christian by his mother, was well-acquainted with the Punic paganism of his father, had converted to and left Manichaeism, and had become an intellectual skeptic.

> *Right away, Augustine was impressed by Ambrose. He was 30 when he arrived in Milan, and Ambrose was 44...In fact, the bishop's preaching dazzled Augustine— not so much the style as the substance. Faustus, the Manichean, had been more fun to listen to, but in content, he couldn't hold a candle to Ambrose. The bishop's deft handling of Old Testament stories easily answered the Manichean objections. Ambrose's famous sermons on Genesis may have been preached in Augustine's hearing and the bishop definitely taught the younger rhetorician to appreciate the Apostle Paul.[149] As he listened he was smitten by something that exceeded eloquence. Here was a man who grappled with the problems of faith and who showed that one could be an intellectual and a Christian.[150]*

All of this was occurring in the midst of Augustine's still sinful life. In the spring of 386 AD, when he was 32 years of age, he found himself under deep conviction. At that time he received Pontitianus, a fellow North African, as his guest. Pontitianus talked of his own Christian experience and commented upon the importance of St. Paul's epistles which he saw on Augustine's desk. Shortly after having received Pontitianus, Augustine became a Christian, and explains in his own words what happened.

> *But when a deep consideration had from the secret bottom of my soul drawn together and heaped up all my*

> *misery in the sight of my heart, there arose a mighty storm within me, bringing forth a mighty shower of tears... Solitude was suggested to me as fitter for the business of weeping, so I retired... I cast myself down I know not how, under a certain fig tree, giving full vent to my tears; and the floods of my eyes gushed out an acceptable sacrifice to Thee. And though not actually in these words, yet to this purpose, I spoke much unto Thee, saying, "O Lord, how long? How long, Lord? Wilt Thou be angry forever? Remember not our former iniquities, for I felt that I was held by them. I sent up the sorrowful words: 'How long, how long, tomorrow and tomorrow?' Why not now? Why is there not this hour an end to my uncleanness?"*[151]

While in the midst of this prayer, he reports that he heard a voice which sounded like that of a child, saying, "Take up and read, take up and read." Knowing that there were no children in the area, he took it to be God speaking to him. "So checking the torrent of my tears, I arose; interpreting it to be no other than a command from God, to open the book, and read the first chapter I should find."[152] Returning to the house where he had been, he picked up the book of Paul's epistles which he had left on his desk. Augustine describes what happened in his own words: "I seized, opened, and in silence read that section, on which my eyes first fell: 'Not in carousing and drunkenness, not in sexual promiscuity and sensuality, not in strife and jealousy. But put on the Lord Jesus Christ, and make no provision for the flesh in regard to its lusts'"[153] (NASB). Augustine continues:

> *No further would I read; nor needed I; for instantly at the end of this sentence, by a light as it were of serenity infused into my heart, all the darkness of doubt vanished away.*[154]

Following his conversion, Augustine displayed a true change in both character and the direction of his life. He wrote a letter to Ambrose explaining his conversion and then, for a time, went to a country retreat in northern Italy where he was joined by his friend Alypius, by his mother, Monica, and his son, Adeodatus. This seemed to be an important period in his life as he continued his studies, discussed philosophy with his friends, continued to write, and was being formed by a growing Christian viewpoint. The whole arrangement was much like what Augustine had planned before his conversion—an enclave of philosophers, living a life of thoughtful leisure.[155]

> *After six or seven months, around Easter of 387, Augustine emerged from his retreat and returned to Milan. There, along with Alypius and Adeodatus, he was baptized by Ambrose.*[156]

Soon, along with his family and friends, he left Italy and life in Milan and returned to his home of Thagaste in North Africa to continue the type of life they had experienced while living in northern Italy. However, soon after their arrival, both his mother and his son died within one year of each other.

Back home, Augustine and his friends thought they would serve the church, not as priests and bishops, but as writers and thinkers.[157] But Augustine's influence and reputation grew and, in 391 AD, he was ordained a presbyter of the church. Four years later he became Bishop of Hippo. From this time on his influence and accomplishments were many. He opened the first monastery in North Africa, wrote powerfully against the heresies of Manicheans, Donatists, and Pelagians, and through his pen produced writings that would permanently affect the direction of Christian thought for hundreds of years. His most well-known works are *The Confessions* and *The City of God*. The first describes his life of sin and the subsequent work of God's grace to bring Augustine to salvation. It has been noted that both Catholicism and Protestantism find roots in Augustine. Catholicism takes from him its high view of the Church and sacraments, and Protestantism its understanding of the sovereignty of God, man's lost condition in sin, and salvation only by the grace of God. It was from Augustine that medieval thought inherited its framework of ideas.

Augustine's most elaborate writing, *The City of God*, written as the Empire was crumbling, portrayed the Church as a new civic order in the midst of the ruins of the Roman Empire. Augustine died while the Vandals were besieging the very gates of Hippo, AD 430.[158]

Confirmation of the Canon

Hermeneutics is important in gaining an accurate understanding of the Bible. The term may be defined as "the art and science of Biblical interpretation." One of the first steps in interpreting the Bible is the study of canonicity, which is the differentiation between those books that bear the stamp of divine inspiration and those that do not. In other words, before we begin to interpret the Scriptures, we need to know which books are indeed Scripture. Essentially, the process that gave us the Bible was a historical one that went on for quite a long time, and one in which the Holy Spirit guided the Church to recognize that certain books bear the impress of divine authority.

Canon

When used theologically, the word *canon* refers to the compilation of books we call Scripture. The first recorded use of the word *canon*, denoting the authoritative list of books that comprise the New Testament, came in the year 367 AD from Athanasius, bishop of Alexandria in North Africa.

Our English word *canon* is derived from the Greek work *kanon*. The word has several meanings: (1) a straight rod, or bar, used especially to keep things straight; a straightedge or bar of wood or metal having one side true to a straight line, and used for testing surfaces, edges, etc.; (2) a measuring rod; (3) a rule or line used by carpenters and masons for measuring or for keeping things straight; (4) as a metaphor, it means anything that serves to regulate or determine the accuracy of something; a rule of conduct or doctrine; (5) a boundary line or limit.

As applied to Scripture, the word canon means: (1) the testing rule, or critical standard by which each book of the Bible must be tested before it may be admitted as part of the Sacred Scriptures; (2) the title, *Canon*, is the name given to the collection of books that met the standard and have been accepted as the reliable and authoritative Word of God.

It took a process of more than two centuries to define the precise shape of the New Testament. The fixing of the New Testament canon was an extremely important step in stabilizing the early church.

Factors that caused the recognition of the New Testament Canon

There were several influences that forced, or brought about, serious consideration and recognition of the New Testament writings.

- Spurious writings, as well as attacks upon genuine writings, were a factor. For instance, Marcion (second century) rejected the Old and New Testaments, except for Paul's writings and part of Luke.
- The content of the New Testament writings testified to their authenticity and they were naturally collected, being recognized as canonical.
- The writings of the apostles were used in public worship; hence, it was necessary to determine which of those were canonical.
- Ultimately, the edict by Emperor Diocletian in 303 AD, demanding that all sacred books be burned, created the necessity of collecting what was thought to be the genuine New Testament books.

The process of recognition and collection in the first few centuries of the church

Very early the New Testament books were being recognized (in the first century, *Apostolic Period*). Paul, for example, recognized Luke's Gospel as being on a level with the Old Testament (I Tim. 5:18 quotes Deut. 25:4 and Luke 10:7, and refers to both texts as "the Scripture says"). Peter recognized Paul's writings as Scripture (II Pet. 3:15,16). Letters that we now recognize as canonical were being read and circulated among the churches (Col. 4:16; I Thess. 5:27).

In the *post-Apostolic Period*, various church leaders put their stamp of approval upon various books. Clement of Rome (95 AD) mentioned at least eight New Testament books in a letter. Ignatius of Antioch (115 AD) also acknowledged about seven books. Polycarp (108 AD), a disciple of John the Apostle, acknowledged 15 books. Irenaeus (185 AD) wrote, acknowledging 21 books. Hippolytus (170-235 AD) recognized 22 books.

A very important witness was that of the Muratorian Canon (170 AD), which was a compilation of books recognized as canonical. The Muratorian Canon included all the New Testament books except Hebrews, James, and one epistle of John.

In the fourth century, there was important recognition given the New Testament Canon. When Athanasius wrote in 367 AD, he cited the 27 books now present in the New Testament canon as being the only true books. This was the first recognition of the 27 we presently have. In 363 AD the Council of Laodicea stated that only the Old Testament and the 27 books of the New Testament were to be read in the churches. The Council of Hippo in 393 recognized the same 27 books. The Council of Carthage in 397 AD affirmed that only those previously recognized canonical books were to be received as Scripture and read in the churches. Seemingly, the last council to address the issue of canonicity was the Council of Chalcedon. At this council in 451, those present merely approved and gave uniform expression to what was already an accomplished fact generally accepted by the Church over a long period of time. Two of the last books adopted into the canon were Hebrews and Revelation. The slowness with which the Church accepted these two books is indicative of the care and devotion with which it dealt with the question of canonicity.

The Tests of Canonicity

The Old Testament is easily identifiable because of its history and acknowledgement by the Jewish people and because of its recognition by Christ (Luke 24:44). Since the question of the formation of the New Testament canon is a matter of historical inquiry, it is necessary to find the tests employed by the early leaders of the church and those known as "church fathers." These tests are gathered from early Christian writings. H. S. Miller catalogues the following tests used by the early church for the approval of canonical books.[159]

Apostolicity

The word apostolic or apostolicity can be taken in different senses. *Apostolic authorship* simply means books written by apostles. Most of the New Testament books have this distinction. *Apostolic authority* refers to books that were not written by apostles themselves, but by "apostolic men," companions of the apostles, those who came from apostolic circles and taught apostolic doctrines. This would include men like Mark and Luke. There is evidence that before the apostles died there was discussion and recognition amongst themselves concerning books to be accepted as Scripture.

Mark Noll, author of *Turning Points*, a book about important periods or events in the history of the church, states the following about the canon:

> *The key throughout was apostolicity. Where a writing was held to come directly from a disciple of Christ, to arise from the circle or direct influence of one chosen personally by Jesus (for example, the Gospel of Mark was widely held*

to derive from Peter's eyewitness reports), or to express in a pure form the message of the apostles about Christ, that writing was accepted as canonical. For those Christian writings where the apostolicity of either author or content was in doubt, recognition as a canonical book could take much longer. Thus, the fact that the Book of Hebrews does not begin by announcing the name of its author retarded its full acceptance as Scripture....[160]

"Read in the churches"

This statement is emphasized repeatedly in the writings of the church fathers. This does not mean "read in some churches," but in the churches as a whole. The disputed books were read in some churches, but they were not acknowledged until they were accepted by the Church as a whole. At first, a few apocryphal books were read in a few churches, but upon further examination, they were discarded.

Contents of a book

In the days of the apostolic church (first century), doctrine had been received orally from the apostles, and had been passed on orally (along with the letters they wrote) and in small written creeds. The Church had its rule of faith, and each book received the same question: "Does it agree with the doctrine, or rule of faith?" This is the reverse of the way the question is asked today: "Does the doctrine agree with Scripture?"

Recognition and use by the early church fathers

This was an important test in the early church. Eusebius speaks of accepting *I Peter* because "the ancient presbyters used it freely in their own writings as an undisputed work."[161] He refused to include other writings because they were not quoted by early church fathers. Out of the collections of the early church fathers we find the books that were considered canonical. A simple survey will show that by the middle of the second century every book of the present New Testament was quoted, referred to, and presumed to be canonical.

The ability of a book to edify

This test was a minor consideration because tests for canonicity were of a more objective nature, but if a book did not appear to edify at all, it would scarcely have been considered. It was believed that Scripture would build up and give life to people even though containing teaching that could appear negative. This was not a sufficient test in itself and could be seen in the rejection of other books which, for a time, seemed to be edifying.

The witness of the Spirit

The early fathers believed it was the Holy Spirit who gave common consent to the Church and is witnessed in the creeds and confessions of the church. The same Spirit who inspired the writers in producing the New Testament also guided the Church step-by-step in the growth of the canon. While the Church did not give official recognition to the canon prior to the later fourth century, it is misleading to say there was no recognition. Recognition was dynamic, demonstrated in the prior ways listed.

The Old Testament Canon

The traditional Jewish division of the Old Testament is three-fold: *Law*, *Prophets*, and the *Psalms* (or, *the Writings*). This coincides with the delineation Jesus gave in Luke 24:44-45: "These are my words which I spoke with you while I was still with you, that all things which are written about Me in the *Law of Moses* and the *Prophets* and the *Psalms* must be fulfilled. Then he opened their minds to understand the *Scriptures*" [italics mine].

The Old Testament division that Jesus knew was as follows:

The Law (five books): Genesis, Exodus, Leviticus, Numbers, and Deuteronomy.

The Prophets (eight books):
- Former: Joshua, Judges, Samuel, and Kings.
- Latter: Isaiah, Jeremiah, Ezekiel, and The Twelve.

The Psalms, or Writings, or Hagiographa (eleven books):
- Poetical: Psalms, Proverbs, and Job.
- The Five Rolls: Song of Solomon, Ruth, Lamentations, Ecclesiastes, and Esther.
- Three Books: Daniel, Ezra-Nehemiah, and Chronicles.

Various theories are advanced as to why such a division exists. One theory is that the three divisions represent three stages of inspiration: the first and highest being that of Moses, who spoke directly from God; the second, that of the prophets who wrote by the Spirit of Prophecy; and the third, that of the other writers who were inspired by the Holy Spirit. An explanation given by many conservative scholars is that the books of the first section were written by Moses, God's appointed lawgiver and founder of the Old Testament economy. Those books included in the second section were composed by men who held the prophetic office as well as the prophetic gift. Those who composed the third section were the writers who had the prophetic gift but not the prophetic office.

Another explanation is based upon the premise that there were three stages of collection and canonization. This is the predominant modern view. The critics do not agree on dates, but do agree that the Law, so-called "the first canon," was canonized around 444 BC, in Nehemiah's time; the Prophets, the so-called "second canon," was canonized somewhere between 300 and 200 BC. About 200 BC, we are told, the Old Testament contained only two parts. Various scholars agree that the Psalms (the Writings), known as the "third canon," were formed between 160 and 105 BC and were finally ratified with the completed Canon in 90-110 AD.

The problem with knowing details in this process is due to the fact that so little extra-biblical data is available. Even so, it seems that there were at least three steps in the canonization of the Old Testament: (1) divine inspiration and authority, (2) human recognition of inspiration and authority, and (3) collection process. It seems that the Jews received the books of the Old Testament for the following reasons with respect to the various divisions.

Pentateuch

- Preservation. Although little is known of the canonization process of the Old Testament books, its preservations stands as a testimony to its authenticity. While preservation is not canonization, the two are closely related. When a writing is so carefully preserved, it may be assumed that it was highly valued as a sacred and authoritative document.
- The Law was written by Moses. Chosen by God and commanded by Jehovah to write the *Ten Commandments* as well as the first five books, Moses must be recognized as an authoritative writer of Scripture. Jehovah and Moses are linked in such a way that Moses became the authoritative voice of Jehovah. "Jehovah spoke unto Moses," "the commandment of Jehovah by Moses," and equivalent expressions, occur hundreds of times.[162]
- The Book of the Law. The first five books of the Old Testament are also known as *the Book of the Law*, and, as such, are understood to possess divine authority. The reasons given are as follows: First, the Law was commanded to be read publicly before all of Israel at the end of each seven years at the Feast of the Tabernacles (Deut. 31:10-13); second, the next leader, Joshua, must teach, meditate upon, and do the things contained therein (Josh. 1:7, 8); the future kings of Israel must possess a copy of it, read it, and be governed by it (Deut. 17:14-20).[163]

The Prophets

The recognition of the Prophets comes from two sources: internal evidence and external evidence. *Internal evidence* is based upon claims the books make for themselves, their own accuracy, their consistency with other known Scripture, and the credentials of their authors. It can be said that all 15 of the Old Testament prophets, when examined carefully, bear proper credentials. *External evidence* was applied by those responsible for assembling the Old Testament canon. Ancient and persistent traditions teach that the first collection of prophetic books was completed by Ezra (himself a scribe) and a band of helpers known as "the Great Synagogue." It is hard to say exactly what their external tests might have been, since there is little extra-biblical data available, but it was no doubt something like tests applied by those who developed the New Testament canon (i.e., evidence of inspiration and authority, reliable content, well-read and accepted, recognition by religious leaders in Israel).

The Writings (or Psalms)

We can assume that many of the same tests were applied to these writings as to the other two divisions. When examining the books that comprise this section, one can see how easily the tests above can be applied here as well.

Additional support is given to the present Old Testament canon by Christ's endorsement (Luke 24:44-45) and the witness of the Jewish nation over the last 3,000 years.

Institutionalization of the Church

It is clear that a massive change took place when Christianity was "popularized" following Constantine's rise to power in the early fourth century. A church which had been suppressed and persecuted, found itself being protected, accepted, and promoted by political leadership. Constantine not only favored Christianity, but went to lengths to attend to the safety of the church. He extracted state taxes for the purpose of restoring church buildings and erecting new ones, as well as training clergy and placing them throughout the empire.

The favoring of the church gave greater freedoms and power to bishops. It might be observed that the churches began to structure themselves politically after the empire. All of this gave rise to greater organization and proficiency in operating the church. The rise in the power of leadership provided the inertia to develop the church, which began institutionalization.

Dr. Loraine Boettner, in his book, *Roman Catholicism*, provides a chronological list of actions within the Catholic Church. He points out that these developed over a long period of time and came to be known as the doctrines and practices of the church. Not all of the ones he points out in his book are listed, but the following list gives an idea of time and development of certain practices now found in the church.

1. Prayers for the dead began — 300 AD
2. Making the sign of the cross — 300 AD
3. Veneration of angels and dead saints, use of images — 375 AD
4. The Mass as a daily celebration — 394 AD
5. Beginning of the exaltation of Mary, the term "Mother of God" first applied to her by the Council of Ephesus — 431 AD
6. Priests began to dress differently from laymen — 500 AD
7. Extreme unction — 526 AD
8. The doctrine of purgatory, established by Gregory I — 593 AD
9. Latin language used in prayer and worship, established by Gregory I — 600 AD
10. Prayers directed to Mary, dead saints and angels — 600 AD

The Church and Western Culture

11. Title of Pope ("Papa"), or universal bishop, given to Boniface III by Emperor Phocas	610 AD
12. Kissing the Pope's foot began with Pope Constantine	709 AD
13. Worship of the cross, images, and relics, authorized in	786 AD
14. Holy water (water mixed with a pinch of salt and blessed by a priest)	850 AD
15. College of Cardinals established	927 AD
16. Canonization of dead saints, first by Pope John XV	995 AD
17. Fasting on Fridays and during Lent	998 AD
18. The Mass, developed gradually as a sacrifice, attendance made obligatory in the eleventh century	1000 AD
19. Celibacy of the priesthood, decreed by Pope Gregory VII	1079 AD
20. The Rosary, praying with beads, invented by Peter the Hermit	1090 AD
21. Sale of indulgences	1190 AD
22. Transubstantiation	1215 AD
23. Auricular confession of sins to a priest	1215 AD
24. Adoration of the wafer (Host), decreed by Pope Honorius III	1220 AD
25. Bible forbidden to laymen, placed on the Index of Forbidden Books by the Council of Valencia	1229 AD
26. Cup forbidden to the people at communion by Council of Constance	1414 AD
27. Purgatory proclaimed as dogma by the Council of Florence	1438 AD

28. Doctrine of Seven Sacraments affirmed (Baptism, Eucharist, Confirmation, Penance, Extreme Unction, Holy Orders, Marriage)	1439 AD
29. Jesuit order founded by Loyola	1534 AD
30. Tradition declared equal authority with the Scriptures by the Council of Trent	1545 AD
31. Apocryphal books added to the Bible by the Council of Trent	1546 AD
32. Immaculate Conception of the Virgin Mary	1854 AD
33. Papal infallibility	1870 AD
34. Assumption of Mary	1950 AD

Many people are surprised at the late dates of some of these actions. This only emphasizes that these developments occurred over a long period of time, and were not in the church from the beginning. Consider the following.

Immaculate Conception

> *We declare, pronounce and define that the Most Blessed Virgin Mary, at the first instant of her conception was preserved immaculate from all stain of original sin, by the singular grace and privilege of the Omnipotent God, in virtue of the merits of Jesus Christ, the Saviour of mankind, and that this doctrine was revealed by God, and therefore, must be believed firmly and constantly by all the faithful.*[164]

Papal Infallibility

> *We teach and define that it is dogma divinely revealed that the Roman Pontiff, when he speaks ex cathedra, that is when in discharge of the office of pastor and doctor of all*

Christians, by virtue of his supreme Apostolic authority, he defines a doctrine regarding faith and morals to be held by the universal church, by the assistance promised him in blessed Peter, is possessed of that infallibility with which the divine Redeemer willed that His Church should be endowed for defending doctrines regarding faith and morals, and that therefore such definitions of the Roman Pontiff are irreformable of themselves, and not from the consent of the Church...But if anyone—which God may avert—presume to contradict this our definition: let him be anathema." [165]

Assumption of Mary

On November 1, 1950, Pope Pius XII pronounced that Mary's body was raised from the grave shortly after she died, that her body and soul were reunited and that she was taken up and enthroned as Queen of Heaven. Roman tradition puts it this way:

On the third day after Mary's death, when the apostles gathered around her tomb, they found it empty. The sacred body had been carried up to that celestial paradise. Jesus Himself came to conduct her thither; the whole court of heaven came to welcome with songs of triumph the Mother of the divine Lord. What chorus of exaltation! Hark how they cry, "Lift up your gates, O ye princes, and be ye lifted up, O eternal gates, and the Queen of Glory shall enter in." [166]

The Fall of Rome

Christianity was born and developed within the boundaries of the Roman Empire. The first expression of Christianity outside the Roman Empire was not until the fifth century in Ireland when St. Patrick carried the gospel to what was thought to be the "end of the earth." Thus, it is difficult to comprehend early Christianity without understanding its relationship to this great empire. Its history is usually understood in a variety of stages.

First, April 22, 753 BC, is the date given for the founding of Rome. Events following this date were reckoned A.U.C.—*anno ubis conditai*—"in the year from the city's founding." Apparently Romulus was the founder although it is hard to separate fact from fiction in the stories told about him. It seems there was a clan leader prominent enough that a small community was named for him. This community continued for a couple of hundred years until it became more organized.

Second, 508-30 BC covers the period in which the *Roman Republic* developed. Three tribes united and their clan heads formed a senate of some 300 members. From this the Roman Republic evolved and continued strong until the times of revolution beginning around 145 BC Most historians recognize this as the greatest stage in Rome's history.

Third, 145-30 BC are the dates for the Revolutionary Period which ended with the monarchies under the Caesars and the decline of the Republic. Julius Caesar, emperor from 60 BC until his death in 44 BC ("Ides of March"), was declared "Pontifex Maximus" during his reign which meant that he was chief of the senate and high priest of the empire. As emperor, and demi-god, he stood between the people and the senate. As high priest, he stood between the people and the gods. Julius Caesar put an end to civil wars, which had raged since 133 BC. He conquered Pompeii, saw the necessity of blending the multi-ethnic population into one people, and encouraged giving more freedom and privileges to the people. In exchange for their freedoms, he persuaded the people to abdicate to him their rights of self-government and the right of election. Thus, in Julius Caesar, the Roman Republic reached its end.

The fourth stage began during the reign of Octavius Caesar (Julius Caesar's son by adoption). Civil war erupted after Julius Caesar's death, and when Octavius won the decisive battle on the field of Actium, he became emperor on September 2, 31 BC. On January 16, 27 BC he officially did away with the old Roman Republic and became founder of The Roman Empire. His title became "Augustus Caesar," which meant that he was "a god among the gods." Julius Caesar had been a demi-god, but not Octavius—he, himself, was a god.

Sometimes the official dates of "The Empire" are dated from 145 BC-192 AD. This takes into account the events that led to the time of Octavius and the continued decline following his reign. The significance of the Roman government moving away from a republic was that it became an authoritarian form of government.

The "period of the Caesars" is usually thought to include the following 12 Roman emperors with the dates of their reigns: Julius Caesar (49-44 BC), Marc Antony (44-31 BC), Augustus Caesar, or Octavius (31 BC-14 AD), Tiberius (14-37 AD), Caligula (37-41 AD), Claudius (41-54 AD), Nero (54-68 AD), Galba (68-69 AD), Otho (69 AD), Vitellius (69 AD), Vespasian (69-79 AD), Titus (79-81 AD), and Domitian (81-96 AD).

Fifth, the decline and fall of the Roman Empire is dated 30 BC-500 AD. The official date given is 476 AD. The last Roman emperor in the West was Flavius Romulus Augustus whose reign ended on September 4, 476, when he was defeated by the Goth, Odovacar, also called Skyrian.

Great Thinkers

The whole Roman world, especially the Republic, was influenced by great thinkers and great ideas from the Greeks. There were many ideas formed at this time that helped lay foundations in civil, political, moral, and ethical areas, and subsequently benefited many nations that followed. Some of the great thinkers of this time were:

    Pythagorus (580?-? BC)
    Socrates (469?-399 BC)
    Plato (427?-347? BC)
    Aristotle (384-322 BC)

Euclid (around 300 BC)
Cicero (106-43 BC)
Plutarch (50?-120 AD)

What made the Roman Republic and Empire great?

The family
Religion
The moral code
Education
Roman law and government
The Roman army
Organization

St. Augustine, in his well-known book, *The City of God*, written at the time Rome was crumbling, explains the greatness of the Romans.

> *The original Romans were honorable people. Their achievements sprang from a love of liberty and a desire for domination. Roman literature shows that the second urge grew out of the first. The contrast with the peaceful tendencies of the early Christians is striking.*[167]

In chapter 15 of *The City of God*, Augustine expands upon his views of the Romans and the great contributions they rendered for so many centuries. Observing that even though they were pagans, the Romans understood what made a society great and were willing to make sacrifices to insure the public good.

> *After all, the pagans subordinated their private property to the common welfare, that is, to the republic and the public treasury. They resisted the temptation to avarice. They gave their counsel freely in the councils*

of the state. They indulged in neither public crime nor private passion. They thought they were on the right road when they strove, by all these means, for honors, rule, and glory. Honor has come to them from almost all peoples. The rule of their laws has been imposed on many peoples. And in our day, in literature and in history, glory has been given them by almost everyone.[168]

There was sadness in Rome's fall. Reflecting upon the conditions that brought about the collapse of the Empire, Thomas Cahill writes, "What we can say with confidence is that Rome fell gradually and that Romans for many decades scarcely noticed what was happening."[169]

Decline and Fall of Rome

What caused the decline and fall of Rome? "The two greatest problems in history [are] how to account for the rise of Rome, and how to account for her fall." [170]

Various reasons are given for Rome's fall: inner weakness, both social and spiritual, as well as outer oppression contributed to Rome's decline. What can be said is that Rome fell gradually and that Romans for many decades scarcely noticed what was happening. But, what must also noted is that Rome lasted, in various forms, for 1,200 years.

Generally, scholars have come to agree upon three different influences that caused Rome's fall.

First, there was inner decay. Edward Gibbon (1737-1794) in his well-known work, *The Decline and Fall of the Roman Empire*, stated that the following five characteristics marked Rome at its end:

- ✦ A mounting love of show and luxury.
- ✦ A widening gap between the very rich and the very poor (this could be among countries in the Roman family of nations as well as within a single nation).
- ✦ An obsession with sex.

- ✧ Freakishness in the arts, masquerading as originality, and enthusiasms pretending to be creativity.
- ✧ An increased desire to live off the state; excessive taxation.

Second, there was oppression from without. More and more historians have come to realize the heavy pressure that came from the barbarian hordes. The fifth century was characterized by these armies coming against the city of Rome. Though it is easy for us to recognize the instability that typified Rome in its final years, it was not clear to the Romans. Rome, the Eternal City, virtually had been untouched since the Celts of Gaul had sacked the city by surprise in 390 BC. Although there were other conflicts at the gates of Rome, three major sacks of Rome can be noted in the 400's.

- ✧ In 410 AD, Alaric, king of the Visigoths, arrived at Rome with his massive army. Jerome, from his monastery in far off Bethlehem, wept: "The city that which has taken the whole world is itself taken!"[171]
- ✧ In 452 AD, Attila the Hun came to take Roman booty.
- ✧ In 455 AD, the Vandals from Scandinavia, who had "parked" on the shores of North Africa waiting their opportunity, came to sack Rome.

Third, the strength of Christianity contributed to Rome's end. Will Durant explained that Christianity helped with Rome's death—because Rome was already decaying, Christianity's strength added to her fall. And, Edward Gibbon maintained that Christianity was the chief cause of Rome's fall. Christianity disrupted the unity of the empire. It gave life in place of a system that was dying.

With the breakdown of Roman order, came a time of political, social, and intellectual turmoil, as well as general apathy. Francis Schaeffer summarized this as follows:

As the Roman economy slumped lower and lower, burdened with an aggravated inflation and a costly government, authoritarianism increased to counter the apathy. Since work was no longer done voluntarily, it was brought increasingly under the authority of the state, and freedoms were lost. For example, laws were passed binding small farmers to their land. So, because of the general apathy and its results, and because of the oppressive control, few thought the old civilization worth saving... and Rome gradually became a ruin.[172]

With the fall of the Roman Empire came the birth of the "Dark Ages." Classical learning, which had been born out of, and cradled in the Greco-Roman world, died. When the barbarians came they destroyed the libraries, public education died, and learning was reserved only for the very privileged or very fortunate.

Part Three
The Middle Ages: 500 - 1500

Overview

The Middle Ages is a term employed to designate the period that stands between ancient and modern times. It begins with the collapse of the Roman Empire in the fifth century, includes the transition from the Greco-Roman civilization to the Romano-Germanic civilization which arose out of the chaotic world of northern European barbarism in the Middle Ages, and takes us to the birth of modern Christianity in the sixteenth century. The reign of emperors in Rome shifted to the rule of kings and emperors in the north of Europe. The connecting link between the two was Christianity, which helped preserve the best elements of the old and gave direction to what was to come. A dream that never died following the fall of Rome was the idea of a united, single empire. Attempts at "revival of the glory that was Rome's" were tried several times. In the periods where this was most successful, it was due to the combined efforts of both church and state. Whereas in previous periods of history there was a courtship and close connection between church and state, it was during the Middle Ages that the two were married. The first years of this period are generally referred to as "the Dark Ages" (500-1200) and the later years as "the Renaissance" (1200-1600).

CHAPTER 9

The Rise of the Papacy: 500 - 600

Leo I

In June of 452 AD, Attila the Hun, known by the Romans as the "Scourge of God," marched up the Danube. A sudden raid over the Alps brought him and his army into northern Italy, where they met with resistance at only a few places.[173] He perceived that the Roman army was weak and decided to march toward Rome. At the Po River, Attila met up with an embassy sent from Rome. When he learned that the Roman Bishop, Leo I, was in this group of peace negotiators, he decided to meet with them. Attila and Bishop Leo sat face to face to discuss the matters before them. In the course of their discussions, Attila granted to Leo that he would spare Rome. Not only this, but he would also withdraw from Italy. Through this achievement the Bishop of Rome assumed a new role and elevated influence in the Christian world.

The papacy has been a highly controversial subject and hardly any other institution has been so loved and so hated. Some have revered the pope as the "Vicar of Christ" while others have denounced him as the "Anti-Christ." All who have studied the history of the Church agree that Leo represents an important step in the development of this historic institution. The papacy has shown an ability to adapt to many different situations throughout its existence. We see this demonstrated in the closing years of the Roman Empire, in its survival among the Germanic kingdoms of the Middle Ages, and in the national states of modern times.

According to the official teaching of the Roman Catholic Church, defined at the First Vatican Council (1870), Jesus Christ established the papacy through the Apostle Peter, and the Roman bishop, as Peter's successor, bears supreme authority over the whole Church. Both Eastern Orthodox and Protestant denominations deny these claims. Historian Bill Austin writes:

> *It is impossible to document a precise date for the beginning of the papacy. While the Catholic Church insists that Peter was the first pope, others look to Leo the Great or perhaps Damasus, but hardly ever anyone earlier than Stephen of Rome (third century).*[174]

Whatever the claims of church authorities, history shows that the concept of papal rule was established by slow and painful stages. Leo is a major figure in the process because he provided for the first time the Biblical and theological arguments for the papal claim. That is why many believe it is misleading to speak of the papacy before his time. Philip Schaff speaks pointedly, "But the first pope, in the proper sense of the word, is Leo I…In him the idea of the papacy, as it were, became flesh and blood."[175]

The term *pope* comes from the Latin *papa*, and in the fifth or sixth century time period we are considering, did not carry the same weight or distinction that it does in our modern world. The word actually has a long and somewhat varied history. The title "papa" originally expressed the fatherly care of any and every bishop of his flock.[176] It would be something comparable to our modern term "senior pastor" and was used to identify the main or primary church leader in each major city in a region. However, as time passed, the title began to be reserved only for the bishop of Rome, coming into almost exclusive use in the sixth or seventh century.

There are many reasons the bishop at Rome came to be known as "the pope." Bruce Shelley, in his book, *Church History in Plain Language*, suggests the following reasons on pages 134-135 of his book. Following is a summary of his thoughts.

First, Rome was the imperial capital, the Eternal City, and the Church of Rome was the largest and wealthiest church, with a reputation for orthodoxy and generosity. It stood without a rival in the West. Rome naturally attracted ecclesiastical influence as well as economic activity and political power.

Second, despite all of the persecutions of the Christians that took place in Rome, the Roman congregation grew in numbers and significance. By the middle of the third century, its membership probably totaled 30,000. It counted around 150 ordained pastors and 1,500 widows and poor people who were cared for by the church. Back then, just as today, size meant wealth and influence.

Third, several early Christian writers, beginning with Irenaeus in the second century, referred to Peter and Paul as founders of the church in Rome. Such identifiable roots in the second century were important in a day when gnostic teachers appealed to a secret "apostolic succession" arising from Christ. Many Christians of this time thought that a list of bishops tracing back to Peter and Paul would help protect apostolic succession and apostolic teaching.

Fourth, as the Church grew, it adopted, quite naturally, the structure of the empire. This meant that the main town in a province became the Episcopal town of the church. As these church centers grew, certain cities became prominent. Larger towns and churches assumed rule throughout different regions. Rome exercised rule in Italy, Carthage in North Africa, Alexandria in Egypt, Antioch in Syria, and so on. The bishop of Rome rose to major importance through these developments. The bishops of Rome succeeded even when the empire failed. In 401 AD, Innocent I had declared the supremacy of the Roman bishop over the rest of the church.

Fifth, when Leo I was inducted into office as Bishop of Rome, he preached a sermon that extolled the "glory of the blessed Apostle Peter...in whose chair his power lives on and his authority shines forth."[177] Leo advocated the supremacy of the Roman bishop on the basis of a threefold Gospel testimony: Matthew 16:13-19; Luke 22:31-32; and John 21:15-17. In this testimony, the new pope laid the theoretical foundation for papal primacy: Christ promised to build his church on Peter, the rock for all ages, and the bishops of Rome are his successors in that authority. "Leo the Great," as he is also known, was bishop in Rome from 440-461 AD.

Gregory I

The next major step in the development of the papacy came when Gregory I became the leader of the church in Rome in 590. He continued there as bishop until 604. He was a leader of great accomplishments. Born into one of the oldest noble and wealthy families of Rome, he was given a legal education to fit him for government service. In 573, he was made prefect of Rome, a position of importance and honor. Shortly thereafter, he gave up a fortune he had inherited from his father and used the proceeds to build seven monasteries in Italy, the most important of which was set up in his father's palace. Between 579 and 585, he was an ambassador representing the Roman bishop at Constantinople. Upon his return to Rome, he was made abbot of St. Andrew's monastery, one he had founded after his father's death. When pope Pelagius died of the plague in 590, Gregory was chosen to take his place.

He became one of the noblest leaders of the Roman Church and, soon after his death, came to be known as "Gregory the Great." His renunciation of great wealth impressed the people of his day and he thought of himself as "the servant of the servants of Christ." He was zealous for missions, winning many of the English to Christianity. His legal training, tact, and common sense made him one of the ablest administrators of the Roman Church. Through his work, the power of the Roman bishop was expanded. Because he was such an able and respected leader in the Church, he made the bishopric of Rome one of the wealthiest of his day. Gregory refused the title of "pope," protesting it as a blasphemous anti-Christian assumption; however, his successor, Boniface III (606-607), assumed the title and it has been the designation of the bishops of Rome ever since. Though he disliked and disclaimed the title of "pope," he exercised great power and set the stage for the continued development of the position of "universal bishop of the Church" (the papacy). After Gregory, the pope was no longer only a Christian leader; he was also an important political figure in European politics—God's Consul.[178] Gregory was an outstanding theologian, a great preacher, and also contributed to the advancement of music in the Church. He developed what is known as "the Gregorian chant." Gregory I is generally thought to be the first medieval pope.

The development of papal power is the great outstanding fact in the 10 centuries of the Middle Ages.[179]

Chapter 10

Mohammedanism: 622 AD

Islam, or Mohammedanism, can be understood by looking at its history, learning the meaning of a few words, and understanding some basic concepts. In fact, one of the appeals of Islam is its simplicity.

> *"Islam" is an Arabic word meaning "surrender," or "submission." It is a religion embraced by one-fifth of the world's population. A person who follows the religion of Islam is called a Muslim. A person becomes a Muslim by reciting the following creed: "There is no God but Allah, and Mohammed is the messenger of Allah."*[180]

Islam had its origins in the Arabian Peninsula in the early part of the seventh century AD. At the time of its beginning, Semitic Bedouin tribesmen wandered from oasis to oasis with their camels, flocks and herds, trading with the townsmen of Mecca and Medina. Tribal warfare was frequent except during periods of truce each year when the tribes went to worship at Mecca. At this time in the Arabian peninsula, there were numerous tribal religions and cults, but not a major religion.

One of these tribesmen was Mohammed (570-632). Orphaned at age 6, he grew up under the guardianship of an uncle in the Qureish tribe and later made his living as a camel driver. Going with his uncle to Syria and Palestine, he came into contact with Christianity and Judaism. He became the business manager and caravan leader for a wealthy widow named Khadijah. When he was 24 and she was 40, they married. Through this union he gained the wealth that made it possible for him to devote his time to religious meditation. Mohammed, who was appalled at the idol worship prevalent in his day, was in the habit of meditating each evening.[181]

> *One night in the hills near Mecca, in a cave on Mt. Hira, he said that he had a vision of the angel Gabriel telling him to recite. He went home and produced the entire ninety-sixth sura of the Koran. In a second appearance, Gabriel commissioned him a prophet of the Lord, and subsequent revelations that constitute the Koran came frequently.*[182]

It is reported that Mohammed received several other revelations. All of these were compiled and they became the Koran, which means "recitation," based upon Gabriel's command. Muslims believe this happened in the year 610. That same year, he felt divinely called to proclaim monotheism and in the course of three years won 12 converts, mostly among his own kinsmen. In his preaching, Mohammed called people to submit to Allah, stop their idol worship, repent of their selfishness and materialism, and warned them of the coming "Day of Judgment." Stirring up opposition through his preaching against idolatry, he was forced to flee in 622 from Mecca to Medina. This flight, known as the "Hegira," became the first year of the Mohammedan calendar. By 630, the movement had grown so much that Mohammed was able to capture Mecca. Two years later all of Arabia had "surrendered" to Allah and his followers were ready to expand outside of the Arabian Peninsula. In the year 632 he made his last pilgrimage to Mecca at the head of forty thousand followers, and soon died of a violent fever in the sixty-third year of his life.

Between the years 632-732, this new religion expanded dramatically. Syria and Palestine were won in the fourth decade of the seventh century, and the Mosque of Omar was soon erected in Jerusalem. Egypt was won in the next decade, and Persia fell under

Mohammedan control by 652. Islam spread into Arabia, Persia, across northern Africa and into Spain.

Mohammedanism became a threat to European Christianity in the early 700s but was halted by the armies of Charles Martel at Tours in 732. By 750 the era of Mohammedan conquest came to an end and, influenced by Greek culture, they set out to build a splendid Arabic civilization centered in Baghdad.

The main source of the Mohammedan religion is the Koran, or Qur'an. The Qur'an, in Arabic, is the perfect Word of Allah. This work, two-thirds the length of the New Testament, is arranged in 114 suras, or chapters. The longest chapter comes at the beginning of the book, and the chapters become successively shorter until the last chapter consists of only three verses. It was composed between 610 to 632, the year Mohammed died, with the final compilation about 650. To the Westerner, the Koran is repetitious and unorganized.

Belief in one God, known as Allah, is the central theme of Islam. Allah made his will known through many prophets, including such people as *Musa* (Moses) who gave the *Taurat* (Torah), *Dawud* (David) who gave the *Zabur* (the Psalms), and *Isa* (Jesus) who gave the *Injil* (Gospel). To Muslims, all these writings became corrupted so God gave the Qur'an to Mohammed to correct corruptions. Thus, Mohammed became the latest and greatest of the prophets. The religion is fatalistic with its idea of passive submission to the will of Allah. After judgment, men will enjoy a sensual Paradise or face the terrors of hell. The good Mohammedan prays five times a day, facing toward Mecca. He also recites his creed daily. Fasting and almsgiving are important, and the holiest Mohammedan makes a pilgrimage to Mecca at least once during his life. The vital differences between Christianity and Islam are:

- ✧ Christians believe in the triune nature of God, affirming that God is one in essence (nature) and three in person. Mohammedans are monotheistic, believing in a god of singular nature and person. This is the crucial difference between Christians and Muslims. The term "god" does not refer to the same being. Never are Muslims and Christians referring to the same god when the term is used. Allah is clearly not triune. For Islam, there is no second person of the Trinity who becomes incarnate and affects our salvation; furthermore, there is no third person who applies that redemption to us.

- ◇ Another major difference is that in Islam there is no cross and no need of the cross, since salvation is essentially a matter of works. Mohammed made no atonement for sin.
- ◇ In Islam, there is no resurrection of Christ, proving that he was the Son of God and completely adequate for our salvation.

Both the Eastern and Western sections of the Church were weakened by losses of people and territories to Islam, but the greater losses were those in the Eastern Church. In 1453, Constantinople fell to the Ottoman Turks which opened the way for Islam to penetrate deeper into Eastern Europe.

What are the tenets of Islam? Muslims believe that their doctrinal system is internally consistent, simple to understand, and devoid of the mysteries that surround the Christian faith, including Protestantism, Catholicism, and Eastern Orthodoxy. Islamic theology can be described in five main points.

God

Central to Mohammedanism is the unshakable belief in the absolute oneness, sovereignty, and transcendence of god. In a key *sura* (chapter) of the Koran, followers of Allah are commanded: "Say: he is god, the one and only; god, the eternal, absolute; he begetteth not, nor is he begotten; and there is none like unto him" (sura 112). God, to them, is known as the "one of inscrutable divine will," which ultimately remains unknown to human beings. He is the one who leads astray as well as guides. He can bring damage and trouble as does Satan. He can also be described as "the Bringer-down," "the Compeller," or "Tyrant, the Haughty." If these terms were used of men, they would have an evil sense, but used of god, this is not so. All of these descriptions co-exist with Allah's attributes of mercy, compassion, and glory. They all work together to bring about the will of Allah, and describe God's acts in history more so than His attributes. Mohammedanism is dogmatically monotheistic and completely denies the existence of the Trinity of Christianity.

Angels and Jinns

God's work is carried on among men by angels, the mediating spirits of God.[183] Allah has created two classes of spiritual beings known as angels and jinns. Angels are intelligent creatures formed from light who serve and worship God continually, record the deeds of people, receive the souls of people when they die, witness for or against them in the Day of Judgment, guard the gates of hell, and serve the faithful in paradise. The most prominent of the angels is Gabriel. Most Muslims identify him with the Holy Spirit and he is the angel through whom God sent His revelation (the Koran) to Mohammed. The other class of spirit beings is the jinn. It is commonly believed that they are powerful, intelligent creatures that fall into two groups—good and evil. Satan, the most powerful of the evil group, chose to disobey God in the far past.

Prophets

According to the Koran, God has "sent amongst every people an apostle (with the command), 'Serve God, and eschew evil'" (sura 16:36). Therefore, God has continually sent prophets among men, and every nation has had a prophet that has preached the one true message. Muslim tradition says there have been 124,000 prophets. The most well-known have been Adam, Noah, Abraham, Lot, Isaac, Jacob, Joseph, Moses, Aaron, David, Solomon, Elisha, Jonah,

Zachariah, John the Baptist, and Jesus. Of these, six are singled out as the great prophets: Adam, Noah, Abraham, Moses, Jesus, and Mohammed. The latest and most important is Mohammed who brought God's final and complete revelation to mankind. He was the seal of the prophets. According to Muslim teaching, all the prophets prior to Mohammed were limited in their teachings and mission and were not universal as is Mohammed. With him, God's final will is known for all times and places. Muslims believe that Mohammed was sinless, but not divine. They also believe that Islam started with Adam, not Mohammed. Though Jesus was a prophet of God, he was not the Son of God. He was born of the virgin Mary, performed many miracles, did not rise from the dead, but did ascend to heaven, and will return to earth. He was a faithful Muslim or follower of Allah.

The Scriptures

The Koran (Qur'an) is seen by Muslims to be the uncorrupted and final revelation of God to humans, transmitted by way of dictation to Mohammed. The will of Allah is written down in the Koran, which contains all a Muslim needs to know to obtain salvation.[184] Muslims believe that all previous revelations of God (Scriptures) have been corrupted or tampered with over time. These would include what tradition calls "the scrolls of Abraham" (considered lost) or copies of those that still remain, like "the Torah of Moses," "the Psalms of David," and the "Gospel of Jesus." In fact, the Koran tells Muslims that they should read these previous revelations and refers to the Scriptures of the Jews and Christians as "the Word of God," "light and guidance," and "illumination." It is simply that over time they have become corrupted. This charge of corruption is not found in the text of the Koran, but developed in the tradition and other writings of Islam. Consequently, because of this attitude of the Muslim toward previous "Scriptures," the absolute importance of the Koran becomes quite evident. Not only is it seen as the last inspired book, but also the only one which has been miraculously preserved uncorrupted to this day. It is complete, trustworthy, and the fulfillment of all previous revelations. Whatever was true in previous revelations has been repeated in the Koran and whatever error crept in has been purged. Therefore, the Koran is all that is needed for mankind to have a true and sufficient knowledge of God.

The Day of Judgment

Mohammedans are preoccupied with the Day of Judgment. Even casual reading shows the Koran's concern and preeminence regarding the Day of Judgment at the end of history when all will be held accountable for their beliefs and actions. There are graphic depictions of heaven and hell and catastrophic events surrounding the final resurrection and appearance of humans before the judgment seat of God. One image conveyed in the Koran is that of a scale used for balancing an individual's good thoughts, desires, and deeds against his bad ones. "Then those whose balance is heavy—they will attain salvation: but those, whose balance is light, will be those who have lost their souls; in Hell they will abide" (sura 23:102-103). Islamic theology is very emphatic that salvation is gained by means of the right faith and right deeds, such as performing the obligatory acts of reciting the confession of faith, prayer, fasting, alms-giving, and pilgrimage to Mecca. Despite the fact that God is considered gracious and merciful, a Muslim cannot have any assurance of salvation until the Day of Judgment.

Islam means "surrender" or "submission" to the will of God. A Muslim is a follower of Islam, literally meaning "one who submits." Classical Islam is based on five foundations, called "pillars," which include the witness, prayer, giving alms, fasting, and pilgrimage.[185] Sometimes, *jihad* is included as a sixth pillar.

The Witness or Confession of Faith

The first pillar is the creed or "Shahada" that all Muslims must recite: "There is no God but God, and Muhammad is the Apostle of

God." All it takes to become is Muslim is making this confession in a meaningful way. Since it is used in all daily prayers, it is the most frequently repeated sentence in Islam. It is the first thing whispered into the ear of a newborn Muslim baby and the last thing heard and spoken at death.[186]

Ritual Prayer

The second pillar is the pillar of prayer, or the "Salat." These are the ritual prayers spoken five times a day: at dawn, noon, mid-afternoon, sunset, and late evening. Loyal Muslims face Mecca (a city in southwest Saudi Arabia) and assume the correct posture or bodily position described in the Koran. Ritual cleansing of certain parts of the body is required before these prayers. Praying may be done individually, but whenever possible, it is done in a group with one respected Muslim leading the prayers.[187]

Obligatory Alms

The third pillar is the giving of alms, known as the "Zakat." Muslims are expected to give a percentage of their possessions every year as a constant reminder that there are others in the world that are worse off than they are, and the Zakat goes toward helping those who are less fortunate. Good Muslims must give at least 2.5 percent of their total wealth to the poor and needy.

The Fast of Ramadan

The fourth pillar is fasting, or the "Saum," during the ninth month of the Islamic lunar calendar, the month of Ramadan. Muslims go by the lunar calendar, which is 11 days shorter than the West's solar year, and so Ramadan falls on different days every year. Ramadan is the month Muslim's believe Allah sent his word down from heaven to Mohammed. During the holy month of Ramadan Muslims are to refrain from eating, drinking, smoking, swallowing saliva, and sexual intercourse from sunrise to sunset. The faithful are encouraged to use the month of fasting to draw closer to God and renew their spiritual strength.

The Pilgrimage

The fifth pillar is the Pilgrimage to Mecca, known as the "Hajj." Every Muslim who can afford to and is not sick must complete the Hajj sometime in his lifetime. If unable to make the pilgrimage, it may be done by proxy. It is a time when all are deemed equal before God regardless of social or financial position, and everyone is dressed alike (in white). As part of their purification process, participation in the pilgrimage heightens their social status.

The Jihad

Jihad has a much wider meaning than most Westerners understand. Most people living in the western world understand it only as "a holy war."

> *Jihad simply means "struggle," but it can be interpreted in various ways. It certainly denotes an internal struggle as a person strives against his or her own sinful nature or bad habits while trying to gain religious merit. (Western Christians call this a struggle against the "flesh.") A second form of jihad is the struggle within Islam to better the community (through education, for example). It can also mean external struggle (outside Islam) against anyone or any group that threatens the safety of Islam or Muslims. The most extreme interpretation comes when a respected Muslim leader believes that all Islam is in danger and calls for a general jihad, or holy war, to be fought against "unbelievers"(non-Muslims). This is not, however, the most common meaning of jihad.*[188]

Although the word *jihad* does not mean "holy war," it does allow for the use of the sword to accomplish Allah's purposes.

CHAPTER 11

Charlemagne: 800 AD

After the fall of Rome, Europe divided into multitudes of small kingdoms. From time to time, these kingdoms varied and their borders changed depending upon who happened to be the most powerful ruler or rulers at the time. Various warring tribes and small kingdoms were constantly on the march, with much movement—even of entire communities—throughout Europe. Because of localized authorities and social arrangements, disorder marked life at that time. Autonomy, variety, and decentralization describe the characteristics of this age. Even though this was the case, the splendor of Rome's single empire never ceased to enthrall the imagination of people living in the West.

By the middle of the eighth century, around 750, events began to occur that would move the Western world back toward a large, unified kingdom based upon Roman ideals. The initial phases of this struggle involved two forces concerned with the restoration of order and unity; the Church and state became allies for mutual benefits.

The first stage of this attempt at a "new order" involved the Anglo-Saxon missionary, Saint Boniface (680-754) and the Frankish king, Pepin (741-768). Boniface provided the religious impetus and Pepin was the magistrate who would prepare the way for the establishment of a strong united kingdom in Europe.

Boniface
Boniface was born in Devonshire, England, but would have a huge impact among the Germanic tribes. He was commissioned by Pope Gregory II in 729 and sent to Germany. Irish Celtic missionaries had already made their way to Europe, upsetting the

pope's plan to unite Roman and European Christianity. Boniface enlisted many missionaries from his native England who became outstanding leaders in the European churches. He had exceptional organizational skills and was a great integrating force. He traveled widely, beginning in Frisia (Netherlands) and continued on to Saxony (part of modern Germany), Hesse, and Bavaria and became known as "the apostle to the Germans." He was very successful in that he baptized many new converts, established new churches, and did away with pagan practices. In his Germanic tongue, Boniface's name was Winfrith, which means "the lover of peace." But he preferred the Latin name, Boniface, "the doer of good." Although he was not the originator of missionary work in Germany, it is proper to call him the organizer of Christianity in that area. Boniface's influence reached into England and brought England and the Continent together. It also brought together France and Germany since the kings from both regions protected and supported his efforts. His work also joined Rome and the churches of northern Europe. In the end, Boniface had a great influence in creating unity between church and state. It can be said that it was he who cemented an alliance of the papacy with the kingdom of the Franks. Believing his first missionary efforts in Frisia had not been very successful, in his old age he undertook another missionary tour in 754 and was martyred by tribesmen.

Charles Martel

Along with the influence of Boniface, there was a succession of three kings from the same family that moved Europe toward becoming a unified kingdom: Charles Martel (688?-741), Pepin the Short (715-768), and Charles I, also known as Charlemagne (742-814). Charles Martel was one of the most able of rulers. Through his administrative and military powers, he showed his strength when he beat back the Saracens (Muslim nomadic peoples from the deserts between Syria and Arabia) at Tours. He inflicted heavy losses upon them, so that during the night they retreated back into Spain and were never again a major threat to central Europe. His power enabled him to expand his kingdom over a wide area. He earned the title "martel," which means, "the hammer."

Pepin

Charles Martel's son was Pepin the Short. Pepin supported Boniface, the great missionary to the Germanic tribes in baptizing German chieftains and tribes into the Christian faith.[189] Nineteen years after the battle at Tours, Pepin, who had succeeded his father, decided that it was imperative to have his rulership and title come under divine sanction. But how? The answer was through the papacy, the only institution that could give divine sanctions. Had not the power of "binding and loosing" been given to the pope? But exactly how would this be done? Rome was far away. Fortunately, an emissary happened to be at hand in the person of Boniface. With the approval of the pope, Pepin was anointed, like the Kings of Israel, with holy oil by Boniface and, in this, was formally recognized as king. Two years later this act would be repeated by the pope, himself. Without papal sanction, it was inferred that the monarchy might be invalid. This was an important event because it was a demonstration of the papacy's power in setting up a government. Years later, Pepin would repay his debt. When the Lombards rose up against Rome and the pope, Pepin marched to Rome to fight against and subdue the Lombards. At that time, in 754, he conferred upon the pope political authority over a strip of land that ran from Rome to Ravenna. Pepin's act is called the "Donation of Pepin." This was significant because it is regarded by many historians as the beginning of the temporal or political power of the papacy in Europe. The truth is, popes had long exercised political functions, but this act gave formal or official recognition. Through Pepin's efforts, the Frankish kingdom expanded further.

Charlemagne

An even more dramatic display of papal and state alliance would come years later, and the two principle parties involved would be Pope Leo III and Pepin's son and successor, Charles I, also known as Charlemagne. In spite of Pepin's military ventures into Italy, the Lombards continued to threaten Rome. After Charlemagne assumed the throne, he made two military campaigns into Italy, and on the second, put an end to the Lombard kingdom. Then, in 799, Pope Leo III was beaten by a Roman mob, accused of many crimes and vices, and was imprisoned. Again Charlemagne marched into Italy, imposed order on Rome, and reinstated Leo to the papacy. On Christmas day, 800, when Charlemagne was kneeling and praying in the Basilica of St. Peter's in Rome, Pope Leo III placed a crown on his head and declared him emperor of The Holy Roman Empire. It is reported that the people present shouted the following: "To Charles, the most pious Augustus, crowned of God, to the great peace-giving emperor of the Romans, life and victory."[190] Thus, the "Christian Roman Empire" was born.

How did this "Holy Roman Empire" come about? Since the fall of Rome, men still longed for a recovery of the good things of the Roman Empire. They longed for the unity that had marked the empire and actually looked forward to the day when a new Roman Empire would appear. From the time of the invasion of Rome by the Germanic tribes in the early fifth century, there had been a blending of Roman and Germanic peoples and cultures. The Franks (people of Germany and France) became strong and led the way in cultural development in Europe. It was into this world that Charlemagne came. He was born in 742 and named Karl der Grosse. As has been pointed out, his father was Pepin I, also known as Pepin the Short, and his grandfather was Charles Martel. Both had been outstanding rulers. It was in this family environment that Charlemagne grew. However, he was destined to be greater than his father or grandfather.

Charlemagne, also known as Charles I or Charles the Great, was one of the most imposing figures in all of history. He had a commanding and winning presence. He was tall, strongly built, and well-proportioned. His height was seven times the length of his foot, which meant he was about seven feet tall. As he aged, his hair turned white, which gave him an even greater appearance of dignity or godlikeness. Einhard, a contemporary and his biographer, wrote, "His appearance was also stately and dignified, whether he was standing or sitting…his gait was firm, his whole carriage manly, and his voice clear, but not so strong as his size led one to expect."[191]

He was naturally eloquent and spoke with great clearness and force. He was simple in attire and temperate in eating and drinking and, says Einhard, "he abominated drunkenness in anybody, much more in himself and those of his household…He rarely gave entertainments, only on great feast days, and these to large numbers of people."[192] He enjoyed physical exercise, especially swimming and hunting, and enjoyed robust health until the last few years of his life. During mealtimes, he enjoyed hearing readings from Augustine's *City of God*, his favorite book, and stories of "olden times."

Charlemagne had a great zeal for education and religion. He could speak old Teutonic literary Latin, and understood Greek. Though he could read, he could not write. He saw to the compiling of a German grammar and gave German names to the months. With him, education and religion tied together. Charlemagne founded the palace school and other schools connected to convents and visited them in person. One of his laws required general education for all male children. He surrounded himself with religious leaders, scholars, poets, and historians from many places. His biographer, Einhard, was a Swabian. Warnefrid, known as "Paul the deacon," was a Lombard. One of the outstanding teachers who was close to him was the great Alcuin. Alcuin was an Anglo-Saxon who earlier had been educated at the outstanding and well-known cathedral school in the northern English city of York. There he had become a teacher and librarian. When he and Charlemagne met in 781, he so impressed the emperor that he was invited to become his adviser in education and religious matters. He told Charlemagne it was his desire that in the land of the Franks there might be reared "a new Athens enriched by the sevenfold fullness of the Holy Spirit."[193] In this, he could picture something greater than Rome had been. He revived the ancient disciplines of grammar, rhetoric, and dialectic as the basics of education and saw the teacher as a better propagator of Christianity than the warrior.

Charlemagne was a firm believer in Christianity and a devout and regular worshipper, "going morning and evening...." He was kind to the poor and a generous almsgiver. He supported the clergy, saw to it that worthy Christian pastors were appointed, assisted in the building of churches, and built the beautiful cathedral at Aix-la-Chapelle where he was buried.

Charlemagne was also a great military leader and his life was comprised of no less than 53 military campaigns conducted by himself or his sub-commanders. This led to his rule over "all" of Europe with the desire to establish a Christian theocracy. Einhard, in his famous biography of Charlemagne, pictured his king as a natural leader of men—tall, physically strong, and a great horseman who was always in the vain of the hunt. Although he was preeminently a successful warrior-king, leading his armies on yearly campaigns, Charlemagne also sought to provide an effective administration for his realm.[194] He expanded his kingdom as conqueror, but stabilized it as benefactor and educator.[195]

His motivation and goal was to unite all the Teutonic (those of the Germanic language groups) and Latin peoples on the Continent under his crown in close union with the spiritual dominion of Rome—to restore the Christian Roman Empire. Drawing upon Augustine's vision of the "City of God," Charles the Great engrafted the Christian concept of a universal, Catholic Church on the stock of the traditional Roman view of empire and gave to the medieval world Christendom, a unified society mingling religious (or eternal) concerns with earthly (or temporal) affairs.[196] He has been called the "Moses of the middle ages," and the "new Constantine."

Bruce Shelley points out that "four areas were successfully annexed to his kingdom by military might:"[197] First was his southern border. After several expeditions he drove the Muslims back to the Ebro River and established a frontier known as the Spanish Mark (or March) centered in Barcelona. Second, Charlemagne conquered the Bavarians and Saxons who were the last of the independent Germanic tribes. It took 32 campaigns to subdue the Saxons who were very pagan. Charlemagne divided the area into districts with a bishop presiding in each one. He built monasteries and set up harsh laws against paganism. Third, Charlemagne secured the eastern frontier that was constantly threatened by the Slavs and the Avars (Asiatic nomads related to the Huns). After six campaigns, he set up a military province in the valley of the Danube. This was called the East Mark. Later this territory became Austria. Finally, he exercised control over Italy. At the request of the pope, Charlemagne defeated the Lombards in 774 and declared himself their king. Further, he cemented the alliance with the Church of Rome by confirming the Donation of Pepin.

Philip Schaff writes:

> *He seemed to be omnipresent in his dominions, which extended from the Baltic and the Elbe in the North to Ebro in the South, from the British Channel to Rome and even to the Straits of Messina, embracing France, Germany, Hungary, the part of Italy and Spain.... He encouraged trade, opened roads, and undertook to connect the Main and the Danube by canal. He gave his personal attention to things great and small. He introduced a settled order and unity of organization in his empire, at the expense of the ancient freedom and wild independence of German tribes, although he continued to hold every*

year, in May, the general assembly of the freemen. He secured Europe against future heathen and Mohammedan invasion and devastation. He was universally admired or feared in his age.[198]

By the year 800, Charlemagne's success had made him ruler over more of Europe than anyone since Theodosius at the end of the fourth century. When he died, he ruled all of modern France, Belgium, Holland, nearly half of modern Germany and Austria-Hungary, more than half of Italy, and northeastern Spain.[199] The role of Charlemagne cannot be understated when one thinks of the Middle Ages. Mark Noll writes of the magnitude of Charlemagne's coronation on December 25 in the year 800, pointing out that

> *…the event was a dramatic symbol of relationships undergoing permanent change. It stood for a new form of Christian existence that was replacing the Christianity passed on from the time of Constantine…This event also anticipated the future, for the way that the great king Charles and the pope, as the supreme Head of the Western church, conducted their business on that fateful Christmas Day outlined the shape of Christian life in the West for at least the next seven or eight centuries.*[200]

Noll continues:

> *Charlemagne never considered himself a vassal of the pope. Rather, he held himself to be responsible to God alone for the welfare of his people. But whatever Charlemagne thought of his own role, the link with Rome was now secure. For the next 800 years and more, the politics, learning, social organization, art, music, economics, and law of Europe would be "Christian"—not necessarily in the sense of fully incorporating norms of the gospel, but because the fate of the Western church centered in Rome had been so decisively linked with the new "Roman"*

emperor over the Alps...Charlemagne took the notion of the church-state cooperation, which was a legacy from the days of Constantine, and by fixing it to Europe bequeathed "Christendom" to succeeding generations.[201]

Where in previous centuries the church and state had "courted" each other, under Charlemagne they married. Charlemagne reigned from 768-814. After having received communion on January 28, 814, he died from a recent illness. He was 71 years old, and in the 47th year of his reign. He was buried the same day in the cathedral of Aix-la-Chapelle amidst expressions of great sorrow and lamentations from the people.

Chapter 12

The Great Schism of 1054

Though not without tensions, the church continued as a unified institution until the year 1054. In that year, the Eastern Church, with its head in the east at Constantinople, and the Western Church, with its head at Rome, separated from each other.

With that break two great divisions of the Christian religion appeared, and they have had few official contacts with each other since that time. This event is usually referred to as "the East-West Schism." What led up to that schism?

Geographical, political and cultural differences

One of the great influences was the matter of language. In the West, the major language was Latin; in the East the major language was Greek. By the time of the schism, Latin was almost the exclusive language in the West, while Greek was predominant in the East.

Early on, the universal Church operated under one head, the bishop in Rome. The church in the East was never able to be very independent because of this and, also, because she was under the eye of the emperor. The emperor's desire was always for unity throughout the areas of his reign. However, various events brought more and more power and influence under the bishop in Constantinople. One such influence came during Constantine's reign. When he moved his imperial capital to Constantinople in 330 AD, he paved the way for political and, finally, ecclesiastical separation between the East and West.

In 395 AD the Emperor Theodosius made two important decisions. First, he made Christianity the official state religion.

(Constantine had made it the favored religion of the empire.) Second, Theodosius put the administration of the Church under two heads, one in the East and the other in the West. Rome remained as the head in the West and Constantinople became the Eastern head. With the fall of the Roman Empire by the fifth century, this division was strengthened and completely recognized.

The intellectual outlook of the West differed from that of the East. One can truly say that "two minds" existed between East and West. In the West, it can be said, in a general way, the approach was more speculative while, in the East it was more philosophical. Latin thought was influenced more by Roman law, while the Greeks understood theology and life in the context of worship.

Theological and ecclesiastical issues

About the middle of the second century, the problem of when to celebrate Easter arose to mar relations between the two sections of the Church. Differences of opinion on this question always made relations between the two groups difficult. The Church in the East believed that Easter should be celebrated on the fourteenth day of Nisan, the date of the Passover according to the Jewish calendar, no matter what day of the week it fell upon. The western segment believed that Easter should be celebrated on the Sunday following the fourteenth of Nisan. (The month Nisan overlapped our months of March and April.) They remained divided on this until the Council of Nicea in 325 AD, where the viewpoint of the Western Church was adopted.

Another difference that separated the two Churches concerned celibacy. Marriage of all clergy below the rank of bishop was permitted in the East, while in the West all clergy were not allowed to marry. With reference to the clergy, there were even disagreements over the wearing of beards. The priests in the West were allowed to shave, but the clergymen in the East had to wear beards.

Each group had a different view of church government. The church in the West held to the rule of a supreme bishop, the pope. In the East, it was believed that the Church should be overseen by a college of bishops. The Eastern Orthodox Church is not a single church but a family of 13 self-governing churches, with a "patriarch" or "metropolitan" over each one. They are united in their understanding of the sacraments, doctrine, liturgy, and church government, but each administers its own affairs. Though the patriarch of Constantinople (modern Istanbul, Turkey) enjoys the honor of being the ecumenical or universal patriarch, he has no authority to interfere with the other 12 "communions."

The issue, which seemed to ignite the greatest controversy, had to do with the *Filioque*. This concerns itself with the words about the Holy Spirit in the Nicene Creed. The Creed originally read, "I believe…in the Holy Spirit…*who proceeds from the father*…." This original form is still recited in the east to this day, but the Western Church had, over time, added a phrase at the end, so it read, "…who proceeds from the Father *and the Son*." This phrase had begun to be used in Spain in the sixth century to guard against Arian heresy because it emphasized the full deity of Christ. The Eastern Church rejected this because: first, they believed it was a mistake to tamper with the wording of the Creed; second, the Creed is the common possession of the whole church; therefore, if any change is to take place, it should be done by the whole church in council. To arbitrarily change the Creed without consulting the whole church is to commit sin against the entire Church; and third, most Orthodox believe that the West's interpretation of the *Filioque* is wrong, maybe even a heresy, because it changes the delicate balance in the doctrine of the Trinity (the Father as the fountainhead; makes the Holy Spirit subordinate to the Father and Son).

Christian History magazine describes the particulars of the schism.

In 1048 a French bishop was elected as Pope Leo IX. He and the clerics who accompanied him to Rome were intent on reforming the papacy and the entire church. Five years earlier in Constantinople, the rigid and ambitious Michael Cerularius was named patriarch.

Problems arose in Southern Italy (then under Byzantine rule) in the 1040s, when Norman warriors conquered the region and replaced Greek [Eastern] bishops with Latin [Western] ones. People were confused, and they argued about the proper form of the liturgy and other external matters. Differences over clerical marriage, the bread used for the Eucharist, days of fasting, and other usages assumed an unprecedented importance. When Cerularius heard that the Normans were forbidding Greek Customs in Southern Italy, he retaliated, in 1052, by closing the Latin churches in Constantinople. He then induced Bishop Leo of Ochrid to compose an attack on the Latin use of unleavened bread and other practices. In response to this provocative treatise, Pope Leo sent his chief advisor, Humbert, a tactless and narrow-minded man with a strong sense of papal authority, to Constantinople to deal with the problem directly.

On arriving in the imperial city in April 1054, Humbert launched into a vicious criticism of Cerularius and his supporters. But the patriarch ignored the papal legate, and an angry Humbert stalked into Hagia Sophia and placed on the altar the bull of excommunication.[202]

Soon after Humbert had arrived in Constantinople, word came that Pope Leo IX had died unexpectedly. In spite of this, Humbert continued his mission, reminding Cerularius that Rome was the highest See and had jurisdiction over the whole church. Cerularius responded by rejecting Humbert's advances. He questioned whether Humbert was even a properly credentialed legate since the pope had died.

Mark Noll adds the following.

> *Humbert was offended and resolved to leave Constantinople at once. But before he did so, he entered the great church of Hagia Sophia (Holy Wisdom), placed on the altar a bull excommunicating Cerularius, shook the dust off his feet, and left. It is reported that an eastern deacon hastened after Humbert, trying to return the bull, but the overture was rebuffed, whereupon the paper was dropped in the street. Soon thereafter Cerularius excommunicated the papal legation.*[203]

Traditionally, this is called "the Great Schism of 1054." There were two serious attempts made to reconcile the Orthodox and Catholic Churches, but they failed. The first attempt was in 1274 when a reunion council met in Lyon, France. An agreement was reached at the council but was rejected by the Eastern Orthodox when their delegates returned home. The second was another reunion council in Florence, Italy, during 1438-1439. This again failed because of resistance in the Eastern Church. It was never thought that the schism would be permanent; however, other events occurred that drove the western and eastern churches further apart. A major contribution would be the crusades, especially the fourth one.

Recently, there have been renewed conversations between the Greek Orthodox and the Catholic Church. At the beginning of the twentieth century movements were initiated by the Orthodox and the Eastern Rite Catholics in the Ukraine (Eastern Rite Catholics follow the liturgy of the Orthodox Church but are in communion with the pope). Following the Catholic's Second Vatican Council (1962-1965), Pope Paul VI and Athenagoras, the ecumenical patriarch of Constantinople, met in Jerusalem in 1964. This was the first time such a meeting had taken place since the Council of Florence in 1439 and was initiated by the Catholics. In 1965, both churches revoked the anathemas of 1054 pronounced by Humbert and Cerularius. In 1980, formal theological dialogue was begun between Catholic and Orthodox, but these discussions were upset by violence in the Ukraine by Eastern Rite Catholics and Orthodox Christians over the return of church properties following the fall of the Communist regime. This was also aggravated by the fighting between Orthodox Serbs and Catholic Croatians in the former Yugoslavia.

During the leadership of John Paul II (1978-2005), Catholic and Orthodox communication grew. This was due partly to the fact that the Polish background of the pope provided him contact with Orthodox churches. In 1987, the pope and the Patriarch Demetrios I met in Rome where they together recited the Nicene Creed without the *Filioque*. In June of 1995, John Paul II again met the ecumenical patriarch, Bartholemew I, who was the main speaker at a mass celebrated by the pope.

Chapter 13

The Zenith of the Papacy: 1100 - 1300

From 1100 to 1300, the papacy reached the zenith of its power. The papal leader who characterized the period and set the tone for what would follow was Pope Innocent III. The goal of the period was to establish a perfect or near perfect society on earth. With Europe characterized once again by numerous smaller kingdoms, the papacy—after years of organizational development, growth in power, and an emerging philosophy concerning the importance of the papacy—arose as the one, unifying power throughout Europe.

The question addressed during this period was, "If God's will were done on earth as it is in heaven, what would earth look like?" No historical age is characterized more by efforts to achieve this goal than this period. It was perceived that the one to lead the way must be the pope, since he was God's leading representative on earth. Innocent, himself, held a high view of the papal office, and announced, "The successor of Peter is the Vicar of Christ: he has been established as a mediator between God and man, below God but beyond man; less than God but more than man; who shall judge all and be judged by no one."[204]

Most popes before Innocent had been monks and came out of that background to assume the position of pope. Innocent and other popes of the 12th and 13th centuries were trained as canon lawyers and as authorities in church government. Bruce Shelley points out how power was established by the popes:

> *Innocent III told the princes of Europe that the papacy was like the sun, while kings were like the moon. As the moon received its light from the sun, so kings derived*

> *their powers from the pope. The papacy's chief weapon in support of this authority was spiritual penalties. Almost everyone believed in heaven and hell and in the pope's management of the grace to get to the one and avoid the other.*[205]

The Christianizing of Europe had led to the establishment of this power. Over the years, a collective mind had developed in Europe that caused people to bow before God's authority which was represented in the church.

> *The papacy ascended, high above European society, mounting upon the fading glory of the empire. The emergence of unified national states reduced the empire to a show of its former universal power. Emperors continued to call themselves "ever-august Roman Emperors" and continued to go to Rome for their coronation, but they were actually merely the sovereigns of the cluster of kingdoms and municipal republics that constituted the Germany of the late Middle Ages. The papacy, by contrast...emerged as the most powerful office in Europe.*[206]

The rise of the papacy was helped in several ways. A positive contribution came in the aggressive construction of mostly Gothic cathedrals across Europe. In France alone, over 500 of these cathedrals were built between 1170 and 1270. The great Notre Dame Cathedral was built between 1163 and 1235. These cathedrals were designed to draw one toward God. They stretched upward toward heaven. It is still a wonder to journey through the massive church structures that were built during these times. The cathedral at Strasburg rose to 40 stories and the cathedral at Chartes was 30 stories, quite the feats for the times in which they were built. When one entered the interiors, one entered "another world." There were depictions of heaven (angels, saints, Mary the mother of Christ, and Jesus and the apostles). The trained voices that were heard (the music, the readings, and the sermons) had an "other worldly" tone. This is what one was to be drawn into when entering. The effect was profound in a world and times where living conditions were harsh. People felt themselves between heaven and earth.

Another, more negative, control factor came from the power that was possessed by the pope through the understanding people had of his position. Because of the spiritual dimension of his leadership and the widespread belief (in some cases, superstition) in "another world," the pope exercised an extreme amount of leverage over people and states. He had three major weapons he could use in controlling earth for the sake of "God's Kingdom"—excommunication, the interdict, and the inquisition—all of which were part of the larger movement called "the Crusades."

Excommunication gave the pope and the church power over individuals. It involved removal from the membership of the church, exclusion from the sacraments—especially communion, and consequently, exclusion from the communion of the saints. It recognized one as reprobate, lost, outside of the church, with no hope of heaven. Removing a person from the church through excommunication was a solemn ceremony. After a church official read the sentence of excommunication, "a bell rang as for a funeral, a book was closed, and a candle was extinguished—all to symbolize the cutting off of the guilty man. If he entered a church during Mass, he was expelled or the Mass was halted."[207]

> *While under excommunication, persons could not act as judge, juror, witness, or attorney. They could not be guardians, executors, or parties to contract. After death, they received no Christian burial, and if, by chance, they were buried in consecrated ground, the church had their bodies disinterred and destroyed.*[208]

The *Interdict* was a tool that some, according to Shelley, have called an "ecclesiastical lockout." Though excommunication was directed at individuals, the interdict could be aimed at a whole town, diocese, district, or entire nation and was used several times. It also involved the innocent along with those who were guilty. Basically, it was the suspension of the public practice of worship, including marriage and burial. Baptism and extreme unction could be performed, but only behind closed doors. It cast a gloom over a region or a country as people trembled at the thought of rejection at the last judgment and an existence in hell. Pope Innocent III used the interdict 85 times against uncooperative rulers.

The Crusades were initiated in 1095 by Pope Urban II. They were directed at pagan society and promoted the idea of the church taking an area by force that could not be taken by peaceful means. The Crusaders directed most of their efforts toward the Mohammedans, but also at others who resisted the gospel. Throughout history, the church had resisted the idea of a system of gaining evidence by force. But during the time under consideration this changed as church authorities tried to decide what to do with heretics. Heretics usually were considered to be those who left the Roman Church to pursue another avenue of expressing their faith. People who were suspected of having departed from the Roman Catholic faith would be arrested and questioned (or have evidence brought against them) to get them to return to the "mother church." If they refused to recant, then they would be tortured until they repented of their practices.

The Fourth Lateran Council of 1215 authorized cruel crusades against the Albigenses and the Waldenses and, along with this, established the famous courts of *Inquisition*. These authorities believed that torture was the most effective means for punishing heretics. By the famous bull, *ad extirpanda*, of 1252, Pope Innocent IV, authorized torture as a measure for extorting confessions.[209] Canon law forbade the shedding of blood, so all sorts of tortures were devised that mostly resulted in broken bones. New forms of torture were continually invented and were used against those perceived to be heretics and were also used as threats to keep the faithful in line. Gouging out eyes, maiming, burning with hot irons, the rack, burning at the stake, the guillotine, etc., were all forms of torture used to punish heretics. Established at this time, several inquisitions were carried out over the next four centuries.

Chapter 14

The Crusades: 1095 - 1270

Church historian, Philip Schaff, gives the following description of the crusades:

> *The Crusades were armed pilgrimages to Jerusalem under the banner of the cross. They form one of the most characteristic chapters of the Middle Ages and have a romantic and sentimental, as well as a religious and military, interest. They were a sublime product of the Christian imagination, and constitute a chapter of rare interest in the history of humanity. They exhibit the 'muscular Christianity' of the new nations of the West which were just emerging from barbarism and heathenism. They made religion subservient to war and war subservient to religion. They were a succession of tournaments between two continents and two religions, struggling for supremacy—Europe and Asia, Christianity and Mohammedanism. Such a spectacle the world has never seen before nor since, and probably will never see again.*
>
> *These expeditions occupied the attention of Europe for more than two centuries, beginning with 1095. Yet, they continued to be the concern of the popes until the beginning of the sixteenth century. Columbus signed an agreement on April 17, 1492, to devote the proceeds of his undertaking beyond the Western seas to the recovery of the holy sepulchre....There were seven greater Crusades, the first beginning in 1095, the last terminating with the death of St. Louis, 1270.*[210]

The aim of the Crusades was the conquest of the Holy Land and the defeat of Islam. The primary motive of the Crusades was religious and had two directions:

Fighting against the Muslims: the primary element

The Muslims ruled in the Holy Land and disallowed and/or persecuted pilgrims trying to enter Jerusalem. Pilgrimages to Jerusalem were important. Three basic reasons were given as to why one would want to go to Jerusalem: (1) the "holy aura" of the Holy Land; (2) there "is a special presence of Christ"; and (3) to collect artifacts from the Holy Land. The Mohammedans had invaded Eastern Europe and Asia. The crusades were meant to push them back.

Punishment of heretics in Europe: "The Inquisition"

The Crusades were the invention of, and continued to be the concern of, the popes until the sixteenth century. Great preachers such as Bernard of Clairvaux, Peter the Hermit, and Walter the Penniless were employed to arouse the enthusiasm of the masses. The most famous men of the age were identified with these movements. Emperors and kings rode at the head of armies including: Konrad III, Frederick Barbarossa, and Frederick II of Germany; Richard I ("the Lion-Hearted") of England; Louis VII, Philip Augustus, Louis IX of France; and Andrew of Hungary. Priests, abbots, and higher ecclesiastics fought in the ranks and at the head of their troops. These "holy wars" promised special benefits to those who served. Justification was found both in examples from the Old Testament (the wars described in Joshua and Judges) and in the preeminence of the Christian faith. Urban II promised the first Crusaders marching to Jerusalem that the journey should be counted as a substitute for penance. John VIII promised to soldier's complete absolution of sins. Eugenius, 1146, went farther, promising the reward of eternal life. This same reward was promised to parents of those participating in the Crusades. The abbot, Guibert, who was a chronicler of the First

Crusade, said that God invented the Crusades as a way for the laity to atone for their sins and merit salvation.

Bernard of Clairvaux said that pagans should not be slain if they may by other means be prevented from oppressing the faithful. However, it is better that they be put to death…

> …than that the rod of the wicked should rest on the lot of the righteous. The righteous fears no sin in killing the enemy of Christ. Christ's soldier can securely kill and more safely die. When he dies, it profits him; when he slays, it profits Christ. The Christian exalts in the death of the pagan because Christ is glorified thereby. But when he himself is killed, he has reached his goal.[211]

The Crusading armies were designated by such titles as "the army of the cross," "the army of Christ," "the army of the faith," or "the army of the Lord." The cross was the badge of the Crusaders and their favorite name was "soldiers of Christ." Determining to go on a crusade was called "taking the cross" or "taking the sign of the cross." The first crusade was called, "The Deeds of God, accomplished through the Franks." There were seven main crusades and they began and ended in France.

The First Crusade

The direct cause of the First Crusade was the preaching of a sermon against the Muslims by Urban II at a synod at Clemont in November 1095. He was driven by "the grand concept" of the rescue of the Holy Places from Muslim hands. The assembled crowd, mostly Frenchmen, replied with an enthusiastic "Deus vult" ("God wills it"). Urban was able to stir up unbelievable enthusiasm for his "invasion of Jerusalem." Philip Schaff writes:

> It was a heterogeneous multitude of devout enthusiasts.…The priest forsook his cell, the peasant left his plough and placed his wife and children on carts drawn

> *by oxen, and thus went forth to make the journey and to fight the Turk. At the villages along the route the children cried out, 'Is this Jerusalem, is this Jerusalem?'*[212]

William of Malmesbury wrote, "The Welshman left his hunting, the Scot his fellowship with lice, the Dane his drinking party, the Norwegian his raw fish. Fields were deserted of their husbandmen, whole cities migrated...God alone was left before their eyes."[213]

The First Crusade was led by nobles from France, Belgium, and northern Italy who marched across Europe toward Constantinople. Anyone who has read about the crusades knows of the crimes that were committed by these "soldiers of the cross." They slaughtered Jews as they marched through Germany and had occasional skirmishes with local peoples over food and foraging rights. By late 1096, the city of Constantinople was overrun with 50,000 unruly troops. Emperor Alexis of Constantinople was concerned about the safety of the city, so, in exchange for their promise not to harm the city and people, he provided them with food and supplies and sent them on their way. From there, they marched to Nicea, which they took after a short siege. By fall, they found themselves before Antioch. Following a short siege, they captured the city in the spring of 1097. Finally, in June 1099, they captured Jerusalem. This first crusade would be the most successful of all.

The Second Crusade

The occasion for the Second Crusade was a Moslem threat to the northeastern flank of the Kingdom of Jerusalem after the Moslems had captured the small city of Edessa in that region. The King of France and the Emperor of the Holy Roman Empire led the crusade but it proved to be a failure. Their failure was followed by the recapture of Jerusalem by Saladin, the Muslim leader, in 1187. The preaching of Bernard of Clairvaux in 1146 helped inspire this crusade.

The Third Crusade

The Third Crusade (1189-1192), known as "the Kings' Crusade," was under the leadership of Philip Augustus, king of France; Richard of England (surnamed "Coeur de Lion," or the "Lion-Hearted"); and the Emperor Frederick Barbarossa, king of Germany and emperor of the holy Roman Empire. Frederick was accidentally drowned on the way to Palestine and Philip Augustus went home after a quarrel with Richard. Richard continued to fight. Although he was unsuccessful in recapturing Jerusalem, he did get Saladin to agree to give pilgrims access to Jerusalem. Forced to be content with this, Richard made his way home to England.

The Fourth Crusade

Innocent III, who was anxious to retrieve the failure of the Third Crusade, ardently preached the need of a fourth crusade to capture Egypt as a base of operations against Palestine. The crusade lasted from 1200-1204 and was largely a failure. It weakened the Eastern Empire and deepened the hatred between the Latin and Greek Christians.

This crusade is worth noting because it did such damage to the relations between the western and eastern churches that they never recovered. The Western Crusaders who were marching to Egypt decided to take a detour through Constantinople. Because of various circumstances and due to becoming disgusted with Byzantine politics, the Crusaders lost patience and decided to pillage the city. This three-day sack of Constantinople is unparalleled in history. For 900 years this great city had been a center of Christianity. Works of art from ancient Greece and Byzantine masterpieces could be found throughout the city. Many pillagers, especially those from Venice, carried off these art treasures to adorn their town squares and the churches of their towns.

Mobs of soldiers rushed through the streets and into the houses. They took everything of worth and destroyed what they could not take. Churches and libraries were not spared. Estates and modest homes were wrecked. They stopped only to murder, rape or break open wine cellars for refreshment. Bleeding women and children lay dying in the streets. In the Hagia Sophia, the most resplendent church building in the Christian world, drunken soldiers ripped down silk hangings and tore down the huge silver iconostasis (which held sacred icons). Sacred books and icons were trampled under foot. While soldiers drank from the altar vessels, a prostitute sat herself upon the patriarch's seat and sang a bawdy French song. This continued for three days until the city was in a shambles.

Though we in the West may never have heard of this event, Eastern Christendom has never forgotten the slaughter and pillage of those three terrible days in 1204. Though the date given for the Great Schism is 1054, the events in 1204 insured that the Eastern and Western Church would never again be united. It is safe to say that since those three days they have not spoken to one another. One contemporary Orthodox historian protested, "Even the Saracens [Muslims] are merciful and kind compared with those men who bear the Cross of Christ on the shoulders."

The Fifth Crusade

This crusade was the result, and one of the main objects, of the Fourth Lateran Council (1215). It, too, was under the direction of Pope Innocent III. It was kept alive by his ardor for the reconquest of Palestine. The date set for it to start was June 1, 1217. Actually, Innocent III died before the beginning of the crusade, but his successor, Honorius III, promoted it with an amazing passion. This crusade was led by Frederick II and involved losses and triumphs, journeys through Egypt, and negotiations. Finally, Frederick was able to arrange a treaty with Malik-al-Kameel, which was to remain in force for ten years and delivered up Jerusalem to the Christians (with the exception of the Mosque of Omar and the pilgrim route from Acre to Jerusalem). On March 19, 1229, Frederick crowned himself with his own hand in the Church of the Holy Sepulchre. Ten years later Jerusalem was back under Muslim rule.

The Sixth and Seventh Crusades, 1248 AD, 1270

The last two crusades were under the leadership of Louis IX, King of France, commonly known as "St. Louis." It is said that he combined the piety of a monk with the chivalry of a knight. The Council of Lyon in 1254 had as one of its four main points the relief of the holy places in Jerusalem. A summons was set forth by pope and council for a new expedition. Throughout his reign, Louis led the Sixth and Seventh Crusades, both resulting in failures. His last crusade might have had a chance to succeed, but when his army of 60,000 men were encamped outside Carthage, the plague broke out. Among the victims were the king and his son. With the death of "St. Louis," the last hope of a Christian rule in any part of Palestine was gone. At his death, the French army disbanded.

The Children's Crusades

One of the saddest accounts coming from this time period concerns what is known as the children's crusades. An intense interest in the crusades broke out among the children of Germany and France in the year 1212. Driven by visions of recapturing the Holy Land and finding the cross of Jesus, they went to great lengths to fulfill their dreams.

In France, near Chartre, a shepherd boy of twelve, named Stephen, is reported to have had a vision in which Jesus appeared to him and made an appeal to rescue the holy places in Jerusalem. He is said to have traveled to St. Denis where he reported what he had experienced. Other children joined him and their enthusiasm spread from Brittany to the Pyres. It is reported that "the army" grew to around 30,000 with girls as well as boys and adults joining the march. The French children were ill-fated. When they reached Marseilles, they were deceived by slave traders who offered, for the sake of God's service, to carry them across the Mediterranean Sea.

Seven vessels left France, two were shipwrecked, and the rest reached the African shore where the children were sold into slavery.

In Germany, a child named Nicholas, who was ten years old, arose as the leader of the children in that land. Taking vows, both boys and girls along with men and women joined the ranks. Several children from noble families enlisted and joined with others at Cologne, which was the rallying point. Apparently, there were about 20,000 when they began their march from Germany. The children's army reached Genoa, Italy, in August of 1212. By the time they reached that city, their numbers had been reduced to 7,000 due to death and severe hardships. Some children chose to end their march in Genoa while others continued on through Italy to Brindisi. The bishop there refused to let them proceed further.

These pursuits were based upon a highly charged and idealized spirituality, which was not only allowed by adults but also encouraged. Philip Schaff comments on the validity of the accounts given of the children's' crusades:

> *Impossible as such a movement might seem in our calculating age, it is attested by too many good witnesses to permit its being relegated to the realm of legend, and the trials and death of the children of the thirteenth century will continue to be associated with the slaughter of the children of Bethlehem at the hand of Herod.*[214]

CHAPTER 15

Eucharistic Controversies: 1215

During the Middle Ages, two great controversies arose over the Lord's Table, which created major divisions in the Church. The first of these debates took place in the middle of the ninth century, the other in the middle of the eleventh century. The principle parties in the first were Paschasius Radbertus and Ratramnus (also known as Bertrum); the main figures in the second were Berenger of Tours and Lanfranc of Bec.

In both of these controversies, the conflict was between a physical (materialistic) and a spiritual understanding of the sacrament and its effect. One was based upon a physical, literal presence of Christ at the Lord's Table, and the other contended for a figurative, spiritual presence. Both parties agreed that Christ is present in the eucharist as the bread of life to believers, but they differed greatly in the mode of His presence. The one held that Christ was literally and bodily present and was actually communicated to all participants through the mouth; the other held that He was spiritually present and spiritually communicated through faith. The first group believed that the "eucharistic body" of Christ was identical with his historical body and is miraculously recreated when the priest consecrated the elements. The second group denied this and regarded the "eucharistic body" as a symbolic exhibition of his real body once sacrificed on the cross, now glorified in heaven, yet present to the believer with its life-giving virtue and saving power.

These controversies became so great that condemnation of certain writings took place and excommunication from the Church threatened. It is rather sobering to reflect upon the fact that the commemorative feast given by Christ to remember His undying love and sacrifice for sins, which should be the closest bond of union between believers, gave rise to the most violent controversies.

Radbertus and Ratramnus

Radbertus was a learned and devout monk who became the abbot of Corvey in France. He is the first who clearly taught the doctrine of transubstantiation. He did not employ the word *transubstantiation*, which came into use two centuries later, but he taught that the substance of bread and wine is *effectually changed* into the flesh and blood of Christ after the consecration by the priest in the words "*hoc est corpus meum.*" According to his teaching, after the priestly consecration there is nothing else in the eucharist but the flesh and blood of Christ, although the figure of bread and wine remain. This change is brought about by a miracle of the Holy Spirit who created the body of Christ in the womb of the holy virgin, and who, by the same mighty power, creates from day to day wherever the mass is celebrated, the same body and blood out of the substance of bread and wine. Christ's body and blood are sacrificed again each time this is done.

Ratramnus was also a monk at Corvey and a man of considerable literary reputation. He gave more of a symbolic conception to the Eucharist. He wrote a tract against the ideas of his superior, Radbertus, but did not name him. He concluded that the elements in the eucharist, rather than actually becoming the body and blood of Christ, remain in reality bread and wine as they were before the words of consecration—they are the body and blood of Christ only in a spiritual sense through the faith of believers. He calls the elements "figures and pledges of the body and blood of Christ." The souls of believers are nourished in the communion by the Word of God (the Logos), which dwells in the natural body of Christ and in an invisible manner in the elements.

From the middle of the ninth century, these doctrines were taught and each embraced in different places throughout Europe. Some followed the ideas of Radbertus and others the ideas of Ratramnus. The arguments were brought to the forefront again in the eleventh century with the hope of finding a unified position throughout the church.

Berenger and Lanfranc

Berenger was the director of the cathedral school in Tours. He was an able dialectician and a popular teacher. His studies led him to conclude that the eucharistic doctrine of Radbertus was a vulgar superstition contrary to Scripture, to the church fathers, and to reason. He divulged his view to his students and followers throughout France and Germany, and created a great turmoil. Many followed him, but the majority opposed his teachings. The controversy reached its zenith when he wrote a letter to Lanfranc of Bec, a former fellow-student who had taken the opposite position. Berenger communicated to Lanfranc that we cannot literally eat and drink Christ's body and blood, but instead we may have real spiritual communion by faith with the flesh, that is, with the glorified humanity of Christ in heaven.

Lanfranc was a great church leader and later became the archbishop of Canterbury. He advocated the doctrine of transubstantiation and described it as a miraculous and incomprehensible change of the substance of bread and wine into the very body and blood of Christ. More and more, Lanfranc's position became popular and was received in powerful places in the Roman churches. At times, Berenger feared for his life and appeared to recant from his position.

The Fourth Lateran Council

The debates about the Lord's Table continued for about another 135 years. But in the year 1215, at the Fourth Lateran Council, *transubstantiation* was made the official position of the Roman Church. This triumph of transubstantiation is closely connected to the withdrawal of the communion cup from the laity. This was first done from expediency, to guard against "profaning" by spilling the blood of Christ. The removal of the communion cup ended up strengthening the power of the priesthood by taking away the "rights" of the laity.

Further, it furnished the doctrinal basis for the daily sacrifice of the mass and the power of the priest who is able to create and offer the body and blood of Christ in sacrifice for the sins of men. If it is truly the same body of Christ that is sacrificed in the mass to save us from our sins, then a true priest is needed to make the sacrifice. The powerful trio in the Roman mass are *priest, sacrifice,* and *altar.*

The Protestant Reformation (16th century) brought new controversies to the subject of the Lord's Supper. All the prominent reformers rejected the doctrine of transubstantiation. Three other positions arose to stand in contrast to the Roman view: consubstantiation, asubstantiation, and the Calvinist or Reformed view.

Consubstantiation

The seeds of consubstantiation seem to have been planted by the Christian scholastics of the ninth and tenth centuries, and final definition was given by Martin Luther in the sixteenth century. Luther disagreed with the Roman position, but maintained that Christ's real presence was at the table, holding that "the body of Christ in accordance with the will and omnipotence of God and its own ubiquity is really and substantially present in, with, and under the Supper, even as His divine nature is in the human as warmth is in the iron."[215] Luther was sure that no exclusive miracle happened at the altar; Christ was truly present, not taking the place of the elements but in presence with them. "Fire and iron, two different substances, are so mingled in red-hot iron, that in every part of it are both fire and iron. Why may not the glorious body of Christ much more be in every part of the substance of the bread."[216] The word *trans* indicates "a change or transfer of substance." This Luther rejected. The word *con* means "with, or to consolidate." This is how Luther saw the Lord's Supper. Christ's presence was with or consolidated with the material substance of the bread and wine.

Asubstantiation

Ulrich Zwingli, the Swiss reformer, disagreed with Luther. He, too, took a position in contrast to the Roman view. But his view was much more radical than Luther's, and he felt that Luther was heretical for maintaining a position that sounded too much like the Roman. Zwingli interpreted the words "this is" in the statement, "This is my body, this is my blood," to mean "this stands for," or "this signifies." Reduced to its last analysis, the eucharistic concept of Zwingli is one of a symbolic memorial of the suffering and death of Christ...In the supper we confess our faith, we express what that faith means to us, and we do it in memory of Christ's death.[217] In this view, the eucharist is spiritualized and is a means of grace only in the mind with faith being nourished solely by the Holy Spirit. Zwingli's conception of the Lord's Supper rigorously sought to purge the Church of Roman Catholic notions. Zwingli carried this view into practice during Holy Week of 1525, and it resulted in celebrating the Lord's Supper four times yearly. The Zwinglian view has been consciously or unconsciously accepted by a very large portion of the Protestant church.

Calvinist or Reformed View

This view stands somewhere between the view of Luther and the view of Zwingli. It is probably something like Berenger's, who maintained that though we cannot literally eat of Christ's flesh and blood, we have a true spiritual communion with that flesh which is in heaven. Calvin taught that "the virtues and effects of the sacrifice of the redeemer on the cross are made present and are actually conveyed in the sacrament to the worthy receiver by the Holy Ghost..."[218] He seems to mean that the body and blood of Christ, though present only in heaven, communicate a life-giving influence to the believer when he is in the act of receiving the elements.[219]

Chapter 16

The Renaissance: 1200 - 1600

One of the most formative and influential periods in Western history occurred from 1200 to 1600. Called *the Renaissance*, it was a leap forward in terms of intellectual development and human accomplishments, and marks the transition from the Medieval to the Modern world. The period is sometimes dated from Dante (1265-1321) to Michelangelo (1475-1564). The word *renaissance* comes from the Latin words for "birth" and "back," and expresses the idea of the rebirth of culture. The people of this period were characterized by a desire to return to the life and thought found during the classical Greco-Roman civilization prior to the year 500. And it was the people of the Renaissance who coined the term "dark ages" to describe the centuries that had just preceded them—from the fall of Rome in 476 AD to about the year 1200. It was not until the year 1850 that people first used the term *Renaissance* to describe this period.

The Renaissance, or the revival of classical culture, unshackled the minds of men.[220] The collective mind of the Dark Ages was characterized by an "upper story" mentality; that is, one that reflected upon the heavenly and the spiritual, and maintained an idealized view of humanity. The Renaissance mind was more "lower story," and focused upon realism. This realism would be reflected in philosophy, theology, literature, art, and public life in general.

> *The Renaissance began with the revival of classical learning by scholars known as "humanists." Originally, a humanist was someone who taught Latin grammar, but it eventually came to mean those who studied classical writings and molded their lives on what they read.*[221]

The Renaissance began in Florence, Italy, and gradually spread north into Germany, Poland, France, Holland, and other northern countries. It is important to remember that the overarching goal of this period was a revival "of the values of classical Greek and Roman civilization in the arts, literature, and politics."[222] The achievements of the age were life-changing and many great names come to mind when we think of the Renaissance. Almost anyone who looks at the following list will recognize more than one name.

Dante (1265-1321) was the greatest of the medieval poets and brought a new perspective to writing. He was born in Florence, Italy, was a layman, married, and had seven children. As a child he read the great poets—Virgil, Horace, Ovid, and others—and developed an interest in poetic literature. Dante was one of the first men to write important works in the vernacular.[223] Though he wrote several literary pieces, he is most well-known for *The Divine Comedy*, "an imaginary, allegorical trip through hell, purgatory, and paradise"[224] His writing is genius and the insights found in his poetry show a definite transition in thinking, a moving out of the Dark Ages into a new age. His *Divine Comedy* exalts him to the eminence of the foremost poetic interpreter of the medieval world...[and] it sums up the religious concepts of the Middle Ages and introduces the free critical spirit of the modern world.[225]

Giotto (1267-1337) was a friend of Dante. In fact, Dante refers to him in *The Divine Comedy*. Giotto is one of the first to bring a dramatic, human quality to art. His work stood in contrast to the typical religious art of medieval style, which was flat and opaque. Francis Schaeffer has shown that "with Giotto came a radical change."[226] Giotto gave nature a more proper place, and his people were real people...Giotto also began to show the versatility which was to characterize the Renaissance man.[227] His subject matter showed a shocking interest in solid human beings rather than ethereal visions of heaven.[228] He is known for his painting, *Last Judgment*, in which humans are presented more realistically. Possessing a wide interest in art, he also designed the beautiful campanile—the bell tower—next to the cathedral in Florence.

Petrarch (1304-1374) has been called "the first modern man." This is due, partly, to the fact that he saw the tension between the older medieval views of spirituality and the new emerging humanism of the Renaissance. He loved and admired classical thought because he believed it made one a better person. He studied antiquity, not as a philologist or antiquarian, but as a man of taste.[229] His favorite authors were Cicero and Virgil who were "the fathers of eloquence, the eyes of the Latin language"[230] He was one of the first to build a private library and had around 200 books. Recognized as one of the first of the Italian humanists, his passion for classical learning drove him to discover and copy classical manuscripts and books. In 1345, he found several of Cicero's letters at Verona, and also a portion of Quintilian which had been unknown since the 10th century.[231] As Petrarch and his friends studied these manuscripts, they found a new world that placed an emphasis on nature and the present life, and the enjoyment of these things. About 1340 Petrarch climbed a mountain, Mont Ventoux, in the south of France just to climb it—something brand new.[232] Previously, people had climbed mountains to go over them, to get to someplace, not just to enjoy the experience. This showed the change in thinking as men began to place a positive emphasis upon nature.

Petrarch had a wide range of friends among the wealthy and powerful who enjoyed him for his eloquence and wisdom. His graceful Latin verse and zest for learning inspired other Italians in bringing about the renaissance.[233] He has also been called "the father of the new humanism."

> *From Petrarch came a line of professional humanists. These paid men of letters translated Latin, wrote speeches, and acted as secretaries…Their humanism meant, first of all, a veneration for everything ancient and especially the writings of the Greek and Roman age.*[234]

Boccaccio (1313-1375) occupies an important place in the transition from the Middle Ages to the Renaissance. He devoted himself to literature by researching, writing, studying languages, and looking for old manuscripts. He learned Greek in order to have a better understanding of the classics. His translation of Homer was one of the foundation stones of the Renaissance, reviving Greek literature after seven hundred years of neglect.[235] He is a member of the triumvirate of Italian luminaries of the 14th century.

> *With his two great predecessors he was closely linked, with Dante as his biographer, with Petrarch as his warm friend. It was given to him to be the founder of easy and elegant prose. The world has found few writers who can equal him in realistic narration. There is ground for saying that Dante is admired, Petrarch praised, Boccaccio read.*[236]

He was the first to substitute a literature of the people for the literature of the learned classes and the aristocracy.[237] He is also the author of Europe's first novel. *The Decamerone* is a collection of tales written against the backdrop of the Black Death, and reflects themes that are immoral, ironic, amusing, tragic, and earthy, giving vivid pictures of medieval people (in much the same style of Chaucer's *Canterbury Tales* of this same time period).[238]

> *The Decamerone reveals a low state of morals among priests and monks as well as laymen and women. It derides marriage, the confessional, the hypocrisy of monkery and the worship of relics. The employment of wit and raillery against ecclesiastical institutions was a new element in literature, and Boccaccio wrote in a language the people understood.*[239]

Though *The Decamerone* was condemned at the Council of Trent in the mid-16th century, people continued to read it wherever it could be found.

Brunelleschi (1377-1446) was a master of architecture. The style he followed represented a return to the Classical and a move away from the Gothic. This was a dramatic change and also reflected a definite worldview in architecture.

> *The spirit and religion of men are often expressed in their buildings. The Gothic style of pointed arch and soaring vault had expressed medieval man's aspiration of turning from the laborious soil to the exalted sky. But in the rebirth of the Renaissance, men sought to beautify life, not to escape it, and earth was to be embellished as though it was heaven. In 1450, Antonio Filarete cried, "Cursed be the man who invented this wretched Gothic architecture. Only a barbarous people could have brought it to Italy." Believing as they did that architecture should undergo a revival of the classical and utilization of the contemporary, architects of the period created a new physical environment for worshipers and churchmen.*[240]

The Gothic church used spires, pointing to heaven; the Classic church used domes, housing people. Brunelleschi designed the great cathedral dome in Florence, a truly amazing architectural feat.

> *It brought together great artistic triumph with an overwhelming feat of engineering. It was and is one of the wonders of the world in architectural engineering. It was not only an artistic expression, but it showed the high state of his grasp of mathematics. In this dome Brunelleschi went beyond any dome ever built before—including the Pantheon of ancient Rome.*[241]

Brunelleschi is known for many other works, including the churches of Florence of San Lorenzo and Santo Spirito, and the first Renaissance building, the Foundling Hospital in Florence.

Masaccio (1401-1428), though he died at age 27, has been called "the father of Renaissance painting." His work represented another large step forward in the field of painting. Some of the dynamics in his work included the use of space around his subjects, painting in the round, and figures set in the midst of real space. Masaccio also was the first to bring light into his paintings from the naturally correct direction.[242]

> *In Masaccio's work many faces were clearly portraits. He made studies from life and was able to give his work true-to-life quality...In addition, his work had real composition; there was balance to the total work in the relationship of the figures and the whole... Masaccio was the first artist who painted people with their feet actually standing on the ground...In short, in the painting of Masaccio there were a massive number of breakthroughs and firsts.*

These accomplishments were wonderful in the sense of giving new meaning and reality to life in general, and to religious life as well. Masaccio's work reflected a worldview that appreciated the world God had made. Francis Schaeffer observed, "Nature had thus now truly come to its proper place."[243]

Leonardo da Vinci (1452-1519) was the true embodiment of the Renaissance man. He could do almost anything and do it well.[244] His brilliance as a painter is seen in his two most famous paintings, *Mona Lisa* and *The Last Supper*. However, he was more than a painter. He was also a chemist, mathematician, musician, architect, anatomist, botanist, mechanical engineer, inventor, natural scientist, and sculptor. This list is not simply an enumeration of areas that he dabbled in; rather, he was an expert in each of these fields. He was a many-sided genius far ahead of his time. He designed and built a helicopter type of device, but it would not fly. However, he did succeed in many areas, including the invention of the ball-bearing and the sewing machine. The door into the natural world had been opened and Leonardo entered it with purpose, advancing the world of science during the Renaissance. There is an important observation to be made about the life of Leonardo da Vinci. He is a good representative of the philosophical shift that occurred in the Renaissance.

> *The classic work* Leonardo da Vinci, *published in Italy and translated into English in 1963, contained a section by Giovanni Gentile (1875-1944) on Leonardo's thought forms. He spells out the fact that Leonardo really grasped the problem of modern man. Leonardo anticipated where humanism would end.*[245]

At first, Leonardo embraced the Renaissance idea of the greatness of man. But dealing only with particular things—whether in art, science, or daily life—without an over-arching universal truth, led to a split between theory and practice. By the end of his life it appears that the "humanistic ideal" had diminished for Leonardo. Francis Schaeffer observes: He could not bring forth the universal or meaning in either mathematics or painting, and when King Francis I of France (1494-1547) brought Leonardo to the French court as an old man, Leonardo was in despondency.[246]

Michelangelo (1475-1565) was another genius of the Renaissance who excelled as a sculptor, painter, architect, and poet. He portrayed human emotions on a monumental scale in his ceiling frescoes, *Creation of Man* and *The Last Judgment* in the Sistine Chapel[247] It is interesting to see the combined influences in Sistine Chapel paintings. Both Christian images and pagan images borrowed from the classical world of Greece and Rome are represented together. In this we see how he tried to combine the classical with the Christian. His sculptured works, such as *David*, *Moses*, and *The Pieta*, are magnificent representations of physical and anatomical realism, but also of the human strength represented in the Renaissance.

> *In the Academy in Florence is Michelangelo's great room. Here we see on either side Michelangelo's statues of men "tearing themselves out of the rock." These were sculptured between 1519 and 1536. They make a real humanistic statement: Man will make himself great. Man as Man is tearing himself out of the rock. Man by himself will tear himself out of nature and free himself from it. Man will be victorious.*
>
> *As the room in the Academy is arranged, it strikingly sets forth humanistic thought. As we go past these men tearing themselves out of the rock, we come finally, at the focal point of the room, to the magnificent statue of David (1504). As a work of art it has few equals in the world. Michelangelo took a piece of marble so flawed that no one thought it could be used, and out of it he carved this overwhelming statue. But let us notice that the David was not the Jewish David of the Bible. David was simply a title. Michelangelo knew his Judaism, and in the statue the figure is not circumcised. We are not to think of this as the biblical David but as the humanistic ideal. Man is great!... The David was the statement of what the humanistic man saw himself as being tomorrow! In this statue we have man waiting with confidence in his own strength for the future.*[248]

As with Leonardo da Vinci, Michelangelo seemed to come to a similar conclusion at the end of his life: there is no such thing as the humanistic man.

> *Many of his early works show his humanism, as does his David. In contrast stand his later Pietas (statues of Mary holding the dead Christ in her arms) in the cathedral in Florence and in the castle in Milan, which was probably his last. In the Pieta in the cathedral in Florence, Michelangelo put his own face on Nicodemus (or Joseph of Arimathea—whichever the man is), and in both of these Pietas humanistic pride seems lessened, if not absent.*[249]

Raphael (1483-1520), Italian Renaissance painter, is considered one of the greatest and most popular artists of all time. There is no painting that depicts more clearly the thought, purpose, tensions, and the outcome of the Renaissance than Raphael's *The School of Athens*, painted in 1510. It is a complex allegory of philosophy, depicting philosophers, past and present, in a splendid architectural setting. It illustrates the historical continuity of Platonic thought. The two central figures are Plato and Aristotle. Raphael painted Plato with his index finger pointed upward, emphasizing high ideals and absolutes. Aristotle's presence depicts the conflict brought to this period by his thought. Raphael shows him with his fingers spread and pointing downward toward the natural world. This painting showed Raphael's deep understanding of the Renaissance. *The School of Athens* is the most famous of all his frescoes.

His full name is Raffaello Sanzi or Santi and he was born in Urbino, Italy, April 6, 1483. His father, Giovanni Santi, an artist, was also a man of culture who was in constant contact with all the advanced artistic ideas in Urbino. He gave his son his first instruction in art and by the time Raphael was 11, he had introduced the boy to humanistic philosophy in the court school. By the time he was 17, Raphael displayed an extraordinary artistic talent. His training and influence would continue to develop in three important cities: Perugia, Florence, and Rome.

In Perugia he became a student and assistant to the painter Perugino. There he learned to imitate his master in his paintings, and to this day, art historians have found it difficult to determine which were painted by Perugino and which were painted by Raphael. In the autumn of 1504 he moved to Florence where he studied the work of Leonardo da Vinci, Michelangelo, and Fra Bartolommeo. Leonardo and Michelangelo became his principle teachers. Raphael was called to Rome toward the end of 1508 by Pope Julius II. At this time he was little known in Rome, but soon made a deep impression on Julius and the papal court, and his reputation and authority as a master grew day by day. Raphael was endowed with a handsome appearance and great personal charm in addition to his prodigious artistic talents. He eventually became so popular that he was called "the prince of painters." He is known for many works, the most popular being his Madonna series, *The Disputa*, and *The School of Athens*. Raphael died on his 37th birthday, April 6, 1520.

The Renaissance demonstrates two important realities: the greatness of man and the failure of man. Man is great because he is created in the image of God with imagination and creative powers. But these powers are not limitless and man fails in every generation because he is sinful and finite. This surely is one of the important lessons to be learned from the Renaissance.

What caused the Renaissance?

Prior to the year 500 there had been a Platonic resurgence; that is, the thought of Plato made itself more pronounced throughout the Mediterranean world. This Platonic thought emphasized that the only true realities to be found are in the unseen world, and that the world we live in is just an ugly copy of, and inferior to the real. This kind of thinking focused upon the heavenly, unseen world, and tended to diminish the natural or physical world. The Greeks and Romans taught that the world we live in is nothing compared to the world we cannot see. Further, not only is this world nothing compared to the unseen, it is also evil and inferior, since it is material. Mostly, it was the material that made it evil. One can see that ultimately meaning as a human, and the material world as a whole, is minimized or lost because one is driven to ignore or deny what is physical.

This thinking, also called the Greek dichotomy, says "the spirit is good, material is evil," and places the emphasis upon "the spiritual life." These influences of Plato made their way into the church. Consequently, the only things that mattered were those which contributed to, or supported, this way of thinking. Thus, most of life centered in the church.

Worship reflected an "upper story" mentality. The whole aura of church and life was "other worldly." A massive institution grew up during this time which held great power over people. People were divided into two categories: *holy* and *profane*. The clergy were the holy and lay people were the profane. Those doing God's work—the pastors and priests—had "callings." Others merely existed and worked to support God's work through the church. Common work—or secular work—the work of the peasant farmer, the work of the housewife, the carpenter, etc., simply had no value.

Most of the art from this period reflects this Platonic view. People or religious objects were hardly ever portrayed realistically. Important religious figures such as Jesus, Mary, or the apostles were not painted realistically. Rather, they were almost always painted as symbols through the use of an opaque, flat style. Landscape painting did not exist. A study of people living in this period reveals that nature—trees, mountains, streams, countryside, and animals, etc.—held little interest for the artists. The natural world and simply "being human" were inadequate subjects. The "upper story" had to be added through the use of religious symbols.

The centuries from 500-1200 are called the Platonic Period. It is interesting to observe how it came to be and what sustained it. There were probably three main influences.

- ⟡ First, was the general rise of Platonism prior to the Middle Ages.
- ⟡ Second, was the fall of the Roman Empire which brought about the death of classical thought.
- ⟡ Third, was the powerful influence of St. Augustine (354-430 AD).

St. Augustine and Plato

Augustine was deeply influenced by Plato. All who read and study Augustine see the Platonic elements in his work. Augustine, who lived during the revival of Plato's thought, known as "neo-Platonism" (or, "the new Platonism"), developed an affinity for Plato, and turned much of his study towards the philosopher. Thus, Augustine's works are influenced by Plato's love for the unseen world and his disdain for the seen. In his famous work, *The City of God*, we see the "higher" ruling over the "lower" and the perfections of the higher sought over the corruption of the lower. One would not want to minimize the valuable contributions that Augustine brought to the church and to Western civilization—and they are many—but we must observe this influence of Plato in his works.

The importance of this development is seen in that fact that Augustine's writings and theology would be the primary influences in the formation of thought and life over the next 700-800 years in both church and culture. His influence parallels the Platonic Period. Here is how G.K. Chesterton saw the problem with Augustine, and ultimately, in calling on Plato as an ally:

> *Granted all the grandeur of Augustine's contribution to Christianity, there was in a sense a more subtle danger in Augustine the Platonist…There came from it [his thought] a mood which unconsciously committed the heresy of dividing the substance of the Trinity. It thought of God too exclusively as a Spirit who purifies…and too little of a Creator who creates [made the world].*[250]

Scholasticism

Beginning in the tenth century, the medieval period saw the revival of learning through a movement known as Scholasticism. Many outstanding men rose up during this time and came to be called *Schoolmen* because of the emphasis of their work. Among them were Anselm (1033-1109), Peter Abelard (1079-1142), Bernard of Clairvaux (1090-1153), Peter Lombard (1100-1164), John of Salisbury (1115-1180), Albertus Magnus (1206-1280), Roger Bacon (1214-1292), St. Bonaventure (1221-1274), Thomas Aquinas (1225-1274), Duns Scotus (1264-1308), William of Occam (1300-1349).

They developed a systematic approach to scholarship known as *scholasticism*. They had particular approaches to research, teaching, and writing. Their philosophy of learning was called the *dialectic method*. The Scholastic method of teaching involved the *lectio*, the public lecture in which the master explained the text, the *disputatio*, in which a view was expounded and objections to it proposed and answered in syllogistic form.[251] Their method of writing was in the form of commentaries which gave systematic expositions over the entire field of theology. These were called *Summae*. The most well-known and influential of these works is the *Summa Theologica* by Thomas Aquinas.

Thomas Aquinas

The intellectual giant who dominated the thirteenth century, the prince of the school men, and the theologian destined to wield unequaled influence over the theology of Roman Catholicism was Thomas Aquinas.[252] Known as the "Angelic Doctor," Aquinas was brilliant in thought and prolific in writing. He was the outstanding theologian of his day, and ranks among the most influential scholars of all time.

> *During his lifetime, Thomas Aquinas wrote sixty books and many hymns, commentaries, and devotions. His two greatest works were Summa Contra Gentiles, designed to equip missionaries to the Moslems, and Summa Theologica, which crowned his theological thought... The Summa Theologica (written over a period of nine years and still unfinished at his death) deals with the subjects of God, creation, the destiny of man, Christ as the only way to God, the sacraments, and last things.*[253]

Though coming from nobility, he was always humble and considered himself called to the life of the scholar. When offered important positions, he refused in order that he might give himself to study, teaching, and writing. He was passionate in his desire to know truth. Born at Roccasecca, Italy, he was the youngest son of Count Landulf of Aquino, who was related to the king of France. His mother was the sister of Frederick Barbarossa, the king of Germany and emperor of the Holy Roman Empire. He was educated at Monte Cassino, the University of Naples, and Paris. Later, against the wishes of his parents, he became a Dominican monk and devoted himself to a life of scholarship.

Finding Aristotle

While a student at Paris, from 1245-1248, Aquinas studied under the influential Albertus Magnus, who introduced him to Aristotle. Aquinas' discovery of Aristotle changed everything. By joining classical Christian theology to the philosophy of Aristotle, Aquinas affected a synthesis of thought that launched a new revolution. The years from 500-1200 have come to be known as "the Platonic Period." The period ended with what is known as "the Aristotelian Revolution," and was one of the most dramatic changes in world history. It ushered in "the Aristotelian Period," which lasted from 1200-1500. Plato was "upper story." Aristotle was "lower story." In Aristotle the natural world is embraced and seen as a place to discover, build, and enjoy. Aquinas saw that there could be compatibility between Christian theology and Aristotle's teaching.

It is a simple fact that Aristotle's works were virtually inaccessible in the Western world until the 12th century. It was at that time they were discovered and translated into the Latin language. One of the over-riding themes of the Scholastics was the relationship of faith and reason. This remained important for Aquinas and he believed he had found an ally in Aristotle. Though Aristotle had been discovered, he needed to be explained, and this was what Aquinas did in a most effective way. When he was done, the world looked different. Thought was joined to faith and there was an explosion in human achievement.

However, there was an important philosophical shift during the Renaissance. In the beginning there was a much needed emphasis upon the natural world and movement away from the mindset of the previous period (the Dark Ages). From a biblical point of view, nature is important because it was created by God, and is not to be undervalued or despised. It is a world of order and purpose—made that way by God—and is worth exploring, studying, knowing, and enjoying. But somewhere during the Renaissance a corner was turned, and by the end of the period man had put himself at the center, and humanism became the dominant worldview. Francis Schaeffer has pointed out that, at first, it could have gone one of two ways—nature could have had its proper place with real people living in a real world God had made, with value, meaning, and absolutes in place—or, man could put himself at the center. Most of the humanists at the beginning of the Renaissance were Christians and a balance was maintained. However, this changed. A representative figure of the age was Giovanni Boccaccio, and it is written of him, "He was a forerunner of modern writers who ignore Christianity and write of the joys of nature, love, and the flesh."[254] The Renaissance humanism steadily evolved toward modern humanism—a value system rooted in the belief that man is his own measure, that man is autonomous, totally independent.[255]

Part Four
The Modern Period: 1500 - Present

Overview

Generally, two reasons are given as to why we start with the 1500s as the beginning of the Modern Period. First, the beginning of the 16th century witnessed the appearance of modern nations with their distinct borders and political ideas. Second, the Protestant Reformation forced a change in religious thought and public attitudes which changed the face of religion in Europe. Philip Schaff has written, "The Reformation was a republication of primitive Christianity, and the inauguration of modern Christianity. This makes it, next to the Apostolic age, the most important and interesting portion of church history."[256]

Suspicious of the Roman Catholic Church's understanding of the Gospel, and angered by the sale of indulgences for the purpose of building St. Peter's Basilica in Rome, Martin Luther posted his 95 Theses on the door of the Castle Church in Wittenberg, Germany. This occurred on October 31st, 1517, and within four weeks the theses were copied and circulated throughout Germany. Thus, the Protestant Reformation was launched in Europe. The original intent of this movement was to bring reforms within the Catholic Church. But this was not to be, and soon there appeared a new expression of Christianity. The movement was given impetus by other strong leaders: Philip

Melanchthon, along with Luther in Wittenberg; Martin Bucer in Strasburg; Osiander in Nuremberg; Oecolampadius in Basel; John Calvin, William Farel and Theodore Beza in Geneva; Ulrich Zwingli and Heinrich Bullinger in Zurich; John Knox in Scotland; and Thomas Cromwell, William Tyndale, and Thomas Cranmer in England. There were many others as well.

The results were profound and widespread and were not only religious, but political, economic, and social—impacting the entire Western world. Beginning in Europe, and taking root in Germany and Switzerland, the ideas of the Reformation spread to the Scandinavian countries, to Holland, to England and Scotland, and to the colonies, which became the United States.

A reaction to the Protestant Reformation was the Counter-Reformation of the Roman Catholic Church. This movement was initiated by the Council of Trent which met in three sessions from 1545 to 1563 (1545-47, 1551-52, 1562-63). Rather than acquiesce to the demands of the Protestants, the Roman Church clarified its positions on major issues, moved to protect its traditions, and aggressively carried its message throughout the world, ensuring the creation of two major forms of Christianity in the Western world. The ideas of the Reformation were seriously challenged by the Enlightenment ideas of the 18th century. The Enlightenment has been called "the age of reason." It was thoroughly secular in nature, and it has been said that the dream of this period can be summed up in five words: reason, nature, happiness, progress, and liberty. Though from a technical point of view it had a short duration (1720-1780), its effects remain to this day. The combined ideas of the Reformation and Enlightenment led to the period of reason and revival during the 1700s and 1800s. Along with the scientific revolution, the developments of the last 500 years has brought us to a period of theological diversity in our modern world.

CHAPTER 17

The Period of Reformation: 1500 - 1700 AD

Why the Protestant Reformation Occurred

Most scholars agree that Martin Luther's posting of the *95 Theses* on the Castle Church door in Wittenberg on October 31, 1517, can be kept as the birth date of the Protestant Reformation. What happened on that day was a culmination of ideas and events that had been occurring for many years.

At the beginning of the sixteenth century, the stage was set for significant changes—change was "in the air." Ulrich von Hutton proclaimed, "O century! The studies flourish, the spirits awake, it is a luxury to live."[257] Martin Luther seemed to have an understanding and appreciation for the 16th century and wrote in 1522:

> *If you read all the annals of the past, you will find no century like this since the birth of Christ. Such building and planting, such good living and dressing, such enterprise in commerce, such a stir in the arts, has not been since Christ came into the world. And how numerous are the sharp and intelligent people who leave nothing hidden and unturned: even a boy of twenty years knows more than was formerly known by twenty doctors of divinity.*[258]

One historian describes how this period abounded with opportunities that had been unknown for centuries:

> *It was lusty Germany in letters as well as in life and art. Literacy was spreading. Books were pouring forth*

from sixteen publishers in Basel, twenty in Augsburg, twenty-one in Cologne, twenty-four in Nuremberg; there, Anton Koberger, alone employed twenty-four presses and a hundred men. The trade in books was a major line in the busy commerce of the fairs at Frankfurt, Salzburg, Nordinggen, and Ulm. "Everybody nowadays wants to read and write...there is no end to the new books that are written." Schools multiplied in the towns; every city provided bursaries or scholarships for poor but able students; nine new universities were founded in this half-century; and those at Vienna, Heidelberg, and Erfurt opened their doors to the New Learning. Literary academies arose in Strasbourg, Augsburg, Basel, Vienna, and Mainz. Rich burghers...and the Emperor Maximilian himself, opened their libraries, art collections, and purses to eager scholars; and great ecclesiastics like Johann von Dahlberg, Bishop of Worms, and Albrecht of Brandenburg, Archbishop of Mainz, were enlightened patrons of scholarship, poetry, and art. The Church in Germany...welcomed the Renaissance, but emphasized linguistic studies of Biblical and patristic texts. The Latin Vulgate Bible was printed in twenty-six editions in Germany between 1453 and 1500; there were twenty German translations of the Bible before Luther's; the spread of the New Testament among the people prepared them for Luther's challenging contrast between the Gospels and the Church [the Roman Church].[259]

It is important to recognize a relationship between the Renaissance that began in the south of Europe, and the Reformation that was born in Germany.

> *The intellectual changes wrought by the Renaissance both north and south of the Alps created an intellectual outlook that favored the development of Protestantism. The desire to return to sources of the past led the Christian*

Humanists of the north to a study of the Bible in the original tongues of the Scriptures.[260]

Centrifugal Forces

Though the Reformation was, at its core, a religious movement, there were secular influences at work that prepared the way for the Reformation. Mark Noll, in his book, *Turning Points*, indicates that there were several "centrifugal forces" at work within Europe, and Christendom, which paved the way to the Reformation. He states, "In the larger sphere of European history, Protestantism acted as an accelerator for forces or developments that were well underway by 1517 and Martin Luther's posting of the *Ninety-Five Theses*."[261] Consider some of these changes:

Nationalism

This period gave birth to many of our modern states (countries). The emergence of many powerful sovereigns, who possessed money and armies, helped define the territories of many future states. "Whether the expanding authority of the king of France; or strengthening the self confidence among some of Germany's many duchies, principalities, electorates, and imperial cities...the general trend in politics throughout the fifteenth century was to heighten identification with localities."[262] The Hundred Years War, which ended in 1453, established the boundaries of the Kingdoms of England and France. The marriage of Isabella of Castile and Ferdinand of Aragon, in 1469, provided the final unification of Spain, and the power to all but wipe out the Muslim presence in Europe. Though not as clearly defined, but because of the rule of Charles V, Germany's territories began to be delineated.

Naturally, the rise of local authorities gave a sense of identity to particular areas and created tensions and suspicions not known before this time against the authority of the Church of Rome. Religious authority over kingdoms was lessened.

Economic Life

Regional authority helped develop a greater local economic vitality. The Black Death, or plague, had wreaked havoc in the middle decades of the 14th century. Economic depression followed the decline of population, abandonment of fertile land, and curtailing of trade. But by the mid-15th century, economic expansion was once again the order of the day. Trade, population in rural and urban areas, and agricultural production were all generally improving....[263]

As previously noted, local concentrations of power enabled economic development. It is important to point out that this also created tension between the local authorities and the central religious authority that had ruled in Europe for centuries—namely, the Roman Catholic Church.

> *Improving economic activity alongside heightened concentrations of local, political power increasingly made money a point of friction between Rome and the Catholic countries of Europe. Virtually no area of Europe was spared strife over money between the Roman curia and local authorities.*[264]

Social Relationships

The improvement in economic conditions naturally changed the condition of social relationships.

> *Nothing like the modern middle class yet existed, but especially in the cities the increasing numbers of merchants, lawyers, and master craftsmen—all of which grew in strength as the European economy continued to expand—added to social volatility. Peasants increasingly exchanged feudal obligations for contractual and money connections; in western Europe serfdom soon became a distant memory. In the midst of a shifting social world, the roles of the clergy also experienced considerable strain. Whether the lower clergy (who were soon bypassed in*

> *wealth and education by urban merchants), powerful lord-bishops and abbots of wealthy monastic houses, or the prelates who carried out the direct bidding of the popes— all levels of ecclesiastical authority were being forced to renegotiate the honored social status that had long been simply part of the fabric of European life.*[265]

Intellectual Life

At least two influences advanced the intellectual life of the Europeans: the invention of the printing press by Johann Gutenberg of Strasbourg and Mainz in the middle of the 15th century, and the new humanistic intellectual ideas coming out of the south. The printing press made possible the circulation of works that formerly were restricted to a privileged few. The importance of the printing press is highlighted by Jacque Barzun in the following statement:

> *Luther's hope of reform might have foundered like many others of the previous 200 years, had it not been for the invention of printing. Gutenberg's movable type, already in use for some 40 years, was the physical instrument that tore the West asunder.*[266]

Editions of works by ancient scholars and by the church fathers, devotional writings, Bibles, and then the works of the humanist scholars of the Renaissance not only began to be published, but poured forth. A passion for knowledge was evident everywhere. The increase in intellectual life naturally brought into question and created impatience "with authority that rested on settled medieval traditions."[267]

> *They sought instead the freshness of ancient intellectual authority, above all returning to the written sources of European civilization. So it was that earnest searching for authentic ancient text—Latin and Greek, pagan and Christian—was an ongoing European preoccupation*

> *for several generations before Protestants deployed the authority of another ancient text, the Bible, as a justification for rejecting traditional Catholic deference to the papacy.*[268]

It is important to point out how the increased intellectual life specifically called into question the established authorities of the past.

> *Southern forms of the Renaissance came first and produced dramatic innovations in literature (for example, the love sonnets of Petrarch [1304-74]) and painting (for example, Giotto, Fra Angelico, Raphael) as well as science and classical learning (with Leonardo da Vinci [1452-1519] excelling in all). But intellectual energies in northern Europe were not far behind and would, as exemplified by Erasmus of Rotterdam (ca. 1469-1536), also produce prodigies of scholarship. Yet the specific accomplishments of individual luminaries were less important than what might be called the spirit of the Renaissance. Above all, promoters of Europe's "new learning" were impatient with authority that rested on settled medieval traditions and exasperated by intellectual conformity to medieval ideals.*[269]

In all of these factors, one can see the tension that was created by the emerging "local powers" and the authority of the church, which had been present for centuries. Earle Cairns explains:

> *Political historians see the Reformation as a result of nation-states opposing an international church. To them, the Reformation is simply a political event caused by the rise of nationalism.*[270]

Religious Crises: Moral and Doctrinal Failures

Although the dynamics mentioned in the preceding paragraphs help explain how the way was prepared for the occurrence of the Reformation, they were not the effective causes of the Reformation. They have sometimes been called "indirect causes." The "direct causes" of the Reformation were clearly religious.

> *Although edifying spiritual currents persisted among some of Europe's learned clergy and some of the populace at large, the formal concerns of the church seemed always to feature politics, contests for power, and ostentatious display rather than solicitude for godly life and thought.*[271]

In the middle of such concerns, care of the members of the church took second place. The laity, for the most part, existed to serve the needs and wants of the church leaders. Corruption in the church was rampant, followed by unrest and dissatisfaction. Some of the more well-known failures and abuses in the church were:

Immorality Among the Clergy

Most everyone knew of this failure. The enforcement of clerical celibacy had led to clerical concubinage. Erasmus of Rotterdam, himself a bastard child of a priest, wrote against these evils in the church in the early 16th century. His book, *The Praise of Folly*, written when he was a guest in the home of Thomas More in London, was a satire on monasticism and corruption in the church.

The Purchases of Religious Positions

Sometimes obtaining leading religious positions was done at more local levels through bishops or even through the pope himself. It secured prestige, power, and financial gain for those who could find such status. Sometimes those who were able to buy these positions were not even theologically trained.

Financial Pressures

Financial Pressures were placed upon "the faithful" (the church members, which included nearly everyone). Interestingly, this was especially a burden to the rich, who were counted upon to assist the interests of the bishops and priests. Although it was understood that giving to the church was to be voluntary, people resented paying tithes when non-payment meant excommunication. Along with the tithes were the bishop's taxes and the trafficking in indulgences. The bishops were often required to pay taxes on church properties to the ruling king or prince and used this as an opportunity to tax his parishioners. Indulgences were papers purchased from the papacy whereby people might gain remission for their sins and shorten the time that would be required of them in purgatory.

The Sad State of the Local Parishes

So much money was taken from the smaller parishes to support either the state church or the church in Rome that little was left for the local parishes. Many of the "lower clergy" were almost completely uneducated and could barely subsist on what was provided for them. Due to this, many of them served several parishes and often were not "in residence" to serve the local people. Thus, though much was demanded of them, the people were little cared for.

No doubt many of these problems were a result of a deeper issue: failure in the matter of doctrine. Lost in the politics, ritual, and the institutionalization of the church and its ministry was the matter of belief. Mark Noll points out that very foundational questions began to be asked that needed doctrinal definition:

> *What must I do to be saved? Where can I find secure religious authority? How should the church's spiritual interests be balanced by the need to live in the world?*[272]

The problems that existed by the 1500s can be stated different ways. Francis Schaeffer believed that the Reformation, in large part, was a response to the infiltration of humanistic thought that had formed during the Renaissance (but had developed fully by the time of the Reformation.) Elements of "humanism" had come into the church with the following results:

- ✧ The authority of the church was made equal to the Bible.
- ✧ A strong element of human work was added to the work of Christ for salvation so that individuals had to *merit the merit of Christ*.
- ✧ There was an increasing synthesis between biblical teaching and pagan thought (as illustrated in Michelangelo's painting in the Sistine Chapel.)

At its core, therefore, the Reformation was the removing of the humanistic distortions which had entered the church.[273]

Forerunners of the Protestant Reformation

The Reformation was a time that featured the rise of many great and dedicated men. It might be compared, in some ways, to the coalescing of great men at the time of the American Revolution. For many years, the idea had been alive that reform was needed in the church. Beginning about one hundred and fifty years before Martin Luther, John Calvin and their contemporaries began their initiatives for reform, others began to speak out. Three men are worth noting.

John Wycliffe (1320-1384)

Often referred to as "the Morningstar of the Reformation," John Wycliffe, as far as we know, was the first to raise the issues which later resulted in the Reformation. Thus, he is sometimes called "the first reformer." He spoke out publicly against the wealth and worldliness of the church and its leadership, insisted upon the authority of the Bible over the authority of the church, and emphasized the priesthood of all believers. Believing that all

Christians should be able to read the Bible for themselves, he was the first to begin a systematic translation of the entire Bible into English. John Wycliffe was born in the year 1320 at Yorkshire into a family of considerable affluence. His life is easily divided into three parts.

First, his academic life at Oxford (Balliol College) must be considered. He remained in this academic environment until 1371, beginning as a student, rising to become a Master at Balliol, and then going on to be recognized as Oxford University's leading philosopher and theologian. It was during this time that he began to develop what were then perceived as radical doctrines on church government. He argued that only the godly could exercise authority over others. Ungodly, corrupted leaders have no legitimate authority. As early as 1361, while at the university, he began to speak out publicly against the wealth and worldliness of the church hierarchy. At this time the Catholic Church was very wealthy (it owned about one third of the land in England) and claimed exemption from paying taxes.

The second phase of Wycliffe's life began in 1371 when he left the academic community. He always had a relationship to English nobility and members of the secular government. His ideas suited them because of their discontent with an extremely wealthy church. Thus, Wycliffe found support and protection in the secular sphere. In 1374, he represented King Edward III at Bruges, Belgium, in trying to solve a dispute between the king and the Pope over authority. When he observed, first-hand, papal interference in civil affairs, he stepped up his criticisms of the church.

In 1378, Wycliffe was no longer needed in public life so he returned to his life of study. Several people had begun to speak out against abuses in the church, but Wycliffe seems to be the first to explain the abuses as a failure in upholding doctrine. First, he broke with Catholic position and declared that the Bible was sole authority above pope, council, creeds, and traditions. He stated firmly that the Scriptures are the ultimate norm by which the church and popes must be tested. Further, in exalting the Bible, Wycliffe also "demoted" the pope. He stated that the papacy was an office instituted by man, not by God. Wycliffe also opposed the Catholic doctrine of transubstantiation, claiming that it was not consistent with the teaching of Scripture. In conflict with the Catholic Church, and insisting that all believers were priests of God, he believed all should be able to read the Scriptures in their own tongue. Thus, from 1382 to 1384 Wycliffe worked to produce a translation of the Scriptures in English.

Wycliffe founded a group of lay preachers. Their enemies called them "Lollards," which means "mumblers." These disciples disseminated his ideas all over England, keeping his theology alive. Later they were persecuted and became an underground, lower-class movement. Despite opposition, the Lollards prepared the way for the English Reformation by preaching from the English Bible and creating discontent against the Catholic Church. Because of his radical ideas, Wycliffe was banished from Oxford in 1381. He moved to Lutterworth, near Rugby, where he remained until he died from a stroke in 1384. Later, Pope Martin V, incensed at the work of Wycliffe, had his remains exhumed in 1428, burned, and scattered in the waters of the River Swift.

John Hus (1366–1415)

Richard II of England married Anne of Bohemia. This opened the door for students from Bohemia to study in England. Many of them, when they returned to Bohemia, carried with them the ideas and works of John Wycliffe and John Hus read and digested the writings of the earlier "radical." As a professor at the University of Prague in Bohemia (heartland of Czechoslovakia), he helped pave the way for the Reformation in Europe by adopting much of the theology of John Wycliffe. He emphasized the authority of Scripture, spoke out against corruption in the church of Bohemia, and encouraged a movement for preaching and teaching in the language of the people. He made it his goal to bring reform to the church in Bohemia.

Hus resisted the division that existed between the laity and the clergy. He wanted to see more lay participation in the church and proposed a return of the communion cup to the laity. Not long before, the church had restricted the use of the cup to the priest on the basis that the laity could spill "the blood of God." Hus's relations with the Bohemian king were cordial at first, but became more difficult as Hus became progressively involved in controversy. He spoke out against the sale of indulgences, the revenue of which was used to support the pope's war against the king of Naples. Finally, Hus denounced the pope as anti-Christ. All of this became too much for King Wenceslaus of Bohemia.

In 1414, the Council of Constance was convened to try to untangle the theological difficulties in Bohemia. Hus was invited to the conference to defend his views and be examined by the council. He welcomed the opportunity, thinking that the able theologians present would see the validity of his theology. He was promised safe conduct to the council; however, this was not honored and he was seized after his arrival and asked to recant on his views. He stoutly maintained his position.

> *Few scenes in church history are more touching than Hus's fidelity and refusal to swerve from absolute truth, even to save his life.*
>
> *For eight months he lay in prison in Constance. His letters during his last month rank among the great in Christian literature. If the reformer had added nothing to our intellectual heritage, he would still have enriched our moral outlook.*
>
> *"O most holy Christ," he prayed, "draw me, weak as I am, after Thyself, for if Thou dost not draw us we cannot follow Thee. Strengthen my spirit, that it may be willing. If the flesh is weak, let Thy grace precede us... for without Thee we cannot go for Thy sake to cruel death. Give me a fearless heart, a right faith, a firm hope, a perfect love,*

that for Thy sake I may lay down my life with patience and joy. Amen."

Finally, 6 July 1415, the day for his burning came. On the way to the place of execution he passed through a churchyard and saw a bonfire of his books. He laughed, and told the bystanders not to believe the lies circulated about him. On arriving at the execution-ground, familiarly known as "the Devil's Place," Hus knelt and prayed. For the last time the marshal of the empire asked him if he would recant and save his life. Said Hus: "God is my witness that the evidence against me is false. I have never thought or preached except with one intention of winning men, if possible, from their sins. In the truth of the gospel I have written, taught, and preached; today I will gladly die."[274]

He was burned at the stake in the city of Constance in 1415. Even without John Hus, Bohemia was aflame with his beliefs and dedication. His followers became known as "Hussites." Their fervor had both spiritual and social consequences and they even succeeded in carrying their message into Saxony (northern Germany).

Girolamo Savanarola (1452–1498)

Not only were there voices for reform in the northern parts of Europe. As far south as Florence, Italy, Dominican monk, Girolamo (Jerome) Savanarola, began to speak out with the hopes of bringing reform to both church and state. Boldly he denounced the immorality of nobility and clergy. In part, his activities included defying the powerful Italian establishment, including Lorenzo de Medici ("Lorenzo the Magnificent") and Pope Alexander VI. A very effective orator, he gave spellbinding messages that held the attention of his hearers. At the height of his popularity, it is reported that as many as 10,000 to 12,000 at a time came to the cathedral to hear him preach. He insisted upon the authority of the Scriptures and his sermons were full of biblical content. A dominant theme in his preaching was "righteousness," as he called the City of Florence to civil and spiritual righteousness. Savanarola has been described as "the most imposing preacher of the Middle Ages and one of the most noteworthy preachers of righteousness since St. Paul."[275] In his preaching, he was not fearful of speaking out against church and civil leaders.

He gained great popularity. After the death of Lorenzo de Medici, he led an overthrow of the rest of the de Medici family, and set up what amounted to a theocratic dictatorship. He wanted to change the moral constitution of Florence which, though it had reached its cultural height, was known as a hive of wickedness and lewdness. He continued to preach his powerful messages that brought a more biblical understanding to life in Florence. Part of his reform included the "bonfires of the vanities"—a burning of lewd verses, statuary and other works of art, gaudy clothes, musical instruments, playing cards, and "other vanities."

The pope, Alexander VI, made conciliatory advances toward Savanarola to no avail. Instead, Savanarola continued to speak out vigorously against the papacy. In 1497, Savanarola was excommunicated, and Florence was placed under a "papal interdict." The interdict was a tool that has been referred to as an "ecclesiastical lockout." Though ex-communication was directed at individuals, the interdict could be aimed at a whole town, diocese, district, or entire country. It was used several times, with the innocent suffering along with the guilty. It included the suspension of the practice of public worship, including marriage and burial. Baptism and extreme unction could be performed, but only behind closed doors. It cast a gloom over a region or a country as people trembled at the thought of rejection at the last judgment and existence in hell. Savanarola was undaunted and used the situation for his advantage, calling for a general church council to depose Alexander.

Savanarola's firm grip on Florence continued until the general populace began to tire of his control. Civil and religious leaders capitalized upon the situation. Suddenly unpopular, Savanarola was seized, put through a hasty trial, brutally tortured for a week, and then hanged and burned in the public square. Philip Schaff states that he was "...the greatest preacher of his time and the most exalted moral figure since the days of John Hus and Gerson."[276] Further he observes, "He was the best man the world had seen for 200 years."[277]

A Time For "Judgment"?

John Wycliffe, John Hus, and Girolamo Savanarola are examples of men who saw the need and worked for reform in the papal church, even at the cost of their lives. There were others. If the Church of Rome was to be reformed from within, it had ample opportunities in the fourteenth and fifteenth centuries.[278] But the church refused and even fought against the earnest attempts of good men to bring back grace and truth to the church. All attempts at reform were "frustrated or repudiated."[279]

> *The value of the period lies in the demonstration it gives that reform of the papal church from within was impossible. The time of "judgment" had come.*[280]

"Judgment" upon the Roman Catholic Church would come in the form of the Protestant Reformation.

Chapter 18

The Protestant Reformation

Reform was needed in the church. There were many individuals who believed that something should be done about the unrest and dissatisfaction caused by the corruption, immorality, extreme financial demands, neglect of local parishes, and doctrinal issues. When Albert Durer wrote in his diary in 1521 about the work of Martin Luther, he stated that Luther had written more clearly than anyone in one hundred and forty years. This precise number of years was, of course, a reference to Wycliffe and Hus who were calling for reform one hundred and forty years before Luther. Another curious and interesting person who recognized a need for reform was Desiderius Erasmus. He called for a milder reform than Luther but, nonetheless, saw a clear need for changes in the church.

Disederius Erasmus (1466-1536)

Disederius Erasmus was born in Rotterdam, Holland, in 1466. He was the illegitimate son of a priest. At various times he lived in Paris, England, Switzerland, and Italy but his home was mainly in Basel, Switzerland. He was one of the great scholars of the Renaissance and Reformation period and is seen as one of the best examples of the classical spirit. He was trained in a monastery and ordained as a priest in 1492. His main area of study was literature. He became known for a best-selling series of satires, which were highlighted by *The Praise of Folly*, in which Erasmus satirized the scandalous lives of the pope and the clergy, the conditions of the monasteries, and the obscurities and superstitions of Medieval theology.

Known as a Christian humanist, Erasmus believed that the best way to reform the church was through scholarship. He wanted to renew theology by going "back to the sources"—to the study of the Bible in the Hebrew and Greek languages and to the writings of the Church Fathers. No doubt his greatest work was an edition of the New Testament in Greek with a Latin translation. Before the Reformation began, he was an open and somewhat fearless critic of the Roman Catholic Church and worked hard for reform. He was the most famous scholar of his time and did as much to prepare for reform as anyone. It has been said that "Erasmus laid the egg which Luther hatched." When the Reformation began, he remained a Catholic and became a critic of the Protestant reformers as well as the Catholic Church. Though he sympathized with Luther in his desire for reform, he could not support him in his break with the papacy and the division it created in the church. He was looking for a milder reform.

> *Erasmus had welcomed the Evangelical movement and he contributed to it both by his edition of the Greek text of the New Testament and by a variety of popular works. He was the first Humanist to earn his living by his writings, which is a measure of his influence. Nothing like his sway over the minds of his contemporaries has been seen since; not even Voltaire or Bernard Shaw approached it....*[281]

In 1524, a dispute arouse between Luther and Erasmus. In that year Erasmus wrote *The Freedom of the Will*, an attack on Luther's view of the human will. Luther believed that the human will was totally depraved, enslaved, and completely unable, apart from God's grace, to respond, to love, or serve God. Erasmus opposed Luther on the grounds that his doctrine completely relieved humans of any moral responsibility. What Luther believed to be basic to biblical understanding, Erasmus dismissed as an obscure issue.

> *The differences in the Reformation and the Renaissance lie right there, in the view of man. The Reformers preached the original sin of man and looked upon the world as "fallen" from God's intended place. The Renaissance had a positive estimate of human nature and the universe itself. This confidence in man and his powers flowered and filled the air with fragrance during the Enlightenment.*[282]

When Luther replied to Erasmus' attacks on his theology, their relationship was negatively and permanently affected. Erasmus, however, remained on good terms with Luther's colleague, Philip Melanchthon. While at Tubingen University, Melanchthon came under the influence of humanism and became a life-long admirer of Erasmus, the most noted humanist of the day.

Erasmus retained good relationships with several popes, but beginning in 1527 his writings and ideas began to fall on hard times. In that year, his teaching was condemned in Paris. Erasmus died in 1536. During the Council of Trent in 1559, his writings were placed on the *Index of Forbidden Books*.

The German Reformation (The Lutheran Tradition)

The fire that ignited the Protestant Reformation was lit in Germany. All agree that it was Martin Luther who led the way, but there were many others who joined with him in teaching and promoting certain doctrines and practices which served to build the foundations of this great movement. Three played key roles in Germany: Luther, Philip Melanchthon, and Andreas Carlstadt. All these men taught and worked together at the University of Wittenberg in the town of Wittenberg, Germany.

Martin Luther (1483-1546)

Martin Luther was born at Eisleben, Germany, on November 10, 1483, into a very modest family who could almost be classed as peasants. Though not people of means, his father, a copper miner, and his mother, insisted that their son get a good education and sent him to schools at Madgeburg, Eisenach, and then to Erfurt in 1501. Because of his father's wishes, Martin began to pursue a degree in law. He earned his bachelor's degree in 1502 at Erfurt (then considered Germany's greatest university), and three years later earned his master's degree. In 1505, when he was returning to the university from his parent's home, he narrowly escaped being struck by lightening during a severe thunderstorm. He made a vow that if God would preserve him he would become a monk. This occurred at about the same time that he was feeling a great deal of guilt for his sins, occasioned by a religious revival in that part of Europe. Two weeks later he left law school and fulfilled his vow by entering the Augustinian monastery at Erfurt. At this time, he was not quite twenty-two.

He entered the austere life of the monastery and, since he was destined for teaching, he concentrated upon the Bible, the writings of St. Augustine, and the theologians of the Middle Ages. In 1507, he was ordained a priest. At first his stay in the monastery was a respite from his feelings of guilt and despair over his sins, but soon he began again to be tormented by his fear of the wrath of God and the judgment seat of Christ. He became especially aware of his guilt when he said his first Mass, feeling completely inadequate to sacrifice upon the altar the very Savior of the world. Further, according to the teaching of the church, sins had to be recalled, confessed, and absolved one by one. Luther did all he could to find freedom from the guilt of sin. At one point, he confessed his sins for six hours straight only to leave the confessional and remember other sins. He would return to the confessional again and again until the priest hearing his confession became frustrated and actually told him to go and do something worth confessing. Later, Luther realized that even though one might confess every sin, which would seem to make him worthy of God's forgiveness, he still had a sinful nature. What could be done about this? How is one forgiven and cleansed from a nature that is stained and depraved? Experience showed that in this life the believer is never completely free from the influence of sin. When it became clear that the priest to whom he made confession did not understand why Martin had no sense of forgiveness, the thought came to Luther that maybe he was the only one in history so plagued.

In 1508, he was sent to the new university at Wittenberg and assigned a chair in biblical studies as well as responsibilities as a parish priest at the university church (which included preaching and pastoral care). In 1510, he was sent by his superiors to Rome on business and was shaken by the commercialism and ostentatious display at the Vatican. He returned to Wittenberg, and in 1512 was recognized as a doctor of Theology and continued his lectures in Bible. He embarked upon an intensive study of the Scriptures, and from the lectures he gave between 1513 and 1516 (on the Psalms, Romans, Galatians, and Hebrews), Luther became convinced that salvation was not based upon man's efforts but completely upon the work of Christ. He came to see that the justice of God—which he had feared because it seemed to mean that man only deserved punishment—was actually met when Christ bore the punishment for man's sin and made it possible for God to forgive and impute righteousness to man. The full force of this truth hit him in 1516 in the words of Galatians 3: "the just shall live by faith." He said that it was as if the gates of Paradise had opened to him. Luther was released from his haunting sense of guilt to the freedom of God's grace.

During these years, Luther's ideas gained considerable credibility at the university. His theology might have remained in academic circles had it not been for his activities as a parish priest. In his ministry as a pastor, he became aware of a practice that he thought imperiled the souls of his people: the sale of indulgences (papers that were sold which promised relief from purgatory). The sale of indulgences was probably the most abusive practice of the Middle Ages. It found its beginning in Albert of the House of Hohenzollern. At a young age, Albert was already bishop of Halberstadt and Madgeburg, and wanted to be made archbishop of Mainz and primate of Germany. The archbishop of Mainz possessed one of the seven votes in electing the Holy Roman Emperor. The fee required by the pope to install an archbishop at Mainz was very large. Albert borrowed the money from the powerful Fugger banking house in Augsburg and paid the pope in full. But he also made a special arrangement with the pope for paying back his creditors. It involved the preaching and selling of indulgences throughout his territories for eight years. He and the pope agreed to the following: half of the proceeds would go to pay off Albert's debt, the other half would go to build the Basilica of St. Peter in Rome.

One could purchase indulgences for oneself or for relatives or friends. The Dominican, John Tetzel, was put in charge of the sale of indulgences. He proclaimed immediate release from purgatory through his preaching and little jingles such as the following:

As soon as the coin in the coffer rings,
The soul from purgatory springs.

As soon as the money clinks in the chest,
A soul flies up to heavenly rest.

Another soul to heaven springs,
When in the box a shilling rings.

This was too much for Luther. At noon on October 31, 1517, he posted his *95 Theses* on the door of the Castle Church in Wittenberg. The theses were intended for academic discussion, not as a revolt against the pope or the church. As one historian wrote, "Courteously, piously, unwittingly, the Reformation had begun."[283]

The day after Luther posted his document was "All Saints Day," a day that brought people in from the surrounding areas for religious celebration. The *95 Theses* soon were printed and in about four weeks circulated throughout all of Germany. What started out as Luther's concern for indulgences turned into occasions for making known his theological discoveries, namely, that men are not saved by their own efforts but by God's grace alone.

There were varied responses to Luther's statements on indulgences and to his theology. His theses received a wide acceptance throughout Germany. The response from Rome was different. Luther had a copy of his document sent to Albert of Mainz who had a copy sent to Pope Leo X. Luther stood in great disfavor with the court of the Roman Church. For three years, members of his order, the Augustinians, and envoys from Rome, tried to get him to recant on what he had written. From this point on, a series of events took place that shaped an outcome that no one could predict:

- During the summer of 1520, the papal bull, *Exsurge Domine*, was circulated throughout Germany. It began: "Arise, O Lord, and judge thine own cause. A wild boar has invaded your kingdom." The bull, from the Latin *bulla*, which means "seal," condemned forty-one of his theses as "heretical, or scandalous, or false, or offensive to pious ears, or seductive of simple minds, or repugnant to Catholic truth."[284] The bull came into Luther's hands on October 10, along with the communication that he had a sixty-day grace period in which to respond.
- On December 10, 1520, 60 days following its reception, Luther burned the bull.
- In January 1521, the pope declared Luther a heretic and excommunicated him from the Catholic Church.
- In April 1521, the Diet of Worms was held. A diet was a church conference. The young German emperor, Charles V,

was under oath to defend the church and remove heresy from the empire. He presided over the conference. This assembly occurred in order to ask Luther to defend his writings and recant of those points inconsistent with the position of the Roman Church. It was here that Luther uttered his famous words: "My conscience is captive to the Word of God. I will not recant anything, for to go against conscience is neither honest nor safe. Here I stand. I can do no other. God help me. Amen."[285] The emperor was not impressed and declared Luther an outlaw. Luther had twenty-one days before the sentence fell. During this time he was "kidnapped" by the prince of Saxony, Duke Frederick the Wise, who was favorable to Luther and harbored him in the Wartburg Castle near Eisenach.

- Luther stayed at Wartburg for 10 months and during this time translated the New Testament into German (in about a three month period).
- Following his time at Wartburg Castle, Luther returned to Wittenberg in 1522 where, basically, he remained for the rest of his life teaching, preaching, refining the principles of the German Reformation, and building what was to become the Lutheran Church. Here he was protected, first, under the rule of Frederick the Wise, and then, under the rule of Frederick's successor, John, who was even more committed to Luther's position.
- Another important year in the life of Martin Luther and the Reformation movement was 1530. In that year, on June 25, the famous *Augsburg Confession* was read in the German language at the Diet of Augsburg. It has been said that next to October 31, 1517, this is the most memorable day in the history of Lutheranism. Catholics and Protestants (clergy and princes) gathered under Emperor Charles who presided over the council. Luther, still under the ban of

the Diet of Worms, moved to Coburg Castle on the Saxon border where he resided for six months. A four-day journey from Augsburg, he kept in touch with Melanchthon and the Protestant delegation through messengers. Here he wrote several heart-warming letters of encouragement to Philip Melanchthon. It is reported that he spent as many as three hours every morning in prayer, mostly for the proceedings at Augsburg. Apparently it was here that he wrote his most well known hymn, "Ein feste Burg is unser Gott" ("A Mighty Fortress is Our God"). His stay at Coburg also gave him opportunity to continue his Bible translation work. The outcome of the diet was disappointing to the Protestants. The Catholic response to the reading of the Lutheran document was a confutation presented by John Eck. It "insisted on transubstantiation, seven sacraments, the invocation of saints, clerical celibacy, communion in bread alone, and the Latin Mass."[286] The emperor accepted this presentation by Eck. Seeing agreement was impossible, several Protestant princes left for their homes.[287] Soon the council came to a "recess." While they did not arrive the agreement that had been hoped for at this conference, Lutheranism continued to gain ground in Germany through a series of influences—political, military, and religious. Ironically, at Augsburg, on January 18, 1537, the town council issued a decree forbidding Catholic worship, and banishing, after eight days, all who would not accept the new faith.[288] Protestantism had been established in Germany.

It had not been Luther's intention to start a new church; rather, he thought that by bringing back the purity of the gospel the church would reform itself. He believed that the Holy Spirit would lead all responsive hearts to a common belief. But this was not to be.

Though his debates with the Catholic Church began with the issue of indulgences, it soon became apparent that there were other and much deeper issues separating him from the church.

- First, was the matter of *salvation*. Indulgences were part of the entire "merit system" of the church. Men, it was declared, must "merit the merit of Christ." Luther's declaration that "the just shall live by faith" (being saved not by any merit of human work but by God's grace alone) undermined the whole merit system and the church's interpretation of salvation. Salvation did not reside in the church, but in Christ alone.
- Second was the matter of *authority*. Luther's study of the Bible had convinced him that authority did not lie in the church but in the Word of God alone. This stood in opposition to the belief that authority was in the church—long the position of the Roman Church. Pope, councils, creeds, and traditions, along with the church's interpretation of the Bible had stood as the basis for authority. Not only Luther, but other Protestants as well, declared that the Scriptures alone—*Sola Scriptura*—stood as the authority of the church of Jesus Christ.
- A third theme that developed in Luther's teaching, which was a major departure from catholic theology, was the *priesthood of all believers*. This opened the door for wider participation of laymen in worship and service of the church. Although he taught there are some who are called to serve as ministers in the churches as a vocation, he also taught that all baptized believers are priests and any might administer the sacraments.
- A fourth distinguishing mark of Luther's teaching was the issue of *vocation*. Luther taught that all Christians had callings in life, not just priests or other officers in the church. For ages, a two-tiered system based upon the idea of "holy"

and "profane," had existed in the church. Pope, bishops, priests, monks, and others who served in the church were the holy, and lay people were the profane. The holy had "callings" and the others existed to support the church and its work. Luther is known for saying that "the cobbler who cobbles well does as much for the kingdom of God as does the preacher who proclaims the Bible in the pulpit." This gave dignity to laymen in all their areas of work. Unlike the monk, who separates himself from other people, the Christian has a calling, which throws him together with others.[289] Daily work is transformed when the love of God flows through a Christian toward his neighbor.[290] This idea of calling, to Luther, worked itself out in practical and sensible ways.

> *Only look at your tools, your needle, your thimble, your beer barrel, your articles of trade, your scales, your measures, and…they shout this to your face, 'My dear, use me toward your neighbour as you would want him to act toward you with that which he has.'*[291]

This understanding of vocation helped the Christian overcome a "spiritualized Christianity," one that actually kept the believer uninvolved with his neighbor and the world, and one that demeaned normal daily activities.

> *Unlike the monks, who made prayer their first priority, Luther placed his emphasis upon work first and prayer second. Petitionary prayer must only be resorted to when all other possibilities had been tried and found incapable of helping. Only the man who has worked as hard as possible can pray with power, for he alone has a good conscience.*[292]

✧ A fifth conflict with Rome, was over the *sacraments*. In 1520, Luther wrote a tract called *The Babylonian Captivity*, a treatise on the sacraments, in which he said they (the sacraments) were held captive by the Roman Catholic Church. Following his interpretation of the Bible, Luther reduced the sacraments from seven to two. Rome taught that the seven sacraments were: baptism, confirmation, the eucharist, penance, marriage, ordination, and extreme unction (last rites). Luther said that Christ instituted only two: baptism and the Lord's Supper.

These themes emerged in Luther's teaching through the years. In 1529, he published his two catechisms: *The Lesser Catechism* and *The Greater Catechism*. By 1530, Lutheranism was firmly established in Germany and had spread to the Scandinavian countries.

Catholic services continued in Wittenberg along with Lutheran worship until 1524 when the saying of the Mass was abolished in all the churches of the city. Worship in the Lutheran churches included congregational and choral singing, proclamation of the Word of God, and the practice of the sacraments of baptism and the Lord's Supper. Luther also retained the liturgical arts: paintings, some images, and the use of the crucifix to aid piety. He loved music and composed hymns. By the end of his life he had composed more than 400 works and one hundred and twenty-five hymns. Jacques Barzun writes:

> *For 28 years, Luther preached three or four sermons every Sunday, in addition to writing innumerable tracts, Bible commentaries, translations, and the letters already mentioned. They come to 55 volumes in the English edition.*[293]

What about Luther's appearance and demeanor? Philip Schaff provides information that gives a description of Luther earlier in life and one describing him as he aged. The first comes from a description given of him at the Leipzig debates in June and July of 1519:

> *Luther is of middle stature; his body thin, and so wasted by care and study that nearly all his bones may be counted. He is in the prime of life. His voice is clear and melodious. His learning, and his knowledge of Scripture are so extraordinary that he has nearly everything at his fingers' ends… for conversation, he has a rich store of subjects at his command; a vast forest of thoughts and words at his disposal. He is polite and clever. There is nothing stoical, nothing supercilious, about him; and he knows how to adapt himself to different persons and times. In society he is lively and agreeable. He is always fresh, cheerful, and at ease, and has a cheerful countenance….*[294]

A latter description follows:

> *But in latter years he grew stout and portly. The change is characteristic of his transition from legalistic gloom to evangelical cheerfulness. He was of middle stature, had a large head and broad chest, a bold and open face without any dissimulation [dishonesty or falsity] lurking behind, prominent lips, short curly hair, and uncommonly brilliant and penetrating eyes… His countenance makes the impression of frankness, firmness, courage, and trust in God… His feet are firmly planted on the ground, as if they cannot be moved…His voice was not strong, but clear and sonorous. He was neat in dress, modest and dignified in his deportment. He exchanged the monastic gown in 1524 for the clerical robe, a gift of the Elector. He disliked the custom of the students to rise when he entered into the lecture room. "I wish," he said, "Philip would give up this old fashion. These marks of*

honor always compel me to offer a few more prayers to keep me humble...."[295]

On the evening of June 13, 1525, Martin Luther married Katherina von Bora. She was an ex-nun who had escaped from a convent, fled to Wittenberg, and had appealed to Luther for protection. To another reformation leader, she stated that she would be willing to marry him...or Martin Luther. Hearing of it, Luther, age 42 wrote, "I am ready, I believe in marriage, and I intend to get married before I die."[296] Sixteen years younger than Martin, she was described as "not remarkable for beauty or culture, but healthy, strong, frank, intelligent, and high-minded."[297] The Luthers had a loving and happy home filled with fun and activity. They had six children and, almost always, a house full of student boarders and guests along with several orphaned nieces and nephews. It was not uncommon to have anywhere from 25-40 guests for dinner. Luther referred to his wife as "Lord Katey" because of his admiration and respect for her ability to manage their home. The Elector of Saxony gave them an empty monastery in Wittenberg as a present.[298] This became their home. Luther found time to work on his vegetable patch in the cloister farm while Katey tended an orchard and their hens, ducks, pigs, and cows.[299] Martin had a "warm and humorous"[300] love for Katey and depended upon her. "I give more credit to Katherine than to Christ, who has done so much for me."[301] She "is in all things so obliging and pleasing to me."[302]

Table Talk, a popular book on the sayings of Luther, was recorded between 1531-1544 by about ten students who had sat at the family dining table. The poverty of the ministerial and academic life, coupled with the early days of marriage, caused the Luthers to take in student boarders. These students recorded 6,596 entries from conversations over the dinner table with "the good doctor." Later, these would be published as *Table Talk*. It is still available today in various forms. It covers a wide variety of subjects, both sacred and secular.

In 1546 Martin Luther died in Eisleben, the town in which he was born. Many burdens weighed upon him near the end of his life. To the daily burden of business, and the "toil of scribbling," other weights now dragged down his spirits: the roll of drums over Germany summoning recruits for the Imperial regiments enlisting against him, the voices of Protestant radicals shouting him down with arrogant confidence that they alone understood the Bible, and the memory of his beloved daughter Magdalena who had died three years ago.[303]

> *Luther had accepted an invitation to act as an arbitrator between the two counts of Mansfeld in Eisleben his birthplace some 70 miles from Wittenberg. Once there Luther's spirits seem to have revived. To Katey, whom he called playfully a "self-tormentor" because she was worrying so much about him, he wrote to say the beer was very good there. During the next few days he preached to full churches and negotiated a satisfactory settlement. After the reconciliation he sat down to a hearty dinner and enjoyed good company. Later that evening, however, he suffered a series of heart attacks and died in the early hours of 17 February 1546.*[304]
>
> *"O God," Albrecht Durer had once exclaimed when the supposed news of the reformer's death reached him, "if Luther is dead who will expound the holy Gospel so clearly to us?"*[305]

Urbanus Rhegius, the Reformer of Braunschweig-Luneburg, on his way from Augsburg to Celle, called on Luther, for the first and last time, and spent a day with him at Coburg. It was "the happiest day" of his life, and made a lasting impression on him, which he expressed in a letter:

> *I judge, no one can hate Luther who knows him. His books reveal his genius; but if you would see him face to face, and hear him speak on divine things with apostolic spirit, you would say, the living reality surpasses the fame...I, too, have written books, but compared to him I am a mere pupil. He is an elect instrument of the Holy Ghost. He is a theologus for the whole world.*[306]

The importance and magnitude of this man can be recognized from the fact that, in the 400-plus years since his death, more books have been written about him than any other figure in history, except Jesus Christ. It has been said that Luther was "the founder of Protestant civilization."[307] The theological understanding of Luther and the other Reformers led to a new way of looking at the individual, education, government, economics, arts and culture, and society in general.

Philip Melanchthon (1497-1560)

Philip Melanchthon was born in 1497 in southern Germany at the town of Bretten. He was the great nephew of John Reuchlin (1455-1522), the leading German humanist and the foremost Christian Hebrew scholar of his day. Melanchthon's name originally was Schwarzerd, German for "black earth," and was derived from the large number of blacksmiths and armorers in his family. Because of a suggestion from his great uncle, Reuchlin, he changed his name to Melanchthon, a classical Greek word which means "black earth." Philip was a prodigy. In later childhood, his parents sent him off to Latin school in Pforzheim. At age 12 he entered Heidelberg University where he received his bachelor's degree at age 14. From there, he went on to Tubingen where he earned the master's degree at age 17. He remained on the faculty at Tubingen for four years. Interestingly, he never received a doctor's degree and was never ordained into the ministry. Though he taught and developed the areas of oratory and homiletics, he never preached from the pulpit.

In 1518, he received an appointment to teach at the newly founded University of Wittenberg. There, he quickly fell under the influence of Martin Luther. He remained at Wittenberg the rest of his life even though he had opportunities to teach elsewhere. He began at a very young age to become interested in the classical languages and became skilled in Greek, Latin, and Hebrew. Before arriving at Wittenberg—while still on the faculty at Tubingen—he produced an edition of Plutarch and a Greek grammar (at age 21), which remained in use for 200 years. He was also a student of the ancient philosophers and his teaching assignments included Greek, Latin, Hebrew, philosophy, theology, astronomy, astrology, history, poetry, and medicine. Of the 100 courses he taught, only about 30 were in theology. Melanchthon has been called a humanist, a reformer, a theologian, and an educator. As a humanist, he believed that all knowledge led back to God. *"Ad fontes!"*—back to the sources, back to the origins, back to the essence of the truth, was the driving force of the sixteenth century humanists who rejected the scholastic methods and many of the conclusions of the Middle Ages. They returned to classical learning, which they believed had been corrupted by the ideas, traditions, and mystical notions of the Middle Ages.

Melanchthon became Germany's educator in the sixteenth century. Being deeply concerned about education, he organized a number of schools, revamped the German university program, set up written standards for educational institutions throughout Germany, and helped found the universities of Marburg, Konigsberg, and Jena. Because of his reform of the German schools and university system, which became models for other countries, he was given the honorary title of *Praeceptor Germanie*, which means, "Germany's Principal Teacher." It also indicates that he is considered the founder of Germany's educational system. It is not going too far to say that Melanchthon and Luther established both the language and borders of Germany. Luther's translation of the Bible into German helped develop common forms of the language that Melanchthon cultivated through education. Luther's version of the New Testament in the German tongue is regarded the foundation of the written German language. The wide variety of German dialects were pulled together to form the borders of the country.

Will Durant illustrates the differences between Melanchthon and Luther and how they complemented one another primarily due to their different dispositions and perspectives:

> *A man of small stature, frail physique, halting gait, homely features, lofty brow, and timid eyes, this intellectual of the Reformation became so loved in Wittenberg, that five or six hundred students crowded his lecture room, and Luther himself, who described him as having "almost every virtue known to man," humbly sat among his students... Luther enjoyed combat; Melanchthon longed for peace and conciliation.*[308]

Luther wrote of Melanchthon:

> *I have been born to war, and fight with factions and devils; therefore my books are stormy and warlike. I must root out the stumps and stocks, cut away the thorns and hedges, fill up the ditches, and am the rough forester to break a path and make things ready. But Master Philip walks softly and silently, tills and plants, sows and waters with pleasure, as God has gifted him richly.*[309]

Erasmus said, "Melanchthon is a man of gentle nature; even his enemies speak well of him."[310]

Philip Melanchthon was a well-liked person and was especially effective in dealing with people from the upper levels of society. He carried on correspondence with an impressive list of influential people, including Erasmus, King Henry VIII of England, King Francis I of France, the Patriarch of Constantinople, many German rulers, important theologians of varying backgrounds in different countries, and he was in constant contact with John Calvin.

Andreas Carlstadt (1480-1541)

His given name was Andreas Bodenstein but he took on "Carlstadt," the name of his birthplace in Germany. He studied at Erfurt and Cologne and then taught at the University of Wittenberg where he preceded Luther and Melanchthon. He had the privilege of awarding the doctor of theology degree to Martin Luther. Early on, he had an interest in Thomas Aquinas. At age twenty-four he joined the faculty at Wittenberg; and when he was thirty, he was appointed to the chair of Thomistic theology and philosophy. At first, he was "put off" by Luther when he showed up at the university, but later became an ardent supporter of both the man and his ideas. In actuality, Carlstadt and Luther had an up and down relationship. Part of this had to do with the fact that Luther believed that Carlstadt was not able for the tasks he took on.

Certain circumstances involving Carlstadt are noteworthy. The first of these was the Leipzig Debate. Following Luther's posting of the *95 Theses*, several debates on issues he raised took place in various locations. One of the more popular of these was the disputation at Leipzig in June and July of 1519. The topics of this debate included "papal primacy, free will, good works, purgatory, and indulgences."[311] The debate aroused great interest far and wide and lasted about three weeks. The participants were Carlstadt, Luther, and Johann (John) Eck. Eck and Luther were personal acquaintances who became adversaries as time passed. John Eck was a professor at Ingolstadt, where he distinguished himself for thirty-two years, and was a defender of traditional Catholic doctrine. The first sessions at Leipzig involved a debate between Carlstadt and Eck on free will, which the former denied and the latter defended. Carlstadt did not do well. Following this was a contest between Luther and Eck on the subject of the papacy in which Luther proved his ability against

Eck. At the end of the contest, both sides claimed victory. What the debates accomplished was to mark the progress of "Luther's emancipation from the papal system...Here for the first time he denied the divine right and origin of the papacy, and the infallibility of a general council."[312] However, at this debate Luther gained a clearer estimation of Carlstadt's abilities.

A second set of circumstances in Carlstadt's life worth noting occurred in 1521 during Luther's absence from Wittenberg. This took place when Luther was in hiding at the Wartburg Castle.

> *The somewhat unstable Carlstadt tried to turn Luther's reform efforts into a revolution, advocating abolition of confession, the elevation of the host, use of priestly garb, clerical celibacy (he himself married in 1522) and use of pictures and images. Riots broke out, with much needless destruction of church art and property. Luther returned in March, 1522, and Carlstadt left in disgrace. He lived in obscurity and occasional poverty most of the rest of his life, fulminating against Luther for a time, and then in 1530 settled in Switzerland, where he worked with the Zwinglian reformers until his death.*[313]

The Swiss Reformation

When considering the Reformation movement in Switzerland, two names stand out: Ulrich Zwingli, who led the reforms in German-speaking Switzerland, and John Calvin, who led the way in the French-speaking part of the country.

Ulrich Zwingli (1484-1531)

Ulrich Zwingli was born on New Year's Day, 1484, at Wildhaus, a town about forty miles from Zurich. His birth occurred just 52 days after Luther was born in Eisleben, Germany. He had seven brothers and two sisters, he being the third son. His father was the chief magistrate of the small alpine town whose main industry was the raising of flocks. It was there that he was brought up in the Catholic faith by his parents who were known as God-fearing people. Ulrich enjoyed his childhood as a healthy and vigorous boy, seemingly the characteristics of people from that region.

In 1494, when Ulrich was ten years old, he was sent to Basel to attend Latin school where he excelled in Latin grammar, dialectics, and music. In 1498, he entered college at Berne to study under Heinrich Wolflin who was known to be the best classical scholar in Switzerland. Following this, from 1500-1502, he studied at the University of Vienna, which had become a center of classical scholarship.

> *He studied scholastic philosophy, astronomy, and physics, but chiefly the ancient classics. He became an enthusiast for the humanities. He also cultivated his talent for music. He played on several instruments—the lute, harp, violin, flute, dulcimer, and hunting-horn—with considerable skill.*[314]

In 1502, he returned to Basel, taught Latin, and acquired the Master of Arts degree in 1506. Zwingli was ordained a priest by the bishop of Constance and was appointed pastor of Glarus, where he served for ten years, from 1506-1516. During his time in Glarus, he taught himself Greek and learned to read quite well. As a young man, he learned all of St. Paul's epistles by heart and read the church fathers. In 1516, he moved to Einsiedeln to serve as pastor of the church there. It was during his time in Glarus and Einsiedeln that he became interested in reform in the Catholic Church; thus, through his reading and studies, the foundation of his Reformed beliefs were laid. An eloquent preacher, by 1516, he began to preach against indulgences and the veneration of the virgin. Some historians see this as the beginning of the Swiss Reformation, but at this point Zwingli had no intention of separating from the Catholic Church.

In 1519, he moved to Zurich where he became pastor at the Grossmunster (Great Cathedral). There he began to preach systematically through the books of the Bible, a radical innovation at that time. This reflected the understanding that he had come to: the supreme and final authority of the Scriptures. His lectures on the New Testament in Zurich in 1519 sparked off the Reformation in Switzerland.[315] He continued to espouse his reformational ideas and, by 1525, the Reformation in Zurich was nearly complete as the Mass was replaced by a simple communion service. Amazingly, at first, he had been able to introduce reformed ideas with the approval of the Catholic Church. As late as 1523, he had received a warm letter from the pope.

With his success in reform, Zwingli was led to believe that there could be a united evangelical Switzerland. With this in mind, he formed an alliance of evangelical cantons. The Catholic cantons felt threatened and retaliated by forming their own alliance. The outcome was war; and, in 1531, Zwingli, holding the banner of the Zurich forces, was killed on the field of battle at Kappel. During his lifetime, he remained a loyal Swiss patriot. This is reflected in his translation of Psalm 23, in which he rendered the second verse: "he makes me to lie down in an Alpine meadow." Long before he met Luther, it seems that he was affected by Luther's theology, although he had difficulty recognizing Luther as the primary leader of the Reformation. Zwingli's annotated Bible (1522) shows he had read Luther's works.

During his time in Zurich, Ulrich Zwingli found himself in several controversies. First, there were the battles he fought with the Anabaptists, known as "the radicals." They opposed infant baptism, demanded a church of less formality and more lay involvement, and inclined toward extreme separatism. After several debates between Zwingli and the Anabaptists, the town government took Zwingli's side and tried to repress the Anabaptists with sickening cruelty, drowning many of them.

Also, Zwingli engaged in debate with Martin Luther over the Eucharist. At first, they carried on heated exchanges by correspondence and finally met face to face in Marburg in 1529. They managed to agree on 14 out of 15 points, disagreeing only on the mode of Christ's presence at the Lord's Table. Luther and Zwingli were never able to see eye to eye, and failed to patch up their differences; Zwingli drifted away from Lutheranism, eventually becoming part of the movement that would later be called "Calvinism."

John Calvin (1509-1564)

One might say that John Calvin and Martin Luther were the "bookends" of the Reformation. Generally, it may be said that Luther provided the spirit and John Calvin provided the theological underpinnings. The French-born Swiss reformer has been called "the greatest theologian and disciplinarian of the great race of reformers" and "the only international reformer."[316] He was born on July 10 in Noyon (Picardy), France, the son of the secretary and attorney for the bishopric of Noyon. Within five or six years of his birth, his mother died and Calvin and his brothers were left in the care of their father, who, in a short time re-married. Little is known of his step-mother. Early on, it became apparent that he would be a great scholar. According to one source, he "outstripped the others, thanks to his quick intelligence and excellent memory."[317] He first trained for law and studied at Paris, Orleans, and Bourges. During his studies, he became an admirer of Erasmus and the humanists. By the time he was twenty-three, he wrote his first book, the *Commentary on Seneca's Treatise on Clemency*, itself a humanist work. This book failed to make the impact he had hoped for.

At about the same time, he began to frequent the circles of the "evangelicals." During this stage of his life…

> …he experienced what he himself called a "sudden conversion"—an experience he refused to elaborate on except to state that God addressed him through the Bible and it had to be obeyed. Calvin from that time on was a

> *fervent Christian. Later, he adopted as his crest a flaming heart on an outstretched hand with the inscription, "My heart I give Thee, wholly and freely."*[318]

Like other evangelicals of his time, he had no intention of breaking with the Roman Catholic Church but wished for reform. In 1533, his friend, Nicolas Cop, was installed as rector of the University of Paris. Cop's inaugural address, which was influenced by Calvin's thinking, called for church reform and stirred up a controversy. Fearing for their safety, both Cop and Calvin were forced to flee from Paris. After traveling for the next three years in France, Switzerland, and Italy, Calvin finally took refuge in Basel, Switzerland, in 1536.

Calvin's theological understanding became apparent when at age twenty-six he completed his first edition of the *Institutes of the Christian Religion*. It was published in March, 1536, and contained six chapters dealing with the Commandments, the Creed, the Lord's Prayer, True and False Sacraments, and the Church. It was about three-quarters the length of the New Testament. *The Institutes* would go through several edits and enlargements until the final edition in 1559. One of the greatest single compositions of theology, this work is still studied today and has been one of the most influential contributions to literature and to western thought.

In 1536, Calvin decided to make his way to Strasbourg where Martin Bucer was leading the way in reform. There he hoped to find the quietness of the library where he could settle down to a life of scholarly studies. As he made his way to Strasbourg, he had to detour because of a war that was occurring. He hoped to spend a night in Geneva and then continue his journey the next day. He was discovered when a local gentleman recognized him, went to William Farel, the fiery reformer of Geneva, and said, "John Calvin, the writer of the *Institutes of the Christian Religion*, is here."[319] Farel went to Calvin, appealed to him to stay in Geneva, and told him that if he left, "God would curse his peace."[320] Except for a three-year banishment in Strasbourg, from 1538 to 1541, John Calvin would remain in Geneva the rest of his life until 1564.

Calvin crystallized the Reformation.[321] He had a genius for clarifying thought and ordering society.[322] From Geneva, his reputation as a theologian and Bible scholar spread. Many came to Geneva to study under Calvin and his colleagues, including John Knox, the Scottish reformer. In Geneva, Calvin preached, wrote, educated, and led the way in social matters. Though he never held a public office, Calvin influenced the whole community of Geneva. He established a strong Reformed Church in the city and worked to make the city's laws more humane, including better care for the poor and aged. He led the way in establishing a universal educational system. He taught that money was a servant of God and laid out principles for Geneva's banking system. He permitted loaning money at interest, but limited it in theory to five percent, and urged loans at no interest in certain situations. Commerce was the life of the city of Geneva and Calvin did not stand in the way of its development. He recommended state loans to finance the introduction or expansion of private industry, as in the manufacturing of clothing or production of silk.[323] The growth of commerce in Geneva promoted the emergence of a middle class. His goal was to make Geneva a Christian commonwealth. By the middle of the sixteenth century, he became the preeminent figure of the Protestant Reformation.

Laws were clear in Geneva. The difficulties of enforcement must have been extreme, for never in history had such a strict virtue been required of a city.[324] Theological and civil laws seemed to be well-understood in the city and were well-supported by leading citizens. The recurrent fear of invasion and absorption by hostile states (Savoy, Italy, France, and the Empire) compelled political stability and civic obedience; external danger promoted internal discipline.[325] It is hard to tell from reports if people idealized Geneva or if its "shining reputation" were true. Perhaps it was a little of each. Many Protestants found refuge in Geneva. One such person was

Bernardino Ochino, an Italian Protestant, who wrote the following in 1542:

> *Cursing and swearing, unchastity, sacrilege, adultery, and impure living, such as prevail in many places I have lived, are here unknown. There are no pimps and harlots…Games of chance are not customary. Benevolence is so great that the poor need not beg…Lawsuits are banished from the city.*[326]

Similarly, in 1610, Valentin Andreae, a Lutheran minister from Germany, wrote:

> *When I was in Geneva I observed something great which I shall remember and desire as long as I live. There is in that city not only the perfect institute of a perfect republic…All cursing and swearing, gambling, luxury, strife, hatred, fraud, etc., are forbidden, while greater sins are unheard of. What a glorious ornament of the Christian religion is such a purity of morals! We must lament with tears that it is wanting with us [Germans], and almost totally neglected. If it were not for the difference of religion, I would have been chained to Geneva forever.*[327]

The reputation of Geneva attracted refugees from all directions. The city leaders opened the gates of the city to people from France, Holland, Spain, Scotland, Italy, Germany, Hungary, Poland, and elsewhere. This was strategic in that, eventually, these people returned to their homelands as missionaries to spread the Gospel they learned in Geneva. In this way, Geneva became the "Rome" of the Protestant Reformation.

Calvin's banishment to Strasbourg between 1538 and 1541 was due to an opposition party that came to power during that time.

These turned out to be enjoyable and prosperous years for him. The most important event was his marriage to Idelette de Bure. She was a widow, had "several children," was poor, and was in feeble health. He and Idelette had one child, a son who died in infancy in 1542. Calvin loved his wife and they lived happily together for only nine years when she took ill and died in April, 1549. He continued as a widower the remaining 15 years of his life. Calvin died on May 27, 1564, two weeks before his 55th birthday, pulmonary tuberculosis proving to be the end of him.[328] True to his idea that the glory belongs to God alone, he was buried in such an obscure place that to this day no one knows the exact location of his grave.

> *They wrapped his body in a shroud, put it in a simple wooden box, and laid it away in the common burial ground of Plainpalais, as he requested. And since it was also his wish that there be no marker, they merely shoveled a mound of dirt over him, which has long disappeared so that no one knows for sure today where he rests. But a great crowd gathered at his funeral, and the Little Council declared in part, "God gave him a character of great majesty."*[329]

John Calvin's bodily presence was weak. He was of middle stature, dark complexion, thin, pale, emaciated, and in feeble health; but he had a finely chiseled face, a well formed mouth, pointed beard, black hair, a prominent nose, a lofty forehead, and flaming eyes that kept their lustre to the end.[330]

> *But behind the weak frame burned a mind sharp, narrow, devoted, and intense, and a firm indomitable will…His memory was crowded and yet precise…His timidity concealed his courage, his shyness disguised an inner pride, his humility before God became at times a commanding arrogance before men. He was painfully sensitive to criticism…Racked with illness, bent with*

work, he often lost his temper and broke out into fits of angry eloquence; he confessed to Bucer that he found it difficult to tame "the wild beast of his wrath." His virtues did not include humor, which might have softened his certainties…Yet he was no unmitigated kill-joy; he bade his followers be cheerful, play harmless games like bowling or quoits, and enjoy wine in moderation. He could be a kind and tender friend, and an unforgiving enemy, capable of hard judgments and stern revenge. Those who served him feared him, but those loved him most who knew him best. Sexually his life showed no fault. He lived simply, ate sparingly, fasted unostentatiously, slept only six hours a day, never took a holiday, used himself up without stint in which he thought was the service of God. He refused increases in salary, but labored to raise funds for the relief of the poor. "The strength of that heretic," said Pope Pius IV, "consisted in this, that money never had the slightest charm for him. If I had such servants my dominion would extend from sea to sea."[331]

Roland Bainton observes an interesting contrast between Calvinism and Lutheranism.

Calvinism has been credited with giving a great impetus to the spirit of capitalism because it induced men, more than Lutheranism did, to work in their callings for the glory of God—not simply diligently, but relentlessly. Business was not disparaged but was regarded as one of the callings, legitimate alike for workers and for entrepreneurs. Further, Calvinism had an ascetic aspect that endorsed using profits for philanthropy or for building up business, but not for enjoyment. Calvinism was certainly more hospitable to trade and investment than Lutheranism. Luther lived in a peasant community and had a peasant's economic outlook. Geneva, the seat of Calvinism, was on the Rhone River and had plentiful trade connections with southern France. Further, Calvin was confronted

> with the problem of finding maintenance for thousands of refugees with funds to invest…[The] industry and thrift of his followers produced wealth and eventually made of Calvinists a prosperous middle class.[332]

Other Notable Reformers in Europe

William Farel (Guillaume Farel), who lived from 1489-1565, preceded John Calvin at Geneva. As a student at Paris, Farel had studied the Bible and became sympathetic to the evangelical or Reformed position. He was a fiery preacher, more evangelistic than intellectual, who brought the Reformation to the French-speaking part of Switzerland. Farel became an outstanding pulpit personality whose sermons seemed always to make an impact on his hearers, including the cerebral John Calvin. He made a break with Rome and committed himself to the Reformed Church at Basel in 1524. In October 1536, when Calvin stopped overnight while passing through Geneva, Farel demanded that Calvin stay to help with the Reformation there. Calvin wished for a quiet life of study but Farel persuaded him to be his assistant, and then, in 1538, made him his colleague. Soon Farel was overshadowed by the mighty Calvin but had the good grace and sense to recognize Calvin's superior gifts. He remained a part of a powerful team of Reformers in Geneva and throughout Switzerland. In 1538, both Farel and Calvin were banned from Geneva for "meddling in politics." Farel accepted a call to Neuchatel and there he preached for the rest of his life. A public monument stands today in honor of the ministry he carried on in that city.

Theodore Beza (1519-1605) was successor to John Calvin at Geneva, taking over as the leader of the Reformation there. Like Calvin, he was a French-humanist law student who became a Reformer. He spent his student years writing "frivolous verse" and carousing. After a severe illness at the start of his law practice in Paris, he experienced a conversion to Christ. In 1558 he joined Calvin's congregation in Geneva, studied under Calvin, and began a brilliant teaching career in Switzerland. He willingly subordinated himself to the great reformer of Geneva and assisted Calvin in numerous capacities, especially in administrative duties. After Calvin's death, Beza became his biographer and stepped in to assume leadership of the work in Geneva. He had more of a conciliatory spirit than Calvin, which helped offset Calvin's sometimes abrasive manner and advanced the cause of Calvinism in Geneva and throughout Europe. Beza, Calvin, and Farel formed a powerful leadership at Geneva and in the Swiss Reformation.

Martin Bucer (1491-1551) became a Dominican monk but left the order after becoming acquainted with Martin Luther and his ideas. He married an ex-nun and embarked on a career as a Reformer in 1522. He settled in Strasbourg and occupied an influential position there for several years, exercising direction both in the life of the city and in the lives of fellow Reformers throughout Europe. When John Calvin was banished from Geneva in 1538, Bucer received him in Strasbourg where he remained for three years. Bucer's ideas left their mark on Calvin. Following his stay at Strasbourg, Calvin's writings began to reflect content from discussions with Bucer, including an emphasis upon God as being the one for whom all things were created, ideas on election, and an insistence upon the need for man to know and conform to God's will. Interestingly, Bucer is sometimes referred to as "the father of Calvinism." He used all of his persuasive powers to bring about unity and harmony among the Reformers. In 1531, he tried to produce a joint statement of faith among Lutherans, Zwinglians, and various Swiss Reformers, but this proved unsuccessful. In 1549, Bucer accepted an invitation from Archbishop Thomas Cranmer of England to come to Cambridge as a professor. He taught with distinction for the remaining two years of his life. While there he acted as a consultant on the revision of the *English Book of Common Prayer.* Martin Bucer died in March, 1551, and some 3,000 mourners attended his funeral. In this brief time, Bucer had seen the Reformation take root in England.

Johann Oecolampadius (1482-1531) was born in Wurttemberg, studied in Heidelberg where he came under the influence of humanism, was ordained a priest, and became a pastor in his native town. Later he entered St. Bridget's monastery near Augsburg to learn to think more clearly through prayer and meditation. While there, he read some of Luther's materials, left the monastery, and joined the Reformation cause at Basel. Oecolampadius was an outstanding Hebrew and Greek scholar and, in 1515-1516, aided Erasmus in the production of his Greek New Testament. His vigorous and effective preaching, along with his writings, singled him out as a champion of Reformation ideas. During the Lord's Supper debates, he sided with Zwingli and differed with Luther. Considered one of Germany's greatest scholars, he was respected by everyone for his cheerfulness and charity. During his ministry, he served in Basel, Baden, Berne, and Ulm as teacher and pastor.

Heinrich Bullinger (1504-1575) followed Zwingli in 1531 as the chief pastor of Zurich, after Zwingli was killed at the battle of Kappel. In contrast to his predecessor, Bullinger was more conciliatory, and in an age that was marked by strong personalities and doctrinal differences, he sought for points of unity, did not demand rigid conformity, and exhibited charity toward those who differed with him. In 1549, he collaborated with John Calvin to do a careful study of the Lord's Table, which resulted in the publication of the *Consensus Tigurinus*, a work which was read by many and had considerable influence. The work for which Bullinger is most noted is the *Second Helvetic Confession*, completed in 1566. This well-written compendium of the Reformed faith remained for centuries as the basis of the Reformed churches in the Swiss Confederation, in Geneva, and was widely known in the Reformed communities of France, England, Scotland, Poland, Hungary, and Bohemia. It has left its marks on the Presbyterian Church in America.

The Anabaptist Movement (The Radical Reformers)

Most of the Reformers saw a relationship between the church and state, and thus, supported a state church. In the end, this meant that the Christian and the citizen were one and the same. Consequently, as individuals were baptized as infants they were recognized, not only as members of the church, but also as citizens of the city and state. In each of the major thrusts of the Reformation this was true—in Wittenberg, Geneva, and Zurich. Protestantism never developed one ecclesiastical head. In each of the districts an administration was set up to administer the affairs of the church which was supported by the government of the state. In trying to give definition to the Protestant Church, the Reformers felt pressure from two sides: first, from the Catholic Church and, second, from the radical movements within Protestantism.

One of the more prominent examples of this was found in Zurich. To Ulrich Zwingli, a reformation based on the Scriptures would affect the whole religious, political, and social life of the people. One could not be separated from the others. To Zwingli, the good citizen, patriot, and Christian were one and the same. Thus, all of these were tied together in daily life. So, from the beginning, starting with one's baptism, the believer was groomed to embrace all of these areas of life. Since the state was affected by these ideas, it stood by to "enforce" this religious understanding.

Out of this milieu came the Anabaptists. Though there was much variety within the Anabaptist movement, there were several common points that identified them. These believers were more informal than the other Reformers and were, by comparison, "radical" in their beliefs and practices. They preferred to refer to themselves as "brethren," or simply, "Christians." It has been said that they were people who were centuries ahead of their time and paid a terrible price for it. As the Reformation progressed, Zwingli felt that these "radical Reformers" were more dangerous to the movement than were the Catholics. Some of the characteristics of this movement, which became thorns in the sides of the more conventional Reformers, were:

- Baptism is not for infants but only for those old enough to have made a personal and conscious commitment to Christ.
- The Bible was their only rule of faith and practice. The Reformers also agreed that the Bible was their sole authority—*Sola Scriptura*—but also respected the church fathers and the creeds.
- The "breaking of bread" is a fellowship meal in remembrance of Jesus Christ and is only for baptized believers.
- Baptized believers who are found to be in sin and refuse correction are to be banned from fellowship.
- Believers are to "separated" from the evil world, which also includes the Roman Catholic or Protestant "state churches." There is to be a separation of church and state.
- It is wrong for Christians to take oaths, pay tithes, lend money at interest, bear arms, or serve in the military.
- Pastors are to be selected on the basis of Biblical standards and they are to be men of good repute in the world.
- The magistrate's sword is ordained by God for the punishment of the wicked, but he has no right to interfere with matters of religion. In the church, the only force to be used is excommunication. Since Jesus Christ forbids violence, the Christian cannot hold public office due to the need to "wield the sword."

While the Reformers were attempting to found a popular state-church, including all the citizens and their families, the Anabaptists worked to set up independent churches on the voluntary principle, made up of baptized believers separated from the world and state.

Where Zwingli, Luther, Calvin, and others found a relationship between the Christian and society, the Anabaptists drew a hard line. The word "radical" came to be associated with the Anabaptist movement. Whereas, the other Reformers wanted "reform," the Anabaptists wanted "revolution." They wanted a complete reconstruction of the church and, for this, they were scorned and harshly dealt with by both religious and political leaders.

The Anabaptists lived at a time when the world was not ready for the kind of religious liberty and self-government they advocated. The Radical movement began in Zurich and was at its height between 1523 and 1532. During this time, many Anabaptists perished bravely as martyrs of conscience. They found no help from the other Reformers who stood by and even endorsed their sufferings and deaths. In Zurich on March 7, 1526, a law was passed that anyone found re-baptizing would be put to death by drowning. Felix Manz, one of the leaders of the movement in Zurich, was the first Anabaptist martyr, drowned in the River Limmat, which flows through the city. At the Diet of Speyer (in Germany) in 1529, Anabaptism was declared a heresy by both Catholics and Protestants, and called for every court in Christendom to condemn the heretics to death. It has been observed that Catholics burned them and Protestants drowned them. During these years, between 4,000-5,000 Anabaptists were put to death by fire, water, and sword. It should be pointed out that Martin Luther was one of the more tolerant toward the Anabaptists. Though he opposed their doctrine, thinking much of it to be heretical, he disapproved of the cruel treatment to which they were subjected. However, due to his fear of anarchy, in 1531 he agreed to the death penalty for Anabaptists, not because of heresy, but because of sedition. Luther had a high regard for civil authority.

It is important to remember that within the Anabaptist movement there was a wide variety of expression: from the more radical to the more conservative, from the more rational to the more spiritual approach of the "inner light" Anabaptists who relied on special private revelations. The Anabaptists sprang up in Switzerland,

Germany, and Holland. Some of the more well-known leaders of the movement in Zurich were Conrad Grebel, Felix Manz, Georg Blaurock, and Ludwig Hatzer. The radical movement made its way into Wittenberg through the "Zwickau prophets," that included Gabriel Zwilling, Nicolas Storch, Marcus Thomas Stubner, and others. This group was given over to mysticism along with their desire for a radical reform. They made claims of visions, dreams, direct communications with God and the angel Gabriel, and spoke of the near approach of a democratic millennium. Although he was not the founder of the movement in Holland and northwest Germany, Menno Simons was a moderate and respected Anabaptist. He became "the father" of the Mennonites.

Basically, three groups emerged from this movement. First, the Swiss Anabaptists, who survived by retreating to the mountains of Switzerland. From this group, came the Amish who later established colonies in Pennsylvania and various places in the midwestern United States. Second, the Mennonites continued to survive, and today can be found in the United States as well as Holland, Russia, and South America. Third, the Hutterites, named for Jacob Hutter, established colonies in Moravia, Transylvania, and in the United States. Today's distant relatives of the Anabaptists include Baptists, Quakers, and in some sense, Congregationalists. In another sense, they are forerunners of all American Protestants because of their belief in the separation of church and state.

The Reformation in England

The Reformation took on a different look in England. The movement was characterized by progress and retreat due to various political matters, the differing attitudes of successive English rulers, and the conservatism of the English people.

In one respect, reform in England began over a royal problem rather than theological issues. The movement was given help when Henry VIII broke from Rome because the pope would not sanction an annulment of his marriage to Queen Catherine of Aragon, who had given him but one child, a girl, the princess Mary. After 18 years of marriage to Catherine, he secretly married Anne Boleyn and had an English church court declare his marriage to Catherine null and void. When the pope countered by excommunicating him, Henry realized that papal authority in England had to be overthrown, and then began to do what he could to see that this would happen. Henry VIII reigned from 1509-1547. Under the young Edward VI, who had a short reign (1547-1553), there was significant progress in reform. Thomas Cranmer exercised leadership during his reign, aiding in the establishment of the Anglican Church and development the *Common Prayer Book*, rich in thought and speech. Regression occurred when Queen Mary (1553-1558), an extreme Roman Catholic, followed Edward VI. She fought to bring her subjects back to the Catholic Church and used persecution as a means. During her five-year reign about 300 Protestants were martyred. Protestant reform was once again encouraged when Queen Elizabeth (1558-1603) came to the throne. Thought by many to be the greatest of the English sovereigns, she opened prisons to set falsely accused prisoners free, exiles were recalled, and she restored the Bible to a place of prominence in both pulpits and homes. The Church of England was re-established to take the form in which it has continued to exist to the present day.

Thomas Cranmer (1489-1556) is usually regarded the leader of the English Reformation because he was the first Protestant at the head of the English Church. Early on, he gained favor in the eyes of King Henry VIII for his suggestion that the question of the king's divorce be studied by the universities of Europe. He served the king in a number of ways and was appointed Archbishop of Canterbury in 1533. Cranmer assisted the king in turning the English Church's allegiance from the pope to Henry. Changes were made in the liturgy, a new creed was written, and an English translation of the Bible was installed in each parish. After Queen Mary ("Bloody Mary"), who was highly favorable to Roman Catholicism, came to the throne, Cranmer was deposed from his archbishopric, imprisoned, and later burned at the stake.

William Tyndale (1494-1536) was a significant leader in the English Reformation. He was driven by a great desire to put the English Bible in the hands of the common man. After studying at Oxford and Cambridge, he was forced to flee from England to the Continent to live, work, and begin his labor to get the Bible printed in English. In 1524, he began working on his translation at Wittenberg, Germany, where he met Martin Luther. In 1526, he began smuggling the first copies of his English translation of the Bible into his homeland. Constantly harassed, threatened, and pursued, he worked in several different cities. In 1534, he published Bibles at Worms, Germany. Attempts were made to stop these efforts and arrest him. To save his life, he sought refuge in Marburg where he began work on the Old Testament, completing the first five books. In secret, he moved to Antwerp, Belgium, seeking safety and a place to work quietly. He was turned in by an English informer and arrested near Brussels in 1535. In 1536, he was condemned for heresy, brutally strangled, and burned. His memorable last words were, "Lord, open the King of England's eyes."

The Reformation in Scotland

The Reformation was not quick to catch hold in Scotland. The land was secure under the hands of the Catholic Cardinal Beaton and Queen Mary of Guise. But a series of events unfolded that opened the door for reform. The cardinal was murdered, the queen died, and John Knox entered the land. The story of reform in Scotland is about John Knox.

John Knox (1505-1572) was born in the Scottish lowlands in or about 1505 and was educated at the University of St. Andrews. He studied for and was ordained to the priesthood. Due to political and religious unrest, Knox experienced a number of unusual circumstances. About the time he was forty-two years old, around the year 1547, he began to embrace the ideas of reform. He was made a prisoner with other Reformers and, after serving 19 months as a galley slave, he settled in England (then under the rule of Protestants at the beginning of Edward VI's reign). There he served as a royal chaplain. When Catholic Queen Mary came to the throne in 1553, Knox fled and found refuge in Geneva where John Calvin was leading the Reformation. There, he learned from Calvin and became convinced of his theology and form of church government. In 1559, he returned to Scotland and became more or less the absolute ruler in reforming both the religious and the political shape of the country. John Knox was not only founder of Scottish Presbyterianism, but also is recognized as "The father of Scotland."

> *A modest unassuming man personally, Knox's grave today appropriately is marked merely by small initials on a paving stone in Edinburgh's High Street. He is honored as the man who influenced not only the faith, but character of the Scottish nation more than any other in Scottish history.*[333]

The Force of the Protestant Reformation

> *At the opening of the sixteenth century, the only church in western Europe was the Roman Catholic, apparently secure in the loyalty of every kingdom. Before the end of that century every land of northern Europe west of Russia had broken away from Rome and had established its own national church.*[334]

The Results

The results of the Reformation were profound and affected the entire western world. Reformation thought spread through Germany, Switzerland, Holland, parts of France and Belgium, the Scandinavian countries, England and Scotland, Colonial America,

Australia and New Zealand. Its effects were many and widespread. Francis Schaeffer wrote:

> *Let us emphasize again that the Reformation was no golden age; and our eyes should not turn back to it as if it were to be our perfect model. People have never carried out the biblical teaching perfectly…The Reformation did not bring social or political perfection, but it did gradually bring forth vast and unique improvement.*[335]

The obvious result of the Reformation was a return to a theology based upon the Bible. Life and practice in the church found a basis in biblical theology. The Reformers produced new works of theology based in the Scriptures. They wrote comprehensively, clearly, and produced materials for the general public. They accepted the Bible as the Word of God with the belief that it spoke to all areas of life. Their biblical understanding was applied to all elements of culture.

> *Luther kept addressing the Germans on every issue of religious, moral, political, and social importance. Pamphlets, books, letters to individuals that were "given to the press" by the recipients, biblical commentaries, sermons, and hymns kept streaming from his inkwell. Disciples made Latin translations of what was in German and vise versa…A torrent of black-on-white wordage about the true faith and the good society poured over Christian heads. It did not cease for 350 years: 1900 was the first year in which religious works (at least in England) did not outnumber all other publications.*[336]

Another outcome of the Reformation was more biblically based preaching. It was important that the actual texts of the Bible be developed by ministers. Sermons were generally longer, expository in nature, and practical in application. Reformers believed that the Bible spoke to all areas of life and this was reflected in their teaching.

Another area affected by Reformation thought was art. Much of the art from this period reveals biblical content and a biblical understanding about life. Dutch Reformation art is one of the high points in the history of art. With a proper understanding of man and his world, art was promoted and poured forth during this time. Examples found in men like Lucas Cranach, Albrecht Durer, Altdorfer, Hans Baldung-Grien, Hans and Barthel Beham and, of course, Rembrandt, should remind us of the great work that came from this period. All of these men, and others with them, were Reformational in their orientation and their work reveals it.

Music was a major contribution of the Reformation. The Reformers brought singing back to the congregations, enabling them to sing again for the first time in centuries, and promoted music throughout culture. The church led the way and encouraged the development of different styles of music.

> *There was the lively Geneva Psalter, the 1562 hymnbook made up of the Psalms. The tunes were so vivacious that some people in derision called them "Geneva Jigs." The great Theodore Beza, who followed Calvin as leader of the Reformation in Geneva, translated the Psalms' texts, and these were set to music by Louis Bourgeois. Later this Psalter was used in England, Germany, the Netherlands, and Scotland, as well as in Switzerland. But it was in Luther's Germany where the effects of the Reformation on music are best seen.*[337]

Creating "wholesome" songs, and, it is alleged, at times borrowing tunes from the culture, Luther and his colleagues were quite innovative in creating a wide range of music. Luther wrote: "I am not of the opinion that all the arts shall be crushed to the earth and perish through the Gospel, as some bigoted persons pretend, but would willingly see them all, and especially music, servants of Him who gave and created them."[338] Along with his translation of the Bible into the German language and his published sermons and pamphlets, Luther also provided a hymnbook that contained several of his compositions.

> *I have no use for cranks who despise music, because it is a gift from God, he wrote. Next to the Word of God only music deserves to be extolled as 'mistress and governess' of the feelings of the human heart.*[339]

One cannot speak of the Reformation's influence in the realm of music without mentioning Johann Sebastian Bach (1685-1750). There were other composers, as well, but certainly his work represents the zenith of the music at that time, perhaps of all time.

> *His music was a direct result of the Reformation culture and the biblical Christianity of the time, which was so much a part of Bach himself. There would have been no Bach had there been no Luther. Bach wrote on his score initials representing such phrases as: "With the help of Jesus"—"To God alone be the glory"—"In the name of Jesus." It was appropriate that the last thing Bach the Christian wrote was "Before Thy Throne I Now Appear."*[340]

With a return to biblical Christianity, a new political freedom was brought to the world. Reformation thought laid a basis for the development of law in the western world.

> *The Reformation did not bring social or political perfection, but it did gradually bring forth a vast and unique improvement. What the Reformation's return to biblical teaching gave to society was the opportunity for tremendous freedom, but without chaos. That is, an*

individual had freedom because there was a consensus based upon the absolutes given in the Bible, and therefore real values within which to have freedom, without these freedoms leading to chaos. The world had not known anything like this before.[341]

The idea of constitutional government grew out of Reformation thought. Following in the stream of the Reformation thinkers, Samuel Rutherford (1600-1661) wrote his influential book, *Lex Rex*, which means "Law is King." As a result of this thinking, the ordinary citizen would find protection and freedom from the arbitrary or whimsical rule of a sovereign. It would eventually mean that even the King himself was accountable. Rutherford's work had a direct influence on the writing of the United States Constitution, as well as other documents of governance throughout the western world.

The biblical understanding that came from the Reformation provided for a system of checks and balances.

The Reformers were not romantic about man. With their strong emphasis upon the Fall, they understood that since every person is indeed a sinner there is a need for checks and balances... Each Reformation country showed the practice of checks and balances in different forms. Switzerland (whose national political life was shaped by the Reformation tradition even though not all its cantons followed the Reformation) is especially interesting in this regard. Since the mid-nineteenth century, the Swiss have separated geographically the legislative and executive parts of government from the judiciary, placing the former in Bern, the latter in Lausanne. In Great Britain came the checks and balances of a king, two Houses of Parliament, and the courts. Today the monarch has less authority than when the division of power was made, but the concept of checks and balances continues. The United States has a slightly different arrangement, but with the same basic principle. The White House covers the executive administration; Congress, in two balanced parts, is the legislative; the Supreme Court embodies the judiciary. In the Reformation countries, there was a solution to the "form" or "chaos" problem in society.[342]

Present day economics finds a connection to the Reformation. In Geneva, John Calvin taught that money was the servant of God and should be used for the good of society. He laid out biblical principles on economics and encouraged well-organized banking systems, investing, saving, and lending money at interest. These ideas have been carried over into our modern western world with great benefit.

Wherever the Reformers traveled, schools were born. They revived education and established it on a biblical understanding. Beginning in Germany, with the work of Philip Melanchthon, and spreading through the other countries of the Reformation, great institutions were born. For centuries, these schools operated upon the foundations provided by the biblical absolutes born in the Reformation. This does not mean that they studied the Bible only. While the basis was religious, their content was the liberal arts. Though many were prepared as clergy, education became wider and prepared people for cultural participation. Luther wrote to the civil leaders in Germany:

> *If I had children and could manage it, I would have them study not only languages and history, but also singing and music together with the whole of mathematics....The ancient Greeks trained their children in these disciplines... they grew up to be people of wondrous ability, subsequently fit for everything.*[343]
>
> *Calvin was similarly committed to the liberal arts. In his academy at Geneva, of the twenty-seven weekly lectures, three were in theology, eight in Hebrew and the Old Testament, three in ethics, five in Greek orators*

and poets, three in physics and mathematics, and five in dialectic and rhetoric. Texts included works by Virgil, Cicero, Ovid, Livy, Homer, Aristotle, Plato, and Plutarch.[344]

It has already been mentioned that Philip Melanchthon was considered a humanist; that is, a man given to liberal learning. The idea of liberal learning was promoted and secured under the protection of a biblical umbrella.

> *The humanist movement in Germany was at first— and after its flirtation with Luther—more orthodox in theology than its Italian counterpart. Germany had no classical past like Italy's; she had not had the privilege of being conquered and educated by Imperial Rome; she had no direct bond with non-Christian antiquity. Her memory hardly went beyond her Christian fathers; her Renaissance was a revival of early Christianity rather than of classical letters and philosophy. In Germany the Renaissance was engulfed in the Reformation.*[345]

In large measure, it was out of the Reformation that the western world was educated. Their integration in education was due to their view of truth. They believed God was the source of all truth in all the disciplines.

The Catholic Counter-Reformation

The strength of the Protestant Reformation of the 16th century can be seen in the response of the Roman Catholic Church. Not long after the Reformation began, a major effort was made by Rome to regain lost ground and subvert the work of the Protestants. Much of the Catholic world had been asking for a council from the time Luther appeared at the Diet of Worms. Many within Catholicism sensed a need for reform, and for statements clarifying the beliefs and practices of the Roman Church. The young emperor, Charles

V, concerned over the religious divisions in Europe, made repeated efforts to get the popes to convene a council.

The Council of Trent (1545-1563)

Finally, reform in the Catholic Church was sought through the Council of Trent, which met in several sessions from 1545-1563. It was the longest church council ever convened. The council was called by Pope Paul III, to examine and condemn the errors promulgated by Luther and the other Reformers, and to reform the discipline of the church. It actually met in more than one place, though mainly in the city of Trent, in Austria, about 75 miles northwest of Venice, Italy. It lasted through the reigns of five popes (Paul III, Julius III, Marcellus II, Paul IV, and Pius IV) and under two emperors (Charles V and Ferdinand). All the bishops and abbots of the church were invited. At the opening, there were only 34 participants at a time when there were about 500 bishops in the Catholic Church. During the several meetings of the council, the number grew to a total of 237 participants by the last sessions. An over-arching hope was that the chasm between Catholics and Protestants could be bridged, and Christianity reunited, but this was not to be. However, many reforms were brought about, the doctrines of the Catholic Church were more clearly defined, and a mighty effort followed to promote Catholic missions in foreign lands. Many Protestant scholars believe that the popes since the Council of Trent have been better than most before. The net result was a conservative reform within the Roman Catholic Church.

The Results

The first series of sessions, between 1545-1547, were directed toward several doctrinal questions. The outcome included the following:

The council declared that it was not the Bible alone that served as authority for the church, but the canonical Scriptures along with the Apocrypha (in the Latin Vulgate prepared by Jerome), and the creeds and traditions of the church, all of which constituted final authority. Martin Luther and the other reformers had said that final authority for the church was *sola Scriptura*—"the Bible alone!"

With regard to the doctrine of justification, the council declared that humans were made right before God by faith plus subsequent works rather than by faith alone. The reformers taught that justification was *sola fide*—"by faith alone!"

The third action of the council in the first sessions was a reaffirmation of the seven sacraments. Catholic theology taught that the seven were: baptism, confirmation, the Eucharist (mass), penance, marriage, ordination (orders), and extreme unction. The Protestants had reduced the number to two: baptism and the Lord's Supper. Clearly, the conclusions from the Council of Trent were a response to the Protestant position. The decree read as follows:

> *If anyone says that the sacraments of the new law were not all instituted by Jesus Christ, or that there are more or less than seven, or that any of the seven is not truly and strictly speaking a sacrament, let them be anathema.*[346]

During the second series of sessions, 1551-1552, the dogma of transubstantiation was reaffirmed. The Reformers had denied the doctrine of transubstantiation and put a variety of other interpretations on the Lord's Supper. To this the Catholic Church responded forcefully. From the thirteenth session, October 11, 1551, with 54 voters present, the following is stated:

> *If anyone denies that in the venerable sacrament of the Eucharist the whole Christ is contained under each species, and in each separate part of each species, let them be anathema.*[347]

During this second series of meetings, other important decisions were made. The translation of the Bible was forbidden and it was placed on "the index of forbidden books." Of course, the Protestant reformers had been busy translating the Bible into the common languages of the people. The Bible was first forbidden to the people and put on "the index" by the Council of Valencia (in Spain) in 1229. The decree reads as follows:

> *We prohibit also the permitting of the laity to have the books of the Old and New Testament, unless any one should wish, from a feeling of devotion, to have a Psalter or breviary for divine service, or the hours of the blessed Mary. But we strictly forbid them to have the above mentioned books in the vulgar tongue.*[348]

The "psalter" was the Book of Psalms that we find in the Old Testament and the "breviary" was a small book of devotions (which had to be in Latin) written by the Catholic Church. The Council of Trent reaffirmed the decree from the Council of Valencia and further prohibited the use of the Scriptures by any member of the church unless he obtained special permission from a superior. The statement from the Council of Trent reads as follows:

> *In as much as it is manifest, from experience, that if the Holy Bible, translated into the vulgar tongue, be indiscriminately allowed to everyone, the temerity of men will cause more evil than good to arise from it; it is, on this point, referred to the judgment of bishops, or inquisitors, who may, by the advice of the priest or confessor, permit the reading of the Bible translated into the vulgar tongue by Catholic authors, to those persons whose faith and piety, they apprehend, will be augmented, and not injured by it; and this permission they must have in writing.*[349]
>
> *Even as late as 1816, Pope Pius VII issued a Bull against Bible societies, making it clear that "the Bible printed by heretics is to be numbered among other prohibited books, for it is evident from experience that the Holy Scriptures, when circulated in the vulgar tongue*

> have, through the temerity of men, produced more harm than benefit." And a Catholic priest, even later than that, remarked publicly that "he would rather a Catholic should read the worst works of immorality than the Protestant Bible, that forgery of God's Word."[350]

In the final sessions between 1562-1563, discussions took place concerning the other sacraments—rules concerning marriage, issues concerning purgatory, the priesthood, and other matters of reform. Some of the statements of affirmation are as follows:

On the Mass, in the twenty-second session, September 17, 1562, with 183 voters present:

> *If anyone says that the rite of the Roman Church in which part of the canon and the words of consecration are recited in a low voice, must be condemned, or that the mass may only be celebrated in the vulgar tongue, let them be anathema.*[351]

On the priesthood, in the twenty-third session, July 15, 1563, with 237 voters present:

> *If anyone says that there is no visible and external priesthood in the New Testament, or that there is no power to consecrate, to offer the true body and the true blood of the Lord and to forgive or retain sins, but only a function and a simple ministry of the preaching of the Gospel; or that those who do not preach are no longer priests, let them be anathema.*[352]

Of course, emphasized in the teaching of all the reformers was the priesthood of the believer—that there is not a special class of priests, but that all believers are priests.

On marriage, in the twenty-fourth session, November 11, 1563, with 231 voters present:

> *If anyone undertakes to contract marriage other than in the presence of the parish priest or some other priest authorized by the parish priest…and before two or three witnesses, the Holy Council declares them absolutely incompetent to make a contract of this kind and declares that such contracts are null and void.*[353]

No council in the history of the church had ever accomplished so much. It lasted the longest, issued the largest number of dogmatic decrees, and produced the most benefits for the Catholic Church. To this day, many of the decisions made at the Council of Trent still hold in the Catholic faith. One cannot study the Catholic Church, nor understand its present state, without studying this council. It can also be observed that it was the Protestant Reformation which gave impetus to the Catholic Church to face its own failings and improve its theology, practices, and disciplines.

The Jesuits

A powerful instrument of influence in the Counter-Reformation was found in the Order of the Jesuits, also known as "The Society of Jesus." The order emphasized preaching by well educated monks which became a positive means for spreading Catholic teaching, especially that which was clarified at the Council of Trent. Founded by Ignatius Loyola (1491-1556) in 1540, the main functions of the organization were education, fighting heresy, and foreign missions.

Ignatius Loyola was born into a wealthy, aristocratic family. When old enough he became a soldier and learned and appreciated the disciplines of military life. In 1521, his leg was severely wounded in a battle against the French and he was forced into a long period of recuperation. During his time of recovery in a hospital, he began to read and study religious literature, which resulted in a spiritual experience in 1522. This led him to dedicate his life to the service of God and the church. He began a period of intense discipline and study, including a trip to the Holy Land, the writing of his famous *Spiritual Exercises*, and absorbing an enormous amount of education between 1528 and 1535 at the University of Paris. While at the university, he joined with six other outstanding young male scholars to form a highly disciplined military unit. Their goals included developing strict spiritual disciplines, maintaining purity and chastity, practicing unquestioning obedience to superiors, and fighting heresy. These seven young men won the approval of Pope Paul III in 1540 to form the Society of Jesus.

The principle purpose of the Order of the Jesuits was to fight the Protestant movement with methods "both open and secret." During the times of Inquisition, heretics could be punished several ways. The Roman Inquisition was established by a papal bull of Paul III in 1542 and was intended to deal with heresy anywhere.

> *Those accused were always presumed guilty till they proved their innocence; they were never confronted with their accusers; they could be made to testify against themselves; and they could be tortured to extract a confession. If sentenced, they were punished by a loss of property, or imprisonment, or burning at the stake, unless they confessed and recanted. These punishments were carried out by the secular authorities, under the watchful eye of the inquisitors.*[354]

The intensity of the times and the direction of these efforts against the Protestants are illustrated in the instructions of Ignatius of Loyola to Peter Canisius, the emperor's advisor:

> *Once a man has been convicted of heretical impiety or is strongly suspect of it, he has no right to any honour or riches: on the contrary, these must be stripped from him. To make a few examples by condemning some to death*

> *or exile along with confiscation of their goods, will show that one is taking religious affairs seriously… If public professors or administrators at the University of Vienna or other universities have a bad reputation in relation to the Catholic faith, they must be deprived of their degrees.*
>
> *All heretical books must be burned or sent beyond all the provinces of the kingdom. This is appropriate treatment for the productions of heretics, even if their content is not heretical, as with the grammar, rhetoric, or dialectic of Melanchthon. It is necessary to be able to exclude them as a sign of antipathy to the heresy of their author.*[355]

Through their preaching, large portions of Germany were won back to Catholicism. The Jesuit order became so powerful, and so severe, that at times it was opposed even by the Catholic Church. In 1773, Pope Clement XIV forbade the operation of the order throughout the church. It continued in secret and then was again recognized and reorganized in 1814 by the pope. Since that time, it has continued as one of the most potent forces for the Catholic Church throughout the world, leading the way in education and missionary activity.

The Council of Trent is considered pivotal and highly important in the history of the Catholic Church. Its clarification and restatements of Catholic doctrines and practices continues to influence and guide the Catholic Church today.

CHAPTER 19

The Age of Reason and Revival: 1700 - 1870 AD

From its beginnings, the Protestant Reformation continued its influence in the western world, especially in northern Europe, England, and in Colonial America. Though its influence remained powerful over a long period of time and in different places, it would be challenged by a movement that began in France in the early 18th century, known as "The Enlightenment." In the Reformation, faith and reason had proved a good marriage. In the Enlightenment faith would be left behind in favor of reason alone. From the period of the Enlightenment, two influential streams would flow together in western culture: the ideas of the Reformation and the ideas of the Enlightenment.

The Enlightenment

On November 10, 1793, in the city of Paris, an amazing event took place in Notre Dame Cathedral that was meant to present a visual demonstration of the triumph of reason.

> *For over six hundred years, from the time this magnificent gothic structure began to be constructed in the mid-twelfth century, it served as a symbol for the Christian identity of the nation. But now in the enthusiasm of revolution the cathedral had been renamed the Temple of Reason. A papier-mâché mountain with Greco-Roman motifs stood in the nave. Historian Simon Schama describes what happened next: "Liberty (played by a singer from the Opera), dressed in white, wearing the Phrygian bonnet and holding a pike, bowed to the flame of*

> Reason and seated herself on a bank of flowers and plants." This inverted "worship service" was a high point in the French Revolution's program of de-Christianization, whereby leaders of the Revolution attempted to throw off what they felt to be the heavy, dead hand of the church. In Paris, the revolutionaries renamed 1,400 streets in order to eliminate references to saints as well as monarchs. Priests, bishops, and other religious leaders were forced to leave their posts.[356]

There is no question that the efforts made were intended to free France from the religion that had been established there for centuries. The event of raising the "Goddess of Reason" stood as a statement, and remains a symbol of what was perceived as a victory, in the Age of Enlightenment. Other "temples of Reason" were established in other French cities. To make their outlook clear, the French changed the calendar and called 1792 "the year one," and destroyed many of the things of the past, even suggesting the destruction of the cathedral at Chartes.[357]

Also called the Age of Reason, the Age of Enlightenment…

> …was so named for an exultant intellectual movement that shook the foundations of Western civilization. In championing radical ideas such as individual liberty and an empirical appraisal of the universe through rational inquiry and natural experience, Enlightenment philosophers in Europe and America planted the seeds for modern liberalism, cultural humanism, science and technology, and laissez-faire capitalism.[358]

Roughly, the dates for the Age of Enlightenment might extend from the 1680s to the 1790s. Some, wishing to be more technical, set the dates from 1720-1780 since much of the philosophical formation took place during that period.

> *The beginnings are marked in Britain by the Glorious Revolution in 1688, which provided a constitutional arrangement repudiating Stuart aristocracy and ushering in religious toleration, as well as by the writings of Locke and the publication in 1687 of Newton's Principia. The French beginnings are signaled by the Revocation of the Edict of Nantes in 1685 and the writings of Bayle and Fontonelle. The end of the Enlightenment is best linked to the realization of its ideals in the revolutionary fervor that swept through America, France, and even England in the last quarter of the eighteenth century.*[359]

The French Revolution (1787-1799) came at the end of the Enlightenment period. These were times of significant change in Europe. Commerce and industrialization were bringing major changes to the western world and, with them, the emergence of the middle class. Theirs was also an age of increasing literacy, as for the first time in history reading ceased to be a monopoly of the very few, the rich, and the clergy.[360] It was also an age when intellectuals eagerly wrote for and to this wider audience of new readers.[361] Revolution came in France because censorship by state or church was so strong that the imprisoned mind could expand only by the violent destruction of its bonds.[362]

> *Tensions before the beginning of the Revolution in 1789 were manifold. Strain existed between political form (absolute monarchy) and political reality (the power of the king checked on every side by the hereditary privileges of nobles, corporations, and the Roman Catholic Church). Intellectual strain grew out of the tension between the traditional authoritarianism of Catholic Church and monarchial rule, on the one hand, and, on the other, a surging confidence in human reason and human capabilities (exemplified in different ways by Voltaire [1694-1778], the philosophers who published the great Encyclopedia between 1751 and 1780, and the brilliant*

eccentric Jean-Jacques Rousseau [1712-1778]). Social strain divided aristocrats from a rising "middle class" of commercial interests and both of those groups from a large peasant sector, which, although very poor, was required to bear the heaviest taxes.[363]

Though from a historical point of view the Enlightenment had a short duration, its effects remain to this day.

In a short essay written in 1784, Immanuel Kant asked the question, "What is Enlightenment?" In his essay, he states the Enlightenment's creed, *Sapere aude*!—"Dare to know!"

> *Enlightenment is man's release from his self-incurred tutelage. Tutelage is man's inability to make use of his understanding without direction from another. Self-incurred is this tutelage when its cause lies not in lack of reason but in lack of resolution and courage to use it without direction from another. Sapere aude! "Have courage to use your own reason"—that is the motto of the enlightenment...It is so easy not to be of age. If I have a book, which understands for me, a pastor who has a conscience for me, a physician who decides my diet, and so forth, I need not trouble myself. I need not think, if I can only pay—others will readily do the irksome work for me.*[364]
>
> *For this enlightenment, however, nothing is required but freedom...It is freedom to make public use of one's reason at every point.*[365]

Religion was understood to be the major oppressor. It was seen to promote mysticism, superstition, and prevented the use of the mind. Kant continues:

> *I have placed the main point of enlightenment—the escape of men from their self-incurred tutelage—chiefly in matters of religion because our rulers have no interest in*

playing guardian with respect to the arts and sciences and also because religious incompetence is not only the most harmful but also the most degrading of all.[366]

Alexis de Tocqueville, who lived from 1805-1859, wrote:

> *In France…Christianity was attacked with almost frenzied violence, there was no question of replacing it with another religion. Passionate and frenzied efforts were made to wean men away from the faith of their fathers, but once they had lost it, nothing was supplied to fill the void within…There is no question that the nation-wide discredit of all forms of religious belief which prevailed at the end of the eighteenth century had a preponderant influence on the course of the French Revolution. This was, in fact, it's most salient characteristic, and nothing did more to shock contemporary observers.*[367]
>
> *The spirit of the Age of Reason was nothing less than an intellectual revolution, a whole new way of looking at God, the world, and one's self. It was the birth of secularism. The Middle Ages and the Reformation were centuries of faith in the sense that reason served faith, the mind obeyed authority. To a Catholic it was church authority; to a Protestant biblical authority, but in either case God's Word came first, not man's thoughts. Man's basic concern in this life was his preparation for the next. The Age of Reason rejected that. In place of faith it set reason. Man's primary concern was not the next life, but happiness and fulfillment in this world; and the mind of man, rather than faith, was the best guide to happiness—not emotions, or myths, or superstitions. The spirit and purpose of the Enlightenment were eloquently expressed by one of its spokesmen, Baron von Holbach, who wrote: "Let us endeavor to disperse those clouds of ignorance, those mists of darkness, which impede man on his journey…which prevent his marching through life with a firm and steady step. Let us try to inspire him…*

> with respect for his own reason—with inextinguishable love of truth...so that he may learn to know himself... and no longer be duped by an imagination that has been led astray by authority...so that he may learn to base his morals on his own nature, on his own wants, on the real advantage of society...so that he may learn to pursue his true happiness, by promoting that of others...in short, so that he may become a virtuous and rational being, who cannot fail to become happy.[368]

Though often associated with and located in France, the Enlightenment was a worldwide movement. Many important names are connected with its thought and influence, including: Francis Bacon, John Locke, and Isaac Newton as influencers; and Voltaire, Rousseau, Montesquieu, Condorcet, Diderot, Turgot, D'Alembert, Condillac, Helvetius, Holbach, Thomas Jefferson, Benjamin Franklin, Thomas Paine, and James Madison as contributors.

> *The Enlightenment was an international movement that included French, English, Scottish, American, German, Italian, Spanish, and even Russian schools. Voltaire and Montesquieu visited England and wrote extensively about its institutions. Franklin and Jefferson visited England and France and were well connected with writers in both countries. The intellectual ferment was transnational.*[369]

It is appropriate, therefore, to speak of the German Enlightenment, the British Enlightenment, the Scottish Enlightenment, and the American Enlightenment, as well as the French Enlightenment.

A group in France, known as *philosophes,* were influential in promoting the ideas of the Enlightenment, especially through their 17 volume *Encyclopedie*. Dennis Diderot (1713-1784) and Jean Le Rond D'Alembert (1717-1783) were the principle editors of this large work. It summarized the rational scholarship of the time, included contributions from skeptics, materialists, atheists, and deists, and had a profound influence on political, social, and cultural trends in France and in many other countries in the eighteenth century.

> *While it is French eighteenth-century thought that is conventionally depicted as best embodying Enlightenment principles, with the writings of the philosophes and their magisterial seventeen-volume Encyclopedie given pride of place, the Enlightenment was, in fact, an intellectual movement that knew no boundaries. The philosophes themselves saw three Englishmen as the prophets of Enlightenment, and they dedicated the Encyclopedie to Bacon, Locke, and Newton. Jefferson, an American disciple of the Enlightenment, agreed, ordering for his library in 1789, a composite portrait of the same three Englishmen. They had, he wrote to a friend, laid the foundation for the physical and moral sciences of modernity and were "the three greatest men that ever lived, without any exception."*[370]

Although there certainly were others, Thomas Jefferson, Benjamin Franklin, Thomas Paine, and James Madison would be the primary individuals to carry Enlightenment ideas to America; and is so doing, influence the documents, foundations, and attitudes of the new country's civil and cultural life.

What were the major elements in the efforts of the Enlightenment thinkers? What were they trying to accomplish? In his introduction in *The Portable Enlightenment Reader*, Isaac Kramnick points to human reason, radical individualism, human perfection, nature, science, progress, complete secularization, and deism as the trademarks and ideals of the eighteenth-century movement.

Human Reason, Radical Individualism, Human Perfectibility

> *What was the message of these Enlightenment intellectuals? What were their ideals? They believed that unassisted human reason, not faith or tradition, was the principle guide to human conduct. "Have courage to use your own reason—that is the motto of Enlightenment," Kant wrote in 1784. Everything, including political and religious authority, must be brought to a critique of reason if it were to commend itself to respect of humanity. Particularly suspect was religious faith and superstition. Humanity was not innately corrupt as Catholicism taught, nor was the good life found only in a beatific state of otherworldly salvation. Pleasure and happiness were worthy ends of life and realizable in this world.*[371]
>
> *His [Condorcet's] optimistic hope for the "future condition of the human race" was "the abolition of inequality between nations, the progress of equality within each nation, and the true perfection of mankind.*[372]
>
> *There is a profound radical individualism at the heart of Enlightenment thought. Its rationalism led Enlightenment philosophy to enthrone the individual as the center and creator of meaning, truth, and even reality…He as the I, the irreducible thinking being, existed at the core of reality…Government's purpose was to serve self-interest, to enable individuals to enjoy peacefully their rights to life, liberty, and property, not to serve the glory of God or dynasties, and certainly not to dictate moral or religious truth.*[373]

The emphasis upon the human individual with his personal rights had large implications economically, morally, and politically. In Enlightenment thought governments exist to protect and defend the rights of the individual. Public law no longer enforced God's higher truths nor any ideal of the moral life; it merely kept order.[374]

As Enlightenment liberalism would free the individual from intellectual constraint, so it would also liberate that individual from economic restraints on private initiative. Rejected were the ideas of a moral economy in which economic activity was perceived as serving public moral ends of justice, whether these be realized through church-imposed constraints on wages and prices, or through magistrates setting prices and providing relief to insure that the poor not starve. Church, state, and guilds were no longer to superintend economic activity; individuals would be left to seek their own self-interest in a free voluntary market.[375]

Morally, each individual must be left to decide for himself how he would live and what would make him happy.

> *In reaction to the religious view that in this life and under its veil of tears a virtuous person lived a life of self-denial and privation, Enlightenment writers emphasized enjoyment and happiness, not the least of which was sensual pleasure...In his Encyclopedie entry on "Enjoyment" (jouissance), Diderot praised sexual pleasure as the most noble of passions.*[376]

So it was that the 18th century became the fountain of modern pornography, be it the Marquis de Sade or John Cleland's *Fanny Hill*. Montesquieu, Diderot, and even Franklin, wrote their share as well.[377]

> *Happiness was an explosive political ideal as well, for it was closely linked to the new world of individualism and the legitimacy of self-interest. Jefferson knew exactly what he was doing when he changed Locke's trilogy "life, liberty, and property," to "life, liberty, and the pursuit of happiness." Property, and the individual's right to it, was but one expression of the larger human right to individual happiness. The emphasis is properly on the individual's happiness, for the Enlightenment's*

revolutionary objective, enshrined in Jefferson's text for the Declaration of Independence, was to place at the heart of politics the sacredness of each separate individual's own quest for happiness and the good life. No longer was there assumed to be a Christian conception of the good life or the moral life, which the church and state defined and to whose common values it led all men and women. The Enlightenment assumption was that each individual pursued his or her own happiness and their own individual sense of the good life—so long, that is, that in doing this they did not interfere with other people's life, liberty, or pursuit of happiness—or, as Jefferson put it, so long as "it neither picks my pocket, nor breaks my leg."[378]

The Enlightenment had a utopian dream: the perfectibility of man. Voltaire wrote of four stages of history in which man moved toward perfectibility—and saw the age in which he was living as the apex or last stage. Marquis de Condorcet (1743-1794), wrote:

> We have witnessed the development of a new doctrine which is to deliver the final blow to the already tottering structure of prejudice. It is the idea of the limitless perfectibility of the human species...[379]

Nature, Science, Progress

To the people of the Enlightenment the perfectibility of man was to be found, in part, in the advances being made in understanding the natural world, and in the discoveries of science. It was Benjamin Franklin who wrote that science might even eliminate mortality.

> The rapid progress the sciences now make, occasions my regrets sometimes that I was born so soon. It is impossible to imagine the heights to which may be carried in a thousand years, the power of man over matter...All diseases may by sure means be prevented or cured, not

excepting even that of old age, and our lives lengthened at pleasure even beyond the antediluvian standard.[380]

Condorcet saw progress for humankind in every area. His optimistic hope for the "future condition of the human race" was "the abolition of inequality between nations, the progress of equality within each nation, and the true perfection of mankind."[381]

Joseph Priestley and Edmund Burke carried on a debate through correspondence. Priestley defended the Enlightenment ideals and Burke, in large part, opposed them. In a letter to Burke in 1781, Priestly wrote the following:

> *I cannot conclude these letters without congratulating, not you, Sir, or the many admirers of your performance who have no feeling of joy on the occasion, but the French nation, and the world—I mean the liberal, the rational, and the virtuous part of the world—on the revolution that has taken place in France, as well as on that which some time ago took place in America. Such events as these teach the doctrine of liberty, civil and religious, with infinitely greater clearness and force than a thousand treatises on the subject. They speak a language intelligible to all the world, and preach a doctrine congenial to every human heart.*
>
> *These great events, in many respects unparalleled in history, make a totally new, a most wonderful and important, era in the history of mankind. It is, to adopt your own rhetorical style, a change from darkness to light, from superstition to sound knowledge and from a most debasing servitude to a state of the most exalted freedom. It is a liberating of all the powers of man from that variety of fetters by which they have been hitherto held…*
>
> *How glorious, then, is the prospect, the reverse of all the past, which is now opening upon us, and upon the world.*[382]

Priestley's last statement reflects the general Enlightenment view of history.

> *Such faith in progress required a jaundiced view of the past, and once again Voltaire was the Enlightenment's guide. History, he wrote in 1754, was "little else than a long succession of useless cruelties" and "a collection of crimes, follies, and misfortunes." Progressive, perfectible humanity disdained the superstitious past and traditions in general, for it could not pass the skeptical test of reason. The American philosophe Jefferson summed up well this Enlightenment ideal in a letter to his friend, Priestley, attacking what the former labeled "the Gothic idea," which has one "look backwards instead of forwards for the improvement of the human mind."*[383]

Progress was the leitmotiv of the Enlightenment.[384] Just as Priestley had insisted that "those times of revered antiquity have had their use and are now no more," so Jefferson agreed that Americans would have nothing to do with such errors.[385] He wrote:

> *To recur to the annuls of our ancestors for what is most perfect in government, in religion, in learning, is worthy of those bigots in religion, and government, by whom it is recommended, and whose purpose it would answer. But it is not an idea which this country will endure.*[386]

Secularism and Deism

Historian Owen Chadwick wrote, "Enlightenment was of the few. Secularization was of the many."[387] It would be wrong to suggest that the Enlightenment was a total failure. It was an admixture, just as we find in all movements. Much of the attitude displayed at the time was a response to legitimate social concerns. It was a time when many areas of life were affected by superstitions that carried over into religious beliefs.

> *The Enlightenment had made some positive contributions to Christendom and the world in general. The campaign against superstition put an end to witchcraft trials; the ideal of humanity advanced democracy over totalitarianism; the slogan of liberte, egalite, fraternite raised a banner against slavery; the idea of progress challenged the mood of despair; and moral consciousness experienced a general awakening.*[388]

The overall effect produced a secular attitude. With man's ascendancy, God became less important. A religion was needed to fit the general mood, "a rational religion in which God became no more than the supreme intelligence or craftsman who had set the machine that was the world to run according to its own natural and predictable laws."[389] Religion was removed from public life, and public authority would be reserved for the private sphere of individual preference and individual practice.

The religion of the Enlightenment was deism and it was both embodied and promoted by several prominent 18th and 19th century men. Many could be mentioned but we will consider four: Voltaire, Rousseau, Franklin, and Jefferson.

Francois Marie Arouet de Voltaire (1694-1778)

Occasionally someone comes along who has an immediate social impact. This was Voltaire. At a time when French culture dominated Europe, Voltaire dominated French culture.[390] His writings include a vast amount of work in almost every literary form, including 56 plays, dialogues, historical writing, stories and novels, poetry and epic poems, essays, scientific and learned papers, pamphlets, book reviews, and more than 20,000 letters.[391] All told, his collected writings run to well over 30,000 pages.[392] For 50 years, Voltaire dominated the French stage. His tragedies broke new ground in continental literature.[393] It was through these means, along with his intelligence, stylishness, cleverness, sense of humor, and his sense of justice and need for cultural reform that made him popular. Will and Ariel Durant, in their eleven-volume set on the history of western civilization, titled the volume on the 18th century, simply, *The Age of Voltaire*. It is probably accurate to say that one cannot understand 18th century Europe without understanding Voltaire.

Francois Marie Arouet, whose pen name was Voltaire, was born on November 21, 1694, in Paris. He lived to be 84 years of age. His family was wealthy and maintained many social contacts in Paris.

> *He chose a career as a writer against the wishes of his father who said he could not earn a living as a writer. However, by the time he was forty years old, Voltaire was both a well-known writer and a wealthy man. Voltaire is known for his philosophical writing, his great wit, and as a crusader against injustice, intolerance, cruelty, and war. In France, in the 1700s, he was the most outspoken writer who supported political and social reform. Because his writing criticized the king and the Church, he lived most of his life in constant fear of being jailed. Thus, he spent comparatively few years of his life in Paris, where his stay was either forbidden or too dangerous.*[394]
>
> *Voltaire was perhaps the dominant and dominating intellectual of the Age of Reason…he set the tone for the new way of looking at the world, by rejecting traditional religion and authoritarianism, and by acknowledging limited reason as providing the only way of understanding the cosmos and improving man. Voltaire's irony, ridicule, satire, polemics, and arguments were central in bringing about the great change of outlook in the eighteenth century. For his age Voltaire was the conscience of the civilized European world.*[395]

His main ideas focused upon the following: to try to reconcile the Newtonian scientific world with the moral world; that the order in the universe indicates that there is a Designer, but not necessarily a moral or immoral one; that there is a natural basis for ethics and justice; that all religions that focus on the supernatural are based upon ignorance and superstition and fanaticism; that the human situation can be improved by eliminating superstition; that although we have no complete explanations of nature, the best accounts of nature are empirical and materialistic.[396] He embraced a kind of deism and saw no relationship between a Designer and the God of Christianity.

From age nine to 17, Voltaire attended the Jesuit College, Louis-le-Grand. His father was a lawyer, with many influential friends, and desired that his son train for a career in law. When he left school, his father found work for him in a law office. However, Voltaire did not like this employment and was drawn to devote himself to literature. From about 1715, he began moving in aristocratic circles, amusing people with his poetry and wit. He was outspoken and critical of people in important positions and of the injustice of French society.

> *In 1717, Voltaire was arrested and sent to the Bastille for insults to the regent, Philippe II D'Orleans. He was freed eleven months later when it was found that he was wrongly accused. While he was in prison, he wrote his first play, "Oedipe," which won him great recognition when it was staged following his release from prison. Voltaire continued to write for the theater...In 1726, while at the theater, Voltaire made a clever remark to the Chevalier de Rohan, a young nobleman, who resented that Voltaire made him look like a fool. To get even, Rohan had several men give Voltaire a beating, while he watched the assault from his carriage. Though he was not the athletic type, Voltaire took fencing lessons and planned to challenge Rohan to a duel. To avoid a problem, the powerful Rohan family had a lettre de cachet issued and Voltaire was arrested and taken to the Bastille. He was released from prison by promising that he would leave the country and go to England.*[397]

The *lettre de cachet* was a letter issued by administrative order at the request of powerful persons in Parisian society. Through this instrument leading people in society could have other lesser persons "automatically" put in prison. To Voltaire, this was one of the many social injustices requiring reform. Individuals should not have to live under the threat of such abuse by the powerful in society. His own experiences contributed to his crusading against what he perceived to be the failures and abuses of society.

> *The Rohan incident left an indelible impression on Voltaire and from that point onward he became an advocate for judicial and social reform. While in England for more than two years, Voltaire met the important literary men of the country. He was impressed by the greater freedom of thought in England, and was deeply influenced by Isaac Newton and John Locke.*[398]

While in England he regularly attended the theaters and playhouses and saw several performances of Shakespeare's plays. Also, he mastered the English language and took a deep interest in the works of John Locke and Isaac Newton. He found that Locke questioned the divine right of kings and thought that limits should be placed upon the authority of the state. He was also impressed by the English constitutional ideas. The scientific discoveries of Sir Isaac Newton also attracted his attention and for the rest of his literary career he would do all he could to popularize the ideas of Locke and inform people of the discoveries of Newton. In these two men, he found justification to encourage people to have faith in their own powers of reason and physical senses (in contrast to religious faith).

> *When he was allowed to return to France, Voltaire established himself financially, and then continued his literary career with the goal of seeking truth and writing about it, and in promoting social reform.*[399]

Voltaire returned to France in 1728 after being in England for a period of two to three years. He would reside in Paris for the next several years and devote most of his time to literary activities. His main work during this period was his *English or Philosophical Letters*. In these, he sought to show the advantages of the English liberal democratic developments for human improvement and happiness, commenting on how the educated commoners could take up occupations and professions, suggested the freedom of the press, equality in taxation, and respect and freedom for the individual.

As he analyzed the ills of society, Voltaire saw the church and the state in France as the main enemies. One of the issues that he confronted was that of the divine right of kings.

> *Through his writing, Voltaire attempted to bring about reform of the social and legal structure that existed at the time. In eighteenth century France, all power lay in the hands of the king and the church. The church taught that all authority to determine what was right and wrong was given to the king by God. The law did not affect the king in any way; his will was law. In return for establishing the divine right of kings in the minds of the people, the king supported the authority of the Catholic Church in France. Thus, it was a system of mind control, and as long as the masses believed in the divine right of kings, the king and the church, and those who held positions in their service (the nobles and upper clergy) maintained their privileged position over the general population.*[400]

Another matter that needed to be addressed, according to Voltaire, was the French judicial system.

> *In the eighteenth century there were 350 different bodies of law in the different regions of France. It was difficult for a citizen to discover what the law was in his*

> *particular place and case. Judiciary appointments were for sale and no prior experience was necessary. Judges passed sentence based on existing laws because the king had delegated to them power that was divinely his. An arrested person could be held in jail for months before a trial was held. There was no trial by jury, torture could be used to get a confession and, if found guilty, the person's property was confiscated by the king. The penal laws were in chaos. New laws passed revoked old laws, and they were often contradictory. Almost any decision made by a judge could be enforced and justified under some law. Thus, judge's power was unlimited. When an arrest was desired, and no law had been violated, a person of influence could obtain a secret warrant called a lettre de cachet that was countersigned by the secretary of state and stamped with the royal seal. The person named in the lettre de cachet was ordered to go to a certain prison or into exile, either abroad or in a certain town in France. The victim stayed in prison or exile for an undetermined amount of time. The person could not clear himself since he had not been accused and there had been no trial.*[401]

Though one might not agree with Voltaire's philosophy at many points, or his methodology, one must agree that the issues he addressed would have been a concern for any moral and thinking person. However, he had a difficult task to accomplish.

> *It was not easy to be a social reform writer in eighteenth century France. All written work had to pass the official censors before it could be published. An edict of 1723 stated: "No publishers or others may print or reprint, anywhere in the kingdom, any books without having obtained permission in advance by letters sealed with the Great Seal." In 1741 there were seventy-six official censors. Before a book was given "permission and privilege du roi," the censor was required to testify that the book contained nothing contrary to religion, public order,*

> *or sound morality. A book that was published without the permission of the government might be burned by the public executioner, and the printer arrested and sent to prison...In 1757, a man named Damiens attempted to assassinate Louis XV. In response to this threat to the king, a new edict decreed death for "all those who shall be convicted of having written or printed any works intended to attack religion, to assail the royal authority, or to disturb the order and tranquility of the realm." In 1764 another decree forbade the publication of works on the finances of the state. Books, pamphlets, even prefaces to plays, were subjected to the most detailed scrutiny and control. Sentences varying from the pillory to flogging to nine years in the galleys were imposed for selling or buying published work that criticized the establishment. During most of his life Voltaire found it necessary to have an escape route planned should he receive word that the police were looking for him. Due to the censorship laws, Voltaire wrote anonymously, and the sale of most of his writing was forbidden. However, due to his writing talent and wit, a work written by Voltaire that was banned was in great demand.*[402]

Throughout his career, many of his works would be burned by the public executioner. Writing anonymously served as his protection on several occasions.

> *Voltaire and other French writers who wanted to elude censorship had their work printed in Amsterdam, The Hague, or Geneva, and then had it smuggled into France. Voltaire denied being the author of much of his writing, and at times wrote criticisms and denunciations of his own work. He also used other means to disguise his statements that promoted social reform. Plays and stories (with examples of social injustice that were similar to what was happening in France) were often set in ancient times, or in foreign or fictional countries. Another technique he*

> *used was to present an issue, make no judgment, and let the reader decide how he or she felt about the issue. Voltaire was often called "the Genius of Mockery." He used logic and humor to show that opposition to his viewpoint was totally ridiculous—and in this technique Voltaire was the master.*[403]

In 1734, he was again exiled from Paris and moved to Cirey, an independent duchy, in eastern France. He lived there in the Chateau of Marquise du Chatelet. It is reported that he became the lover of Madame du Chatelet, the wife of the marquise. He lived there for the next 15 years and then, in 1750, after her death, he moved to Germany at the personal invitation of Frederick the Great of Prussia. After three years in Frederick's court in Potsdam, Voltaire and Frederick had a quarrel, and Voltaire left Germany in 1753. From there, he went to Geneva where he lived on an estate, but his liberal views made even Switzerland an unsafe place for him. In 1758, he moved to Ferney on the French-Swiss border. He thought that if trouble arose, he would have two directions in which he could flee. He lived there for 20 years, entertained visitors, and continued to write, pouring out massive amounts of work.

In 1778, when he was 83 years of age, he returned, and was enthusiastically welcomed back in Paris.

> *Voltaire returned to Paris, where he attended the premiere of his new play, Irene. Large crowds applauded him as the "grand old man" of the French Enlightenment. Hundreds of admirers, including Benjamin Franklin, visited him. But Voltaire's life was soon over. He died in Paris on May 30. 1778. Because of his outspoken anticlericalism, he could not receive a Christian funeral in Paris; but thirteen years later, victorious French revolutionaries had his remains dug up and reburied in the Pantheon in Paris.*[404]

The Pantheon is the national mausoleum of French heroes. His burial took place during the French Revolution, and as the internment took place, it was proclaimed, "He caused the human spirit to take a great leap forward. He prepared us to be free."[405] Probably no one in his lifetime served as a greater symbol for toleration and freedom than Voltaire. And much of this was done through his literary influence. "He is the greatest writer in the world in one way—he wrote more good stuff in more different genres—non-fiction, essay, tragedy, comedy, than any other author."[406]

He's not the greatest in any one field, but he goes into so many different fields, that no one can really rival him in terms of the breadth and depth of the variety of what he wrote. And his spirit moved over the entire continent of Europe and over the entire eighteenth century. He stirred millions—millions of people—to want to seek freedom and toleration because of his writings. As soon as he was dead he was translated into English by Ben Franklin…and by people in other countries, as well, so his works were read all over the world, and they were always categorized by the spirit of reform that permeates everything he wrote. It's not that we owe Voltaire a "thanks" for being such a great author, but in our own way we owe him for the schools we have today, libraries, universities, humane reforms in both law and government, the treatment of prisoners, the treatment of the sick, the treatment of the insane.[407]

There is no more influential author in terms of everyday living and social consciousness than Voltaire.[408]

Jean-Jacques Rousseau (1712-1778)

"Man is born free, but everywhere he is found in chains,"[409] is the famous statement given us by Jean-Jacques Rousseau. To him, freedom is what man was made for, but freedom is taken away by the impositions and institutions of society. To Rousseau, these chains included the family, institutionalized religion, government, laws, educational institutions, etc. In general, man is by nature good; society is the cause of corruption and vice.[410]

"I was born at Geneva, in 1712, son of Isaac Rousseau and Susannah Bernard, citizens,"[411] is how Rousseau describes his beginning. The term *citizens* is important because only 1,600 of Geneva's population of 20,000 could claim citizenship. Isaac was a master watchmaker and Rousseau describes him as being known for his ingenuity. His mother came from a family of means and it is said that Isaac had some difficulty in obtaining her hand in marriage. However, along with the marriage came a dowry of 16,000 florins (gold coins minted in Europe at this time but patterned after coins first struck in Florence in 1252). All of this indicates that his family was one of some prominence in Geneva. His family was of French origin but had settled in Geneva around 1529. His grandfather on his father's side had been a Calvinist minister and his mother's father was also a minister. It is said that Calvinist strains remained in Rousseau throughout all of his wanderings.

After the birth of a son, Francois, Isaac left his wife in 1705 and went to Constantinople where he lived for six years. Upon his return Jean-Jacques was conceived. His mother died within a week after his birth and he was nursed and cared for by an aunt. His aunt was a fine singer and it is thought that this was the beginning of Rousseau's love of music. His father taught him to read by the time he was five, and together they read French love stories, Plutarch's *Lives*, and Calvinist ideas. In 1722, when Rousseau was ten, his father quarreled with a Captain Gautier, bloodied his nose, was summoned by the magistrate, and left the city to avoid imprisonment. Francois and Jean-Jacques were put in the custody of their uncle, Gabriel Bernard. Francois became an apprentice watchmaker. After a while, he ran away and was never heard from again. Jean-Jacques was sent to a boarding school in the nearby village of Bossey where he learned Latin, and the Calvinist catechism was also a large part of the curriculum. The school was run by a Pastor Lambercier.

The two years Rousseau spent at the boarding school might have been the happiest years of his life for a couple of reasons. First, he liked his teachers, especially one—Mrs. Lambercier, the pastor's wife—who he "fell in love with." She was 30 years of age when he arrived, and in his *Confessions* he notes the "sensuality" he felt when with her. Also, he loved the countryside that surrounded him. "The country was so charming...that I conceived a passion for rural life which time has not been able to extinguish." In 1724, when he was 12 years of age, he returned to Geneva and the Bernard household. He was not happy there and consoled himself by borrowing books from the library and taking walks into the countryside.

In 1728, he left Geneva and began his wanderings that were to last for years. After a few days he went to a catholic priest in Catholic Savoy and appealed for charity. The priest introduced him to Madame de Warens, a woman known for good deeds, and who lived at Annecy. She took him to a hospice in Turin where he stayed for several days and was instructed in the Catholic faith. He renounced his Protestantism, and on April 21, 1728, was baptized into the Catholic faith. After working as a servant-boy for several months, he returned to Madame de Warens who took him in. He lived there for approximately ten years.

During the years he lived with Madame de Warens, Rousseau embarked on several attempts to find a vocation. First, he thought of, and studied for the priesthood. This did not materialize. Next, he tried music. This failed. Prompted by Voltaire's *Philosophical Letters*, he thought he would make a survey of different fields of knowledge, thinking this would lead to some vocation. He studied 17th century philosophers, mathematics, anatomy, astronomy, history, theology, and the Latin poets. These times of study were interrupted by his wanderings. When he returned from one of these trips, he discovered that his place in the household had been filled by another. This prompted him to take a position as tutor in a family of nobility in Lyons. There, he discovered that he did not like teaching.

In 1741, he went to Paris. During these years, many things materialized. In Paris, he met Denis Diderot, Jean Le Rond D'Alembert, and other French philosophers. This was during the writing of the *Encyclopedie* and Rousseau actually contributed some pieces on music. In 1745, while he was living and working in Paris (copying music for a living), he began to live with Therese le Vasseur. She is described as a "plain and ignorant" servant girl. He met her at the hotel where he stayed. We are told that he remained with her throughout his life. She bore him five children, all of whom were passed on, at their births, to the foundling hospital (an orphanage).

Rousseau's philosophy and approach to life is easily summarized in four major works: *Discourse on the Arts and Sciences, Discourse on Inequality, Emile,* and *The Social Contract.*

In 1749, Rousseau saw an advertisement from the Academy of Dijon in which a question was asked regarding the effect of the arts and sciences upon culture. It read, "Has the progress of the arts and sciences contributed more to the corruption or purification of morals?"[412] People were asked to answer this question in an essay; Rousseau won the contest as well as immediate fame.

> *The Discourse on the Arts and Sciences is a sweeping condemnation of modern society...Rousseau's central claim is that virtue is found "engraved on the heart" of every person. No special knowledge is necessary, so the advance of knowledge suggested in the question does nothing to improve morals. Rather the reverse is true. One is more likely to find virtue in the simplest laborer than in the philosopher or artist. The problem, as Rousseau saw it, is that when a society achieves the leisure to pursue knowledge in art and philosophy, its members become caught up in appearances and illusion. The need to appear correct becomes more important than the truth, and people are led away from the honesty that characterizes more primitive, natural societies.*[413]

As one can see, the essay concerns itself with the superiority of the savage state and promotes a "back to nature" theme. Most thinkers of this time agreed that any government should correspond to the "nature of man," and have the consent of the governed. Not all agreed on how this should happen. Rousseau proclaimed the gospel of "back to nature." This stood in conflict with the theories of Thomas Hobbes who agreed that people are by nature free but also possess self-interest. This self-interest creates "war" in the state of nature because each person's self-interest conflicts with every other human's self-interest. Though Hobbes believed that man should be governed according to his nature, he also believed that each individual should agree to submit his natural rights and freedoms to the laws of a sovereign in order to maintain order.

> *Rousseau's Discourse on Inequality is in part a critique of Hobbe's views. Where Hobbes sought to justify existing governments, Rousseau once again offers a condemnation. Like Hobbes, Rousseau argues that people are by nature free and self-interested. But in this case, self-interest is accompanied by a natural compassion that makes people reluctant to hurt each other. The state of nature is not a state of war but one of robust indifference. There are natural inequalities of strength and intelligence, but these are unimportant when taken with natural freedom. They become important only in society. For in society, people start to compare themselves with one another. Vanity, pride, and contempt appear, and so the corruption of people by society described in the first Discourse begins. Rousseau argues that people err and mislead each other in their first efforts to construct a government. Their fatal error is to give up their freedom for the illusion of protection. Instead of achieving protection, they become slaves. The origin of inequality is preoccupation with appearances; inequality then leads to loss of freedom. Both steps lead people away from their true nature.*[414]

Rousseau stated clearly what he thought was at the foundation of the inequality that existed among humans.

> *I conceive that there are two kinds of inequality among the human species; one which I call natural or physical, because it is established by nature and consists in a difference of age, health, bodily strength, and qualities of the mind or of the soul: and another, which may be called moral or political inequality, because it depends on a kind of convention, and is established by the consent of men. The latter consist of the different privileges, which some men enjoy to the prejudice of others; such as that of being more rich, more honored, more powerful or even in a position to exact obedience.*[415]

Following the publication of this second essay, his fame was assured. In 1754, he returned to Geneva and was received with great acclaim. From that time he called himself "a citizen of Geneva." From these first two essays it can be seen that several basic themes emerge in Rousseau's philosophy. Human beings are by nature good; society corrupts them.[416] The worst corruption is the loss of freedom brought on by social inequality.[417] It is clear, too, that Rousseau believes people should look within themselves to find answers to life's questions.

> *I confess that, as the events I am going to describe might have happened in various ways, I have nothing to determine my choice but conjectures; but such conjectures become reasons, when they are the most probable that can be drawn from the nature of things, and the only means of discovering the truth.*[418]

In his next two works, *Emile* and *The Social Contract*, Rousseau tries to provide solutions to the problems he saw in individuals and society. *Emile* was published in 1758.

Emile describes Rousseau's vision of a youth's education. It is above all an education of the will, designed with two ends in mind. The first is to avoid the corrupting influence of contemporary society. The second is to create an individual ready to assume the moral and political responsibilities of the new state described in *The Social Contract*. Both books are about the development of freedom, from the natural freedom of the child to the moral and political freedom of the citizen.

> *Given Rousseau's views on sophisticated society, it is not surprising that the first requirement of the education of the true individual is a rural setting. There the child will be free from the influence of the "arbitrary" will of socialized adults. Rather than learning to conform to the whims of society, the child learns to test himself or herself against the physical necessity of nature. In this way the limits of natural freedom are discovered by direct experience.*
>
> *Rousseau thought that education should be progressive. The child's education he proposes calls for a prolonged experience of things rather than an introduction to ideas. The only book he allows is Robinson Crusoe. Formal religion and in fact all abstractions are postponed until a time when the individual's will and reason have already developed independently.*
>
> *Although the child's education begins in a state of nature, the aim is not simply to recapture an idyllic, more primitive past, even were that possible, for the adult. Social interaction represents for Rousseau both the potential for human corruption and the possibility of human perfection. The achievement of autonomy— or moral freedom—is, for Rousseau, the perfection of the human will. The transition from natural to moral freedom is based on reason. The individual learns to let reason be the master of passion and thus to free himself from the tyranny of immediate desire.*[419]

The Social Contract, published in 1762, is designed to show how humans can live in a social setting that supports moral freedom and responsibility without corrupting the individual. It is based upon the premise that all men are born free and equal. It regards the state, in its best form, as a contract in which individuals surrender none of their natural rights, but rather, agree for the protection of them. It is designed to resolve the tension between the individual and the state.

> *The difficulty if one accepts Rousseau's description of the true individual as autonomous and moral is to construct a society that promotes and solicits such citizens. Rousseau thought it necessary that a society's members be willing, active members of their community. The Social Contract is Rousseau's attempt to provide a blueprint for such a society. Perhaps the most striking and controversial element of the political theory outlined in the book is his conception of the "general will." Rousseau's critique of existing governments centered on the loss of freedom. Fundamental to his views on politics is his insistence that people cannot be made to alienate their freedom...On the other hand, Rousseau recognized, the sheer numbers of members of modern society precludes true democracies. The general will is his answer to this conflict of demands. It is the result of the terms of a contract in which each individual transfers all of his or her natural rights and freedom to everyone else in order to create a new corporate person. The corporate person...becomes the sovereign of the new state.*[420]

This corporate person can only exist as each person alienates himself from his own individual, natural freedom; but, this can happen only when all persons alienate their rights equally, "thus avoiding inequalities that lead to the loss of freedom."[421] The next step is to discover, or rediscover, individual autonomy in the shared sovereignty of the general will. "As sovereign, the general will decides the founding laws of the society. It always decides for the 'good of the whole.'"[422] All of this implies a process. To Rousseau, the general will became the sovereign. To Hobbes, sovereignty resided in the ruler or government.

> *Rousseau's conception of the general will has been both admired and criticized. He himself claimed that the general will is not the same thing as the voice of the majority. A majority may be simply a collection of the shared particular interests of a group of individuals. The general will, however, must always will the good of the whole. Unfortunately, this distinction may be clearer in theory than in fact. How is one in practice to know the general will apart from the voice of the majority?*[423]

One cannot minimize the effect of this work. *The Social Contract* became the handbook of the French Revolution and provided ideas and insights in the further development of the entire western world.

Naturally, Rousseau's views on society, politics, and religion put him in conflict with the French authorities. Soon after its appearance in 1758, *Emile* was condemned by the parliament of Paris, and Rousseau knew he would be arrested if he did not go into exile. He spent years of exile in Neuchatel, then Berne, and in 1766 accepted an invitation from David Hume to join him in England. After a quarrel with Hume in 1767, he went back to France where he learned that he could reside unmolested. In 1770, he moved to Paris and resumed his former occupation of copying music. During these latter years, he wrote his *Confessions* and this work was completed after he moved to Paris.

> *In the Confessions Rousseau tries, with brutal honesty, to tell the story of his life—times of happiness and despair, success and failure. He recounts sexual affairs and his guilt after having given up his children to foundling*

> homes. *The book is above all an attempt to explain himself to himself and his public. It has become a classic of self-analysis, but it was not well received at the time.*[424]

Jean-Jacques Rousseau died in the home of a friend in Ermenonville, France in 1778, the same year Voltaire died.

The Enlightenment in America

We cannot leave a discussion of the Enlightenment without mentioning how its thoughts and spirit entered the American colonies. With America being the land of freedom and opportunity, Enlightenment ideas such as reason, natural rights, human achievement, individualism, freedom of conscience, science and progress, free inquiry, and even the free practice of religion, found a natural home. Influential people from around the world saw an opportunity in this new land for these ideas to take root and grow. Alexis de Tocqueville later saw in America the realization of the Enlightenment spirit that he traced to Descartes.[425] The Marquis de Condorcet described America as "the most enlightened, the freest and the least burdened by prejudices of all nations."[426] Its respect for human rights, he wrote, was a lesson for all the peoples of the world.[427] Denis Diderot, in turn, saw America as "offering all the inhabitants of Europe an asylum against fanaticism and tyranny." It was Baron Turgot who thought the American people were "the hope of the human race, they may well become the model."[428] Tom Paine joined the chorus, writing that the cause of America was "the cause of all mankind."[429] Free of clerical and political tyranny, America was "an asylum for mankind."[430]

Several names come to mind when one thinks of those who adopted this spirit on American soil. Two influential figures stand out: Benjamin Franklin and Thomas Jefferson.

Benjamin Franklin (1706-1790)

If America was the embodiment and natural home of the Enlightenment, according to Europe's advanced thinkers, then the American who best personified the Enlightenment ideal was Benjamin Franklin.[431] Born into a Puritan home, his father, Josiah was a candle maker and a skilled mechanic and, along with his wife, Abiah (Folger), maintained a consistent work ethic. In the course of his lifetime, Ben Franklin excelled as a writer, printer, publisher, scientist, philanthropist, political leader, and diplomat. He was the first great self-made man in America, and the most famous and respected private figure of his time. The Scottish philosopher, David Hume, referred to Franklin as America's first great man of letters. After only two years of formal education, he began working alongside his father in order to learn his trade. During this time, he began to devour books found in the family library. Some of his favorite authors included John Bunyan, Plutarch, Daniel Defoe, and Cotton Mather. Later he was apprenticed to his brother James, a printer, and during this time he read virtually every book that was brought into the print shop. His favorite author was Joseph Addison, a leader in the English Enlightenment, who wrote in the *Spectator* and whose essays Franklin actually memorized. Along with his interest in Addison, he also read John Locke, Lord Shaftsbury, and other Enlightenment writers. In this way, he absorbed the values and philosophy of the English Enlightenment.

The thoughts that he picked up early on developed throughout his lifetime. He traveled abroad where he advanced in Enlightenment thought. From 1757 to 1762, he lived in London as a representative of the Pennsylvania Assembly. In 1764, he traveled to London again. In 1767, he traveled to France. In October of 1776, Franklin and his two grandsons sailed for France where he became a "hit" on the social scene (especially with the ladies), and also gained French support for the Revolutionary War. In 1779, he was appointed minister (ambassador) to France where he remained for nine years.

During his life he lived in Boston, Philadelphia, London, and Paris. A veritable cult of Franklin developed: English baby boys were named Benjamin and French artists painted Franklin.[432]

Combining the ideas of human improvement and advancement with the earnestness of his family's Puritan background, prepared him for a life of greatness and immense influence. Though he respected religion and maintained a religious interest, he often broke with his Puritan roots when they conflicted with the ideals of free inquiry, justice, liberty, pursuit of happiness, and equality, as the natural rights of man. He rejected his family's Calvinistic views that stood against one's free will to improve himself.

Benjamin Franklin's religious view has most commonly been recognized as deism. This belief does not reflect the general disposition of most of the founding fathers. Most were theists and held strong beliefs from the Bible. Very few deists were influential. He can be said to have been a religious man but his views of God and the work of redemption, however, were less than biblical. His own words provide insight into his theology.

> *Here is my creed. I believe in one God, Creator of the universe. That he governs it by his Providence. That he ought to be worshipped. That the most acceptable service we can render to him is doing good to his other children. That the soul of Man is immortal, and will be treated with justice in another life respecting its conduct in this.*[433]

His view of salvation seems to be based upon doing good. His break with his Puritan background and a biblical viewpoint is also seen in the following statement:

> *As to Jesus of Nazareth, my opinion of whom you particularly desire, I think the system of morals and his religion, as he left them to us, the best the world ever saw or is likely to see; but I apprehend it has received various corrupting changes, and I have, with most of the present*

> *dissenters in England, some doubts as to his divinity; tho' it is a question I do not dogmatize upon, having never studied it, and think it needless to busy myself with it now...I see no harm, however, in its being believed, if that belief has the good consequence, as probably it has...*[434]

It becomes clear that at the heart of Franklin's religion is moral belief and not a conversion experience. This was a departure from his Puritan roots. To minimize the deity of Christ and show little interest in pursuing an understanding of the doctrine, shows his disregard for historic Christianity and its cardinal beliefs.

It is important to be clear that Franklin believed in the free practice of religion because he believed that each person should be free to follow his personal beliefs and conscience. His position, as was the position of the founding fathers, was against a state religion. He writes:

> *All sects here, and we have a great variety, have experienced my good will in assisting them with subscriptions for building their new places of worship; and, as I have never opposed any of their doctrines, I hope to go out of the world in peace with them all.*[435]

Having been influenced as he was with Enlightenment ideas, and because of his great influence, he helped bring a stream of Enlightenment thinking into the American colonies.

Thomas Jefferson (1743-1826)

Thomas Jefferson is the most notable champion of political, personal, and religious freedom in American history. He believed in reason and free inquiry and that each individual, as far as it is possible, should follow his own conscience. He believed in limitations on government and had a lifelong emphasis on local government. His life is full of accomplishments and he served in public life for about 40 years. He graduated from William and Mary College in 1762 with a degree in law; he served his own locality (in Virginia) as burgess and lieutenant of his county; he wrote the Declaration of Independence and helped frame the Constitution of the United States; he was his country's minister (ambassador) to France; he served as Secretary of State; he served as Vice-President; he served two terms as President of the United States; he engineered the Louisiana purchase, thought by may to be the greatest achievement of Jefferson's presidency; he mostly wrote the Statute of Virginia for Religious Freedom; and he is known as "the Father of the University of Virginia."

His concern for freedom, undergird by education, is seen in all he did and wrote. In writing his own epitaph, he did not mention that he was President of the United States, but listed the following three accomplishments as those of which he was most satisfied: Author of the Declaration of American Independence, of the Statute of Virginia for Religious Freedom, and Father of the University of Virginia.

There is a clear relationship in these three accomplishments. His quest for independence of a nation was not separated from the independence of a man.[436] Jefferson saw that education, free thought, and a free society were related.

What formed Thomas Jefferson's thinking? He was a Virginian and devoted to seeing his ideas established in his own state. His parents were Anglicans, which was the established religion of the State of Virginia. The first settlers of this colony were Englishmen, loyal subjects to their king and church, and the grant to Sir Walter Raleigh contained an express proviso that their laws "should not be against the true Christian faith, now professed in the Church of England."[437] Any other groups, such as Presbyterians, Methodists, Baptists, or any others, were considered heretical. Anglican ministers were state-supported as they had been in England. Taxes provided for the support of Anglican pastors which all citizens were required to pay. Jefferson opposed this and later worked hard to do away with the practice in Virginia (which occurred in 1785), and allow each religious group to support its own pastors. Much of Jefferson's early education came under religious auspices. His first schooling was under the Reverend Douglas A. Scot, who had strong Calvinist convictions.[438] He thought deeply and continuously about the practice of religion and the part it played in the scheme of freedom. It would play a large role in the formation of his thoughts. In later years, Jefferson said that the fight for religious freedom was perhaps the bitterest of his life.[439]

> *No cause in which Jefferson became involved represented more of a challenge to him or called for a greater intellectual and emotional investment than the cause of religious freedom in Virginia. His case was that religion was being stifled by religion itself; that a state that identifies itself with one denomination makes it difficult or impossible for other denominations to exist. Religions had to be protected not so much against the irreligious as against the government itself, acting in the name of religion.*[440]

Following is one of Jefferson's popular statements regarding the role of government and the freedom of religion:

> *The legitimate powers of government extend to such acts only as are injurious to others. But it does me no injury for my neighbor to say there are twenty gods, or no God. It neither picks my pocket nor breaks my leg. If it be said, his testimony in a court of justice cannot be relied on, reject it then, and be the stigma on him. Constraint may make him worse by making him a hypocrite, but it will never make him a truer man. It may fix him obstinately in his errors, but will not cure them.*[441]

When Thomas Jefferson entered college at age 17, he would find an influence that would both inspire and guide his future.

> *At seventeen Jefferson entered William and Mary College at Williamsburg, Virginia. Here he met one of the strong influences of his life, Dr. William Small, a young scholar who had come from Scotland, then undergoing an exciting flowering of intellect with reflections and repercussions throughout the western world…The outpouring in ideas brought with it a reaction against the rigorous Calvinism of recent years.*[442]

These "ideas" and the resulting "flowering of intellect with reflections," of course, refers to the influence of the Enlightenment that was occurring throughout the continent and England. Small and Jefferson became good friends.

> *William Small carried this sense of intellectual adventure with him to the new world. He was Jefferson's teacher but still young enough to be his close friend. And it was Small who helped Jefferson to start building his personal library that is still one of the finest of its kind.*[443]

Though he would later serve as America's ambassador to France, enter into conversations with intellectuals in Europe about the Enlightenment, and watch developments that led to the French Revolution, these did not influence his ideas as much as his already formed ideas. He was a man connected to history, literature, philosophical thought, and contemporary issues.

> *If a man is known by the books he reads and keeps, then the library at Monticello can tell us a great deal about Thomas Jefferson. There are sections on art, architecture, music, history, science, poetry, belles-lettres, religion, and philosophy. Of these, no books were pondered more carefully*

> *than the books dealing with the perfectibility of man. He returned time and again to Homer, Euripides, Cicero, Chaucer, Milton, Pope, Dryden, Hume, Adam Smith, Locke, Hobbes, Rousseau, Blackstone, Bolingbrooke, Voltaire, Montesquieu, Buffon, and Palladio.*[444]

In many ways, he became an American version and embodiment of the Enlightenment man. Called a "Renaissance Man" by many, he was an author, lawyer, diplomat, educator, politician, farmer, architect, scientist, inventor, surveyor, cartographer, and had a great interest in music. Because of his suspicion of the supernatural in religion, and because he was a man of wide and deep understanding, embracing Enlightenment ideas came easily.

It is clear that Thomas Jefferson did not oppose religion. A close look at what he wrote would indicate that he was a deist. There were those who called him a Unitarian. He called himself a Christian, but what did he mean by this?

> *Jefferson did not permit himself to become personally involved in controversy over his religious beliefs or affiliation. When the question came up, he would handle it…with complete tact and respect for the views or affiliations of others, but avoid debate. In a letter written while in retirement, he said that he had "never told my own religion, nor scrutinized that of another. I never attempted to make a convert, nor wished to change another's creed. I have ever judged of the religion of others by their lives"…To his good friend Benjamin Rush he wrote that his religious beliefs were the "result of a life of inquiry and reflection, and are very different from the Anti-Christian system attributed to me by those who know nothing of my opinions. To the corruptions of Christianity I am opposed, but not to the genuine precepts of Jesus himself. I am a Christian, but I am a Christian in the only sense in which I believe Jesus wished anyone to be, sincerely attached to his doctrine in preference to all*

> *others; ascribing to him all excellence, and believing that he never claimed any other."*[445]

What Jefferson seems to be emphasizing is the moral teaching of Jesus. Many have heard of *The Jefferson Bible* in which he removed the supernatural aspects of the Bible and left the moral and ethical parts. How we treat others seems to be at the heart of his belief in the teachings of Jesus. He believed in the universalism of Jesus' teachings, uniting all mankind in "one family in the bonds of love, peace, common wants, and common aids."[446] There is no mention of sin and redemption and the need for personal conversion. The following statement represents Thomas Jefferson's philosophy.

> *Reason and free inquiry are the only effectual agents against terror. Give a loose to them, they will support true religion, by bringing every false one to their tribunal, to the test of their investigation. They are the natural enemies of error, and of error only.*[447]

The Puritans

Puritanism was not a denomination but a movement that began in England and made its way to America. The Puritans desired to bring reform to the state churches. In their view, these churches had lost vision and zeal for the things of God and practical religion. They wished to purify the church of the remaining vestiges of Roman Catholic ceremony, ritual, and hierarchy. Puritanism began as liturgical reform, but it developed into a distinct attitude toward life—or as we would say today, a worldview.

Some of the better-known Puritans were John Bunyan, Richard Baxter, John Milton, William Bradford, Richard Mather, Cotton Mather, Increase Mather, Samuel Rutherford, William Perkins, John Owen, Anne Bradstreet, and Jonathan Edwards. Their teachings and writings influenced both the church and society. The Puritans were responsible for the founding of excellent schools, such as Harvard (1636), William and Mary (1639), Yale (1701), New Jersey which became Princeton (1746), College of Philadelphia (1751) which became Pennsylvania University, King's College (1754) which became Columbia University, Brown (1765), Rutgers (1766), and Dartmouth (1769).

It is true and sad that the Puritans are largely misunderstood in today's culture. Critic H. L. Mencken once said, "Puritanism is the haunting fear that someone, somewhere, may be happy."[448] Another has written that Puritanism "damages the soul, renders it hard and gloomy, deprives it of sunshine and happiness."[449] These assessments fail in the light of scholarly research.

> *On the contrary, Puritans read good books and enjoyed music. They drank beer with their meals and rum at weddings. Puritans swam and skated, hunted and fished, and played at archery and bowling.*[450]

George Fox, a Quaker, and contemporary of the Puritans, despised their "ribbons and lace and costly apparel," their "sporting and feasting."[451] No doubt the modern slang term, "puritanical," has done its work in the minds of most moderns. A. G. Dickens has pointed out:

> *When you think about Puritanism you must begin by getting rid of the slang term "Puritanism" as applied to Victorian religious hypocrisy. This does not apply to seventeenth-century Puritanism.*[452]

C. S. Lewis wrote: "We must picture these Puritans as the very opposite of those who bear that name today."[453] Further, he states, the early Puritans were "young, fierce, progressive intellectuals, very fashionable and up-to-date."[454] Leland Ryken adds that "The Puritans 'thought young,' whatever their chronological age."[455] Most Americans have no concept or little appreciation for the contributions made by the Puritans to the foundations of their country. Had it not been for the Puritans, one wonders whether or not the beginning of the United States would have been as successful as it was. Puritans were numerous and influential in the beginning of the colonies in North America.

> *The American colonies became, in one historian's words, "the most Protestant, Reformed, and Puritan commonwealths in the world." When American colonists declared their independence in 1776, a full 75 percent came from Puritan roots.*[456]

Along with their religious commitment, the Puritans were committed to education which was reflected immediately in the first settlements.

> *Within only six years of their arrival, while still trying to hew out an existence, the Puritans founded a religious college named Harvard. Puritans wanted highly educated ministers, not "Dumme Doggs," as they called the less-trained examples.*[457]
>
> *The early settlers of Massachusetts included more than 100 graduates of Oxford and Cambridge. One historian termed Massachusetts "the best educated community the world has ever known."*[458]

It is important to note the significance Puritans placed upon education and the life of the mind in general. When John Calvin brought reform to the city of Geneva, education became mandatory because it was believed that a Christian's responsibility was civic as well as spiritual. The Puritans, likewise, committed themselves to building an educated public. Ryken highlights the emphasis that the Puritans placed upon education.

> *No Christian movement in history has been more zealous for education than the Puritans. The adjective "learned" was one of their most frequently used positive titles for a person. A modern scholar describes Puritanism as "a movement of the 'learned godly,' the religious intellectuals of the day, a movement that found its strongest support in university circles."*[459]

Before the revolutionary war, Colonial America supported nine colleges. Each of these was a variation on Oxford and Cambridge, the two British universities. This type of education was very particular. In the American colleges, the ancient languages were kept alive along with classical ideas of education. The students attended to logic, rhetoric, ethics, metaphysics, astronomy, physics, and mathematics. The four years at Harvard were structured as follows:[460]

- ✧ First Year: Latin, Greek, Hebrew, Logic, Rhetoric.
- ✧ Second Year: Logic, Greek, Hebrew, Beginning Natural Philosophy (physics).
- ✧ Third Year: Natural Philosophy, Mental Philosophy (Metaphysics), Economics, Ethics, Political Science, and Sociology.
- ✧ Fourth Year: Review of Latin, Greek, Logic, Natural Philosophy, Mathematics.

To say that the Puritans were ignorant, or superstitious, or opposed to education, would be an inaccurate statement.

Puritan Origins

Puritanism flourished in America, but what were the origins of the movement? It is commonly believed by scholars that its beginnings can be traced to William Tyndale who was not himself called a Puritan, but is considered the father of the movement.

Tyndale died in 1536, but by 1560 the word "puritan" was a coined term of derision being used toward those who seemed disgruntled with the religious establishment. Thus, through his leadership and teaching, the Puritan movement began in England.

> *Puritanism was part of the Protestant Reformation in England. No specific date or event marks its inception. It first assumed the form of an organized movement in the 1560s under the reign of Queen Elizabeth, but when we identify the traits of the movement we can see that its roots reach back into the first half of the century. Its intellectual and spiritual forebears include figures like the Bible translator William Tyndale, the popular preacher-evangelist Hugh Latimer, and Thomas Becon. And surely the roots of Puritanism include the Protestant exiles who fled to the Continent during the persecution under the Catholic Queen Mary (1553-1558).*[461]

These exiles would include such notables as John Knox who fled to Geneva, Switzerland to learn and be trained under the reformers there—Calvin, Beza, and Farel.

The development of Puritanism in England ran parallel to important church developments in England. First, Henry VIII broke from Rome because the pope would not sanction annulment of his marriage to Queen Catherine of Aragon. She had given him only one child, a girl—the princess Mary—so after 18 years of marriage to Catherine, Henry secretly married Anne Boleyn and had an English church court declare his marriage to Catherine null and void. When the pope countered by excommunicating him, Henry decided to overthrow papal authority in England and founded the Church of England. He reigned from 1509-1547. Then came Edward VI who reigned for only a short time (1547-1553) but did much to advance the English Church. During his reign, he was assisted in bringing reforms to the church by Thomas Cranmer, usually regarded as the leader of the English Reformation because he was the first Protestant head of the English Church. The movement went into regression under the reign of Queen Mary who was a devoted Roman Catholic. During her reign, about 300 Protestants were martyred and she became known as "Bloody Mary." She reigned from 1553 to 1558. She was replaced by Queen Elizabeth, thought by many to be the greatest of English sovereigns. Elizabeth brought several reforms to re-establish the Church of England. In fact, it took the form in which it has continued, for the most part, to the present. But her reforms did not satisfy the Puritans.

Queen Elizabeth, acting as the head of the church, and trying to balance the high church views of Anglicans, and the views of the Puritans, who were looking for greater reforms, established what is known as "the Elizabethan Compromise." The compromise drew together Reformed or Calvinistic doctrine, the continuation of a liturgical and (in the eyes of the Puritans) Catholic form of worship, and an Episcopal church government.[462] This took place in 1558 when she became queen.

To the Puritans, this action of the Queen greatly impeded or halted the Reformation. To them, such interference from the state had a definite impact upon the purity of the church. In their eyes, as long as the relics of Rome remained, the true Church of Jesus Christ could not find a home within the Church of England. To the purists in the movement, medieval vestments, kneeling at communion, making the sign of the cross, use of images or shrines, or anything resembling the mass, got in the way of true religion. Many of these practices were encouraged and retained under Queen Elizabeth's compromise. Movements began to occur in order to rid the church of these vestiges. In Stratford-upon-Avon, for example, in 1564—the year of his son William's birth—John Shakespeare, the town's bailiff, put his mark beside a council order to deface the images and whitewash the frescoes in the guild chapel of the parish church.[463]

Shortly after Queen Elizabeth came to the throne, she appointed Matthew Parker, a Cambridge don in his mid-fifties, as See of

Canterbury and it became his responsibility to "keep an eye" on the English Reformation. It was probably Parker who first used the terms "irritable precisions" or "puritans" and gave them the name that was to follow them wherever they went.

Trying to balance between the establishment of a state church—the Anglican Church—and the aggressive initiatives of "the puritans" created tensions in England for years. The Puritans were often persecuted by the state church and eventually would look to America for a new home.

Why the Puritans Left England

The reign of Charles I, who reigned in England from 1625 to 1649, illustrates the tensions between the Puritans, the state church, and the state. Charles William Laud was appointed archbishop of Canterbury in 1633. Laud was a Protestant reformer but he turned out to be a leader who greatly disappointed the Puritans.

> *Laud's program differed fundamentally from the Puritan's. Following the theory of the Elizabethan settlement, Laud believed there should be latitude in doctrine but uniformity in polity and liturgy. The liturgy was set forth in the Book of Common Prayer, which required that the Communion table always be at the east end of the church and not in the nave... He also believed that the clergy should be attired in the vestments prescribed by the changing seasons of the Christian year. Laud cared more that every Englishman should eat the same kind of wafer at the Lord's Supper than that all should have the same theory as to the real Presence.*[464]

Stipulations such as these created difficulties for the Puritans. Their desire was for simpler forms of worship along with more democratic forms of church life, including more participation and leadership on the part of the laity. As a result, the Puritans would suffer for their faith.

> *Laud punished non-compliance with his measures by mutilation and imprisonment. The Star Chamber, which had been instituted to force compliance with the state, and the Court of High Commission, which since Elizabeth's day had been employed against non-conformists to the established Church [Church of England], were both called into use against the Puritans. An individual might suffer at the hands of both. Alexander Leighton, for example, who had issued Sion's Plea Against the Prelacie, was defrocked by the Court of High Commission and then was sentenced by the Star Chamber to be whipped, his ears cropped, his nose slit, and his forehead branded, and in addition, to be fined and imprisoned. The like treatment of other dedicated Puritans…provoked intense resentment. Despite the outcry against barbarous penalties, Laud would grant no concessions and no relief.*[465]

After the pilgrims landed at Plymouth in 1620, William Bradford became their second governor in 1621. The first governor, John Carver, had died in that same year. Except for five brief year-long respites, Bradford would serve as governor until his death in 1657, a total of 36 years in public service. He explained why the Puritans left England and came to the new world.

> *Why did they leave England? In his history Of Plymouth Plantation William Bradford hinted at the atmosphere of hostility, which surrounded them as well as the features of English life which they found unacceptable… Bradford described the 'inveterate hatred against the holy disciples of Christ in his Church' still displayed by their enemies which rankled at the Puritans. 'And to cast more upon the sincere servants of God, they opprobriously and most injuriously gave unto and imposed upon them the name of Puritans, which it is said the Novatians [an obscure sect in the third century] out of pride did assume and take unto themselves. And lamentable it is to see the*

effects that have followed. Religion has been disgraced, the godly grieved, afflicted, persecuted, and many exiled; sundry have lost their lives in prisons and other ways. On the other hand, sin has been countenanced, ignorance, profaneness, and atheism increased, and the papist encouraged to hope again for a day.[466]

Bradford's remarks indicate two reasons for leaving England. First, was the persecution that the Puritans suffered. Second, was what they perceived as the "worldliness" they encountered in English life.

In 1620, the Mayflower arrived at Plymouth carrying 102 persons. Due to childbirth and the arrival of other ships, the population grew to around 2,500 by 1630. In 1630, John Winthrop's fleet arrived with an additional 1,000 Puritans. In the next 12 years, 20,000 Englishmen sailed to Massachusetts. This great movement of people has been called "the Puritan Exodus" or "the Puritan Immigration." This was the first "en masse" immigration to the Americas. Their location in New England would have great influence in the development of the colonies and in the establishment of a new nation.

Because the Puritans were "learned people," they would have great influence in the development and founding of the new nation that would come. They developed communities of law and order characterized by democratic participation. Theirs was a spirituality that combined heart and mind. Further, they saw a greater relationship between the church and culture than most Americans, including other Christians, would see today. To those who have studied the Puritans and the development of the Colonial States, most would agree that America is still borrowing upon the capital provided by these pilgrims and founders.

Ironically, the very freedoms provided through the influence of the Puritans may have been part of the reason for the loss of the values they initially provided. Their influence seems to have remained strong from their early arrival in America and throughout the eighteenth century, but by the end of that century, and the beginning of the next, new sentiments began to replace their positive contributions.

> *During the First Great Awakening, Jonathan Edwards had insisted that Christian experience must have intrinsic relation to the workings of the mind and thus to Christian doctrine. Edwards, himself a Puritan, warned of the dangers of being caught up in the emotionism or experience orientation of such great movements as an awakening. He did this both in writing and in preaching. No doubt he saw the seeds of something that would come if experience replaced theology and tradition.*[467]

> *The Second Great Awakening—the enormous burst of revivalistic fervor that swept the nation in the early years of the nineteenth century—was largely responsible for this newfound suspicion of dogma and tradition. Its pietistic and moralist ardor helped set fire beneath the frigid faith of the eighteenth century. Yet it also made inherited convictions seem inimical to the life of the intellect.*[468]

The shift from the First Great Awakening in the eighteenth century to the Second Great Awakening in the early nineteenth century gave a new face to evangelicalism and a new emphasis to Christian experience.

> *…Charles Finney and Barton Stone were much less concerned about Christian thought. The schools sustained by revivalist experience exalted personal morality and devotion over hard Christian thinking. These two main evangelical gifts—the strangely warmed heart and the ethically straitened conscience—seemed to make the church colleges into mighty fortresses of Christian learning. They proved to be houses made of cards. Burtchaell shows that,*

without rootage in Christian thinking, faith seeking understanding, the good of the intellect—Christian piety and morality eventually die, though they may thrive for awhile.[469]

Charles Finney, Barton Stone, and others of the same persuasion—with good intent—created a shift in Christian experience from which the church in America has not yet recovered. As others have pointed out, either a diminished or forsaken life of the mind has existed for the last 170 years. The "warmed heart" and desire for holiness may enliven one's sense of God, but practiced alone, result in rather devastating consequences.

With a loss of the Puritan emphasis, a different kind of Christianity was produced in America. A continued disengagement with the culture at large, and a marginalization of faith, gradually grew in the United States.

At the close of his book, *Worldly Saints*, Leland Ryken reminds us that the Puritans were not perfect. Though they contributed much, they had their weaknesses. He points to the following as areas of concern:[470]

- ✧ An inadequate view of recreation.
- ✧ Too many rules.
- ✧ Too many words.
- ✧ Too much pious moralizing.
- ✧ Male chauvinism.
- ✧ Partisan spirit.
- ✧ Insensitivity to the religious feelings of other groups.
- ✧ Puritan extremism.

To gain a balanced assessment of the items listed above, one should read those pages from Ryken's book. The final chapter of the book is titled, "The Genius of Puritanism: What the Puritans Did Best." He lists the following:[471]

- ❖ The God-centered life.
- ❖ All of life is God's.
- ❖ Seeing God in the commonplace.
- ❖ The momentousness of life.
- ❖ Living in a spirit of expectancy.
- ❖ The practical impulse in Puritanism.
- ❖ Getting back to basics.
- ❖ The balanced life.
- ❖ A simplicity that dignifies.
- ❖ A sure foundation.

Leland Ryken's book is a must read for anyone wishing to gain a better understanding of the roots of American order and an appreciation for the greatness of its founders. Here is a final word from Ryken:

> *Puritanism can give us a place to stand. The Puritans believed that all of life is God's. This enabled them to combine personal piety with a comprehensive worldview. Beginning with the premise that the Bible is a reliable repository of truth, the Puritans had a basis from which to relate their Christian faith to all areas of life—to work, to family, marriage, education, politics, economics, and society. In Puritanism, a theology of personal salvation was wedded to an active life in the world.*[472]

Evangelical Awakenings

Beginning at the end of the 17th century and extending through the mid-19th century, Western Christianity saw a renewed spiritual interest. Today we call this the period of "the Evangelical Awakenings," and three regions in particular were affected: Germany by the rise of Pietism, the British Isles by the preaching of the Methodists, and the American colonies by the impact of the Great Awakening.[473] It is also important to remember that awakenings were not only times of heightened spiritual sensibilities; awakenings had social impact. There was cultural restoration. Laws became more just and morals and manners replaced corrupt, dishonest, and unjust behavior and conditions.

Pietism

Pietism was a movement which arose in Europe during the last half of the 17th century. It stressed spiritual renewal of the individual, belief in the Bible as the only true guide to faith and life, and promoted a devotional life as the means for achieving Christ-likeness. Pietists surrounded themselves with reminders of piety, such as plaques and printed sayings, and they used various devotional aids in the form of booklets, printed sermons, and hymns, in order to encourage spirituality. They likewise emphasized the love of Christ as a solution to societal ills. Pietists created the model of orphanages for both church-related and public programs.[474] They would later create homes for widows and single women, medical dispensaries, and other organizations that had social significance. Modern missions found a beginning among the Pietists.

Though originating in Germany, Pietism spread across Europe, to England, to North America, and beyond. The Pietists did not see themselves as a new church, but as an extension of the Reformation within Reformation churches.[475] It should also be noted that there was a relationship between Pietism and Puritanism.

> *Pietism and Puritanism, while usually considered two separate movements, were actually related. Puritanism was one of the formative influences on Pietism. The American Puritan Cotton Mather carried on correspondence with the Pietist leader Spener.*[476]

They promoted the creation of conventicles (cell groups), that is, little churches within the church.[477] Pietists in the Netherlands were the first to use the term "huis kirk" or house church for their renewal meetings.[478]

> *While there is no official or recognizable "Pietist" church or denomination as such, nevertheless the movement left its mark on much of contemporary Christianity. The influence of the "Pietists" can be clearly traced in contemporary expressions of missions, ecumenism, revivalism, social activism and Bible study groups. Pietism has also influenced how we worship through its rich hymnology, how we give, and how we conduct devotional life.[479]*

The formation and development of Pietism was made up of two phases. The first phase revolved around two figures: Philip Jacob Spener and August Hermann Francke, and the second phase was carried forward under the leadership of Count Nicolaus Ludwig von Zinzendorf.

Philip Jacob Spener

Philip Jacob Spener (1635-1705) grew up under strong spiritual influences and became a Lutheran pastor who emphasized a deep personal awareness of Christ's presence based mainly upon careful devotional habits. First, he was influenced by the writings of Johann Arndt (1555-1621), a German mystic, who many consider to be the true father of Pietism. Then he read the writings of the Puritans. Later, he met teachers at Strasbourg who introduced him to the works of Martin Luther. Through Luther, he understood the doctrine of justification by faith in which he saw the basis for true spiritual birth. During his life, he served churches in Strasbourg, Frankfort, Dresden, and Berlin. Each city played a key role in his personal development and in the development of his ministry. In Strasbourg, foundations for his theology were laid. In Frankfort, he preached for years with few results. Then, in 1669 he preached a series of messages from the Sermon on the Mount with a response that was "sudden and surprising."[480] People were converted and family life changed.[481]

It was during his years in Frankfort that Spener began holding meetings twice weekly in his home for Bible study, prayer, and for discussion aimed at application. These meetings were soon, in derision, called "gatherings of the pious," and "pietism" was born.[482]

> *As interest in devotional literature grew Johann Arndt's sermons were published and Spener wrote an introduction to them. He called it Pious Desires. In it he recommended the establishment of Bible study groups for spiritual development; a strenuous, rather ascetic, Christian life [and] simpler and more spiritual preaching. Spener's thought was that a cell of experiential Christians should be gathered in each congregation to cultivate a stricter and warmer Christian life. He hoped that this leaven would permeate the whole church.*[483]

By the term "experiential Christians," he meant those who had experienced true conversion, had a genuine walk with Christ, and could model the life of pietism.

In 1686, Spener received the prestigious appointment of court chaplain at Dresden. However, his stay in that city did not last long, mainly due to his uncompromising preaching which put him in conflict with the civil authorities. In 1692, he accepted a call to move to Berlin. During his time in Berlin, he helped found the new University of Halle, which would become a center of Pietism. He maintained an influential pastorate until his death in 1705.

August Hermann Francke

August Hermann Franke (1663-1725), a teacher at Leipzig and one already attracted to pietism, paid a visit to Dresden where he met Spener and was deeply influenced by him. When his "evangelical activities" were objected to at Leipzig, he was able to get an appointment in 1691 as a professor at the University of Halle. This occurred directly through Spener's influence. Though Spener would continue to write and preach, it would be Francke who would rise to lead the Pietist movement. Philip Spener showed a great deal of wisdom and humility in allowing Francke to assume this role.

Francke's work would be characterized by a strong desire to show a Christianity motivated by love that would result in service to others.

> *He traced his zeal to a life-changing conversion that had come after two years of inner struggle and doubt. While writing a sermon on John 20:31, Francke dropped to his knees in great fear. I implored, he said, "the God, whom I did not yet know and whom I did not believe, that, if there really is a God, he should save me from this wretched condition." God heard him! Sadness left his heart and he was "suddenly overwhelmed by a flood of joy." When he arose, he knew he was saved and from that time on, it was "easy to live righteously and joyfully in this world."*[484]

Throughout the next two decades he created a model educational community, led the way in moral and social concerns, and encouraged a spirit for missions with Halle becoming a center for missionary activity. Those educated at the University of Halle became pastors and teachers for other communities. Francke organized the Paedagogium, a free elementary school for poor children, in 1695, and a secondary school two years later.[485]

> *He also established an orphanage and bought a tavern and adjunct land to build a hospital. His on-going work included a Latin school for talented boys, a house for widows, a house for unmarried women, a medical dispensary, a book depot, a printing establishment, and a Bible house. When King Frederick IV, of Denmark,*

wished to establish one of the earliest missions in India in 1705, it was among Francke's disciples in Halle that he found his first missionaries.[486]

Auguste Hermann Francke's *Autobiography* lays out the characteristics of a ministry, which he describes as "a life changed, a church revived, a nation reformed, and a world evangelized."[487]

Count Nicolaus Ludwig von Zinzendorf

Count Zinzendorf (1700-1760) was born at Dresden, Germany, of Austrian nobility. Since Austria was dominated by Catholicism at that time, his grandfather, a nobleman, left Austria because of his religious convictions and settled in Germany. As a child, Nicolaus was exposed to pietistic preaching and literature and studied in Francke's Paedagogium at Halle. All of this fostered within him a desire to pursue a theological education and become a missionary. However, his family wanted him to go into government; so he studied law at Wittenberg and entered civil service in the Court of Saxony. Zinzendorf is probably a good example of someone called by God for a specific work, but due to family pressures, took a different route. His desire for ministry never went away, and while still a young man, he acquired a substantial estate at the town of Berthelsdorf in southwest Saxony in 1722.

> *An opportunity for service came in an unexpected way with the remains of the old Hussite movement, the Bohemian Brethren (Unitas Fratrum). The brethren flourished in Bohemia and Moravia at the time of the Reformation but had been nearly crushed during the Thirty Years War, and were subject to severe persecution. Under a Moravian carpenter, Christian David, the Brethren had experienced the stirring of revival and were casting about for some place of refuge in Protestant lands. They found it in Zinzendorf's estates, and in 1722 David*

established a community called Herrnhut, "The Lord's Watch." (Or, "the Lord's Protection.")[488]

In receiving these refugees from Bohemia and Moravia (modern Czech Republic), who had been driven out of their countries by Catholic authorities, Zinzendorf had the door of ministry opened to him. He entered the community, and because of his winsome spirit and Christ-centered faith, people from various backgrounds began to flock to Herrnhut. By the summer of 1727, over 200 people had accepted Count Zinzendorf's invitation to settle on the estates, some from Moravia and Bohemia, but others from throughout the German-speaking lands.[489] In 1727, he retired from civil life and gave himself entirely to the work at Herrnhut. This community gave him a place to express his deep commitment to Christ, and it became a place for his missionary zeal to take shape.

> *From 1727 Zinzendorf was the guiding spirit of Herrnhut, and ten years later he received formal ordination in the reorganized Moravian Church. Zinzendorf's impulses were always strongly missionary. As a result the Moravians became the first large-scale Protestant missionary force in history.*[490]

They joined the Halle Pietists in inaugurating the modern missionary movement, sending missionaries to the West Indies, Greenland, North America, Guiana, Egypt, South Africa, Labrador, Holland, England, and the Baltic States.[491] Zinzendorf went on three missionary journeys himself: to the West Indies from 1738-1739, to England in 1741, and he spent two years overseeing Moravian efforts in the American colonies from 1741-1743. While in America, he conducted journeys to the Iroquois and Delaware Indians. It was Herrnhut Moravians who went to Pennsylvania and founded the town of Bethlehem. Today they are known as the Moravian Church.

Lasting Influences of the Pietists

There were emphases in the Pietist movement that have remained part of evangelical ministries throughout the world. Bruce Shelley cites ways the Pietist movement influenced evangelical Christianity: Pietism made regeneration a dominant theme, not as a theological doctrine, but as a particular and indispensable experience of the Christian.

> *The intensely personal way the Pietist described regeneration often made Christianity a drama of the human soul. The heart of man was the scene of a desperate struggle between the powers of good and evil. In this sense Pietism was the fountain of all modern revivals. For this reason it is impossible to think of evangelical Christianity without the imprint of Pietism.*[492]

Pietism made *preaching and pastoral care* central concerns of the Protestant ministry. It also enriched *Christian music* enormously. Pietism underscored the importance of a *spiritual laity* for a revived church. In addition, it promoted the idea of the *devotional life*, which has remained a part of evangelical tradition.

Further, Shelley points to two important traits that evangelicals have inherited from the Pietists.

> *First, emotion played so large a part in the Pietists religious life that reason was endangered. Since the mind of man could not fathom the mysteries of human destiny, feelings were left to carry the meaning of faith. Consequently Pietism had little to say about God's place in nature or human history and it presented few challenges to the spread of secularism.*[493]
>
> *Second, Pietism assumed the existence of the institutional church...[but] it shifted what was essential to Christianity—the new birth and the spiritual life—from*

the traditional state churches to intimate fellowship groups or voluntary associations of believers.[494]

Wesleyan Revivals

England had experienced two awakenings in her history, the English Reformation in the 16th century, and the 17th century Puritan movement. In the first half of the eighteenth century, the churches in England, both Established and Dissenting, sank into a state of decline, with formal services, cold intellectual belief, and a lack of moral power over the population.[495] In the Established Church—the Anglican—and in the Nonconformist denominations, such as the Baptists and Congregationalists, the zeal of the Puritans seemed to be a thing of the past.[496] In general, life in England was at a very low ebb, with much poverty, immorality, and squalid conditions.

By this time, the Enlightenment was showing its effects in England, and religion, though still alive, was being pushed from the prominent place it once occupied in daily life, to the margins. Church life was formal, and "enthusiasm" was frowned upon. John Tillotson, the Archbishop of Canterbury, is an example of how people thought about and practiced religion at that time. Rather than emotionalism and extremes, Tillotson and others emphasized instead, proper behavior. Men should reform their conduct; they should be generous, humane, and tolerant, and avoid bigotry and fanaticism.[497] Being good people and doing good was emphasized with little or no emphasis placed upon man's sinfulness and need of redemption.

With the diminishing of the influence of the Puritans in the late 1500s and the 1600s, and the rise of Enlightenment thought in the 1700s, life had become more secular, and spiritual life more disenfranchised. From this condition, England would be awakened by a group of earnest preachers led by the brothers John and Charles Wesley, and their friend and fellow minister, George Whitefield. A third awakening was coming.

John Wesley

John Wesley (1703-1791) became the undisputed leader of the awakening that began in England and moved through the British Isles and into other parts of the world. In fact, apart from Christ, no single leader in Christian history has obtained so large a personal following as John Wesley.[498] Although a high church Anglican pastor, his ministry would appeal to, and revolutionize, the lives of lower-class Englishmen. Though recognized as the founder of the Methodist Church, his aim was not to start a new denomination; rather, he wanted to create a movement or society within the English Church.

The parents of John Wesley, Samuel and Susanna Wesley, had 19 children, eight of whom died in infancy. John Wesley was their 15th child, and his brother Charles, was the 18th. The children were raised in the rectory at Epworth, Lincolnshire, England where their father was an Anglican clergyman. From early in their lives it seemed apparent that God had a plan for the Wesley brothers.

> *When only six, he and his younger brother Charles were rescued from the flames which destroyed the rectory—an event that left a deep impression on John and led him to describe himself as "a brand snatched from the burning."*[499]

Being a part of Samuel and Susanna Wesley's family was an education in itself, but beyond this, John received schooling at Charterhouse in London, and then, at age 17, he left for Oxford University where he studied first at Christ Church College and then at Lincoln College. He was a diligent student and became adept in several languages.[500] He was also athletic and quite healthy, and remained so throughout his life. After his education at Oxford, he was ordained an Anglican deacon in 1725, and a pastor (priest) in 1728. He served as his father's assistant from 1726 to 1729, and gained standing at the university—and a steady income—when he was elected a fellow of Lincoln College in 1726.

His brother Charles followed in his brother's footsteps, entering Oxford in 1726. When John returned to the university in 1729 to assume certain duties, he found that his brother and some other students had formed a Bible study and prayer group. This group had been given various nicknames, including "the Holy Club," "the Godly Club," "Bible Moths," "Reforming Club," and "Methodists." One of the books studied by the club was William Law's *A Serious Call to a Devout and Holy Life*, which was published the same year the "Holy Club" was formed.[501] The group did not mind that they were made fun of, or thought a bit weird by others at the university. Upon his arrival, John immediately became leader of the group.

From the time John entered Oxford, he read widely, including in his literary diet the early church fathers and the great devotional literature of the past. Being impressed by the highly disciplined lives of those he read, he determined to grow in the devotion and holiness he found in them. He listed his own sins and weaknesses and formulated his own rules to overcome them. This fit well with the desires of the group he had joined. Along with the other members of the "Holy Club," rules and disciplines were initiated to help them grow into Christ-likeness and "save their own souls."

> *Wesley and the circle of Oxford students, painfully obsessed about their own salvation, set out to discipline themselves to live intensely strict lives. They examined their own motives, made rules for themselves, assigned precise chores such as visiting the Oxford jail, fasted, prayed by schedule, met regularly, and did everything humanly possible to achieve a sense of personal salvation.*[502]

Yet the "Holy Club," for all its methodical morality, experienced little peace and joy in the enterprise.[503] Although John Wesley had sought to know God and be the right kind of Christian, he lacked peace and his life was filled with spiritual struggles. From his days at Oxford, to his ministry within the church, and in his participation in the "Holy Club," he lacked the assurance and joy that his soul desired. This would continue for several years until he came to a particular point in time that he would point to as the day of his "new birth."

The story of his conversion is one that has interested many, and is characterized by its own drama. 1735 was an important year for John Wesley. Still lacking assurance of salvation, John began intensive reading of the Greek New Testament, fasted on Wednesdays and Fridays, received communion weekly and ministered to the prisoners in the local jail.[504] As usual, this was an attempt to find peace of mind in his relationship to God. Also, in 1735, George Whitefield joined the "Holy Club." Late in the same year, John and Charles set sail for the Colony of Georgia. They were sent as missionaries in response to an invitation from the governor of Georgia, James Oglethorpe.

Near the end of January in 1736, at age 33, John Wesley was aboard the British ship *Simmonds*, sailing to Savannah, Georgia, when the ship encountered a series of violent Atlantic storms. By his own admission, his motive in going to Georgia was "the hope of saving my own soul."[505] Though he had preached the gospel to others, he found he was suffering great fear from the prospect of dying.

> *He was deeply awed, however, by a company of Moravian Brethren from Herrnhut. As the sea broke over the deck of the vessel, splitting the mainsail in pieces, the Moravians calmly sang their psalms to God.*[506]

Wesley observed the "cheerful confidence" of the 26 Moravians aboard ship, which included men, women, and children. Following the storm, he interrogated these Moravian missionaries to find that it was their "assurance" in Christ that enabled them to overcome their fears. Deeply impressed, Wesley wrote in his journal, "This was the most glorious day I have ever seen."[507]

By all accounts the trip to Georgia was a fiasco. Though he worked tirelessly to be the right kind of pastor, John was not well received by the colonists, being described as "priggish," "tactless," and a "joyless bore." This situation was complicated when he became romantically involved with a Georgia girl, Sophie Hopkey. She was open to receiving a proposal of marriage from him, but soon became put off by his "sillyness" and married someone else. Later John refused to give communion to Sophie, which only caused greater resentment toward him from the colonists.

> *It was in Georgia, however, that John Wesley had his famous encounter with the Moravian leader, Augustus Spangenberg, an encounter from which he could not escape as he wrestled with his soul's discontent. Spangenberg pointedly asked Wesley, "Do you know Jesus Christ?" John could only reply, "I know he is the savior of the world." Spangenberg countered with, "True, but do you know that he has saved you?"*[508]

At that time the emphasis upon assurance of salvation both troubled and caused conviction for Wesley. Later, however, it would become one of the key features of Methodism. After this failed missionary effort in Georgia, he returned to London where his journey to conversion would continue.

> *On his way home, he had a chance to ponder the whole experience. "I went to America," he wrote, "to convert the Indians, but, oh, who shall convert me?"*[509]

On February 1, 1738, after two years in Georgia, he landed back in London. On February 7, just six days after his return, he met a group of five Moravians who were seeking to establish a mission among African Americans in the Colony of Georgia. Their leader was Peter Bohler who had worked with Count Zinzendorf in several evangelistic efforts in Germany. Wesley and Bohler engaged in several discussions in which Bohler impressed upon Wesley the need for "a new birth." Up to this point, Wesley had been on a journey toward "holiness" or "perfection." Bohler pointed out that people are "justified by faith" immediately when they come to God through Christ and could experience assurance of salvation. Wesley could not understand how salvation could be given in a moment of time. This issue was resolved on May 24, 1738.

> *In the evening I went very unwillingly to a society in Aldersgate Street, where one was reading Luther's preface to the Epistle to the Romans. About a quarter to nine, while he [the speaker] was describing the change that God works in the heart through faith in Christ, I felt my heart strangely warmed. I felt that I did trust in Christ, Christ alone, for salvation; and an assurance was given me that he had taken away my sins, even mine, and saved me from the law of sin and death.*[510]

The basic Reformation doctrine of justification by faith had gripped Wesley.[511] From that time, his ministry grew. Two things marked his ministry. First, he was tireless in his efforts. He preached more than 40,000 sermons and traveled more than 225,000 miles before he "first began to feel old at 85." Second, he was an ingenious organizer. He organized his converts into classes, developed a strong lay ministry, which included lay ministers, and began having annual conferences in London to foster vision and maintain continuity in the efforts. It was out of his dedication, and "methodism," that the Methodist Church was born.

Wesley always thought of himself as a loyal Anglican and never left the Church of England. Despite Wesley's intentions to keep his societies within the Church of England, an independent organization developed, with its own network of chapels or congregations and separate institutional apparatus.[512] For years, he resisted encouragement from his own followers that "the Methodists" separate from the Church of England. Interestingly, the influence that turned the tide was the beginning of Methodism in colonial America. John Wesley asked Philip Embury, who had been converted under Wesley's preaching in 1752, if he would go to America and start a Methodist society. It is commonly held that Wesleyanism arrived in America in 1766 with the landing of Embury. He arrived in New York and began the work in his living room with five people. From this, the first American society of Methodists began. Upon this small foundation, others would come, and continue to build. One, in particular was Francis Asbury (1745-1816). Wesley commissioned him to America, and when he arrived in Philadelphia in 1771, there were only 300 Methodists in all the colonies. He worked tirelessly at starting new societies, and by the time Asbury died, Methodism in America had grown into the hundreds of thousands. At the request of John Wesley, Thomas Coke (1747-1814) left England to join the work in America. At an annual conference in Baltimore in 1787, Coke and Francis Asbury would be made the first bishops of the "Methodist Episcopal Church" in America. It was on American soil that a new, distinct denomination was born—something more easily done in the colonies than in England.

John Wesley died in London on March 2, 1791. He was nearing 88 years of age. After his death, the English Methodists followed the example of their American counterparts and separated from the Anglican Church to begin the Methodist Church in England.

In studying the work of John Wesley, and the establishment of the Methodist Church, it is evident that there were many influences in his development: Anglican, Lutheran, Catholic, the influence of the mystics, and, of course, the Moravians. When examined closely, it seems that there is justification for placing the Methodist movement within the Pietist fold. The small societies, the broader structure of the Methodist churches, and the hymnology that developed, contain a strong Pietistic language and influence.

Charles Wesley

Charles Wesley (1707-1788) was the eighteenth child of Samuel and Susanna Wesley. He is described as "more somber," and his brother John as "more exuberant," yet their lives and ministries worked together in very dynamic ways. John was the leader and preacher, and Charles made his mark on the church mainly through hymn writing. He wrote more than 6,000 hymns and gospel songs, including "Jesus, Lover of My Soul," "O For a Thousand Tongues to Sing," "Love Divine, All Loves Excelling," "Rejoice, the Lord is King," "Soldiers of Christ, Arise," "Christ the Lord is Risen Today," and "Hark the Herald Angels Sing." Some historians believe that Charles Wesley's hymns are the greatest legacy from the 18th century awakenings.

It was Charles who, along with two other Oxford undergraduates—Robert Kirkham and William Morgan—started the "Holy Club." Though the group had many negative traits, it also served in the development of the young men who were participants. Another benefit came in the form of a young visitor to their group who had recently graduated from Pembroke College—George Whitefield. An association began with him at Oxford and would bear abundant fruit throughout the years.

Following ordination as an Anglican clergyman, Charles accompanied John on his mission trip to Georgia. He experienced the same storm at sea, observed the spirit of the Moravians, joined in the work, but became ill and immediately returned to England in 1736 (the same year they had arrived in Georgia). Having been impressed with the spirituality and assurance of the Moravians during the trip to Georgia, Charles sought them out on his return to England, hoping to find a more meaningful faith. When John returned from Georgia, both brothers began meeting with Peter Bohler to inquire into his beliefs. It was during this time that Charles became critically ill and, on May 21, 1738, experienced a joyous personal conversion. Interestingly, this was just three days before his brother John came to faith in Christ on May 24.

The following years would set in motion a movement that would change the world. Joining with their friend from Oxford, George Whitefield, John and Charles Wesley looked for opportunities to preach wherever they could find an audience. Following Whitefield's example, they took to preaching in fields and factories, taking their message to the English lower classes. There were many converts and Methodism grew. Charles was never as healthy and robust as John, and, in 1756, after 20 years of itinerant work, he was forced to stop traveling.

Charles was conservative by nature and remained loyal to the Church of England. As the work of Methodism expanded, he found himself in disagreement with John over various issues. To him, too much leniency was allowed in both doctrine and practice. Ordinations and sacraments had always been done under the administration of Anglican clergymen. Due to the rapid expansion of Methodism, especially in America with its wide open spaces, it became necessary to ordain men to the ministry who could administer the sacraments of baptism and communion. With very few Anglican pastors in these areas, there were large numbers of church members who would go long periods without receiving communion. When John ordained Francis Asbury and Thomas Coke, he did so without consulting Charles. This was done in order to give them authority to ordain ministers in America. These were referred to as "non-episcopal" ordinations. Charles was greatly disturbed over this for a number of reasons, one of which was his belief that John had taken "upon himself the prerogative of a bishop, and he commissioned Coke to act with similar powers."[513] Charles wrote:

So easily are Bishops made
 By man's, or woman's whim?
W_____ his hands on C_____ hath laid,
 But who laid hands on him?...
 For lo! ye see contained in John
 The whole of Presbytery.[514]

Of course the W_____ stands for "Wesley" and the C_____ stands for "Coke." In this way Charles Wesley questioned his brother's claim to apostolic succession.

A final commentary on their lives might be seen in the places the brothers were buried. Charles was buried in an Anglican Church yard. John was buried beside a Methodist chapel. Though they had their disagreements, they remained loyal to one another. As within most movements, especially in the beginning, there were tensions that needed time for resolution. The Wesleyan movement awakened Christians within both the state church and the dissenting churches to a greater spirituality and a greater sensibility to the meaning of Christianity.

Both John and Charles Wesley were used in very unusual ways in this time of spiritual awakening. Their work had great social consequences as well as spiritual. Concern for the poor, establishment of orphanages, visiting the imprisoned, and addressing issues which gave rise to the abolition of slavery in England are but a few.

George Whitefield

George Whitefield (1714-1770) gave a dynamic voice to the awakenings in England. Never an organizer, Whitefield was preeminently an awakener.[515] Though only 22 years of age, he was ordained by the Church of England in 1736 and embarked on a meteoric preaching career that would take him to both sides of the Atlantic. He was the undisputed "preacher par-excellance" of the awakenings in both England and America. Whitefield's preaching was unforgettable.[516] David Garrick, the actor stated, "I would give a hundred guineas if I could only say the word *Oh!* like Mr. Whitefield."[517] "George Whitefield could pronounce the word Mesopotamia so as to bring tears to the eyes"[518] Not only was he a gifted orator, but he had such a strong, resonant voice that Benjamin Franklin, who became his friend, calculated could be heard and understood by 30,000 gathered people.

He was born and grew up in Gloucester, England, where he worked in his parents' inn and tavern. His parents were poor, but he entered Oxford in 1733 where he met the Wesleys and became acquainted with their "Holy Club." This encounter led to a lifelong friendship with the Wesley brothers, and it can be said that it was through his relationship with Charles Wesley, that he was converted. Whitefield was the first to be called a "Methodist" by students at Oxford University, who wanted to make fun of the small group that met for prayer and Bible study, went to church, and helped the poor.[519] Although eleven years younger than John and seven years younger than Charles Wesley, he was respected and easily accepted into their group.

> *His extraordinary speaking ability was noticed at a young age; he would have liked to become an actor, but instead his voice would be used to call thousands to Christ in Britain and America. Whitefield played a major role, along with the Wesleys, in the awakening that swept across Britain in the first half of the 1700s. His powerful preaching caused a great stir wherever he went. He is mostly remembered, however, for his part in the First Great Awakening in America, where his preaching had a tremendous impact. Before George Washington, George Whitefield was the most popular figure in America.*[520]

As the Wesleyan movement spread through England, it was Whitefield who first conceived of the idea of preaching in open-air services. It was through this method that tough Bristol, England, miners were converted. At first, Wesley was skeptical about this approach, but was finally convinced by Whitefield and took up the practice himself with great results.

> *After that spring of 1739 in Bristol, Wesley set out to carry the gospel to the poor wherever they were willing to listen. In June he wrote: "I look upon the world as my parish; I judge it my bounden duty, to declare unto all that are willing to hear, the glad tidings of salvation. He preached in jails to prisoners, in inns to wayfarers, on vessels crossing to Ireland. At a natural amphitheater in Cornwall he preached to 30,000 at once, and when he was refused admission to the Epworth Church he preached to hundreds while standing on his father's tombstone.*[521]

Whitefield inspired John Wesley and everyone who heard him. Though his ministry was extremely effective in England, it is for his part in the First Great Awakening in America that he is mostly remembered.

John Wesley and George Whitefield remained good friends throughout their lifetimes, although not without difficulties. It should be noted, and perhaps there is a lesson to be learned from a particular element in their friendship, that theologically, John Wesley was Arminian and George Whitefield was Calvinist. They debated over predestination, and even exchanged polemical letters, but remained friends to the end. There were two significant breaks in Wesley's ministry. One was with the Moravians whom he thought were given over to antinomianism (license, or too much liberty). In fact, Wesley wrote tracts exposing this condition in Moravian theology. The Moravians responded in 1745 by making it clear they had "no connections" with either John or Charles Wesley. The other break was with Whitefield.

> *The same fear of antinomianism caused a breach in his friendship with George Whitefield...he [Wesley] could not*

> *accept a doctrine of extreme election and predestination. He was afraid that antinomianism could be the possible end result of such a stance and in 1770 he openly denounced Calvinism as a "poison to faith"...Although they were reconciled in friendship and supported each other's ministry, Whitefield and Wesley traveled different paths doctrinally and theologically.*[522]

The break in their ministries occurred as early as 1740 so they traveled these separate doctrinal and theological paths for about 30 years. However, the affirmation of their friendship was demonstrated at George Whitefield's funeral. When Wesley gave the sermon at Whitefield's funeral in 1770, he spoke of the evangelist's "most generous and tender friendship."[523]

There is no doubt that George Whitefield had a special relationship to America. Apart from a highly successful ministry, he gained many friends as he traveled through the colonies. And, it was on his seventh preaching tour in America that he took ill and died on September 30, 1770. It is fitting, that he was buried at Newburyport, Connecticut.

Great Awakenings in the American Colonies

America is noted for two Great Awakenings, one in the middle of the 1700s and the other at the beginning of the 1800s. Historians often point to a third awakening from 1857-1859. The third was of shorter duration and brought about, it is believed, by a combination of crises and prayer meetings throughout the United States and Canada. Awakenings in America have played a major role in shaping the religious, moral, intellectual, social, and economic foundations of the country. Foreign missions were driven forward by these spiritual awakenings. In 1800, Christians were concentrated in Europe and North America; by 1900, many Christians were in China, India, and Africa.[524] Of the nine colonial colleges, six were born as a result of the awakenings.[525] Social reforms were initiated. The anti-slavery movement in America was mainly a part of the reform movement generated by the Second Great Awakening, as were movements for prison reform, child labor laws, women's rights, inner-city missions, and many more.[526] Preachers of this time addressed family, social, and political issues as well as spiritual, with the result that a large portion of the population was "awakened." The first Great Awakening took place in the first half of the 18th century; the Second Great Awakening began just before and continued well into the first half of the 19th century.

America was built upon strong spiritual foundations. Beginning in the early part of the 17th century, as the colonies began to develop, religion was central in the formation of their families and the communities they established. As someone has said, "The pilgrims arrived 'awakened.'" However, as in England, the colonial Americans moved from the biblical foundations built by their forefathers. Shortly after 1700, there was a marked decline in morals and in religion. Due partly to an expanding frontier and the dynamics of a population "on the move," faith was taking less and less of a prominent place in American life.

Forerunners to the First Great Awakening

The dates for the First Great Awakening are usually designated from 1735 to 1750 or beyond. By all measurements, it seems apparent that the first awakening began on a grand scale in 1740 under the preaching of George Whitefield; however, it is not always easy to define a precise beginning or end to such times. As with all such movements, there were forerunners, "voices" that prepare the way for what would follow.

Solomon Stoddard

Solomon Stoddard (1643-1729) was one such forerunner. As a congregational pastor, he labored and preached at the First Church (Congregational) of Northampton, Massachusetts, for 60 years—from 1669 until he died in 1729. Stoddard's writings carried immense weight in the late 17th and early 18th century. Situated on the Connecticut River, Northampton was considered the western frontier. His influence "dominated the political and ecclesiastical affairs of western Massachusetts for half a century."[527]

Stoddard and other Puritan leaders became concerned about the declining spiritual conditions in New England since the arrival of the colonial founders. Their concern was such that in 1679 they called together a "Reforming Synod," to address these issues. It was noted that a great preaching style had developed in the New England, but that preachers had become more concerned about delivery than with the content in their messages. Stoddard believed that if there could be a return to true biblical preaching and teaching, coupled with prayer, and biblical principles were applied at both the individual and corporate levels, it might be expected that there would be a return to true spirituality. Joining with others, and believing that the Bible had the true answers for all man's problems, Stoddard thought the church and New England could be brought up out of the "valley" they were in.

> *Stoddard was known as a powerful preacher, and followed his own advice completely. In response to his strong preaching and pastoral methods, five awakenings, or "harvests" as he called them, came upon his church and the area of Northampton: in 1679, 1683, 1696, 1712, and 1718. More souls were added to Christ than any other time in New England before the Great Awakening.*[528]

Despite the "harvests" or awakenings at Northampton, most New England churches continued in their old ways. In many, there was a pattern of spiritual decline as well as diminishing memberships. Some pastors began to learn from Stoddard and to preach for revival in their own churches. One such pastor, Eliphalet Adams, of New London, Connecticut, began urging prayer and preaching for revival. As time passed, there seemed to be certain "outpourings of the Spirit" throughout northern New England. On a preaching tour to Windham, Connecticut, in 1721, Adams announced that revivals "were no longer a rarity, and that a Great Awakening seemed to be at the threshold."[529] Historian Michael Crawford has found records of at least 15 other such New England spiritual harvests, mostly in towns along the Connecticut River, in the two decades between 1712 and 1732.[530] No doubt many of these were due to the influence of Solomon Stoddard.

> *Solomon Stoddard completed an amazing pastorate of sixty years. Due to his failing health, the church, in 1727, called for an assistant to aid him. They selected Stoddard's grandson, Jonathan Edwards. This was a momentous decision.*[531]

Jonathan worked for a couple of years as assistant pastor to his grandfather and then assumed responsibilities as pastor of First Church of Northampton.

Theodorus Jacobus Frelinghuysen

Theodorus Frelinghuysen (1691-1747), at age 27, sailed from Holland to New England in 1719 aboard the ship King George. He was born in Germany, the son of a minister, and educated in the Netherlands. Having come under the influence of the Dutch Pietists, he came to the Raritan Valley of New Jersey to minister to Dutch immigrants who had formed themselves into four churches. In Holland, he had been ordained and served one small Dutch church. Devoted to the teachings of Pietism, in his ministry he emphasized personal conversion and a life of obedience demonstrated in faith and love.

What he found in Raritan in 1719 disappointed him. He felt that his parishioners had only a "form of godliness" and no true, vital faith. In fact, he believed that most of the church members were unconverted. He wrote that "great laxity of manners prevailed throughout his charge...that while horse-racing, gambling, dissipation, and rudeness of various kinds were common, the [church] was attended at convenience, and religion consisted of the mere formal pursuit of the routine of duty."532

> *The Dutch farmers must have been stunned when their new pastor called on them to repent and be converted to Christ. In some of his first New Jersey sermons Frelinghuysen set the tone for his evangelistic preaching for years to come. He portrayed the beginning of the conversion experience as a great "conviction" of one's lost condition. Frelinghuysen declared that only those who have undergone such a conversion have salvation, and that no one else, even the most upright and moral may entertain hope for heaven. The proper Dutch members of his congregations did not find such doctrine unacceptable in itself, but their new pastor seemed to regard many of them as unregenerate, as self-righteous, as hypocrites.*533

Amid controversies he continued and soon the entire area was affected by his powerful preaching. Numbers were baptized and others began to see a connection between their profession of faith and the way they led their lives. True to his Pietist training, he began to organize his congregations "into small groups for Bible study and prayer, urging them to pray publicly and extemporaneously..."534 Under his ministry the church was being revitalized and prepared for greater stirrings of the Spirit of God.

> *The Great Awakening had its beginning in the preaching of Theodore Frelinghuysen to his Dutch Reformed congregations in New Jersey in 1726. When George Whitefield came to preach in America, he recognized Frelinghuysen's work as an important source for the Great Awakening. It should be noted that it was Frelinghuysen who was responsible for laying foundations*

for the formation of the Dutch Reformed Church in America.[535]

Gilbert Tennent

Gilbert Tennent (1703-1764) became a key figure in preparing the soil of New England. When George Whitefield came to the colonies, he and Gilbert Tennent traveled together, and shared preaching responsibilities. When Whitefield heard Tennent preach, he said, "[I] never heard such a searching sermon. He convinced me more and more that we can preach the Gospel of Christ no further than we have experienced the power of it in our own hearts...He is a son of thunder, and does not fear the faces of men."[536]

Gilbert Tennent's father, William Tennent (1673-1746), was trained in Edinburgh, Scotland, and came to America as an ordained Presbyterian minister. Bothered by the lack of centers for theological education, he decided to start a school to train pastors. He did this by taking young men into his own home in Neshaminy, Pennsylvania. Later, he built a log building to house the school. It came to be called the "log college" by those who opposed his work. Gilbert Tennent attended his father's school and then helped in the operation of the school until his father died. At that time, it was decided to close the school and start a Presbyterian school, which was called the College of New Jersey, now called Princeton University. Gilbert was a trustee of the College of New Jersey for many years.

In 1726, Gilbert Tennent met Theodore Frelinghuysen and they became friends, even though he was 12 years younger than Frelinghuysen. At this point, Tennent had a sense of barrenness in his own ministry and became impressed with Frelinghuysen's ministry and the effects of his powerful preaching. Tennent was inspired and learned much from his older friend. In 1727, he became pastor of the Presbyterian Church in New Brunswick, New Jersey, and having been influenced by Frelinghuysen as he had, sought to employ the same methods in his church. Before long, Tennent had convinced several other young Presbyterians that Frelinghuysen's piety was exactly what their churches needed also.[537] In this way, Frelinghuysen had an effect upon clergymen as well as the lay population.

Tennent was an eloquent, scholarly preacher who called for a genuine change of heart in his hearers. He promoted the idea of revival and became one of the most outspoken defenders of George Whitefield.

The Great Awakening

Jonathan Edwards (1703-1758) and George Whitefield (1714-1770) are the names that come to mind when the First Great Awakening is mentioned. Each contributed in major, yet different ways, and with unique styles.

Jonathan Edwards and George Whitefield

Thought by many to be America's finest theologian ever, Jonathan Edwards is regarded the faithful leader of the Awakening. He possessed the combination of keen logic, utmost diligence and insight in theology, and a warm and devout spiritual life. Highly intelligent, he entered Yale at age 13 and graduated in 1720 when he was 17. By that time, he had already read most of the great philosophic literature of the past and that of his own time. Following graduation, he taught at Yale for a short while, then served as a pastor for a time in New York. In 1727, he became associate pastor alongside his well-known grandfather, Solomon Stoddard, at the First Congregational Church in Northampton, Massachusetts. When his grandfather died in 1729, Edwards continued on as pastor and remained in the church for 27 years. During this time, he became known as an advocate for a genuine and true spiritual life. From his pulpit, messages were given that first brought small awakenings to Northampton, and then the Great Awakening to New England.

In 1734, Edwards gave a series of messages on justification by faith. No immediate effects became apparent, but after some time, in December 1734 "The Spirit of God began extraordinarily to set in and wonderfully work among us...."[538] On one occasion in 1735, 300 people professed faith in Christ for the first time. Soon the whole town became spiritually aware and revival began to spread to other towns. Other pastors began to promote the Awakening, and it spread to more than 20 communities in western Massachusetts and Connecticut, lingering for a few years in some villages.[539] Jonathon Edwards made an important contribution during this time through his writing and record-keeping. In 1737, he produced a publication, *A Faithful Narrative of the Surprising Work of God*, which gave an account of the awakenings experienced in Northampton and the other cities. This became a bestseller in America and England, and helped spread the ideas which fostered the Great Awakening.

The crest of the First Great Awakening was from 1740 to 1745. Edwards' popularity increased and he began to travel outside his local parish to preach and foster the ideas of the Awakening. His well prepared sermons and keen thought enlightened and convicted people, moving them to true conversion. His work was important, and done well, but the Great Awakening did not come through the efforts of one man. Jonathan Edwards had plowed the ground by favorably preparing New England with his *Faithful Narrative*, but it was the powerful preaching of George Whitefield that brought the Great Awakening springing to life.[540] Until his arrival in the colonies, there had been revivals referred to as "regional awakenings." After his arrival, there churned up "a spiritual hurricane called the Great Awakening."[541] He has been referred to as "the Great Awakening's traveling lightning rod...the fireball who set things ablaze in New England...."[542]

From 1738 to 1770, Whitefield would engage upon several extended preaching tours throughout the colonies, which produced profound results. He made seven trips to America and preached in virtually every important town on the Atlantic seaboard during 1738, 1739-41, 1744-48, 1751-52, 1754-55, 1763-65, and 1769-70.[543]

> *In 1738, Whitefield made his first of seven exhausting but productive preaching tours in the American colonies. His dynamic preaching in New England in 1740 detonated the spiritual revival known as the "Great Awakening." Free from denominational bias (unusual for a time when sectarian loyalties ran deep), Whitefield cheerfully preached in all pulpits. His remarkable voice and compelling presence affected vast audiences and boosted membership in all Protestant churches.*[544]

From February through the spring of 1739, Whitefield was in Bristol, England, conducting successful preaching campaigns in the open fields, but he left for America in October.

> *George Whitefield arrived in the Middle Colonies,*[545] *coming ashore at Lewes, Delaware, on 30 October, 1739. Whitefield claimed that he had stopped only to pick up supplies for an orphanage he planned to build in Georgia.*[546]

No one knew what was coming. Upon his arrival, he was invited to speak in Philadelphia and did so with overwhelming success. Diverse groups such as the Congregationalists, Baptists, Presbyterians, Anglicans, Moravians, and Quakers began setting differences aside and cooperating. It was here that he met Benjamin Franklin who became a life-long friend and admirer of Whitefield. From Philadelphia, he traveled through New York, New Jersey, and Pennsylvania. On these tours he met Gilbert Tennent and Theodore Frelinghuysen. He and Tennent traveled together. Whitefield was impressed with the men he met on this tour, thinking them to be gentlemen of great quality. Finally, on January 9, 1740, he "arrived at his orphanage—his colonial home base—in Savannah, Georgia."[547] After three months in Georgia, he sailed north. During April and May, he preached in Philadelphia and New York, to numbers upwards of 15,000 in each city. Whitefield returned to

Savannah and Charleston to catch his breath—if overseeing an orphanage that grew to about 70 residents in a large new building that cost nearly 4,000 pounds, supervising the services of Savannah's Church of England congregation (where he was the incumbent), and making short preaching tours into the countryside could be called relaxation.[548] It is of note that the orphanage Whitefield founded, and raised the money for in Georgia, still operates today on the south side of Savannah. Bethesda orphanage and school, established in 1740 as the result of Whitefield's efforts, and a land grant of 500 acres from the king of England, is the oldest existing program for boys of its kind in America. Following his summer in Georgia in 1740, he sailed for Newport, Rhode Island, and arrived there in September.

> *Whitefield preached from Maine to Connecticut during the period 14 September to 29 October 1740. As the historian Edwin Gausted wrote, he "came, bristling, crackling, and thundering" to an area "electrified with expectancy."*[549]

He preached in Newport and then went to Boston. His arrival in Boston moved the Great Awakening forward. On a weekday, he preached "forenoon" at the South Church to a "packed house," then in the afternoon he spoke to about 5,000 people on the Boston Common. On Sunday afternoon, he went to the Old Brick Church to preach to an over-packed building, and then went from there to preach to 8,000 in an open field. For more than a month he preached up and down the New England coast. On Sunday evening, October 12, he gave a farewell sermon on the Common, in Boston, with an estimated 23,000 in attendance (some say as many as 30,000). The entire population of Boston at the time was 13,000. From there, he turned west across Massachusetts, preaching his way through the central part of the state as he went.

On Friday, October 17, he arrived in Northampton, Massachusetts, where he met Jonathan and Sarah Edwards and preached four times in the Northampton Church. Immediately he developed an affection for Jonathan and Sarah. He was impressed with their church, with the couple, and their family. George Whitefield recorded the following in his journal, dated "Friday, October 17, 1740:"

> *Mr. Edwards is a solid, excellent Christian, but at present, weak in body. I think I have not seen his fellow [his likes] in all of New England. When I came into his pulpit...to remind them of their former experiences, and how zealous and lively they were at that time, both minister and people wept much.*[550]

After spending a couple of days with them, another entry in Whitefield's journal, dated "Sunday, October 19":

> *Felt great satisfaction in being in the house of Mr. Edwards. A sweeter couple I have not yet seen. Their children were not dressed in silks and satins, but plain, as become the children of those who, in all things, ought to be examples of Christian simplicity. Mrs. Edwards is adorned with a meek and quiet spirit; she talked solidly of the things of God, and seemed to be such a helpmeet for her husband, that she caused me to renew those prayers, which for some months, I have put up to God, that he would be pleased to send me a daughter of Abraham to be my wife.*[551]

Over the three days he spent with the Edwards, he, too, left an impression. Sarah Edwards summed up what she called "the mixture of spiritual zeal and raw charisma that created Whitefield's unforgettable presence:"[552]

> *He makes less of doctrines than our American preachers generally do, and aims more at affecting the heart. He is a born orator. You have already heard of his deep-toned, yet clear and melodious voice. It is perfect music. It is wonderful to see what a spell he casts over an audience by proclaiming the simplest truths of the Bible. I have seen upwards of a thousand people hang on his words with breathless silence, broken only by an occasional half-suppressed sob.*[553]

Whitefield left Northampton and traveled south where he met Gilbert Tennent on Staten Island. There he urged Tennent to make a preaching tour through New England and cover many of the same places where Whitefield had preached in the last couple of months in order "to blow up the divine fire lately kindled there."[554]

> *Tennant arrived in Boston December 1740, and proved as popular to many as Whitefield had been. The Awakening continued to blossom.*[555]

Through the itinerant work of such men as Whitefield, Tennent, and others, and with the prayer and preaching that was taking place in the churches throughout New England, the next five years would be the high period of the First Great Awakening.

On July 8, 1741, at Enfield, Connecticut, Jonathan Edwards gave his famous sermon, "Sinners in the Hands of an Angry God." The response from the congregation was amazing. People were overcome with guilt and fear, and began to cry out. Edwards' response revealed his own disposition and intent in preaching.

> *When the congregation at Enfield could not control themselves as they listened to "Sinners in the Hands of an Angry God," and Edwards could not be heard for the commotion, he stopped and requested that they be quiet to*

> *hear the rest of the sermon, and refrain from weeping and crying out!*[556]

Jonathan Edwards has often been portrayed as a "hellfire and brimstone" preacher, primarily because of this one sermon. However, a careful look into his life and methods reveals otherwise.

> *His preaching, he determined, was to appeal to the mind, and not to encourage outbursts of emotion. He was by all accounts never a spellbinding speaker, and he did not wish to be. All of his sermons were delivered in the same calm fashion—but with penetrating force.*[557]

Some revival preachers thought that emotional displays or outbursts were signs of something supernatural occurring within an individual. Edwards countered, saying that such displays were not "sure evidence" of anything. He wanted the Christian message to be clearly understood, and thought that the mind could inform the heart in such a way that there could be a sustained commitment to Christ, rather than the short-lived "commitments" he had already observed. In fact, he believed that true religion resided in the affections, but true affections were produced in the joining of mind and heart. His success, and the depth of influence in his ministry, clearly was not due to dramatic style.

> *It was not due to theatrics. One observer wrote, "He scarcely gestured or even moved, and he made no attempt by the elegance of his style or the beauty of his pictures to gratify the taste and fascinate the imagination." Instead he convinced "with overwhelming weight of argument and with intenseness of feeling."*[558]

Word of the awakening at Enfield spread, and through his preaching, writing, and careful analysis of what was happening in New England, Jonathan Edwards was becoming more important to the cause. The Great Awakening was at its zenith, and Edwards was at the peak of his fame.[559]

Following his sermon at Enfield, he was invited to speak at Yale College, and surprised everyone by not giving a usual "revival message." His intent was to defend the Awakening and show it was clearly from God. He called upon everyone to embrace and not do or say anything that would hinder the work God was doing throughout the land. He warned that there were two dangers that could threaten or undo this work of God. The first would come from ministers who could not embrace the awakening. There "is a secret Kind of Opposition, that really tends to hinder the Work…silent Ministers stand in the Way of the Work of God."[560] The second danger would come from those who favored what was happening but would disrupt through errors or excesses. Those in favor of the revival must "give diligent Heed to themselves to avoid all Errors and Misconduct, and whatsoever may darken and obscure the Work, and give Occasion to those that stand ready to reproach it."[561] Edwards was exactly right. The chief criticisms came from those two sources.

Jonathan Edwards had a deep belief in the Great Awakening because of his theological beliefs. As with many others at that time, he did not see a separation between church and state in the way people do today. In his mind, it made perfect sense that religion and state would co-exist and that each was necessary to the other.

> *Edwards' enthusiasm for the Great Awakening was fired by his vision of hope for the establishment of God's kingdom on earth. He believed that the Great Awakening could be the doorway to the Messianic Kingdom, the Millennial period foretold in Isaiah and Revelation 20, during which the redeemed of God "Lived and reigned with Christ a thousand years." It is not surprising that he felt this way, for all over New England a remarkable transformation was taking place.*[562]

In more than one way, Jonathan Edwards was a gift to America. His life, his ministry, his theology, and his family, are all examples of what can happen when people know God and follow his teachings. His Calvinist theology, especially with its emphasis upon man's sinfulness and God's love and sovereignty, gave directions, not only for how the gospel was to be proclaimed, but in how people should be governed. His theology came to be known as "New England Theology" and it dominated Protestant theological thinking for generations. Though Edwards died approximately 20 years before the founding of the new nation, his thought influenced political leaders and churchmen alike in establishing the United States of America.

Jonathan and Sarah Edwards

Jonathan and Sarah Edwards had a good marriage and home life. Marriage was given a high place in the thinking of the Puritans, and the Edwards' life together demonstrated this belief. Their courtship occurred over four years, due mainly to their age difference, Sarah being seven years younger than Jonathan. He was twenty when they met, and she 13. There is an amusing anecdote which shows that Jonathan's studious mind was not always on its studies. He had a great deal of studying to do as he prepared for his master's degree. He had already met Sarah and the following is what he wrote on the front page of his Greek grammar book.

> *They say there is a young lady in New Haven… She has a strange sweetness in her mind, and singular purity in her affections; is most just and conscientious in all her conduct… She is of wonderful sweetness, calmness and universal benevolence of mind…She will sometimes go about from place to place, singing sweetly and seems always to be full of joy and pleasure; and no one knows for what!*[563]

Jonathan's hope was that he was the "what." Four years later they were married on July 28, 1727. The contributions accrued from the lives of Jonathan and Sarah Edwards is noteworthy:

> *Their eleven children have been a gift to American cultural history. In 1900 a reporter tracked down 1,400 descendants of Jonathan and Sarah Edwards. He found that they included 13 college presidents, 65 professors, two graduate school deans, 100 lawyers, 66 physicians, 80 holders of public office, including three senators and three governors of states. Members of this clan had written 135 published books, and the women were repeatedly described as "great readers" or "highly intelligent." These people seemed to have a talent for making money: their numbers include a roster of bankers and industrialists. Of course there were platoons of missionaries. The report asserted: "The family has cost the country nothing in pauperism, in crime, in hospital or asylum service: on the contrary, it represents the highest usefulness."*[564]

Apparently both Jonathan and Sarah came from good genetic stock. Additionally, it is noted that Sarah had an acute understanding of nutrition and health for the time in which she lived.

> *It was extraordinary that all eleven Edwards babies lived. At that time, infant mortality was high. The survival of the Edwards in that precarious era says something about Sarah's instinctive sense of nutrition, her clean house, her good health during pregnancy, and about the remarkable eugenic combination this couple represented.*[565]

Jonathan and Sarah Edwards were married for 31 years. In 1758, Jonathan was invited to become president of Princeton. A short time after taking office, he died from the effects of a smallpox vaccination. He received the vaccination as an example, hoping it would save others from the dreaded disease. Historian, Sydney Ahlstrom, wrote: "In the long run the influence of Jonathan Edwards...is the most enduring result of the New England Awakening...."[566]

Outcomes of the First Great Awakening

Others contributed to the expansion of the Great Awakening which blessed all of New England.

> *Presbyterians from the Middle colonies carried the revival fires to the South. Samuel Davies became the leader of the revival among the Presbyterians in Virginia. The Baptist phase of revival in the South grew out of the work of Shubal Stearns and Daniel Marshall of New England...Revivalistic Methodism also took deep roots in the South through the efforts of Devereux Jarrett, an Episcopalian minister, and lay preachers during the revival...Whitefield unified the efforts of all these revival preachers as he traveled in all the colonies....*[567]

From 1740 to 1742, during the First Great Awakening, it is estimated that there were as many as 50,000 converts added to New England churches. By 1760, 150 new churches had started in New England. All of this occurred in a population of around 300,000. It is easy to see what a profound influence this movement would have had upon the country. It is worth noting that the leaders of the First Great Awakening, besides being great preachers and leaders, were churchmen. Not only were people "saved," churches were strengthened and new ones started. When analyzing the results of the First Great Awakening, historian Bill Austin suggests the following:

First, there was a general arousal of religious life, a renewed emphasis on personal conversion, a large increase in church membership, and a higher standard of morality. This increased awareness would have long-lasting effects in American life. Second, the Great Awakening aroused awareness for education and led to the establishment of important educational institutions.

> To this end, the Presbyterian synod of New York, in 1745, established the College of New Jersey, which became Princeton University. The University of Pennsylvania was founded in 1753 on a non-denominational basis. King's College (now Columbia University) was started in 1754 as an Anglican institution. Rhode Island College (Brown University) was established by the Baptists in 1764. The Dutch Reformed opened Rutgers College in New Jersey in 1766, and the Congregationalists founded Dartmouth College in New Hampshire in 1769. Numerous parochial schools were established, the common public school was upgraded, and the English Latin grammar school was replaced by the American academy with its more practical studies.[568]

For the most part, the leaders of the First Great Awakening were well-educated people. Edwards was trained at Yale. The Wesley brothers and George Whitefield received their educations at Oxford. To them, there was no division between spirituality and a good education.

Third, missionary activity that focused upon Native Americans and African Americans, arose during this time, as well as the beginning of the modern missions movement. When Jonathan Edwards' pastorate terminated at the church in Northampton, Massachusetts, he became a missionary for a short time to the Indians living in the region. David Brainard, who was engaged to marry Edwards' daughter, had a passion for the Indians and literally burned himself out trying to reach them. He died before he could marry. His story became an inspiration. When Jonathan Edwards published Brainard's biography, it became a major influence for missions. Many young people read it and were motivated to a life of missionary service. One of those inspired by the biography was

William Carey, missionary to India, who would come to be known as "the father of modern missions." It is this point in history that is recognized as the beginning of the modern missions movement.

Fourth, there was important influence upon the thinking of the founders of the new republic, which was about to be born. The fact that the Great Awakening preceded the Revolutionary War and the founding of the nation, was very fortunate for colonial America. There was a definite "Christian influence" that prevailed during this period. Not only did Christian sensibilities influence the thoughts of the founders, but the ideas within colonial Christianity supported the political ideas that were incorporated into the *Declaration of Independence*, and later, into the *Constitution of the United States*. The belief in "religious liberty" reigned strong and fit with the beliefs inherent in democratic ideals. In short, two distinctive principles of the Reformation, salvation by faith of the individual and the priesthood of all believers, characterized the Great Awakening and undergirded the principles of democracy, which would be incorporated in the coming new republic, the United States of America.[569]

The Second Great Awakening

Though the impact of the First Great Awakening was significant, religious life in the colonies diminished dramatically by the end of the 1700s. There were several influences that combined to reduce religious awareness, including the Revolutionary War, Enlightenment thought, religious division and suspicion, and the migration to the west.

It is no surprise that the American Revolution (1775-1783) created problems for the colonial churches. As a religious leader, should one remain loyal to the Crown, or endorse the revolution? Churches needed to decide, and in doing so, ended up on both sides of the question.

> The Anglican Church remained loyal to the revolutionary cause in the Southern colonies, such as Maryland and Virginia; in the Middle colonies its loyalty was about equally divided between the revolutionists and the English; in New England it was generally loyal to England...The Quakers, Mennonites and Moravians were at heart patriotic, but their pacifist principles kept them from any participation in the war. Congregationalists, Baptists and Presbyterians espoused the cause of the revolution with ardor....[570]

Methodists, by contrast, were hamstrung during the conflict by the taint of loyalism—not only were they suspect for their connection with the Anglican Church, but John and Charles Wesley, along with other British Methodists, had made widely publicized comments denouncing the American rebellion as a cynical assault on Britain's mild and godly authority.[571] When patriotic feeling rose against the Methodists...all of the itinerants whom Wesley had recruited for service in America, except Francis Asbury, returned home, and Asbury was forced to lie low in the Delaware countryside.[572] Division and suspicions were rampant.

Timothy Dwight, the grandson of Jonathan Edwards, made the observation that "war is fatal to morals."[573] He described the time just prior to, and during the American Revolutionary War:

> The profanation of the Sabbath...profaneness of language, drunkenness, gambling, and lewdness, were exceedingly increased; and, what is less commonly remarked, but is not less mischievous, than any of them, a light, vain method of thinking, concerning sacred things, a cold, contemptuous indifference toward every moral and religious subject.[574]

The war itself created economic, social, and political conflicts as well as spiritual problems.

> *Ironically, although the Revolution owed much of its inception to religious motives and forces, the war for independence had an immediate adverse effect on Christianity in the United States. All of the denominations had suffered severely, with churches destroyed, congregations scattered, ministers and members slain, and with very few ministers trained. Spiritual religion had been neglected, with the resulting increase of crime and immorality. Excessive debts were threatening and demoralizing to individuals and churches, as well as the government. Added to these negative internal conditions was the imported influence of popular agnosticism. The bitterness and cynicism which always accompany a war prepared the way for English deism, French naturalism, and the growing fad of atheism. Skepticism and infidelity were encouraged by the anti-Christian writings of Voltaire and Thomas Paine. At the close of the Revolution, less than 10 percent of the American population professed to be Christians. Atheism was especially fashionable among students and educated men.*[575]

The time just following the war has been described as "the period of the lowest ebb-tide of vitality in the history of American Christianity."[576]

As indicated, another major influence at this time came from the ideas being born in America out of the French Enlightenment. During the French Revolution, the goddess of Reason became a Fury.[577] By comparison, in England deism was more timid, less aggressive. In the North American English colonies, deism had the French complexion.[578] These ideas had been bred in some of America's leaders, and at the time of the American Revolution, Europeans were citing America as a living example of Enlightenment thought.

> *Many of the Sons of Liberty were infected with the spirit of the Enlightenment. Like their French*

> *and English tutors these patriots—Jefferson, Franklin, Madison—assumed that man could use his reason and by it he could arrive at a reasonable or "natural" understanding of himself and his world.*[579]

But the revolution was more than an example; it also became an inspiration to many in Europe and England who had embraced Enlightenment ideas and were observing the developments in America.

> *To European observers, the American settlers were true men of the Enlightenment—rational yet passionately concerned about equality, peaceful yet ready to go to war for their freedom. By wresting independence from a formidable imperial power, the colonists had proved that the Enlightenment ideas worked. They had been tested in the hardest laboratory of all, the laboratory to which the Enlightenment liked to submit all its ideas: experience.*[580]

Enlightenment thought provided a breeding ground for modified versions of Christian faith, such as Deism, Unitarianism, and Universalist doctrine, all of which began to make their way into American thinking. Becoming more accepted by intellectuals, these beliefs "caused a widespread drift from the settled religious customs and practices in New England and throughout the colonies after 1750."[581] This influence was probably much greater than one might be inclined to believe. The word "widespread" is an accurate word. Timothy Dwight became president at Yale College in 1795 and when he arrived at the school, it was his opinion that there was not one Christian student on campus and that the prevailing doctrine was Deism.

> *The deists nevertheless considered themselves Christians. Their God was not the personal God of the theists, a God who operated through history and concerned*

> *himself continually with the affairs of men. Their God was the great Great Artificer of the universe... The Mighty Architect had done his work so well that he could withdraw into the vast silences and leave men rightly to order their own affairs by reason, that "candle of the Lord."*[582]

Authority lay in human reason, not in God's Word. Man had the privilege to judge for himself what was right and wrong and how the world worked. Not only was the Bible being explained away as irrelevant, but it was being attacked even by some of America's favorite sons.

> *In 1784 Ethan Allen, the Revolutionary War hero who captured Fort Ticonderoga, published "Reason the Only Oracle of Man". In 1794 Thomas Paine, who had helped America in the cause of freedom, wrote "The Age of Reason," a book that ridiculed the Old and New Testaments as unworthy of a good God...It would be more consistent that we called it the word of a demon than the word of God...A large edition was published in France and sent to America to be sold for a few pennies a copy, or given away.... While the other Deists aroused Christian anger, it was Thomas Jefferson who came to represent Deist views to the minds of many. Religion for him was simply a moral code, not a divine revelation.*[583]

With these influences being promoted and spreading in America, Christian beliefs and behavior were greatly diminished.

Another influence that had an eroding effect upon the Christian foundations of American life was the western migrations. People traveled into the Blue Ridge Mountains, on into Kentucky and Tennessee, and into the Indian territories. This separated families, depleted the populations of some cities, and undermined church influence. This situation made the work of the church and clergy more difficult. Many towns were without churches or ministers. Whisky became a curse in these new settlements and was the cause of most frontier social and moral problems.[584] In 1803, under Thomas Jefferson's presidency, the Louisiana Purchase was made, doubling the geographical size of the United States and giving a huge boost to the western expansion. By the year 1800, nearly a million people made their way west.[585] One can only guess how many of them never read, or heard the Bible read, or heard the gospel, or were in anyway exposed to the Christian message. In many ways, this is one of the most lamentable periods of American history.

Stirrings in the South

How would the church respond to the conditions created by expansion into these wide open spaces in post-revolutionary America? In the southern states the Baptists and Methodists went to work.

> *Baptists had come into the southern colonies only in the 1760s; by 1790 half of all American Baptists lived in the five most southern states. Baptists founded an average of about fifty new churches each year during the 1780s. Although historiography on Baptists is not as advanced as it should be, there is no doubt that evangelical energy drove Baptist preaching into the open spaces of post-establishment America.*[586]

There can be no doubt about the contributions made by the Baptist, and by other denominations such as the Presbyterians and Congregationalists, but when all is said and done, it must be admitted that much of the story of the Second Great Awakening is the story of the Methodists. This time period surely is the high point of Methodism.

> *Important as the Baptist action was, the great engine behind what has been called "the phenomenal advance of evangelical Protestantism" that began in the mid-*

> 1780s was Methodism…Only the excitement attending Whitefield's early preaching can match what happened next when the Methodists were unleashed on the new American nation.[587]

Francis Asbury and Thomas Coke

An important leader at this time was Francis Asbury (1725-1816). Though the Methodists "lay low" during the American Revolution, they regrouped under Asbury's leadership at the conclusion of the war. He was not the only person responsible for this dramatic upsurge, but his role as organizer, encourager, preacher, delegator, and mediator of John Wesley's form of evangelical Christianity was critical.[588] Francis Asbury was converted through the preaching of John Wesley when he was a 16-year-old boy living in England. Later, as a young man, he became a lay itinerant preacher within the movement. Although he had little formal education, he was a fluent speaker and a good leader and organizer. As previously stated, Wesley commissioned him to America, and when he arrived in 1771, there were only 300 Methodists in all the colonies. At his death 40 years later, there were more than 300,000.[589] Asbury is known as "the father of American Methodism." Thomas Coke (1747-1814) would join Asbury in 1774. In England, he had joined the Wesleys and was personally discipled by them. Trained, and deeply influenced by this association, he committed himself to the Methodist cause. While still in England, he had been "set apart" by John Wesley as a "superintendent" for work in the Methodist movement. When sent to America, he came with the power to ordain. The term "superintendent" at that time was preferred over "bishop" in order to avoid conflict with the Anglican Church. Methodism was not yet a denomination, and was still considered a movement within the Church of England.

> Coke, with letters of introduction from Wesley, arrived at Baltimore in 1774 and energetically set to work.

> *Coke called the first American Methodist Conference in December, 1774, ordained Asbury as a "superintendent," and formally established the Methodist Episcopal Church in America. In 1787 the American Methodist Conference changed Coke's and Asbury's titles to "Bishop."*[590]

The Methodist's "methods"—or organization—came into play as the movement marshaled its forces. They were characterized by the usual Methodist "disciplines" such as classes, conferences, and the itinerant or "circuit riding preachers," who were well trained and committed to reaching the lost, and strengthening and organizing churches.

> *Coke and Asbury led by example through indefatigable travel and insistent gospel proclamation… Beginning in the late 1780s Asbury regularly made a giant circuit each year throughout the whole United States to convene local Methodist conferences, assign itinerants to their own circuits, recruit new preachers and encourage the veterans…From the start he was joined by a host of itinerant evangelists as dedicated to the cause as he was.*[591]

Significant progress was made in reaching people in the western expansion. As the American population burst from the sea coast, Methodist itinerants marched along stride for stride, even as other Methodists worked just as assiduously in settled areas for the conversion of the lost and the organization of the convicted.[592] The statistics provided from that time reveal the effectiveness of their efforts.

> *In 1780 there were 42 itinerants ministering to 8,500 society members in 21 circuits. Ten years later it was 227 itinerants for almost 58,000 society members in*

101 circuits. Almost one fifth of the society members were African American.[593]

The Methodist strategy and commitment is almost unparalleled in history. The beginning of the Second Great Awakening is said to have started around 1800, but it is not difficult to see what provided the momentum that carried to that date, and well into the 19th century. Francis Asbury and Thomas Coke mustered together an army of workers who dedicated themselves to the cause of Christ under the Methodist banner. Both would live to see the beginning of the Second Great Awakening and enjoy the benefits it brought. 50 years later (in 1850) more than one in three Americans who belonged to a church was a Methodist.[594]

Awakenings in the West

From these initial revivals and movements, several events followed. The Presbyterians in the southern states began to sense a movement of God's Spirit in the work they were doing. Around the year 1799, some dramatic changes began taking place. In that year, a Presbyterian pastoral letter stated that although there was still much immorality and vice,

> *We have heard from different parts the glad tidings of the outpourings of the Spirit...*[595]

The following was expressed in another letter.

> *From the west, the Assembly has received intelligence of the most interesting nature. On the borders of Kentucky and Tennessee, the influences of the Spirit of God seem to have been manifested in a very extraordinary manner.*[596]

These letters would prove to be reports of the actual beginnings of the Second Great Awakening in America.

> These were the beginnings of the Second Great Awakening. God had not abandoned his people. The heritage of the Great Awakening of the 1740s, was surfacing again.[597]

James McGready

In the west, the Second Great Awakening began with James McGready (1762?-1817).[598] McGready was the Presbyterian frontier preacher who originated the idea of the "camp meeting." The camp meeting featured continuous preaching services along with "camping out." He had been the pastor of three small churches in Logan County, Kentucky. In order to create an extended time for intensive instruction and preaching, he brought the three churches together for a "camp meeting," which lasted several days. During this time, there was a powerful "demonstration" of God's Spirit. This happened in June 1800.

> *Convinced that God was moving, McGready and his colleagues planned another camp meeting to be held in late July 1800 at Gasper River. They had not anticipated what occurred. An enormous crowd—as many as 8,000—began arriving at the appointed date from distances as great as 100 miles. Tents were set up everywhere, wagons with provisions brought in, trees felled and their logs cut to be used as seats.*[599]

After three days of meetings it seemed apparent that the Spirit of God was doing something of a very significant nature. Commenting on a sermon given by the Presbyterian minister, William McGee, McGready wrote:

> *The power of God seemed to shake the whole assembly. Toward the close of the sermon, cries of the distressed arose almost as loud as his voice. After the congregation was dismissed the solemnity increased, till the greater part*

of the multitude seemed engaged in the most solemn manner...eternal things were the vast concern. Here awakening and converting work was to be found in every part of the multitude; and even some things strangely and wonderfully new to me.[600]

The "awakening and converting work" that was experienced at these camp meetings did not stop there. From there it spread across Kentucky and Tennessee. The "camp meeting" quickly became a part of the American religious experience, especially in the south and the west. McGready devoted his entire ministry to reaching lonely families and unchurched villages in the raw frontier.[601] The Gasper River camp meeting was the turning point of the Awakening in the West.[602]

Barton W. Stone

The full force of the movement was yet to be experienced, and it came about through the activity of Barton W. Stone, Presbyterian pastor of Cane Ridge and Concord churches, northeast of Lexington, Kentucky.[603] He would capitalize upon the "camp meeting" strategy devised by McGready. After visiting the work in Logan County, Kentucky, Stone planned for his own camp meeting. In August 1801, he hosted the most famous camp meeting in America's history. It is estimated that up to 25,000 attended the event that lasted several days. At that time, Lexington's population was 1,800. No one expected such a large crowd, but preparations had been made for such an eventuality. One of the wise strategies was that invitations had been sent to pastors from various denominations. Baptist, Presbyterian, Methodist, and others were present, which made it possible for the crowds to be divided into separate "congregations" while at the meetings and be under the supervision and counsel of these pastors.

Cane Ridge became famous not only for its numbers, but also for its excesses of enthusiasm. Hysterical

> laughter, trances, and more bizarre forms of behavior were seen occasionally. This wildness was of course greatly exaggerated and often used to discredit the camp meetings…Most clergy opposed this but it was beyond their power to control, and in some ways it was inevitable. The roughness of frontier life, its absence of social controls, and the scarcity of social contacts for those living in isolated cabins, made such people very susceptible to uncontrolled displays when they found themselves in the company of large numbers. And under the intensity of much powerful preaching within just a few days, emotions boiled over.[604]

The west was wild, and it is hard to imagine what the movement into the western Carolinas, Kentucky, Tennessee, and the Indian territories, would have produced without the gospel close on the heels of such expansion.

It should be noted that it was at this time that "The Christian Church" was founded in America. Barton Stone became disenchanted with denominationalism and decided to start a church that had no doctrinal statements or creedal documents but depended upon the Bible alone as its standard of faith. He withdrew from the Presbyterian Church and organized a church at Cane Ridge, Kentucky, that would have only the name "Christian." Later, he met Alexander Campbell, a Presbyterian minister from England who became convinced of baptism by immersion, resigned from the Presbyterian Church, formed a Baptist Church, but soon withdrew, and formed a church in which his followers were called "Disciples of Christ." In 1832, Stone's group and Campbell's group combined and went under the names of either "Disciples" or "Christian."

Peter Cartwright

Peter Cartwright (1785-1872) was born on the Kentucky frontier and went on to become a circuit-riding Methodist preacher. As a youngster, he was poorly educated and was known as a gambler. After a dramatic conversion in 1801, he became one of the most successful evangelists and church planters in the western expansion. In 1806 he was ordained by Francis Asbury as a deacon in the Methodist Church and worked in Kentucky, Tennessee, and Illinois. He became known for his eloquent and bold preaching, and baptized approximately 10,000 converts. He came to be known as the "Kentucky Boy," and W. W. Sweet named him "The Friar Tuck of American Methodism."[605]

Along with the development of the Methodist Church, especially in Kentucky and Illinois, Cartwright developed an interest in education which he promoted in these states. He left the circuit in Kentucky and Tennessee in 1824 because of his distaste for slavery, and transferred to Illinois.[606] Developing an interest in politics, he ran for and was twice elected to the state legislature. In 1846, he ran for Congress and lost to Abraham Lincoln. His ministry helped keep the Second Great Awakening alive on the frontiers of the young country.

Awakenings in the East

As awakenings continued in the west, a movement began in New England as well. Two groups were involved initially, the Presbyterians in the south and the Congregationalists in the north.

The Presbyterian phase in New England began at the small Hampden-Sydney College in Hampden-Sydney, Virginia, in 1786 and continued strong through 1789. The movement began among the students who had a concern for their own spiritual condition, then spread through the school, out to other colleges, and throughout the Presbyterian Church in the south.

The New England phase, and the more influential of the eastern awakenings, began in Connecticut at Yale College, in 1802. Whereas, the revival at Hampden-Sydney College began among the students, the revival at Yale began from the initiative of one man.

Timothy Dwight

In 1795, Timothy Dwight (1752-1817), the grandson of Jonathan Edwards, was appointed president of Yale. Dwight had been a chaplain in the Revolutionary War, and had served successfully as a Congregational church pastor. Upon his arrival at Yale he found the school to be a center of infidelity.

> By 1789 the influence of the [First] Great Awakening had been largely dissipated by the Deism that had been brought to the colonies by British army officers during the French and Indian War [1754–1763] and by the import of deistic literature, and by the influence of the French Revolution. Yale illustrates the decadent religious spirit in this period. Few students professed regeneration; gambling, profanity, vice and drunkenness was the order of the day among students, who prided themselves upon being infidels.[607]

Yale was such a hot-bed of infidelity that the students called each other by the names of Voltaire, Rousseau, and other French intellectuals.[608] Apart from having no use for the Christian faith, the students were also rebellious and undisciplined. It had been required of professors that they be Christian, but by 1795 it seemed that many of them had given up their Christian faith.

Timothy Dwight wasted no time in beginning to correct the disbelief and the other problems he found at Yale. Besides having an infectious personality, he proved himself to be a versatile leader. He was an effective preacher, an outstanding educator, and had a special talent for entering into dialogue with the students and professors. After a while, the students learned to admire and appreciate Dwight's abilities, his openness in discussing sensitive subjects, and his concern for their souls.[609]

As a result of Dwight's dynamic leadership and persistence, things began to change. Campus discussions in dorms and around the campus, as well as around the town of New Haven, Connecticut, began to center on the subject of salvation. Through their president's teaching, the idea was alive that a person could experience forgiveness and assurance of salvation. Finally, in 1802, a revival broke out on campus and the atmosphere at Yale changed. About a third of the student body professed conversion during the revival, which later spread to Dartmouth, Williams, and other colleges.[610]

This revival at Yale happened just before the college spring vacation. Many wondered if the dynamic found in the revival might come to an end during the students' time away from campus.

> *The students carried home with them the news of Yale's turnabout, and the impulse spread. When they returned after the summer, more offered their lives to God. Dwight witnessed the conversion of 80 out of the total enrollment of 160 students.*[611]

The entire state of Connecticut, and areas beyond, would be influenced as a result of this awakening that began at Yale in 1802. But this was not the end of spiritual revitalization at Yale. A new awakening came in April 1808, which was almost as powerful as that of 1802, and succeeding revivals came to the students in 1813 and 1815.[612]

Because of his effective leadership at Yale, and through his preaching and writings, Timothy Dwight enjoyed wide influence. Though he wrote several books, he was also a hymn-writer and is known for several compositions, including one sung today, "I Love Thy Kingdom Lord." When he was chaplain during the Revolutionary War, he wrote the song, "Columbia," which became well-known at that time.

It should be pointed out that, as a key figure in the Second Great Awakening, Dwight brought a new view to the matter of revivals. His grandfather, Jonathan Edwards believed that a revival or awakening was something that could not be planned. One simply continued faithfully in his daily responsibilities, and in prayer and preaching, and it would be the Holy Spirit who determined when revival or awakening would come. Dwight believed that human initiative played a role. In fact, he "established the desire for awakenings as a permanent feature of American Protestantism."[613]

> *As for revivals, Edward's connection with the First Awakening was much different from Dwight's connection with the Second. Edwards preached sincerely and vividly of what he had experienced and apparently was genuinely surprised when the revival began. Dwight deliberately set out to start a revival…to Edwards the revival was a by-product of his shared experience: to [Dwight] revivals were the calculated means to an end.*[614]

In this we find a difference in emphasis between the First and the Second Great Awakenings. The first was more Calvinistic, the second was more Arminian. The first placed more emphasis upon the sovereignty of God; the second placed more emphasis upon human responsibility or initiative.

Through Dwight's ideas, "revivalism" became a part of American culture. To our present time revivals are planned into the yearly schedule of many churches. What was behind this? Was it related to the scientific and industrial revolution with its emphasis upon the idea that we can now understand how things work? Was this an outcome of the educational environment where science was playing more of an important role? Was it due to the emphasis upon positive thought and technique in business and personal success? Was it truly new insight from God?

The Third Phase and Charles Finney

Amazingly, the Second Great Awakening continued through the first 25 years of the 1800s. And, when it seemed that it would diminish or come to an end, new life was breathed into the movement and it continued for another 15 years, making the length of the Second Awakening about 40 years.

Charles Finney

The third and final phase of the Second Great Awakening stemmed from the aggressive evangelism of Charles G. Finney (1792-1875).[615] The first phase was both preparatory and initiatory, and can be dated from around the end of the 1700s into the early 1800s with the western expansion and the "camp meetings," featuring the ministries of James McGready, Barton Stone, Peter Cartwright, and others. It was characterized by emotionalism and "spiritual demonstrations." The second phase occurred in the east through Timothy Dwight and others, and is dated from around 1800 to 1825. These "second phase" revivals were more conservative and less emotional than the first. The third phase (1825-35) was largely involved with the activities of Charles G. Finney, who began his revival work in small towns in western New York in the 1820s but eventually conducted revival meetings in the largest cities in America and Britain.[616] This phase was characterized by order and more "technique" than the first two. It is worth thinking about the characteristics of the different phases and what made them distinct.

Charles Finney was born at Warren, Connecticut, in 1792. He studied law, but began his professional career as a teacher, then became a lawyer. As a young attorney practicing in Adams, New York, from 1810 through 1820, he became interested in the Scriptures due to the fact that so many legal authorities referred to them. Though he was a skeptic, after his interest in the Bible was aroused, he began attending the Presbyterian Church. Though somewhat confused and put off by what he thought was hyper-Calvinism, his lawyer's mind became enamored with the meaning of theological words in the Bible that seemed to have a judicial sound or relationship. For example, he was fascinated with such words as "repentance," "justification," "regeneration," and "sanctification."

Through a study of these words and concepts he became agitated and concerned about his soul.

> *On October 10, 1821, at age twenty-nine, Finney gave himself to Christ. The night before, he had felt "as if I was about to die. I knew that if I did die I should sink down to hell. I felt almost like screaming." But the next day he realized that "instead of having, or needing, any righteousness of my own to recommend me to God, I had to submit myself to the righteousness of God through Christ. Indeed the offer of Gospel salvation seemed to me to be an offer of something to be accepted, and that it was full and complete; and that all that was necessary on my part, was to give my own consent to give up my sins, and give myself to Christ." Dazzled by his insight, he went into the woods to tell God of his new dedication.*[617]

He returned home, and after spending some time playing his bass viol and singing hymns, later that day Finney believed he had a personal encounter with Christ and experienced a "mighty baptism of the Holy Ghost."[618]

Following this dramatic conversion in 1821, he immediately believed that he was called to be a preacher. When a client asked him to appear in court on his behalf, Finney replied, "I have a retainer from the Lord Jesus Christ to plead His cause and I cannot plead yours."[619] Right away he left his law practice to become an evangelist, and in 1824 was ordained by the Presbyterian Church. In that same year, he began preaching in upstate New York in small towns and communities. In 1825, he held revival campaigns in the New York cities of Utica, Western, and Rome, where there were numerous conversions with the result that church membership rolls in all these regions increased.

Finney's fame grew and, as he was given more opportunities, great numbers of converts were gained wherever he spoke. Sometimes his meetings would go on for weeks in one city. His career seemed to reach a peak in 1830 and 1831 when a long evangelistic campaign was held in Rochester, New York. Beginning in the fall of 1830, the meetings continued through March 9, 1831. This made Finney an international figure. Historian Whitney R. Cross wrote:

> *No more impressive revival has occurred in American history. Sectarianism was forgotten and all churches gathered in their multitudes...but the exceptional feature was the phenomenal dignity of this awakening. No agonizing souls fell in the aisle, no raptured ones shouted hallelujahs. Rather, despite his doses of hell-fire, the great evangelist, 'in an unclerical suit of gray,' acted 'like a lawyer arguing before a court and jury,' talking precisely, logically, but with wit, verve, and informality. Lawyers, real-estate magnates, millers, manufacturers, and commercial tycoons led the parade of the regenerated.*[620]

The awakening at Rochester produced significant effects, gained international attention, and seemed to initiate a revival spirit across America. Under the ministry of men influenced by Finney, and through the ministry of others touched by belief in revival, awakenings occurred throughout the United States, beginning in 1831, and continued for many years.

In 1832, Finney became pastor of the Second Free Presbyterian Church in New York, but this did not mean that his evangelistic career was waning. While pastor in this church, he regularly held revivals that went on for long periods of time. Soon, he found that there were theological issues in Presbyterianism with which he disagreed; thus, he moved on from Presbyterianism and embraced Congregationalism. He then erected what was known as the Broadway Tabernacle, a large structure that would hold the large crowds that attended his meetings.

In 1835, he became a professor at Oberlin College in Oberlin, Ohio, as well as pastor of the First Congregational Church in the town. His scholarly abilities were recognized in that he was asked to form and head up the theology department at the newly founded school. From 1851 to 1866, he served as president of the college and continued as minister of the First Congregational Church in Oberlin.

In some ways, Finney's ministry was an extension of Timothy Dwight's idea that revivals could be planned.

> *Soon he clashed with older views, for Finney's entire concept of awakening was new. He taught that awakening was not a miraculous act of God, but a simple use of human choice. He saw revivals very differently from Stoddard, Edwards, Whitefield, or Wesley, who understood that Christians could do nothing about periods of sin and backsliding until the Holy Spirit brought about renewal. Finney put the initiative in the hands of Christians: if they did the right things, revival would come. There was nothing at all miraculous about the coming of revival. Many said then—and have since—that Finney changed American religion from God-centered to man-centered.*[621]

His ministry, therefore, though characterized by order and carefully planned meetings, was not without its controversies. These controversies revolved around the "new measures" Finney introduced into evangelism, especially the idea of "the anxious seat." The anxious seat was part of the "invitation system" in which people were invited forward to take their place in the anxious seat (usually the pew or seats in the front row) where they would pray and be prayed for until true conversion took place. This was a new idea to most churchmen who believed that God had already established a way of publicly professing Christ, and that way was baptism.

> *C. G. Finney, apparently the first professed evangelist to call people forward during a service to a position which he called "the anxious seat," defended the practice on the*

grounds that it answered the purpose which baptism had in the days of the apostles. Professor [Albert] Dod of Princeton commented on this argument: "Though he supposes that the anxious seat occupies 'the precise place' that baptism did, we can by no means consent to receive it as an equivalent. Baptism was, indeed, a test of character, since obedience or disobedience was exercised in view of a divine command; but the anxious seat cannot operate thus, except by arrogating to itself a similar authority."[622]

Praying for people by name, and allowing women to pray and give testimony, were some of the other "new methods" introduced by Finney. But it was not only his methods that were unconventional. Others found doctrinal errors in Finney's theology. To Finney, the will of man was the key in living righteously or in continuing in sin. His emphasis upon the freedom of the will eventually led him to deny the doctrine of original sin. He taught that children are not born with sin natures but that sin came into humans through choice. This did not mean that he believed there were some humans who were not sinners. Rather, because of the facts of temptation and the desire for human gratification, all humans do choose to sin when they reach the age of accountability. But this did leave the door open for the possibility of human perfection through choice. Regardless of his "new measures" and questionable theology, there is no doubt that Charles Finney impacted Christianity of his time and initiated practices that have influenced the church to the present day.

Outcomes of the Second Great Awakening

The Second Great Awakening wove faith and religion well into the fabric of American cultural life. The people of the United States would live on the moral and spiritual capital gained for at least another 100 years (until the 1950s). When one thinks of the Second Great Awakening, Charles Finney's name is the first to come to mind. He stands as the recognized leader of this great spiritual movement in America during the first half of the nineteenth century. Thousands professed to become Christians under his ministry and others were influenced and motivated by him. But it must also be pointed out that there were major social adjustments in American life due to this awakening. Armies of people were brought together in the movement and organized to address and bring change in the following areas: slavery, education, prison reform, temperance, vices, public profanity, morals and manners, Sabbath observance, and even world peace. Improvements were made in all these areas.

A simple example of how humane laws were established can be seen in the abolishment of dueling.

Revivalism created an atmosphere antagonistic to the prevalent practice of dueling with pistols or swords. The tragic death of Alexander Hamilton in a duel with Aaron Burr, coupled with propaganda from the pulpit, soon brought the practice to an end.[623]

The use of alcohol prior to and during the beginning of the Second Great Awakening was epidemic. During his 1830-1831 revivals in Rochester, New York, Finney addressed the matter of temperance and its accompanying issues of debt and family neglect. The church also took an interest in the needs and abuse of the poor, and saw to it that laws were passed banning imprisonment due to debt. And, of course, there was the matter of slavery. As early as 1769, Congregationalists in Rhode Island spoke out against slavery. In fact, it may be stated that Abolitionism grew out of the second great awakening. The American Anti-slavery Society was founded in 1833.[624] These steps were difficult and church denominational splits occurred over the issue. The Wesleyan Methodist Church was organized in 1843 on the basis of no slave-owning membership after many withdrew from the Methodist Episcopal Church.[625] Though tensions existed, the position taken by leading revivalists (including Finney) opposed slavery, and worked toward its eventual end.

Other results from the Second Great Awakening include the birth of "revivalism," the beginning of the midweek prayer service, the birth of the Sunday School movement, an upsurge in missions, which included the founding of the *American Board of Commissioners for Foreign Missions* in 1810; the *American Bible Society* in 1816; the *American Sunday School Union* in 1817; the *American Tract Society* in 1826; and the *American Home Missions Society* in 1826.

America's Third Awakening

The third awakening, sometimes called the "Third Great Awakening," occurred from 1857 to 1859 and centered largely in prayer meetings that took place throughout the United States and Canada. As with the other awakenings, it was preceded by a time of spiritual decline. Despite all of the advances made during the first 40 years of the 1800s...

> *...The religious life of America was in decline from 1840 to 1857. Many causes were responsible. Agitation over the issue of slavery in both the North and South had reached fever pitch, and hatreds boiled. Great numbers were disillusioned over spiritual things because of the extremes of the Millerites, a radical group that had widely proclaimed that Christ would return to earth between 21 March 1843 and 21 March 1844. When this did not happen, William Miller, the leader, reset the date at 22 October 1844, and again those who had trusted his prediction were disappointed and infuriated.... In October 1857 a financial panic occurred, with banks failing, railroads going into bankruptcy, and financial chaos arising everywhere. A civil war seemed unavoidable to many because of the slavery question. America tottered on the brink of disaster.*[626]

On September 25, 1857, the Bank of Pennsylvania in Philadelphia failed. On October 10, 1857, the New York stock market crashed. Businesses closed. Corporations and individuals declared bankruptcy. People were out of work. This financial panic, it seems, was the catalyst that triggered the awakening.[627] Interdenominational prayer meetings had already begun to occur in a few places due to uncertainties that had prevailed throughout the nation—economic concerns along with anxiety over the possibility of civil war. Now their attendances swelled. These prayer meetings renewed spiritual interests and also brought about a large number of conversions. At one point during this third awakening, reports were coming in of 50,000 conversions a week. And when the Civil War came, revivals or awakenings continued, especially among the northern and southern armies.

The nation would get through the Civil War and recover from the financial crisis, but this third awakening added to America's spiritual heritage and would bear fruit for years to come. Though America has not seen such awakenings since the middle of the 19th century, revivalism has continued. Following the Civil War, Dwight L. Moody continued the legacy of Finney and the others of the Great Awakenings, and became the most popular evangelist of the second half of the 19th century. In the 20th century, Billy Graham has carried on the tradition of the great "revivalists" and became the most well-known of the traveling evangelists.

CHAPTER 20

The Age of Theological Diversity: 1870 - Present

Challenges to the expansion of God's Kingdom have always existed. The humanism of the Renaissance produced elements in the church that were eventually confronted by the Protestant Reformation. No sooner had the Reformation secured certain beliefs and practices when these were challenged by the rationalism of the Enlightenment. The Puritans and Pietists took issue with Enlightenment philosophy, and fought back to re-establish Reformational foundations.

While America was advancing through periods of awakenings, and developing as a nation, significant ideas were being formulated in Europe that would lessen Christianity's strength on that continent and introduce new challenges to Christianity in America. The theological diversity, which arose by 1870 in the United States, came from ideas introduced a century or so before in Europe. Europe never recovered from the influences of the Enlightenment, as religion was pushed more and more to the periphery of European life throughout the 19th century. And as skepticism grew in Europe, England, and Scotland, religious life in these countries diminished.

Influences in America

In America, three developments in the second half of the 19th century rose to undermine the advances made during the Second Great Awakening. These were the Industrial Revolution, Darwinism, and Higher Criticism.

The Industrial Revolution, which began in America in the late 1700s and early 1800s, represented the advance of science in very practical ways, providing material goods and services previously unknown in the history of the world. There were no sinister motives behind its advancement and it brought great conveniences to the modern world. However, along with these changes, social shifts occurred for which people were not prepared. Not only did the industrial revolution bring a focus on material goods, it led to a change in life. The development of factories for the production of these goods moved people into the cities to get jobs and find a better way of life. From 1850 to 1950, the location of populations in the United States changed dramatically. In 1850, 90 percent of the nation was rural. By 1950, only 10 percent was rural, meaning that 90 percent of the population had shifted into cities over a relatively short period of time.

City life created challenges as multitudes of people were brought together in urban settings. Large cities began to develop, and in every one of them slums could be found. Fathers were gone from their families for long periods of time and new stress put upon the family in general. The "traditional family" model, where all members of a family spent most of their time living and working in the same environment, was altered. As an outcome, there were major increases in crime, and juvenile delinquency (almost unknown previously) became a new social phenomenon. With all of this came indifference to life in general and a diminishing of faith.

Darwinism introduced evolution as a plausible explanation for the existence of man, denying the biblical account of creation. In 1859, Charles Darwin introduced his book, *Origin of the Species*, in which he explained that his studies led him to believe in biological evolution; that man, in fact, had a common ancestor with the animals. Causing a furor, but finding support among scientists, naturalists, and atheists, the evolutionary theory undermined biblical authority. It also raised questions regarding the issue of sin. Rather than being something in man's nature as a result of the fall, sin was merely the residue of the animal instinct in man. The hope offered in evolution was that man would some day "outgrow" his tendency toward sinfulness or evil as the evolutionary process continued. Given time, mankind would be okay. In Germany, by the early 1900s, evolution also gave credence to the idea of race superiority under Hitler's regime. The introduction of evolution into western culture greatly undermined faith and remains a challenge for the church today.

Higher Criticism was born in Europe. Names associated with its development include Immanuel Kant (1724-1804), Friedrich Schleiermacher (1768-1834), George Hegel (1770-1831), and Albrecht Ritschl (1822-1889). It was Johann Eichhorn (1752-1827) who actually used the term "higher criticism" to describe the methods he thought should be used to judge the veracity of the Bible and theology. This radical critique of the Bible assumes that the Bible is merely a work to be judged by the canons of literary criticism just as any other literary work would be; that there is an evolution of religion; and that natural explanations of the Biblical phenomena should replace supernatural explanations.[628] George Hegel had taught in one area of his philosophy—called *Hegel's Dialectic*—that there is a natural evolution in thought and social development. Darwin, who studied Hegel, was influenced by his ideas. When the historico-critical method was combined with the theory of evolution to religious phenomena, the background for a system of Biblical criticism was completed.[629]

Liberalism

These developments signaled the birth of religious liberalism in the latter half of the 1800s. Up until about 1870, it can be said that all the denominations and churches in the United States believed in the inspiration and authority of the Bible. Though the different groups might have disagreed over interpretation and application of Scriptural truths, nonetheless, they all agreed that the Bible could be trusted as God's Written Word, and that it provided authority for life and practice in the Church. Because of questions raised by science and the development of liberal thought that followed, Biblical authority was diminished and most of the major denominations embraced liberalism. From this time, these two "competing" streams of liberalism and conservatism would exist in American churches.

Liberalism in theology developed in the 19th century, but reached its zenith in the three decades before World War II. Though it may be said that the Industrial Revolution created a condition for change, the direct causes were philosophical (higher criticism) and scientific (evolution). The roots of liberal theology in America can be traced directly to the importation of German idealistic philosophy in the 1800s, and in the doctrine of evolution formulated by Charles Darwin. Liberalism was characterized by an eagerness to discard old orthodox forms if they were judged to be irrational in light of modern knowledge or irrelevant to what was regarded as the central core of religious experience.[630] The German influence can clearly be seen in the writings and teachings of the following men.

Friedrich Schleiermacher

Friedrich Schleiermacher (1768-1834) is generally considered to be the dominant Protestant theologian between John Calvin and Karl Barth.[631] He is also recognized as the founder of the liberal school of theology and the most influential theologian of the early 19th century. As Barth noted, "Schleiermacher is the watershed of modern theology."[632]

The liberal theological position that Schleiermacher came to embrace and promote represented a shift from the influence in his early life. He was born in Breslau, Poland, and was the son of an army chaplain. His father held to Calvinistic theology. Schleiermacher grew up in a pietistic Moravian home in the tradition of Philip Spener, attended a Herrnhut-founded Brethren college, and later enrolled at Halle, the pietist university. He was ordained a Reformed minister in 1794 and received his first appointment as a pastor in the city of Berlin. His background in pietism would have a life-long effect upon him, but would also serve as an element in what developed into liberal theology.

> *His pietist upbringing had taught him that religion is more than merely theology and ethics, knowledge and action, knowing and doing the right thing. 'Piety cannot be an instinct craving for a mess of metaphysical and ethical crumbs.' Religion belongs to a third realm— that of feeling. 'True religion is sense and taste for the infinite.'*[633]

So it was that Schleiermacher had a desire for the supernatural that was connected to personal experience and nature rather than dogma alone. Along with this, there is little doubt that he was influenced by the Romantic Movement, which was at its height from 1760 to 1870. Probably due to the weariness of war and the changes brought on by the French Enlightenment, people were looking for something that went beyond the rationalism and science of the 1700s. It is not that science and rational thought were denied. The Romantics insisted that experience includes more than analytical reasoning and scientific experiment—that it also includes imagination, feeling, and intuition.[634]

We must understand that Schleiermacher did not see the Bible, doctrine, creeds, or dogmas, as irrelevant. In fact, theology could not be avoided when it came to reflecting upon our faith. Our faith is informed by the essential and historical theology of the church. However, to him, true religion was separate from theology. His views are laid out in two major works. The first, presented in 1799, may be seen as the debut of liberal theology. The work, *On Religion: Speeches to Its Cultural Despisers*, was an attempt to win back the educated classes to religion by speaking against skepticism. Its appeal was that one could follow his own intuition and feelings rather than dogma or intellect. One should not look to the actual theology or dogmas of the church, but at the spiritual truth conveyed within them.

> Schleiermacher's criterion for theology is conformity not to the doctrine of the New Testament, but to the experience recorded in the New Testament. The question, which he asked of all doctrine is: what significance does this have for Christian experience?[635]

By following this line of reasoning, which he really believed to be true, he was helping people get over their struggles with the seemingly irrational theology or supernatural elements of the Bible. By looking beyond these, to what is to be learned about Christian experience, people could embrace religion.

In 1811, he was offered the chair of theology at the University of Berlin, and it was there he was able to give time to developing and refining his theology. His second work was called *The Christian Faith* and was first appeared in 1821.

> He began, not with dogmas of the past as most classical theologians did, but with an inward analysis of himself. In his probing, he became aware of a sense of dependence of something beyond himself and he felt that the awareness of this dependence was God-consciousness, the source of all religion. From this God-consciousness, Schleiermacher developed his theory of the feeling of Absolute Dependence. For him, the claims of faith do not represent objective knowledge, but expressions of devout self-consciousness or the Christian's inner experience. The ceremonies and doctrines of religion are always preceded by devout self-consciousness, God consciousness, and the absolute feeling of dependence. It was Christ's perfect God-consciousness that constituted his divinity, and he redeems men by inspiring God-consciousness in them. Thus, we are dependent on Jesus, but orthodox doctrines such as the resurrection and second coming are not essential.[636]

Schleiermacher's statement that "the claims of faith do not represent objective knowledge, but expressions of devout self-consciousness or the Christian's inner experience," meant that all of the Old and New Testament, and all theological texts, were not written as objective statements about the essentials of belief, but were simply expressions of each individual writer's personal inner experience. They were not meant to state "absolutes" when it came to faith, only the relating of one's own experience. Such doctrines as the resurrection, and Christ's coming, become secondary and irrelevant when one takes such a position. Schleiermacher could speak of Christ's deity but did not mean it in the traditional Christian understanding. By it, he meant Christ's perfect humanity. His influence on Protestant thought has been enormous, and his introduction of psychology into systematic theology has influenced all of modern religion. Liberal theology has not always existed.

Many others have embraced and taught theological liberalism. Some of the more well-known and influential include the following men.

Albrecht Ritschl

Albrecht Ritschl (1822-1899) is known as an extreme liberal Protestant theologian who had a significant impact upon theology and biblical scholarship in Germany in particular, and generally throughout Europe in the 1800s. He taught theology at two major German universities: at Bonn from 1846 to 1864 and at Gottingen from 1864 until his death in 1899. His liberal ideas came to be known as the "Ritschlian School." In essence, his theology was free of all supernatural elements. Ritschl even jettisoned such traditional dogmas as original sin, the incarnation, the resurrection, the trinity, and all miracles.[637] He was unwilling to speak of Christ's pre-existence. He agreed with Schleiermacher that the deity of Jesus was found in his perfect humanity. He taught that God did not aim his wrath at our sins, and that the salvation or reconciliation that came through Christ, was mainly a change in our attitude toward God. God did not change his attitude toward us in reconciliation. He did not need to because he loves everyone. Ritschl believed the original Gospel had been corrupted by the early church fathers when they incorporated Greek philosophy into Christian theology. The modern task was to recover the meaning of the early Gospel. To find that out we are driven back again to history, and history can be recovered only through sources.[638] The historico-critical method was important in his system.

Adolf von Harnack

Adolf von Harnack (1851-1930) was a leading Protestant church historian by the turn of the 20th century and a friend and disciple of Albrecht Ritschl. They shared the same liberal theological views and Harnack worked to support them through historical analysis. He agreed with Ritschl that early Christianity had been corrupted by the influence of Greek philosophy. He decided to trace the influence of the "Hellenization" (Greek influence) of Christianity and get back to the pure essence of Christianity. He came to be known as the greatest Patristic scholar (church fathers) of his generation. For Harnack, the essence of Christianity lay in three central truths: the fatherhood of God, the brotherhood of man, and the infinite value of the human soul.[639] In 1899-1900 he gave a series of lectures that were immediately published under the title, *The Essence of Christianity*. Later this series was translated into English under the title, *What is Christianity?* and is considered the finest and most influential statement of liberal Protestant theology.[640] His whole theology was built upon the person of Jesus and his teachings. This meant that the layers of bad interpretations about Christ and his teachings needed to be peeled away through historical methodology so that the true Jesus could be found. Harnack was the son of a German theology professor and followed in his father's footsteps. He spent his life as a professor, teaching at four German universities: Leipzig, Giessen, Marburg, and Berlin.

Walter Rauschenbusch

Walter Rauschenbusch (1861-1918) initiated the "social gospel" movement in the United States. He was the son of a German Baptist professor who taught at the Rochester Theological Seminary in Rochester, New York. Upon completion of his own studies, Walter planned to go to India as a missionary but such plans never materialized. Instead, he became pastor of the Second German Baptist Church on the lower east side of New York City among German immigrants, and where there was much poverty. His church was located next to "Hell's Kitchen," one of the more well-known slums in America. Coming to the conclusion that the Gospel meant more than just "saving souls," he was motivated to develop a theology that would deal with humanitarian concerns. Disturbed by the idea that faith was seen by so many as "personal" and "inner," he began to preach a "social Gospel" in which the main feature stressed concern for others. The kingdom, as preached by Jesus, was not a purely internal, spiritual possession of the individual, but was involved with relationships and responsibilities for our fellowman.[641] His theology is spelled out in three works: *Christianity and the Social Gospel* (1907), *Christianizing the Social Order* (1912), and *A Theology for the Social Gospel* (1917). The weakness analyzed in Rauschenbusch's ideas is: though it rightly emphasized a concern for others, it ended diminishing the salvation features necessary to the Gospel.

Albert Schweitzer

Albert Schweitzer (1875-1965), because of his personal accomplishments and his sacrificial service as a doctor in Africa, became one of the best known and most admired Christians in the world by the middle of the 20th century. He was born at Kaysersburg, Alsace, which was near Strasbourg (then a part of Germany, but today a part of France), and grew up the son of a Lutheran pastor.

At age 21 he very deliberately resolved "to follow the intellectual pursuits of theology, philosophy and music until he was 30, then to lead a life of sacrificial service to his fellow man."[642] Some write that he made this decision at age 19. He never deviated from his plan, and excelled in all three areas of study.

> *First he set about making a name for himself in "scholarship and the arts." He gained a doctorate in philosophy in 1890, and began an intense career of writing and preaching. His workload was so great that he would work all through the night, drinking black coffee with his feet in a bowl of cold water to keep himself awake. His first love, however, was music. A child prodigy at the organ, he continued to perform throughout his life. One of his first books, published in 1905, was about Bach. Schweitzer is one of the few figures in this book whose work can be found in the record shop as well as the bookshop.*[643]

No doubt he could have had a successful career in Europe, but in 1904 he heard a report of an urgent need for physicians in the French African territories. This fit well with his desire to serve humanity and his previously devised goals. Though his desire to go to a remote area of Africa was a shock to his family, friends, and faculty members, after completing his medical studies, he sailed for Africa in 1913. There he opened up a jungle hospital on the Lambarene River in French Equatorial Africa. Many people are familiar with his life, which was characterized by much drama, including imprisonment, his wife's severe illness, his indebtedness, being lost in Africa for three years, and his travels throughout Europe. He has been called "A modern day St. Francis of Assisi in a pith helmet."[644]

However, he also made a major contribution to the development of liberal theology. In 1911, he wrote a book, *The Quest for the Historical Jesus*, which came to be a classic read by liberals and conservatives alike, with positive and negative responses from both sides. Liberals were not entirely happy with his book because of his attack on modern theology, and conservatives were put off by his lack of affirmation for the divinity of Jesus. He contended that the twentieth century picture we have of Jesus is inaccurate because "he is a figure designed by rationalism, endowed with life by liberalism, and clothed by modern theology in historical garb."[645] He contended that the views of Jesus that Schleiermacher and Ritschl had set forth were incorrect.

> *On the contrary, Schweitzer found, that the real Jesus was an eschatological prophet. Jesus wasn't interested in founding a rational, enlightened society here on earth. His work and preaching revolved instead around the coming Kingdom, when he believed that God would intervene dramatically in human history and bring all earthly affairs to an end. Jesus' death was an attempt to hasten this event, and its failure prompted his last utterance, a cry of despair from the cross.*[646]

Schweitzer's main emphasis was that both Jesus and his message were incomprehensible to the modern mind. Until we understand the importance of the kingdom message, and are willing to sacrifice ourselves for it, as Jesus did, we do not understand Jesus. His work seems to signal the beginning of liberalism's failure, but the main critique from others has been that in his diminishing of liberalism he never put anything in its place. In his work, he presents Jesus as a limited person—a good human with good intentions, but not divine. In this, the conservatives found Schweitzer to have failed.

Other books written by Schweitzer include: *The Mystery of the Kingdom of God*, which was his first book, and was published in 1901; *The Mysticism of Paul the Apostle*, written in 1931. *The Quest for the Historical Jesus* in 1911 secured his fame as a thinker and his organ recitals in European capitals won his acclaim as an expert on Bach.[647] He had a deep reverence for life and believed all life must be cherished, including plants and insects. The world admired Albert Schweitzer and showered him with honors, including the Nobel Peace Prize in 1952.

Rudolf Bultmann

Rudolf Bultmann (1884-1976) introduced the idea of "demythologizing" the Bible. By this expression, he means that we must liberate the biblical message from the mythological language in which it is expressed so that modern man who does not share the biblical world view can honestly accept the biblical message.[648] He believed that the first century Christian community that created the biblical records had surrounded it with too much supernatural language for modern man to understand it properly. Modern man's mind misses the core message because of the language the early Christians used to describe what they experienced. We must divest ourselves of the accounts of angels, demons, and all the supernatural events given by the original community of Christians in order to get to the heart of the message. This he called "demythologizing." What man must do is look at the event that brought the original Christian community into being. He calls this the "Christ event." It is in this that humans find meaning. Bultmann has affirmed that what we can know with certainty about Jesus is very slight, because the New Testament, our sole source, presents a picture of Jesus adapted to the religious needs of the early Christian community.[649]

Bultmann contributed to the development of liberal theology mostly because he subordinated the interpretation of the Bible's message to contemporary analysis. Karl Barth criticized him for this method. Bultmann responded that he was removing the mythological framework of the Bible's message and retaining the message.[650] He was a German New Testament scholar who studied at Marburg, Tubingen, and Berlin, and then spent most of his life as a professor at Marburg. Early on, he had an association with Karl Barth and was interested in his theology. Later, he became fascinated with Martin Heideggers' existentialist philosophy and saw it as essential in interpreting the New Testament.

Harry Emerson Fosdick

Harry Emerson Fosdick (1878-1969) became a well known 20th century liberal clergyman. Though he was a popular preacher, it was through his writings that he became well-known in America. By the end of his life, he had published 50 books and was a firm adherent to liberalism and an opponent of fundamentalism.

> *Though "born again" at age 7, Harry Emerson Fosdick early on decided he wanted nothing to do with the born-again movement known as fundamentalism, just then coming into adolescence. Fosdick also rejected Calvinism, which he believed produced "a God who is a devil," and instead relied on his own personal spiritual experiences. The Lord was to be found in living experience, he argued, not at the end of some creed.*[651]

Already in his high school and college days, he was developing the reputation of a theological maverick, and was given the title, "the Jesse James of the theological world." He studied at Colgate College where his formal studies introduced him to the distinctives of liberal thought. In 1903, he was ordained at the Madison Avenue Baptist Church, and in 1911, he joined the Union (Theological Seminary) faculty while accepting the pastorate at the First Baptist Church in Montclair, New Jersey.[652] At Union Seminary, he taught homiletics (the art and science of preaching). In 1918, he was called to a Presbyterian church where, after a time, conservatives put pressure on him because of his liberal views, and he finally resigned in 1924. For a time, he pastored the Park Avenue Baptist Church in New York City, but soon went on to the new 2,300 seat Riverside Church in New York City, a church John D. Rockefeller's money helped build. It was there he became a popular liberal preacher for the next

16 years until his retirement. Upon retirement, he continued for another 28 years espousing his liberal views and addressing issues of the day. He was a staunch opponent of fundamental, conservative Christianity, stating in a sermon titled, "Shall the Fundamentalists Win?" that "the virgin birth was unnecessary; the inerrancy of Scripture, untenable; and the doctrine of the Second Coming, absurd."[653] He was concerned about the practical application of theology and his more popular books include *The Manhood of the Master* (1913), *The Meaning of Prayer* (1915), *The Modern Use of the Bible* (1924), *Successful Christian Living* (1937), *Living Under Tension* (1941), and *A Faith for Tough Times* (1952).

Liberalism's Influence

At the turn of the twentieth century, Protestant liberalism was characterized by an emphasis on the fatherhood of God, the supreme moral and religious example of Jesus, the essential goodness of man, and the duty of doing something to correct the conditions, which denigrated mankind.[654] Most mainline denominations were influenced by liberalism. The Presbyterian Church U.S.A. was infected with issues of "Biblical criticism." Methodists embraced the idea of the "social gospel" with its accompanying liberal views of Christ and the Bible. The American and Northern Baptists went the route of liberalism as did the Congregationalists.

Fundamentalism

The conservatives fought back. At first, unprepared due to the rapid shift in thinking that had taken place, they regrouped and went to work to reestablish a biblical Christianity. The general position taken by these conservative Christians aligned with that of classical Protestant orthodoxy. It sought to preserve the nature of Christianity as a redemptive religion, the place of the supernatural and the miraculous in Christianity, and the nature of the Bible as the authoritative revelation of the mind and purposes of God.[655] Those who have studied this period agree that conservatives responded in at least four ways to the liberalism that entered the church.

The first response was in the form of conferences that were designed to reestablish biblical authority. Emphasizing the inerrancy and literal interpretation of the Bible, these conferences were held widely and featured some of the finest conservative Bible teachers. The Bible conference movement was strongly prophetic and vigorously evangelistic.[656] Another dominant feature was an emphasis upon the pre-millennial return of Christ. This emphasis brought urgency to the movement.

Though these Bible conferences featured strong teaching and evangelism, there was also a deliberate attempt to train lay people in biblical doctrine. In fact, some of the early defining statements of fundamentalism were devised in these conferences. At a conference held in Niagara, New York in 1895, five points of sound doctrine were formulated. These came to be known as the "Five Points of Fundamentalism" and included: the Inerrancy of the Bible, the Virgin Birth, the Deity of Christ, the Substitutionary Blood Atonement of Christ, and the physical Second Coming. It was hoped that the church would be strengthened by training the laity, so these conferences promoted practical Christian living as well as biblical theology. These conferences continued strong for several decades, from 1870 to 1920.

A second response to liberalism was the founding of Christian schools of various types. As time passed, Bible schools, Christian colleges, and seminaries were established. Many believe that these schools grew right out of the Bible conference movement and were intended to continue the education of lay people. In fact, several of the conference leaders became founders of schools. Two of the earliest to be founded were the Nyack Missionary College in 1882 and the Moody Bible Institute, founded in 1886. Nyack was founded by A. B. Simpson who was a pastor, Bible teacher, and the founder of the Christian and Missionary Alliance. Moody Bible Institute was founded by Dwight L. Moody, the great evangelist of the latter half of the 19th century. Other schools founded were Toronto Bible College in 1894, the Bible Institute of Los Angeles in 1908, Columbia Bible College in 1923, Dallas Seminary in 1924, and Bob Jones University in 1926. Westminster Seminary was founded in Philadelphia in 1929. Christian colleges, such as Wheaton College in Wheaton, Illinois, and Calvin College in Grand Rapids, Michigan, have sought to provide higher education that is, at the same time, scholarly, evangelical, Biblical, and God-centered.[657] Today we do not think much about the reason for the origins of such schools, but their existence is a direct result of liberal trends in the church. Liberalism was strong in America from 1900 to 1930 and it is interesting to note what happened in the following decade. Nearly 40 Bible schools were founded between 1930 and 1940. Education was a clear answer to liberal theology.

A third response to liberalism was "the pulpit and the press."[658] Solid Bible teaching was emphasized in conservative churches all over America. Men who were being trained in the Bible schools and colleges were being trained to be good preachers. In fact, many of these schools became known for their "preacher boys." A major contribution to the conservative church in 1909 came from the printing press. It was the Scofield Bible that, more or less, became the official Bible used in churches and in the Christian schools. Though its theology was definitely colored by pre-millennialism, its footnotes were educational and introduced people to a systematic interpretation of biblical doctrine. Christian periodicals began to appear. *Moody Monthly*, *The Christian Herald*, and *The Sunday School Times* are examples of magazines that were read regularly in Christian homes. Another major publication was the *The Fundamentals*. The project arose in the thinking of Lyman Stewart, a wealthy oilman in Southern California, who was convinced that something was needed to reaffirm Christian truths in the face of biblical criticism and liberal theology.[659] Sixty-four authors were chosen to write essays for this collection and they were published between 1910 and 1915 and became 12 volumes. Three million copies of these books were sent to theological students, Christian ministers, and missionaries all over the world.[660] People who promoted these ideas originally were called "Fundamentals." Later they were called "Fundamentalists," but it is important to note that the Fundamentalist movement is usually dated from the publication of these essays.

A fourth response to liberalism came in the development of associations. Conservatives saw the need to band together. The Federal Council of the Churches of Christ in America was founded in 1908 and restructured as the National Council of Churches in 1950. The purpose of this association was to call believers from all denominations together into a Christian ecumenism. Since that organization became increasingly liberal, Bible-believing Christians believed they needed some kind of organization or organizations for common expressions of unity. Various groups approached associations in different ways. For those seeking an interdenominational affiliation, the World Christian Fundamentals Association was organized in 1919. In 1930, the Independent Fundamental Churches of America (IFCA) was formed. This group required its member churches to be independent or dissolve any affiliation with a denomination. In 1942, the National Association of Evangelicals (NAE) was formed with members from more than 40 denominations. The American Council of Christian Churches (ACCC) was formed in 1941 and admitted into its membership only those who were separated from the liberal National Council of Churches. Earlier these associations served to align conservatives in joint efforts, but today their purposes are often questioned. Over the years there have been many other associations formed for the purpose of promoting the evangelical-fundamentalist causes.

In these ways, conservative Christianity marshaled its forces together in order to push back the tide of liberal theology that was so influential in the early decades of the 20th century.

The Fundamentalist-Modernist Controversy

The years from 1920 to 1930 are usually given as the decade of the "Fundamentalist-Modernist Controversy." This can be described as a period of militant activity in which each group fought to gain ground. Among Protestant liberals there were two groups: "evangelical liberals," who had not altogether broken with the tenets of traditional Christianity, and "modernists," who had embraced the liberal brand of 20th century theology. These modernists represented those liberals who waged bitter battles with the fundamentalists. These theological conflicts can be illustrated in three examples.

First was the John Scopes trial in Dayton, Tennessee, in 1925. Scopes, a school teacher, had defied a state law by teaching evolution in his classroom. When the case was brought to court, William Jennings Bryan, a candidate for the U.S. presidency, and an elder in the Presbyterian Church, and one known for his eloquence, led the prosecution. Clarence Darrow defended Scopes. Scopes lost this case, and as an outcome 11 other states established laws prohibiting the teaching of evolution. The trial received worldwide attention and created a furor in the theological and scientific world. Although Bryan technically won his case, he revealed a scientific ignorance and a naïve literalistic understanding of the Bible under sharp cross-examination by defense lawyer Clarence Darrow.[661] The trial indicated fundamentalism's intellectual weaknesses and they were greatly ridiculed. William Jennings Bryan died a few days after the trial. Later, the verdict was reversed by the U.S. Supreme Court.

A second example can be found in the battle fought within the Presbyterian Church U.S.A. The fight between liberalism and conservatism among Presbyterians had been fomenting since shortly before 1900. J. Gresham Machen (1881-1937) was a recognized Greek scholar and New Testament professor at Princeton Seminary (a Presbyterian institution) from 1914 to 1929. Increasingly he became disturbed over the liberal theology making its way into the seminary and related institutions. When these liberal elements were found within the Board of Foreign Missions of the Presbyterian U.S.A., he founded an independent mission board. Machen's solicitation of funds among Presbyterians for his independent board (in money-scarce depression years) and continuing criticism of the denomination's mission program finally brought about his suspension from the Presbyterian ministry after a long, difficult trial.[662] In 1929, he left Princeton Seminary, taking several students with him and founded Westminster Seminary in Philadelphia. Later, in 1936, he and a group of associates founded the Orthodox Presbyterian Church. What happened in the Presbyterian Church also illustrates what happened in other denominations as liberals and conservatives fought for control of their denominations. Generally, fundamentalism lost its thrust in the large denominations and survived mainly in independent fundamentalist churches, many of which were loosely united in the Independent Fundamental Churches of America, organized in 1930.[663]

A third illustration of conservatives and liberals conflict occurred among Northern Baptists. A focal point at this time was the Divinity School at the University of Chicago. This is because Shailer Matthews, dean at the school, was also president of the Northern Baptist Convention. In 1924, he published his book, *The Faith of Modernism*.

> *Matthews contended the modern man's view of the Bible must be based on "scientific investigations." He also applied the evolutionary philosophy to religion, revealed an optimistic view of man, and indicated that God could be "found" by man. In defending his position, Matthews attempted to demonstrate that the Modernism of the twentieth century was to the theological right of nineteenth-century Liberalism. He was not able to convince many of his fellow Baptists that the University of Chicago was either evangelical or on the theological right. [Already] in 1913 the Northern*

> Baptist Theological seminary was founded as a split from the Chicago school.[604]

Fitting into this same picture were events that occurred at Rochester Theological Seminary. A. H. Strong was president at the seminary from 1872 to 1912, and then became president emeritus. In 1918, he visited several of the Baptist foreign mission fields and became alarmed at what were liberal tendencies among missionaries who had been trained at Rochester. Upon his return, he reported his findings.

> In 1920, Curtis Lee Laws, editor of the Watchman-Examiner, called for a conference of "fundamentalists" within the Northern Baptist Convention. Some historians record this as the first use of the term "fundamentalist" which gave the movement its name. Others point to The Fundamentals series as the origin of the name. It is clear that those convened by editor Laws were the first to call themselves fundamentalists. This group worked energetically to stem the tide of liberalism within the denomination, but some more militant Baptists did not think enough had been accomplished and pulled out to form the fundamentalist General Association of Regular Baptists.[665]

Neo-Orthodoxy

In the middle of the controversies between conservatives and liberals in the early 20th century, a theological bomb was dropped that got the attention of the world. This bomb came in the form of Karl Barth's theology, called dialectical theology, or crisis theology, or more popularly, neo-orthodoxy. Liberalism, strong at the turn of the century, was beginning to reveal its weaknesses. Promoting the fatherhood of God, the moral and supreme example of Jesus, and the essential goodness of man who was progressing forward, was beginning to look suspicious. The horrors of a world war and other problems of the 20th century contributed to optimistic liberalism's loss of muscle. On the other hand, fundamentalism, though holding its own and seeming to make progress, had proved itself to be theologically weak. As Jonathan Hill writes, "[The] only options left were unthinking fundamentalism and a weak, watery liberalism."[666]

Into this milieu came Karl Barth (pronounced "Bart") with a hefty theology that got everyone's attention and helped recover a classical approach to theology. He turned his attention to doctrines like revelation, redemption, the nature of God, the incarnation, and the Trinity, which had all been diminished or lost in the rise of liberalism. In fact, Barth saw his task as rescuing these classical doctrines from their demolition by nineteenth century liberalism.[667]

Karl Barth

It is important that we know Barth and his theology because he has come to be regarded as the greatest theologian of the 20th century. Karl Barth (1886-1968) was born in Basel, Switzerland, the son of Fritz Barth, a professor of New Testament and church history at Bern. Though first educated in theology and church history at home, when it came time to go to college, his father, a conservative theologian, insisted that his son study Reformed theology at Bern. This he did, but he also attended schools in Berlin, Tubingen, and Marburg. At Marburg, he became a disciple of Adolph von Harnack and Wilhelm Herrman, the greatest names in liberalism of the time.[668] Wilhelm Herrman, a follower of Ritschl, exerted the greatest influence on Barth. Like others, the young Barth was taken in by liberal theology under the instruction of such influential teachers. Upon graduation, he was ordained a Reformed minister and, after serving as an assistant pastor in Geneva from 1909 to 1911, took his first pastorate in a small farming community at Safenwil, Switzerland, where he remained for 10 years. It was in this simple setting that Barth would become disillusioned with liberalism.

> *Problems began when Barth started systematically studying the Bible in order to prepare his sermons. In its pages he did not find the doctrines of liberal theology with its this-worldly message of progress and reason. On the contrary, he found a voice from beyond the world—a mysterious God who could not be searched out by human reason or religion. The God of the Bible, by contrast, spoke out, actively, unpredictably. The Bible, as Barth was now reading it, was an exciting, fast-moving account of God: who he is and what he does, how he acts in the world, and how he turns around the lives of human beings. Barth could find in the Bible none of the navel-gazing obsession with self and society that he had been taught by liberal theologians.*[669]

He experienced further disillusionment in 1914, a few days after the outbreak of World War I, when he saw the very professors he had studied under signing letters to support the hostilities Germany was involved with. To Barth, this was completely inconsistent with their theology. As the Kaiser stood on his balcony delivering speeches written by Harnack, Barth washed his hands of liberal theology and the moral bankruptcy he now saw associated with it.[670]

One of the greatest influences upon Karl Barth, personally, was his study of the book of Romans. And, as he studied, he wrote. Barth dropped his blockbuster *Commentary on the Epistle to the Romans* in 1918, shattering forever the blithe liberalism of western Protestantism and launching a muscular system of Biblically-based thinking.[671]

Under liberalism, man had ascended to a point of believing that he was able to better himself and discover God on his own. God was found in nature, and God was found in man—in his intuition, imagination, and feelings. In finding God in these places, mankind was able to define God and understand him as people would understand each other. Liberal theology had domesticated God into the patron saint of human institutions and values.[672] To this Barth objected. He wanted to show, as the great theologians before him had done, that one could only know God if God showed Himself to man.

> *The 19th-century liberals had been wrong to think that we could find God by contemplating our own experience or using our own reason. God cannot be found at all: he is not passive. He must find us: he is active. To the whole of human endeavor God simply says "No." He offers, instead, an even greater "Yes" of his own.*[673]

What Barth wanted liberals, and everyone to see, was that humans had no chance without God taking the initiative in revealing Himself.

> *Barth, deliberately provoking a crisis in Christian thinking by stabbing at the subjectivism of Protestant theology which confused man with God, demanded that God be allowed to be God, and that man learn again to be man. Barth penetratingly analyzed man's sin as man's continual attempt to twist truth even in religion to suit his own private ends. Barth's purpose was to force man into a confrontation by the holy, transcendent God of the Bible. Barth's theology came to be called dialectical because his questions led to profound and disturbing contrasts between Holy God and sinful man, Creator and creature, grace and judgment, God's Yes and No.*[674]

Here we learn why his theology was referred to as "crisis theology," or "dialectical theology." As one is faced with the transcendent God of the Bible, a crisis or conflict becomes evident. Man is sinful and needs a solution to his sins; however, God, to whom he is accountable, is far removed in his transcendence. Because of this great gulf between God and humanity, it is impossible to know him unless he makes himself known.[675] Revelation is necessary, and for

Barth, that revelation comes exclusively through Jesus Christ who is the Word of God. In his theology, God is often presented as "Wholly Other." His concept of God as Wholly Other left no way from man to God, but there is a way from God to man, the way of God's gracious self-revelation.[676] In all of man's endeavors to find God, God says a big "no." Then he turns to give a big "yes" as he initiates clearly in Christ who He is and how one may know Him.

One of the greatest strengths in Barth's theology is his Christology. His emphasis is that Christ is the only solution for our sins and the only way to God. Also very strong in Barth's work are the corollary doctrines of the virgin birth, the deity of Christ, his substitutionary death on the cross, grace, and justification by faith. After 1935, Barth's whole theology became focused on Christology, with every doctrine defined in the person and work of Christ, in whom God has declared himself for man, for all men.[677] We cannot reach up to God, but He has reached down to us in a single, dynamic way through Christ. Christ is at once both God's means of salvation and God's exclusive revelation of Himself. It is important to realize what Barth is saying.

> *Barth's theology then is one of revelation. The revelation comes exclusively through Christ, the Word of God. It is mediated through the Bible and the teaching of the church. So, the Bible and church teaching can also be called the Word of God, although in a secondary way.*[678]

In fact, the Bible is a vehicle for the Word of God (Christ) and the Spirit, but cannot replace them. Or, it might be said, the Bible "contains" the Word of God. To Barth, the Bible is not the objective Word of God traditionally found in historic orthodox theology.

> *For Barth, God's word is seen in dynamic, rather than static terms. It is to be thought of not as doctrine or words or statements but as an event, something which*

> *happens. God's word is the event of God speaking to man in Jesus Christ; it is God's personal revelation of himself to us...God's Word confronts us not as an object which we can control, but as a subject which controls and acts upon us.*[679]

It is at this point that Barth departs from traditional orthodox Christian belief. Since Christ is "the Word of God," God's primary and singular revelation, everything else is secondary.

> *Because for Barth, God's word is an event, something that happens, he cannot simply call the Bible God's word. The Bible is the word of God only in the sense that it witnesses to the past event of God speaking and that God speaks through it today.*[680]

So, the Bible is secondary when it comes to revelation. Natural revelation is altogether rejected by Barth. "The Christ event," or "encountering Christ," is the important thing; or, having "a word break through to you" that reveals Christ and gives reality and meaning to one's faith. The Bible particularly becomes meaningful when, through it, you experience "the Word," Christ. This does not mean that the Bible is unimportant in Barth's thinking. It remains the important vehicle for conveying "the Word" to man.

Kierkegaard and Existentialism

Since it is known that Karl Barth studied Soren Kierkegaard (1813-1855), it is believed that Barth was influenced by Kierkegaard's existential philosophy. During his lifetime, Kierkegaard was virtually unknown. After his death, his philosophy began to become known in Europe, and by 1890 to 1900, existentialism had become the popular philosophy on the continent. 20 or 30 years later, it became a major strand of thought in the United States and, many believe, laid the groundwork for the revolution of the 1960s. Kierkegaard came to the conclusion that one cannot arrive at truth or reality through reason; instead, anything of importance—that is, finding meaning "in the moment" one is living—is achieved through a leap of faith.

From this philosophy, we conclude there are experiences to be had that give authenticity to one's life or existence. Disciples of this philosophy, such as Jean Paul Sartre and Albert Camus taught that one had an existential experience when he initiated a "non-rational final experience through an act of the will." Conveyed in this is the idea that the existential experience is not rational, but is based in an act of the will, a choice. One must do something even if it is of a non-rational nature. The Swiss, Karl Jaspers suggested that the "final experience" (the truly meaningful experience) came through a leap of faith—that we are to exercise our wills and "do something!" Not everyone finds meaning in the same way, so the existential experience varies from person to person. When applied (as witnessed in America in the 1950s, 1960s, and years following), the existential experience might involve the use of drugs, eastern religions, the occult, sex, unusual experiences with music (psychedelic), etc., and was usually practiced in a combination of these "experiences." Existentialism became very powerful in western culture because it was conveyed through every form of communication and discipline, including art, music, cinema, the stage, literature, poetry, philosophy, and in theology.

Back to Barth

Many believe that existentialism found its way into Barth's theology. It may be that, rather than Barth consciously incorporating existentialism into his thought, neo-orthodoxy and existentialism simply had a compatibility. To be fair, we must recognize that Barth deliberately laid aside a work he began—*Christian Dogmatics*—because he believed it was characterized by too much existentialism.

Nonetheless, the religious form of existentialism is often ascribed to Barth.

One cannot, and should not, underestimate the contributions Barth made in the field of theology and through his life. Any evaluation should be done in the light of the times in which he lived and the issues he confronted. Barth's theology was a reaction to 19th-century liberalism and ended by blasting a hole in the defense of liberal theology because of its obvious weaknesses. In essence, he said, "You liberals have exalted man at the expense of God, and have studied man's religion rather than God's revelation."[681] Conservatives and fundamentalists were glad for this, but it was as if Barth then turned to them and said, "You are an unthinking group. You need to develop a sound and relevant theology and return to a life of the mind." The introduction of his heavy-weight theology challenged both groups and paved the way for greater development of biblical theology.

There are points in Barth's life worth noting. In 1921, he was appointed honorary professor of Reformed Theology at the University of Gottingen. In 1922, he published a heavily revised six volume set of his *Commentary on the Epistle to the Romans*. In 1925, he moved to the University of Munster to become professor of Dogmatics and New Testament Exegesis. Then, in 1930, he became professor of Systematic Theology at Bonn University. It was after his appointment in 1922 that he published the first half of the first book of the second great work he is noted for, his massive *Church Dogmatics*. He worked on this for more than 20 years, producing 12 volumes, and never actually completed it. It contains over 7,000 pages made up of 6,000,000 words. This was more than Thomas Aquinas had written in *Summa Theologica*. Barth's name began to be included alongside Augustine, Anselm, Aquinas, Luther, and Calvin.

While Barth was teaching at Bonn, Nazism arose in Germany. As he observed the reaction of the church, he was dismayed. The Catholic Church, instead of opposing Hitler, made a truce with him—which he brushed aside.[682] The Protestant Christians formed a movement called the "German Christians" in which they tried to combine Christianity and Nazism. A group opposing these developments arose called the "Confessing Church," and Barth joined. In 1934, members of the Confessing Church met at Barman, Germany, and drew up a document called the "Barman Declaration," which essentially rejected the actions of the German Christians and the Nazi Party. Most of this document had been written by Barth. Later in 1934, teachers were asked to take the oath of unconditional allegiance to the Fuhrer, and he refused. In 1935, as a result of his opposition to the Nazis—and his refusal to salute Hitler at the start of his lectures—Barth was sacked from his job at Bonn University.[683] Within a couple of days he was offered a position in his home town, Basel, Switzerland, and returned and remained there the rest of his life. His life settled into a steady routine of reading, writing, and teaching.[684]

Without question, Barth was the greatest Protestant theologian of the 20th century, and every theological movement of the past 50 years has had to defend itself in the light of his theology. Though he was not a Catholic, Catholic theologians have read, been fascinated by, and learned from Barth. Pope Pius XII, who met personally and discussed theology with Barth, called him the greatest theologian since Thomas Aquinas. Barth personally was a warm, witty human, who never lost his country parson's simplicity. His compassion and social concern is revealed by the fact that in the 1950s and 1960s he preached to those in the prison at Basel. On one occasion he told the prisoners:

> Some of you have heard it said that in the last 40 years I have written a great many books and that some of them have been very fat ones. Let me, however, frankly and openly, and even gladly confess that the four words, "My grace is enough," say much more and say it better than the whole pile of paper with which I have surrounded

myself. When my books have long since been superseded and forgotten, then these words will shine on in all their eternal richness.[685]

Karl Barth visited America once in 1962. On that trip he was asked how he would summarize the meaning to be found in the thousands of pages he had written, and he replied, "Jesus loves me this I know, for the Bible tells me so."

The Composition of Modern Western Protestantism

With the introduction of neo-orthodoxy into western theology, the liberal's contest with the conservatives became a three-cornered struggle. Once introduced into society, each of the three positions has continued to foster certain characteristics.

First, on the soil of America, a Christianity was introduced based upon orthodox Biblical theology and practices. Today we would call this a conservative, evangelical, or fundamental understanding. It featured a belief in the Bible as authoritative, and centered on the long accepted doctrines of Christianity, including the existence of God, the virgin birth and deity of Christ, the blood atonement, justification by faith, and the judgment seat of God. Its strength lay in its commitment to Biblical theology and its communication. Its weaknesses are found in a tendency toward proof-texting, and failure to develop a contemporary theological understanding. A richer theological initiative would equip it to confront new issues as they arise, as when liberalism arose in the late 1800s and early 1900s.

The second religious stream to appear, as we have observed, was liberalism based upon German romantic theologians of the eighteenth century. Though diminished from its initial influence, many of these theological elements have been retained. The Fatherhood of God, optimism about man and his abilities, finding God in the natural world and in man himself, humanitarian acts, an evolutionary understanding applied to culture as well as nature, are all residue from the initial liberal ideas. This fits with the New

Age emphasis found in the second half of the twentieth century. Liberalism has been characterized by humanitarianism, a lessening of the gospel, and a "works mentality" when it comes to salvation.

The third position that resides in Western culture is neo-orthodoxy. Though the term is not often used, its essence promotes religion as experience, as in "experiencing Christ," and faith is secured, not in objective truth, but in one's subjectivity. A large number of theologians and historians believe that neo-orthodoxy is the existential form of Christianity. Many times, when people are asked what they believe, they respond with, "Well, I feel..." which reflects the idea that religion is based more on experience than objective truth. Today, one often hears the term, "leap of faith," which seems to indicated no assurance when it comes to objective truth in spiritual matters...so one must simply leap and hope. It has been noted that in conservative, orthodox belief, the Bible *is* the Word of God; in liberalism the Bible *is not* the word of God; in neo-orthodoxy the Bible *becomes* the Word of God. In the latter, it is one's experience that determines the legitimacy of God's Word.

By mid-20th century, these diverse theological beliefs could be found in various denominations and individual churches throughout the Western world and continue to exercise influence in thought and daily life. In lieu of this, it seems that one of the church's major tasks is to define the essential and vital doctrines and practices that lead to unity. Should this happen, there is little doubt that it will involve looking back. We are "membered" to the past. It is where we came from. The man who understands order does not hack rashly at the roots.[686] The roots of the church's beliefs and life practices are embedded in the soil of history. Whenever people cease to be aware of membership in an order—an order that joins the dead, the living, and the unborn, as well as an order that connects individual to family, family to community, community to nation—those people will form a "lonely crowd," alienated from the world in which they wander.[687]

But the opposite is also true. We need not be a "lonely crowd." As we willingly join ourselves to our human history, there is hope that we will find in our roots the very things that unite and support both the church and society. The benefits of this exercise could be momentous. Throughout our study we have seen the interplay between the church and culture. The church really has been—and is—salt and light, and when the church has been true to biblical teaching and to its purpose for existing, the world has benefited. To use a different metaphor, we might spread a wider net and seine out of the sea of history not only theological but also political, scientific, literary, and military examples of loyalty to Christ.[688] All of these, and more, are ours to explore and discover for the glory of God and for the good of mankind.

BIBLIOGRAPHY

Adair, John, *Puritans: Religion and Politics in Seventeenth Century England and America*, Sutton Publishing Limited, Phoenix Mill – Thrupp – Stroud – Gloucestershire, Great Britain, 1982.

Ante-Nicene Fathers, Apology, Wm. B. Eerdmans Publishing Company, Grand Rapids, Michigan, Reprinted, 1993.

Augustine, *Confessions*, Book VIII.

Augustine, *The City of God*, An Abridged Version for Modern Readers, edited by Vernon J. Bourke, Image Books, Doubleday, New York, 1950.

Apostolic Fathers, translated by J.B. Lightfoot and J.R. Harmer; edited and revised by Michael W. Holmes, Baker Book House.

Austin, Bill, *Austin's Topical History of Christianity*, Tyndale House Publishers, 1983.

Barker, William P., *Who's Who in Church History*, Baker Book House, Grand Rapids, Michigan, 1969.

Barzun, Jacques, *From Dawn to Decadence*, Harper Collins Publishers, New York, 2000.

Bainton, Roland, *Christianity*, Houghton Mifflin Company, Boston, 1964, 1987.

Berkhof, Louis, *Systematic Theology*, Wm B. Eerdmans Publishing Company, Grand Rapids, Michigan, 1932, 1938.

Boettner, Loraine, *Roman Catholicism*, The Presbyterian and Reformed Publishing Company, Philadelphia, Pennsylvania, 1962.

Boice, James and Benjamin Sasse, *Here We Stand,* editors, Baker Books, Grand Rapids, Michigan, 1996.

Boorstin, Daniel, *The Image*, Random House, New York, New York, 1961.

Boyle, Isaac, *A Historical View of the Council of Nicea with a Translation of Documents* (included as an appendix to *The Ecclesiastical History of Eusebius Pamphilus*, Baker Book House, Grand Rapids, Michigan, 1992.

Brown, Colin, *Philosophy and the Christian Faith*, Tyndale Press, London, 1968.

Bruce, F. F., *The Spreading Flame*, Grand Rapids, Eerdmans, 1958.

Brush, John W., *Who's Who in Church History*, Abingdon Press, Nashville, 1962.

Cahill, Thomas, *How The Irish Saved Civilization*, Anchor Books, Doubleday, New York, New York, 1995.

Cairns, Earle, *Christianity Through the Centuries*, Zondervan Publishing House, Grand Rapids, 1954, 1981, 1996.

Catholic Online, *St. Jerome, Doctor of the Church*.

Chadwick, Owen, *The Secularization of the European Mind in the Nineteenth Century*, New York: Cambridge University Press, 1975.

Chatelet, Emilie du, http://www.visitvoltaire.com/voltaire_bio.htm.

Chesterton, G.K., *Orthodoxy*, Dodd, Mead & Company, London, England, 1908.

Christian History, Volume V, Christian History Institute, printed in U.S.A., 1986.

Christian History magazine, Volumes IV, V, VI, VIII, IX, XIII, Christianity Today, Carol Stream, Illinois.

Comby, Jean, *How to Read Church History*, Vol. 2, Crossroad Publishing Company, New York, 1996.

Copleston, Frederick, S.J., *A History of Philosophy*, Volume II: Medieval Philosophy, Doubleday, New York, 1993.

Cousins, Norman, *"In God We Trust,"* Harper & Brothers Publishers, New York, 1958.

Crawford, Michael, *Seasons of Grace: Colonial New England's Revival Tradition in Its British Context*, Oxford University Press, New York, 1991.

Dickens, A. G., *"The Ambivalent English Reformation, in Background to the English Renaissance,"* ed. J. B. Trapp, London, Gray-Mills, 1974.

Durant, Will, *The Age of Voltaire*, MJF Books, New York, 1965.

Durant, Will, *The Reformation,* MJF Books, New York, 1957.

Durant, Will, *The Story of Civilization: The Reformation*, Vol. 6, MJF Books, New York, 1957.

Einhard, *The Life of Charlemagne*, Ann Arbor Paperbacks, The University of Michigan Press, 1960.

Engel, Elliot, *Voltaire's Candide*, a recorded lecture on the life of Voltaire, Session 2, produced by Author's Ink, Raleigh, North Carolina.

Ford, Henry, *Interview with Charles N. Wheeler*, Chicago Tribune, May 25, 1916.

Fox, Richard Wightman, *Jesus in America*, Harper San Francisco, 2004.

Geisler, Norman L., and William E. Nix, *A General Introduction to the Bible*, Moody Press, Chicago, 1968.

Great Books, Volume 38, William Benton, publisher, Encyclopedia Britannica, Chicago, 1952.

Great Thinkers of the Western World, edited by Ian P. McGreal, HarperCollins Publishers, New York, New York, 1992.

Guinness, Os and John Seel, *No God But God*, Zondervan Publishing House, Grand Rapids, Michigan, 1992.

Hart, Michael H., *The 100: A Ranking of the Most Influential Persons in History*, A Citadel Press Book, New York, 1992.

Hill, Jonathan, *The History of Christian Thought*, InterVarsity Press, Downers Grove, Illinois, 2003.

Hoskins, Edward J., *A Muslim's Heart*, Dawsonmedia, Colorado Springs, Colorado, 2003.

Hurlbut, Jesse Lyman, D.D., *The Story of the Christian Church*, Zondervan Publishing House, Grand Rapids, Michigan, 1970.

Irenaeus, *Against Heresies*.

Jesus and the Twelve, Good Will Publishers, Inc., Gastonia, NC, 1969.

Kirk, Russell, *The Roots of American Order*, Regnery Gateway, Washington, D.C., 1991.

Knowing & Doing, A Teaching Quarterly for Discipleship of Heart and Mind, C.S. Lewis Institute, Falls Church, Virginia, Summer, 2004.

Lane, Tony, *Harper's Concise Book of Christian Faith*, Harper & Row, Publishers, San Francisco, 1984.

Letters of John Calvin, selected from the Bonnet Collection, Banner of Truth Trust, 1980.

Lewis, C. S., *Studies in Medieval and Renaissance Literature*, Cambridge University Press, 1966.

McBirnie, William Steuart, *The Search for the Twelve*, Tyndale House Publishers, Wheaton, Il, 1973.

McDonald, Alonzo L., *Introduction to Excerpts from the Lessons of History by Will and Ariel Durant*, The Trinity Forum, 2004.

Melanchthon, Philip, *A Melanchthon Reader*, translated by Peter Lang, Peter Lang Publishing, Inc., New York, 1988.

Miller, H.S., M.A., *General Biblical Introduction*, The Word-Bearer Press, 1937.

Murray, Iain, *The Invitation System*, The Banner of Truth Trust, 78b Chiltern Street, printed by Hunt Barnard & Company, London, June 1998.

Nicene and Post-Nicene Fathers, Series II, Vol. I, *The Church History of Eusebius*, editors Philip Schaff and Henry Wace, T & T Clark of Edinburgh, Wm. B. Eerdmans Publishing Company, Grand Rapids, Michigan, 1989.

Nicene and Post-Nicene Fathers, Series II, Vol. II, *The Ecclesiastical History by Socrates Scholasticus*, editors Philip Schaff and Henry Wace, T & T Clark of Edinburgh, Wm. B. Eerdmans Publishing Company, Grand Rapids, Michigan, 1989.

Nicene and Post-Nicene Fathers, Series II, Vol. III, *The Ecclesiastical History of Theodoret*, editors Philip Schaff and Henry Wace, T & T Clark of Edinburgh, Wm. B. Eerdmans Publishing Company, Grand Rapids, Michigan, 1989.

Niebuhr, H. Richard, *Christ and Culture*, Harper & Row Publishers, 1951.

Noll, Mark, *The Rise of Evangelicalism*, InterVarsity Press, Downers Grove, Illinois, 2003.

Noll, Mark, *Turning Points*, Baker Books, Grand Rapids, Michigan, 1997.

Norton-Taylor, Duncan, *God's Man*, Baker Book House, Grand Rapids, Michigan, 1979.

Papal bull, *Ineffabilus Deus.*

Pascal, Blaise, *The Mind on Fire*, edited by James M. Houston, Multnomah Press, Portland, Oregon, 1989.

Political Sermons of the American Founding Era, edited by Ellis Sandoz, Liberty Fund, Indianapolis, Indiana, 1998.

Portable Enlightenment Reader, edited by Isaac Kramnick, Penguin Books, New York, 1995.

Reid, J. S., *Cambridge Medieval History*, I.

Rousseau, Jean-Jacques, *Confessions*, (Translated from the French by W. Conyngham Mallory, Brentano's, Inc.), United States, 1928.

Rousseau, Jean-Jacques, *On the Origin of Inequality*, found in *The Great Books*, Volume 38.

Ryken, Leland, *Worldly Saints*, Zondervan Publishing House, Grand Rapids, 1986.

Santayana, George, *The Life of Reason*, Vol. 1, 1905.

Schaeffer, Francis, *How Should We Then Live?*, Fleming H. Revell Company, New Jersey, 1972.

Schaff, Philip, *History of the Christian Church*, Wm. B. Eerdmans Publishing Company, Grand Rapids, Michigan, 1984.

Shelley, Bruce L., *Church History in Plain Language*, Word Publishing, Dallas, Texas, 1982, 1995.

Thomas, I.D.E., *William Shakespeare and His Bible*, Hearthstone Publishing, Ltd., Oklahoma City, Oklahoma, 2000.

Vatican Council in Rome, 1870.

Vigeveno, H. S., *Thirteen Men Who Changed the World*, Regal Books Division, G/L Publications, Glendale, CA, 1967.

Wesley, John, *Works* (new), May 24, 1738.

Wood, Ralph C., *Contending for the Faith*, Baylor University Press, Waco, Texas, 2003.

Woodbridge, John D., *Great Leaders of the Christian Church*, Moody Press, Chicago, 1988.

131 Christians Everyone Should Know, from the Editors of *Christian History* Magazine, Broadman & Holman Publishers, Nashville, Tennessee, 2000.

Endnotes

[1] Alonzo L. McDonald, *Introduction to Excerpts from the Lessons of History by Will and Ariel Durant*, The Trinity Forum, 2004, p. 3.
[2] Henry Ford interview with Charles N. Wheeler, Chicago Tribune, May 25, 1916.
[3] George Santayana, *The Life of Reason*, Volume I, 1905.
[4] Will Durant, *The Reformation* (New York: MJF Books, 1957), viii.
[5] Russell Kirk, *The Roots of American Order*, Regnery Gateway, Washington, D.C., 1991, p. XVIII.
[6] ibid., pp. XVIII, XIX.
[7] G.K. Chesterton, *Orthodoxy*, Doubleday, Garden City, New York, 1908, p. 48.
[8] Russell Kirk, pp. XVII.
[9] James Boice and Benjamin Sasse, *Here We Stand*, editors, Baker Books, Grand Rapids, Michigan, 1996, p. 99.
[10] Blaise Pascal, *The Mind on Fire*, edited by James M. Houston, Multnomah Press, Portland, Oregon, 1989, p. 28.
[11] ibid. p. 27.
[12] Os Guinness and John Seel, *No God But God*, Zondervan Publishing House, Grand Rapids, Michigan,
1992, p. 23.
[13] Philip Melanchthon, *A Melanchthon Reader*, translated by Peter Lang, Peter Lang Publishing, Inc., New York, 1988, p. 48.
[14] ibid., p. 54.
[15] Daniel Boorstin, *The Image*, pp. 61-63.
[16] Bill Austin, *Austin's Topical History of Christianity*, Tyndale House Publishers, 1983, p. 13
[17] *The Apostolic Fathers*, translated by J.B. Lightfoot and J.R. Harmer; edited and revised by Michael W. Holmes, Baker Book House, 1989, p. 318.
[18] Eusebius, *Ecclesiastical History*, II, 16, 1.
[19] ibid., III, 1.
[20] Norman L. Geisler and William E. Nix, *A General Introduction to the Bible*, Moody Press, Chicago, 1968, pp. 206, 207.
[21] ibid., p. 206.
[22] Eusebius, *Ecclesiastical History*, III, 172, 173.
[23] Philip Schaff, *History of the Christian Church*, Vol. I, p. 378.
[24] Bruce Shelley, *Church History in Plain Language*, pp. 40-41.

[25] Eusebius, *Ecclesiastical History*, II, 25, pp. 5-7.
[26] F.F. Bruce, *The Spreading Flame*, Grand Rapids, Eerdmans, 1958, p. 156.
[27] Philip Schaff, Volume III, p. 607.
[28] Tony Lane, *Harper's Concise Book of Christian Faith*, Harper & Row, Publishers, San Francisco, 1984, p. 13.
[29] William Barker, *Who's Who in Church History*, Baker Book House, Grand Rapids, Michigan, 1969, p. 73.
[30] Philip Schaff, Volume II, p. 637.
[31] Earle Cairns, *Christianity Through the Centuries*, Zondervan Publishing House, Grand Rapids, Michigan, 1954, pp. 77, 78.
[32] ibid., p. 77.
[33] ibid., pp. 77, 78.
[34] Bill Austin, p. 68.
[35] *The Apostolic Fathers*, Volume I, p. 45.
[36] Roland Bainton, *Christianity*, Houghton Mifflin Company, Boston, 1964, p. 65
[37] Bill Austin, p. 68.
[38] William P. Barker, p. 148.
[39] ibid.
[40] Bill Austin, p. 77.
[41] Bruce Shelley, p. 28.
[42] ibid., p. 68
[43] *The Apostolic Father*, Volume I, p. 45.
[44] Bill Austin, p. 68.
[45] Irenaeus, *Against Heresies*, III, pp. 3 – 4.
[46] Bruce Shelley, p. 37.
[47] Roland Bainton.
[48] *The Apostolic Fathers*, Volume I, p. 42.
[49] Philip Schaff, Volume II, p. 713.
[50] ibid.
[51] ibid., p. 714.
[52] Tony Lane, *Harper's Concise Book of Christian Faith*, Harper & Row, Publishers, San Francisco, 1984, p. 16.
[53] ibid., p. 749.
[54] Philip Schaff, Volume II, p. 751.
[55] ibid., pp. 750, 751.
[56] ibid., p. 751.
[57] Tony Lane, p. 17.
[58] Philip Schaff, Volume II, p. 823.
[59] ibid., p. 18.
[60] Earle Cairns, p. 117.

61 Philip Schaff, Volume II, p. 820.
62 John D. Woodbridge, *Great Leaders of the Christian Church*, Moody Press, Chicago, 1988, p. 50.
63 ibid.
64 *The Ante-Nicene Fathers, Apology*, Wm. B. Eerdmans Publishing Company, Grand Rapids, Michigan, Reprinted, 1993, p.
65 Philip Schaff, Volume II, p. 829.
66 ibid., p. 823.
67 ibid., p. 830.
68 Earle Cairns, p. 120.
69 Philip Schaff, Volume II, p.782.
70 William Barker, p. 72.
71 Bill Austin, p. 79.
72 Bruce Shelley, p. 80.
73 ibid., p. 80.
74 William Barker, p. 212.
75 Philip Schaff, Volume II, p. 787.
76 ibid, pp. 787, 788.
77 Bruce Shelley, p. 85.
78 Philip Schaff, Volume II, p. 792.
79 Tony Lane, p. 23.
80 Bill Austin, p. 79.
81 ibid.
82 Socrates, *Ecclesiastical History*, pp. 1, 2.
83 *The Ecclesiastical History of Theodoret, The Nicene and Post-Nicene Fathers*, William B. Eerdmans Publishing Company, Grand Rapids, Michigan, 1989, Volume III, p. 35.
84 ibid., pp. 35, 36.
85 ibid.
86 ibid., pp. 35, 36.
87 ibid., p. 36.
88 *The Ecclesiastical History of Socrates, The Nicene and Post Nicene Fathers*, William B. Eerdmans Publishing Company, Grand Rapids, Michigan, 1989, Volume II, p. 4.
89 Socrates Scholasticus, *Nicene and Post-Nicene Fathers, The Ecclesiastical History of Socrates Scholasticus*, editors Philip Schaff and Henry Wace (Edinburgh: T & T Clark, reprinted 1989) Second Series, Vol. II, p. 1.
90 Theodoret, *Nicene and Post-Nicene Fathers, The Ecclesiastical History of Socrates Scholasticus,* editors Philip Schaff and Henry Wace (Edinburgh: T & T Clark, reprinted in 1989), Vol. III, pp. 35, 36.

[91] Isaac Boyle, *A Historical View of the Council of Nicea with a Translation of Documents* (included as an appendix to *The Ecclesiastical History of Eusebius Pamphilus*, Baker Book House, Grand Rapids, Michigan, 1992, p. 13.
[92] ibid., p. 11.
[93] Boyle, p. 13.
[94] ibid., pp. 15, 16.
[95] Socrates, p. 11.
[96] Boyle, p. 44.
[97] ibid., p. 27.
[98] Socrates, p. 34.
[99] Theodoret, p. 52.
[100] ibid.
[101] Socrates, pp. 34, 35.
[102] Theodoret, p. 52.
[103] Socrates, pp. 34, 35.
[104] Theodoret, p. 52.
[105] Socrates, p. 35.
[106] William P. Barker, *Who's Who in Church History*, Baker Book House, Grand Rapids, Michigan, 1969, p. 71.
[107] Tony Lane, *Harper's Concise Book of Christian Faith*, Harper & Row Publishers, San Francisco, 1984, p. 37.
[108] ibid.
[109] Earle E. Cairns, *Christianity Through the Centuries*, Zondervan Publishing House, Grand Rapids, Michigan, p. 152.
[110] ibid.
[111] ibid.
[112] Barker, p. 71.
[113] Cairns, p. 153.
[114] ibid.
[115] Barker, pp. 273, 274.
[116] Philip Schaff, Volume III, p. 606.
[117] Barker, p. 25.
[118] ibid.
[119] Cairns, pp. 143, 145.
[120] Philip Schaff, *History of the Christian Church*, Vol. III, Wm. B. Eerdmans Publishing Company, Grand Rapids, Michigan, 1984, pp. 206, 207.
[121] Catholic Online, *St. Jerome, Doctor of the Church*, pp. 1, 2.
[122] Philip Schaff, Volume III, p. 207.
[123] ibid.
[124] ibid.

[125] William Barker, p. 154.
[126] Philip Schaff, Volume III, p. 211.
[127] Philip Schaff, Volume III, p. 212.
[128] ibid., p. 205.
[129] Cairns, p. 155.
[130] *131 Christians Everyone Should Know*, from the Editors of *Christian History* Magazine, Broadman & Holman Publishers, Nashville, Tennessee, 2000, p. 80.
[131] Earle Cairns, pp. 155, 156.
[132] William Barker, p. 18.
[133] Roland Bainton, p. 118.
[134] *131 Christians Everyone Should Know*, pp. 81, 82.
[135] ibid., 82.
[136] ibid.
[137] Tony Lane, p. 36.
[138] Earle Cairns, p. 156.
[139] Philip Schaff, Volume III, p. 963.
[140] *131 Christians Everyone Should Know*, p. 82.
[141] *Great Thinkers of the Western World*, edited by Ian P. McGreal, HarperCollins*Publishers*, New York, New York, 1992, p. 72.
[142] Frederick Copleston, S.J., *A History of Philosophy*, Volume II: Medieval Philosophy, Doubleday, New York, 1993, p. 40.
[143] William P. Barker, p. 26.
[144] Frederick Copleston, p. 40.
[145] Christian History, Volume VI, Number 3, Issue 15, p. 7.
[146] Frederick Copleston, p. 41
[147] ibid., p. 42.
[148] *Christian History*, Volume VI, Number 3, Issue 15, p. 9.
[149] ibid., pp. 8, 9
[150] Roland Bainton, p. 118.
[151] Augustine, *Confessions*, Book VIII, Chapter XII, 28.
[152] ibid., Book VIII, Chapter XII, 29.
[153] ibid.
[154] ibid.
[155] *Christian History*, Volume VI, Number 3, p. 10.
[156] ibid.
[157] ibid., p. 11.
[158] William Barker, p. 26.
[159] H.S. Miller, M.A., *General Biblical Introduction*, The Word-Bearer Press, 1937, pp. 140, 141.

[160] Mark Noll, *Turning Points*, Baker Books, Grand Rapids, Michigan, 1997, p. 38.
[161] H.S. Miller, p. 140.
[162] ibid., p. 99.
[163] ibid.
[164] From the papal bull, *Ineffabilus Deus*.
[165] The Vatican Council in Rome, 1870.
[166] Loraine Boettner, *Roman Catholicism*, The Presbyterian and Reformed Publishing Co., Philadelphia, 1962, p. 162.
[167] Saint Augustine, *The City of God*, An Abridged Version for Modern Readers, edited by Vernon J. Bourke, Image Books, Doubleday, New York, 1950, pp. 111-112.
[168] ibid., p. 12.
[169] Thomas Cahill, *How The Irish Saved Civilization*, Anchor Books, Doubleday, New York, New York, 1995, p.14.
[170] J. S. Reid, *Cambridge Medieval History*, I, p. 54.
[171] Bill Austin, p. 96.
[172] Francis Schaeffer, *How Should We Then Live*, pp. 28, 29.
[173] Bruce Shelley, *The Church in Plain Language*, p. 132.
[174] Bill Austin, p. 107.
[175] Philip Schaff, *The History of the Christian Church*, Volume III, p. 315.
[176] Bruce Shelley, *The Church in Plain Language, p. 133*.
[177] ibid., p. 137.
[178] ibid., p. 167.
[179] Jesse Lyman Hurlbut, D.D., *The Story of the Christian Church*, Zondervan Publishing House, Grand Rapids, Michigan, 1970, p. 82.
[180] Edward J. Hoskins, *A Muslim's Heart*, Dawsonmedia, Colorado Springs, Colorado, 2003, p. 6.
[181] ibid.
[182] Bill Austin, *Austin's Topical History of Christianity*, p. 132.
[183] ibid., p. 132.
[184] ibid., p. 133.
[185] Edward J. Hoskins, p. 3.
[186] ibid., p. 4.
[187] ibid.
[188] ibid., p. 5.
[189] William Barker, *Who's Who in Church* History, pp. 225, 226.
[190] Roland Bainton, *Christianity*, p. 148.
[191] Einhard, *The Life of Charlemagne*, Ann Arbor Paperbacks, The University of Michigan Press, 1960, p. 50.

[192] ibid., p. 52.
[193] Roland Bainton, p. 150.
[194] Bruce Shelly, *Church History in Plain Language*, Word Publishing, Dallas, 1982, p. 176.
[195] Bill Austin, p. 146.
[196] Bruce Shelley, p. 174.
[197] ibid., p. 176.
[198] Schaff, *History of the Christian Church*, Vol. IV, pp. 239, 240.
[199] Bill Austin, p. 146.
[200] Noll. *Turning Points*, p. 109.
[201] ibid. p. 121.
[202] *Christian History* magazine, Issue 28, Vol. IX, No. 4.
[203] Mark Noll, *Turning Points*, p. 133.
[204] Bruce Shelley, *Church History in Plain Language*, Word Publishing, p. 185.
[205] ibid., p. 185.
[206] ibid., p. 184.
[207] ibid., p. 185.
[208] ibid., p. 185.
[209] Philip Schaff, *History of the Christian Church*, Vol. V, p. 523.
[210] Philip Schaff, *History of the Christian Church*, Vol. V, p. 214.
[211] ibid., p. 218.
[212] ibid, p. 232.
[213] ibid.
[214] ibid, p. 268.
[215] *International Standard Bible Encyclopaedia*, James Orr, general editor, William B. Eerdmans Publishing Company, Grand Rapids, Michigan, 1939, Vol. III, p. 1926
[216] Martin Luther, *Against Heavenly Prophets* (1525) and *Confessions Concerning Christ's Supper* (1528), quoted by F.L. Cross, ed., *The Oxford Dictionary of the Christian Church*, London: Oxford, 1958, p. 337.
[217] *International Standard Bible Encyclopaedia*, James Orr, editor; William B. Eerdmans Publishing Company, Grand Rapids, Michigan, Volume III, p. 1939.
[218] Louis Berhof, *Systematic Theology*, Wm. B. Eerdmans Publishing Co., Grand Rapids, Michigan, 1939, p. 654.
[219] ibid., p. 653, 654.
[220] Philip Schaff, *History of the Christian Church*, Vol. VI, p. 3.
[221] Bill Austin, p. 212.
[222] Bill Austin, p. 212.
[223] Francis Schaeffer, *How Should We Then Live*, p. 58.

[224] Bill Austin, p. 213.
[225] Philip Schaff, *History of the Christian Church*, Vol. VI, p. 567.
[226] Francis Schaeffer, *How Should We Then Live*, p. 57.
[227] ibid., p. 57.
[228] Bill Austin, p. 216.
[229] Philip Schaff, *History of the Christian Church*, Vol. VI, p. 575.
[230] ibid., 575.
[231] Philip Schaff, *History of the Christian Church*, Vol. VI, p. 575.
[232] Francis Schaeffer, *How Should We Then Live*, p. 60.
[233] Bill Austin, p. 213.
[234] Francis Schaeffer, *How Should We Then Live*, p. 60.
[235] ibid., 60.
[236] Philip Schaff, *History of the Chrisitan Church*, Vol. VI, p. 576.
[237] ibid.
[238] Bill Austin, p. 213.
[239] Philip Schaff, *History of the Christian Church*, Vol. VI, p. 578.
[240] Bill Austin, pp. 216, 217.
[241] Francis Schaeffer, *How Should We Then Live*, p. 62.
[242] ibid., pp. 65, 66.
[243] ibid., p. 65.
[244] ibid., p. 74.
[245] ibid.
[246] ibid, p. 78.
[247] Bill Austin, p. 216.
[248] Francis Schaeffer, *How Should We Then Live*, pp. 71, 72.
[249] ibid., p. 72.
[250] James V. Schall, *Schall on Chesterton*, The Catholic University of America Press, Washingto, D.C., 2000, p. 233
[251] Bill Austin, p. 174.
[252] ibid., p. 179.
[253] ibid.
[254] Bill Austin, p. 213.
[255] Francis Schaeffer, *How Should We Then Live*, p. 60.
[256] Philip Schaff, *History of the Christian Church*, Vol. VII, p. vii.
[257] Philip Schaff, *History of the Christian Church*, Vol. VII, p. 2.
[258] ibid., p. 2
[259] Will Durant, *The Story of Civilization: The Reformation*, Vol. 6, MJF Books, New York, 1957, p. 320.
[260] Earl Cairns, *Christianity Through the Centuries*, p. 299.
[261] Mark Noll, *Turning Points*, Baker Books, Grand Rapids, 1997, p. 180.

262 ibid., p. 181.
263 ibid.
264 ibid.
265 ibid., p 182.
266 Jacques Barzun, *From Dawn to Decadence*, Harper Collins Publishers, New York, 2000, p. 4.
267 Mark Noll, *Turning Points*, p. 182.
268 ibid., pp. 182, 183.
269 ibid., p. 180.
270 Earle E. Cairns, *Christianity Through the Centuries*, Zondervan Publishing House, Grand Rapids, 1954, p. 303.
271 Noll, p. 185.
272 ibid., p. 188.
273 Francis Schaeffer, *How Should We Then Live?*, Fleming H. Revell Company, New Jersey, 1972, p. 82.
274 Bruce Shelley, *Church History in Plain Language*, Word Publishing, Dallas, Texas, 1982, p. 232.
275 Philip Schaff, *History of the Christian Church*, Vol. VI, p. 685.
276 ibid., p. 707.
277 ibid., p. 704.
278 Bruce Shelley, *Church History in Plain Language*, Word Publishing, Dallas, Texas, 1982, p. 232.
279 ibid.
280 ibid., pp. 232, 233.
281 Jacques Barzun, *From Dawn to Decadence*, Harper Collins Publishers, New York, 2000, p. 12.
282 Bruce Shelley, *Church History in Plain Language*, Word Publishing, Dallas, 1982, p. 313.
283 Will Durant, *The Reformation*, p. 341.
284 Bruce Shelley, p. 237.
285 Bill Austin, p. 241.
286 Will Durant, *The Reformation*, p. 443.
287 ibid., p. 444.
288 ibid., p. 424.
289 John Adair, *Puritans: Religion and Politics in Seventeenth Century England and America*, Sutton Publishing Limited, Phoenix Mill – Thrupp – Stroud – Gloucestershire, Great Britain, 1982, p. 46.
290 ibid., pp. 46, 47.
291 ibid., p. 47.
292 ibid.

[293] Jacques Barzun, p. 18.
[294] Philip Schaff, *History of the Christian Church*, Vol. VII, p. 180.
[295] ibid., p. 472.
[296] John Adair, *Puritans: Religion and Politics in Seventeenth Century England and America*, Sutton Publishing Limited, Phoenix Mill – Thrupp – Stroud – Gloucestershire, Great Britain, 1982, p. 48.
[297] Philip Schaff, *History of the Christian Church*, p. 456.
[298] John Adair, *Puritans: Religion and Politics in Seventeenth Century England and America*, Sutton Publishing Limited, Phoenix Mill – Thrupp – Stroud – Gloucestershire, Great Britain, 1982, p. 48.
[299] bid., p. 48.
[300] ibid.
[301] ibid.
[302] ibid.
[303] ibid., p. 56.
[304] ibid.
[305] ibid.
[306] Philip Schaff, *History of the Christian Church*, Vol. VII, pp. 728, 729.
[307] Jesse Lyman Hurlbut, *The Story of the Christian Church*, Zondervan Publishing House, Grand Rapids, 1967, p. 131.
[308] Will Durant, p. 349.
[309] ibid., 349.
[310] ibid., 349.
[311] Philip Schaff, *History of the Christian Church*, Vol. VII, p. 178.
[312] ibid., p. 182.
[313] William P. Barker, *Who's Who in Church History*, Baker Book House, Grand Rapids, 1969, p. 63.
[314] Schaff, Vol. VIII, p. 23.
[315] John Adair, *Puritans*, p. 53.
[316] William P. Barker, p. 57.
[317] *Letters of John Calvin*, selected from the Bonnet Collection, Banner of Truth Trust, 1980, p. 15.
[318] Barker, p. 57.
[319] *Letters of John Calvin*, p. 21.
[320] ibid.
[321] John Adair, *Puritans*, p. 55.
[322] ibid.
[323] Will Durant, *The Reformation*, p. 475.
[324] ibid.
[325] ibid.

[326] Philip Schaff, *History of the Christian Church*, Vol. VIII, pp. 644, 645.
[327] ibid., 519.
[328] Duncan Norton-Taylor, *God's Man*, Baker Book House, Grand Rapids, Michigan, 1979, p. 293.
[329] ibid., p. 294.
[330] Schaff, pp. 835, 836.
[331] Will Durant, *The Reformation*, pp. 476, 477.
[332] Roland H. Bainton, *Christianity*, Houghton Mifflin Company, Boston, 1964, p. 270.
[333] William P. Barker, *Who's Who in Church History*, p. 167.
[334] Jesse Lyman Hurlbut, *The Story of the Christian Church*, Zondervan Publishing House, Grand Rapids, 1918, p. 125.
[335] Francis Schaeffer, *How Should We Then Live?*, p. 105.
[336] Jacques Barzun, *From Dawn to Decadence*, Harper Collins Publishers, New York, 2000, p. 10.
[337] Francis Schaeffer, *How Should We Then Live?*, p. 89.
[338] ibid., p. 90.
[339] John Adair, *Puritans*, p. 52.
[340] Francis Schaeffer, *How Should We Then Live*, p. 92.
[341] ibid., p. 105.
[342] ibid., pp. 112, 113.
[343] Leland Ryken, *Worldly Saints*, Zondervan Publishing House, Grand Rapids, 1986, p. 164.
[344] ibid., p. 256
[345] Will Durant, *The Reformation*, p. 320.
[346] Jean Comby, *How to Read Church History*, Vol. 2, Crossroad Publishing Company, New York, 1996, p. 27.
[347] ibid., pp. 27, 28.
[348] Loraine Boettner, *Roman Catholicism*, The Presbyterian and Reformed Publishing Company, Philadelphia, Pennsylvania, 1962, p. 97.
[349] ibid., p. 97.
[350] I. D. E. Thomas, *William Shakespeare and His Bible*, Heathstone Publishing, Ltd., Oklahoma City, Oklahoma, 2000, p. 34.
[351] Jean Comby, Vol. 2, p. 28.
[352] ibid., p. 28.
[353] ibid., p. 28.
[354] Earle Cairns, *Christianity Through the Centuries*, p. 378.
[355] Jean Comby, Vol. 2, p. 30.
[356] Mark Noll, *Turning Points*, Baker Books, Grand Rapids, Michigan, 1997, p. 246.

[357] Francis Schaeffer, *How Should We Then Live*, p. 122.
[358] *The Portable Enlightenment Reader*, edited by Isaac Kramnick, Penguin Books, New York, 1995, back cover.
[359] ibid., p. x.
[360] ibid., p. xi.
[361] ibid.
[362] Will Durant, *The Age of Voltaire*, MJF Books, New York, 1965, p. 497.
[363] Mark Noll, *Turning Points*, p. 247.
[364] *The Portable Enlightenment Reader*, ed., Isaac Kramnick, Penguin Books, 1995, p. 1.
[365] ibid., p. 2.
[366] ibid., p. 6.
[367] Mark Noll, *Turning Points*, p. 247.
[368] Bruce Shelley, *Church History in Plain Language*, p. 312.
[369] *The Portable Enlightenment Reader* (Introduction, p. x).
[370] ibid., p. ix.
[371] ibid.
[372] ibid., p. xiv.
[373] ibid., pp. xv, xvi.
[374] ibid.., p. xvi.
[375] ibid., pp. xvi, xvii.
[376] ibid., p. xiv.
[377] ibid.
[378] ibid., xv.
[379] Francis Schaeffer, *How Should We Then Live*, p. 121.
[380] *The Portable Enlightenment Reader*, p. 74.
[381] ibid., xiv.
[382] ibid., pp. 382, 383.
[383] ibid., p. xiv.
[384] ibid., p. xiii.
[385] ibid., p. xiv.
[386] ibid.
[387] Owen Chadwick, *The Secularization of the European Mind in the Nineteenth Century*, New York: Cambridge University Press, 1975, pp. 5, 9.
[388] Bill Austin, *Austin's Topical History of Christianity*, Tyndale House Publishers, Wheaton, Illinois, 1983, p. 327.
[389] The Portable Enlightenment Reader, p. xii.
[390] Emilie du Chatelet, http://www.visitvoltaire.com/voltaire_bio.htm., p. 1.
[391] ibid.

[392] Michael H. Hart, *The 100: A Ranking of the Most Influential Persons in History*, A Citadel Press Book, New York, 1992, p. 369.
[393] Colin Brown, *Philosophy and the Christian Faith*, Tyndale Press, London, 1968, p.85.
[394] www.visitvoltaire.com, p. 1.
[395] *Great Thinkers of the Western World*, edited by Ian P. McGreal, Harper Collins Publishers, New York, New York, 1992, p. 260.
[396] ibid., 257.
[397] www.visitvoltaire.com, p. 2.
[398] ibid.
[399] ibid.
[400] ibid.
[401] ibid., p. 3.
[402] ibid., p. 3, 4.
[403] ibid., p. 4.
[404] Michael H. Hart, *The 100*, p. 370.
[405] Elliot Engel, *Voltaire's Candide*, a recorded lecture on the life of Voltaire, Session 2, produced by Author's Ink, Raleigh, North Carolina.
[406] ibid.
[407] ibid.
[408] ibid.
[409] Jean-Jacques Rousseau, *The Social Contract*, found in The Great Books, Encyclopaedia Britannica, Chicago, 1952, p. 387
[410] *Great Thinkers of the Western World*, p. 271.
[411] Jean-Jacques Rousseau, *Confessions*, (Translated from the French by W. Conyngham Mallory, Brentano's, Inc.), United States, 1928, p. 4.
[412] *The Great Books*, Volume 38, William Benton, publisher, Encyclopedia Britannica, Chicago, 1952, p. 320.
[413] *The Great Thinkers of the Western World*, p. 272.
[414] ibid., p. 272.
[415] *The Great Books*, Volume 38, p. 333.
[416] bid.
[417] ibid.
[418] Jean-Jacques Rousseau, *On the Origin of Inequality*, found in *The Great Books*, Volume 38, p. 348.
[419] ibid., p. 273.
[420] ibid.
[421] ibid.
[422] ibid.
[423] ibid.

424 *Great Thinkers of the Western World*, p. 274.
425 *The Portable Enlightenment Reader*, p. xix.
426 ibid., p. xviii.
427 ibid.
428 ibid.
429 ibid., p. xix.
430 ibid.
431 ibid.
432 ibid.
433 ibid., p. 166.
434 ibid.
435 ibid.
436 Norman Cousins, *"In God We Trust,"* Harper & Brothers Publishers, New York, 1958, p.114.
437 ibid., p. 118.
438 ibid., pp. 114, 115.
439 ibid., p. 116.
440 ibid., pp. 115, 116.
441 ibid., p. 123.
442 ibid., p. 115.
443 ibid.
444 ibid., p. 114.
445 ibid., p. 117.
446 ibid.
447 ibid., p. 123.
448 *Christian History*, Vol. XIII, No. 1, 1994, by Christianity Today, Carol Stream, Illinois, p. 2.
449 Leland Ryken, *Worldly Saints*, Zondervan Publishing House, Grand Rapids, 1986, p. 1.
450 *Christian History*, Vol. XIII, p. 2.
451 Ryken, p. 1.
452 A.G. Dickens, "The Ambivalent English Reformation, " in *Background to the English Renaissance*, ed. J. B. Trapp, London, Gray-Mills, 1974, p. 47.
453 C. S. Lewis, *Studies in Medieval and Renaissance Literature*, Cambridge University Press, 1966, p. 121.
454 ibid.
455 Ryken, p. 4.
456 *Christian History*, Vol. XIII, p. 3.
457 ibid., p. 2
458 Ryken, p. 7.

459 ibid., p. 7.
460 Alison Joseph, article: *The Establishment of Colleges in the Colonies*, http:/// www. columbia.edu/ ~alj10/learn/ curric/colony.html, 2003, pp. 1, 2. columbia.edu/~alj10/learn/curric/colony.html, 2003, pp. 1, 2.
461 Ryken, p. 7.
462 ibid.
463 John Adair, *Puritans*, Sutton Publishing, Great Britain, 1982, p. 86.
464 Roland H. Bainton, *Christianity*, Houghton Mifflin Company, Boston, 1964, p. 298.
465 ibid., p. 298.
466 John Adair, pp. 118, 119.
467 Ralph C. Wood, *Contending for the Faith*, Baylor University Press, Waco, Texas, 2003, pp. 86, 87.
468 ibid., p. 86.
469 ibid., pp. 86, 87.
470 Ryken, pp. 189 – 200.
471 ibid., pp. 205 – 221.
472 ibid., p. 221.
473 Bruce L. Shelley, *Church History in Plain Language*, Word Publishing, Dallas, Texas, 1995, p. 331.
474 *Christian History*, Vol. V, No. 2, Christian History Institute, printed in U.S.A, 1986, p. 6.
475 ibid.
476 ibid.
477 ibid.
478 ibid.
479 ibid.
480 Shelley, p. 326.
481 ibid.
482 ibid.
483 ibid.
484 Shelley, p. 327.
485 Earle Cairns, *Christianity Through the Ages*, Zondervan Publishing House, Grand Rapids, 1961, p. 413.
486 Shelley, p. 327.
487 *Christian History*, Volume V, No. 2, 1986, p. 14.
488 Shelley, p. 328.
489 Mark Noll, *The Rise of Evangelicalism*, InterVarsity Press, Downers Grove, Illinois, 2003, p. 68.
490 Shelley, p. 328.

[491] Austin, p. 331.
[492] Shelley, p. 329.
[493] ibid.
[494] ibid., p. 329, 330.
[495] Jesse Lyman Hurlbut, *The Story of the Christian Church*, Zondervan Publishing House, Grand Rapids, Michigan, 1972, p. 138.
[496] Bruce L. Shelley, p.332.
[497] ibid., p. 333.
[498] Hurlbut, p. 139.
[499] William P. Barker, *Who's Who in Church History*, Baker Book House, Grand Rapids, Michigan, 1977, p. 298.
[500] Austin, p. 334.
[501] ibid.
[502] Barker, p. 298.
[503] Austin, p. 334.
[504] ibid., p. 334.
[505] Barker, p. 299.
[506] Shelley, p. 331.
[507] ibid.
[508] Austin, p. 335.
[509] Shelley, p. 335.
[510] John Wesley *Works* (new), May 24, 1738, 18:249-50.
[511] Baker, p. 299.
[512] ibid., p. 300.
[513] Noll, *The Rise of Evangelicalism*, p. 203.
[514] ibid., p. 204
[515] Baker, p. 303.
[516] Shelley, p. 336.
[517] Shelley, p. 336.
[518] Roland Bainton, *Christianity*, p. 341.
[519] *Christian History*, Volume VIII, No. 3, Issue 23, 1989, p. 17.
[520] ibid.
[521] Shelley, p. 337.
[522] Austin, p. 338.
[523] ibid., p. 338.
[524] *Christian History*, Volume VIII, No. 3, p. 4.
[525] ibid.
[526] ibid.
[527] Baker, p. 263.
[528] *Christian History*, Volume VIII, No. 3, Issue 23, p. 9.

[529] ibid.
[530] Michael Crawford, *Seasons of Grace: Colonial New England's Revival Tradition in Its British Context*, Oxford University Press, New York, 1991, p. 108.
[531] ibid.
[532] ibid.
[533] ibid.
[534] Noll, *The Rise of Evangelicalism*, p. 71.
[535] Cairns, p. 400
[536] *Christian History*, Volume VIII, No. 3, Issue 23, p. 23.
[537] Mark Noll, *The Rise of Evangelicalism*, p. 72.
[538] *Christian History*, Volume IV, No. 4, p. 12.
[539] ibid.
[540] *Christian History*, Volume VIII, No. 3, p. 13.
[541] Shelley, p. 346.
[542] *Christian History*, Volume VIII, No. 3, p. 15.
[543] *Political Sermons of the American Founding Era*, edited by Ellis Sandoz, Liberty Fund, Indianapolis, Indiana, 1998, p. 120.
[544] Baker, p. 303.
[545] The Middle Colonies include Delaware, Maryland, New Jersey, New York, and Pennsylvania.
[546] *Christian History*, Volume VIII, No. 3, p. 16.
[547] Mark Noll, *The Rise of Evangelicalism*, p. 104.
[548] ibid.
[549] *Christian History*, Volume VIII, No. 3, p. 13.
[550] ibid.
[551] ibid., pp. 13, 14.
[552] Mark Noll, *The Rise of Evangelicalism*, p. 106.
[553] ibid.
[554] *Christian History*, Volume VIII, No. 3, p. 14.
[555] ibid.
[556] ibid.
[557] ibid.
[558] *131 Christians Everyone Should Know*, from the Editors of *Christian History* Magazine, Broadman & Holman Publishers, Nashville, Tennessee, 2000, p.44.
[559] ibid., p. 14.
[560] ibid., p. 15.
[561] ibid.
[562] ibid.

563 *Christian History*, Volume IV, No. 4, p. 16.
564 ibid., p. 16.
565 ibid.
566 *Christian History*, Volume VIII, No. 3, p. 19.
567 Cairns, p. 401.
568 Austin, pp. 351, 352.
569 Austin, p. 352.
570 Cairns, pp. 402, 403.
571 Mark Noll, *The Rise of Evangelicalism*, p. 212.
572 ibid.
573 *Christian History*, Volume VIII, No. 3, p. 27.
574 bid.
575 Austin, p. 359
576 ibid.
577 Roland Bainton, *Christianity*, p. 322.
578 ibid., p. 323.
579 Shelley, p. 349.
580 ibid., p. 356.
581 *Christian History*, Volume VIII, No. 3, p. 27.
582 Roland Bainton, *Christianity*, p.322.
583 *Christian History*, Volume VIII, No. 3, p. 27.
584 Cairns, p. 454.
585 ibid., p. 24.
586 Mark Noll, *The Rise of Evangelicalism*, p. 214.
587 ibid., pp. 214, 215.
588 ibid., p. 190.
589 ibid.
590 Baker, p. 76.
591 ibid., p. 215.
592 ibid., p. 216.
593 ibid.
594 ibid., p. 217.
595 *Christian History*, Volume VIII, No. 3, p. 24.
596 ibid.
597 ibid.
598 bid., p. 25.
599 ibid.
600 ibid.
601 Baker, p. 190.
602 *Christian History*, Volume VIII, No. 3, p.25.

[603] ibid.
[604] ibid., p. 26.
[605] John W. Brush, *Who's Who in Church History*, Abingdon Press, Nashville, 1962, p.15.
[606] *Christian History*, Volume VIII, No. 3, p. 26.
[607] Cairns, p. 454.
[608] *Knowing & Doing*, A Teaching Quarterly for Discipleship of Heart and Mind, C.S. Lewis Institute, Falls Church, Virginia, Summer, 2004, p. 21.
[609] *Christian History*, Volume VIII, No. 3, p. 28.
[610] Cairns, p. 454.
[611] *Christian History*, Volume VIII, No. 3, p. 28.
[612] ibid.
[613] ibid.
[614] ibid., p. 29.
[615] Austin, p. 362.
[616] ibid., p. 359.
[617] Richard Wightman Fox, *Jesus in America*, Harper San Francisco, 2004, pp. 176, 177.
[618] ibid., p. 177.
[619] Tony Lane, *Concise Book of Christian Faith*, Harper & Row Publishers, San Francisco, 1984, p. 176.
[620] *Christian History*, Volume VIII, No. 3, p. 30.
[621] ibid., p. 30.
[622] Iain Murray, *The Invitation System*, The Banner of Truth Trust, 78b Chiltern Street, printed by Hunt Barnard & Company, London, p. 10.
[623] Cairns, p. 457.
[624] ibid., pp. 457, 458.
[625] ibid.
[626] *Christian History*, Volume VIII, No. 3, p. 32.
[627] ibid., p. 33.
[628] Cairns, p. 445.
[629] ibid, p. 444.
[630] Austin, p. 378.
[631] Austin, p. 376.
[632] ibid.
[633] Tony Lane, *Concise Book of Christian Faith*, Harper & Row Publishers, San Francisco, 1984, p. 171.
[634] Austin, p. 374.
[635] Lane, p. 172.

[636] Austin, p. 377.
[637] Baker, p. 238.
[638] Bainton, p. 382.
[639] Austin, p. 477.
[640] ibid.
[641] Austin, p. 424.
[642] Baker, pp. 248, 249.
[643] Jonathan Hill, *The History of Christian Thought*, InterVarsity Press, Dowers Grove, Illinois, 2003, p. 259.
[644] Barker, p. 249.
[645] Hill, p. 260.
[646] ibid., pp. 260, 261.
[647] Barker, p. 249.
[648] Austin, p. 478.
[649] Roland H. Bainton, *Christianity*, Houghton Mifflin Company, Boston, 1987, p. 384.
[650] Jonathan Hill, *The History of Christian Thought*, InterVarsity Press, 2003, *p.* 282.
[651] *131 Christians Everyone Should Know,* from the Editors of *Christian History* Magazine, Broadman & Holman Publishers, Nashville, Tennessee, 2000, p. 104.
[652] ibid., p. 105.
[653] ibid.
[654] Austin, p. 477.
[655] ibid., p. 480.
[656] ibid.
[657] Cairns, p. 481.
[658] Austin, p. 480.
[659] Shelley, p. 433.
[660] ibid.
[661] Barker, p. 51.
[662] ibid., p. 182.
[663] Austin, p. 480.
[664] ibid., p. 481.
[665] ibid.
[666] Hill, p. 263.
[667] ibid., p. 270.
[668] ibid., p. 264.
[669] Hill, p. 264.
[670] ibid.

[671] Barker, pp. 30, 31.
[672] *101 Christians Everyone Should Know*, p. 47.
[673] Hill, p. 265.
[674] Barker, p. 31.
[675] Hill, p. 268.
[676] Austin, p. 486.
[677] ibid.
[678] Hill, p. 269.
[679] Lane, p. 187.
[680] ibid., p. 188.
[681] Lane, p. 186.
[682] Hill, p. 266.
[683] ibid.
[684] ibid.
[685] Hill, pp. 267, 268.
[686] Russell Kirk, *The Roots of American Order*, p. 474.
[687] ibid., p. 473.
[688] H. Richard Niebuhr, *Christ and Culture*, Harper & Row Publishers, 1951, p. 231.

Printed in the United States
72776LV00003B/85